Violence against Women and Regimes of Exception

Violence against Women and Regimes of Exception

Undoing Discrimination in Migration Law

CATHERINE BRIDDICK
Andrew W. Mellon Associate Professor of International Human Rights and Refugee Law, Oxford Department of International Development, University of Oxford, UK

OXFORD
UNIVERSITY PRESS

OXFORD
UNIVERSITY PRESS

Great Clarendon Street, Oxford, OX2 6DP,
United Kingdom

Oxford University Press is a department of the University of Oxford.
It furthers the University's objective of excellence in research, scholarship,
and education by publishing worldwide. Oxford is a registered trade mark of
Oxford University Press in the UK and in certain other countries.

Published in the United States of America by Oxford University Press
198 Madison Avenue, New York, NY 10016, United States of America.

British Library Cataloguing in Publication Data
Data available

Library of Congress Control Number: 2025937231

ISBN 9780192867797

DOI: 10.1093/9780191959899.001.0001

Printed and bound by
CPI Group (UK) Ltd., Croydon, CR0 4YY

MIX
Paper | Supporting
responsible forestry
FSC® C013604

The manufacturer's authorised representative in the EU for product safety is
Oxford University Press España S.A., Parque Empresarial San Fernando de Henares,
Avenida de Castilla, 2 – 28830 Madrid (www.oup.es/en or product.safety@oup.com).
OUP España S.A. also acts as importer into Spain of products made by the manufacturer.

For Janet and Colin.
With love and immense gratitude.

Preface

For eight years, I worked for a feminist not-for-profit organisation that provided women in England and Wales with legal advice. During this period, I directly advised hundreds of women on issues in family, criminal, and immigration law. When managing the legal advice service, I reviewed the advice given by our staff and volunteers to many hundreds more. Almost all the women we spoke to had experienced some form of violence, usually domestic or sexual violence. While the majority of those who contacted us were British or resident in the UK, a significant proportion had a migration status in the UK that was not secure. Some had come to the UK to work or to join family. Others sought international protection.

Advising women on both immigration law and violence was, and remains, extremely difficult. In the UK, as in many other jurisdictions, a person's migration status determines almost every aspect of its holder's life. It often makes women dependent, legally and practically, on the person who is violent towards them. It influences the behaviour of perpetrators. Women who seek to end a relationship, or live independently of an abuser, may be threatened with 'prison' (immigration detention) and being 'sent back' (deportation). Migration status determines the legal options women have and the financial and other support that they can receive. To complicate matters still further, legal routes that appear to offer security of residence to women who have experienced gender-based violence seldom provide this remedy. Applying for such protection, and then being denied it, not only increases women's vulnerability to violence, it also exposes them to other risks, including destitution.

One of the last women I spoke to as a practitioner was dependent for her permission to remain on that granted to her husband, a skilled labour migrant.[1] She also worked, and the couple had two children in school. The woman's husband raped her and demanded that she pay him a sizable portion of the money she earned. For a variety of legal and practical reasons, she could better protect their children from both his conduct and other forms of harm in the UK than she could in her country of origin. She wanted to end her marriage and remain here with her children. She had heard that something called the 'domestic violence rule' would enable her to do this.

I advised this woman that while there was an immigration rule that enabled some people who had experienced domestic violence to remain in the UK, it was not one that she could rely on. There were other applications that she could make,

[1] Details have been changed to maintain confidentiality.

including for refugee protection or on the basis of her and her children's human rights. The outcomes of these were, however, far from certain. If she challenged her husband, or sought to separate from him, she could lose the permission to remain that she did have. If she made one of these other applications and it was refused, she might lose her status and with it her ability to work. She and her children could face destitution, separation, and the prospect of leaving the UK. This woman considered the limited options available to her and decided to remain with her husband. She understood that he would, within years, be entitled to permanent residence and that when he did, she would get the same. Once she had that secure migration status, she would divorce him. Until then she would 'live with it'. She would continue to protect and provide for her children. Their lives and education would not be disrupted. They would be safe.

Cases like these were not, in any way, unusual. These and similar situations arise because many women are profoundly disadvantaged by the migration statuses that they hold. Partners are not, for example, alone in being granted a permission to remain that enforces their dependency or restricts their rights. Domestic workers are rendered dependent-in-practice for their migration status on their employer. Both statuses increase their holder's vulnerability to violence. At the same time, restrictions that apply to them specifically, and other migrants generally, prevent those who are subject to violence from escaping from it.

I understood much of the above when I was a practitioner. The rules that applied to partners, domestic workers, and protection-seekers were the rules that I had to navigate and explain. There was much though that, try as I might, I could neither understand nor resolve. The two sets of questions that I had then are now reflected in the two parts of this book. The first concerns how migration statuses are created, distributed, and manipulated. How, for example, are we to understand rules that appear to be gender- or race-neutral, but which actually disadvantage particular groups of people? What impact does migration status have on an experience of violence? What would be reparative of the particular disadvantage that the current rules generate? The second set of questions concerns those rules or regimes that appear to offer residence to some migrant victims of gender-based violence. How do these rules operate? Do they offer victims a remedy for the harm they have experienced?

In asking and answering these questions, this book seeks to understand the legal position of women negotiating circumstances like those I have described above. I offer, in writing and from academia, an understanding of the predicament of being subject to both violence and migration law that I could not provide from practice. When I started my research, my focus was immigration law in the UK. As my work progressed, however, I found that there were a number of similarities between facets of the UK's rules that produced, or sought to remedy, gendered disadvantage and those of other States. This is because within Europe, States' responses to migrant victims of violence are determined by both national and supranational frameworks. This remains the case in the UK, even following its departure from the European Union (EU). Consequently, while it remains rooted in the UK, this book has branches that are comparative and branches that focus on EU law, as well as on European and international discrimination and human rights law. It also draws on feminist jurisprudence and places women's lives, experiences, and legal challenges at the centre of its analysis.

This book was researched and written at a difficult time, legally and otherwise. Significant changes to immigration law have followed the UK's departure from the EU. After a long period, the UK ratified, with a key reservation, the Council of Europe Convention on Preventing and Combating Violence against Women and Domestic Violence.[2] The EU's troubled relationship with this Convention also ended with a contested and partial accession to it. These and other developments took place against the backdrop of the coronavirus pandemic and a populist backlash against migrants' and women's rights. This book charts and reflects on these changes. It also places them within a broader context, identifying patterns and tracing continuities in rules and forms of disadvantage, both over time and between jurisdictions.

Finally, the analysis this book provides may, I know, prove deeply unsatisfying to some. I am not offering readers detailed scrutiny of either UK or European migration law. Chapters that move from the UK to the EU, or from the Immigration Rules to European human rights law, provide evaluation at a level of generality that may frustrate both the scholar of EU law and the immigration practitioner. My focus on violence against women and rules that offer some form of response to it, in the UK and in Europe, may seem to some readers unduly limited and parochial. Wholesale assaults on migrants and their rights, literally and legally, seem to demand more than a discussion of indirect discrimination and the sketching of potential migration status reforms. Notwithstanding these and a myriad of other limitations and objections, there is value in engaging in some non-ideal legal thinking about the relationships between migration status, discrimination, and violence. This book offers readers an understanding of how migration law affects a significant proportion of those whose status it determines. It attributes responsibility, legally and ethically, for the increased vulnerability to violence and intensified experience of it that migrant women are subject to. It explains what might be reparative of such an experience, and how different laws and policies could and should be reformed to prevent it. Finally, this book analyses regimes that purport to offer some migrant victims of violence protection from further harm and deportation, to reveal their role in increasing victims' vulnerability to both.

I am going to end here by saying a few words about hope. This may seem an odd topic in a book about violence against women and migration law. Yet this context,

[2] Council of Europe Convention on Preventing and Combating Violence against Women and Domestic Violence (adopted 11 May 2011, entered into force 1 August 2014) CETS 210.

more than many others perhaps, demands it. Kathryn Sikkink has observed that '[s]ome expectation of hope sustains human rights work. Although hope in itself is insufficient, work sustained by reasoned, well-informed hope is not.'[3] Sikkink made this comment at the end of a discussion about the effectiveness of human rights law and practice. She was concerned that, amongst other things, progress in securing rights could stall if activists lost confidence in their own ability and that of their field to secure emancipatory change. The prospect of securing such change in migration law seems, at the time of writing, very remote. This makes envisaging such a possibility all the more demanding and necessary. To be able to illuminate a problem or set of problems is, of course, in and of itself sufficient. I do that here. I also seek, through legal analysis that is both critical and constructive, to offer reasoned, well-informed hope that progress securing women's and migrants' human rights, within and through law, remains possible.

Catherine Briddick
Oxford
May 2024

[3] Kathryn Sikkink, *Evidence for Hope: Making Human Rights Work in the 21st Century* (Princeton University Press 2017) 180.

Acknowledgements

Much of this book was written during a period that can, at best, be described as 'challenging'. I do not really know how to acknowledge this, or how to thank the many people whose care, support, and love kept me going. What I can say is that this book would not exist, either at all or in its current form, had it not been for the advice, guidance, and encouragement of many people. I do my best to thank some of those people here.

I am incredibly grateful to Cathryn Costello, who supervised the doctoral research that underpinned this book and collaborated with me on *Undoing Discriminatory Borders*, the project that developed it. I have gained so much, intellectually and personally, from working with Cathryn. She has offered both inspiration and support; her supervision and scholarship provide the foundation to my own. Cathryn, thank you so much. My doctoral research was supported by the Arts and Humanities Research Council through the University of Oxford Doctoral Training Partnership. Thank you also to Shreya Atrey, Sandra Fredman, Eric Fripp, Alison Harvey, Carolyn Hoyle, Tarunabh Khaitan, Michelle Madden Dempsey, Siobhán Mullally, Denise Réaume, Nicole Štýbnarová, Colin Yeo, and Adrienne Yong for commenting on various draft chapters, and to the anonymous reviewers who engaged with the manuscript. The book has been shaped and improved by their expertise which was so generously shared. I am also very grateful to everyone at OUP, particularly Rebecca Lewis for helping me bring this project to fruition and to Caroline Valia-Kollery for her insightful copyediting.

I have been very lucky to find, in the Refugee Studies Centre at the Oxford Department of International Development, both an intellectual home and colleagues from whom I continue to learn. I cannot thank Matthew J Gibney and Tom Scott-Smith enough for both the wisest of counsel and the best of friendship. I am particularly indebted to Diego Sánchez-Ancochea for providing the advice I needed at the points I most needed it. Thank you also to Jocelyn Alexander, Ruben Andersson, Simukai Chigudu, and Uttara Shahani for coffee, conversation, and community.

This book is dedicated to my parents, Janet and Colin Briddick. They have given my brother Jonathan and me so much, including the home that we continue to return to and the values I hope to pass on. My children, Raphy and Bella, remain the reasons I both start and stop working. My husband, Henry, is unfailingly brilliant and unhesitatingly generous. Thank you all for the life we share.

Finally, in writing this book, I have sought to do justice, in some small way, to the accounts of violence and migration status that women discussed with me when I was in practice. Their courage has motivated and sustained this work, which I offer in return, with gratitude and in solidarity. Thank you.

Contents

Table of Cases

COURT OF JUSTICE OF THE EUROPEAN UNION (CJEU) (NUMERICAL)

COURT OF JUSTICE OF THE EUROPEAN UNION (CJEU) (ALPHABETICAL)

EUROPEAN COURT OF HUMAN RIGHTS (ECTHR)

INTER-AMERICAN COMMISSION ON HUMAN RIGHTS

INTER-AMERICAN COURT OF HUMAN RIGHTS

UN COMMITTEE ON THE ELIMINATION OF DISCRIMINATION AGAINST WOMEN (CEDAW COMMITTEE)

NATIONAL/UNITED KINGDOM

Table of Legislation

EUROPEAN UNION DIRECTIVES

INTERNATIONAL TREATIES AND INSTRUMENTS

NATIONAL LEGISLATION

Abbreviations

AG	Advocate General
CEAS	common European asylum system
CEDAW	Convention on the Elimination of All Forms of Discrimination against Women
CFREU	Charter of Fundamental Rights of the European Union
CGD	conclusive grounds decision
CJEU	Court of Justice of the European Union
DDVC	Destitute Domestic Violence Concession
EU	European Union
EUSS	EU Settlement Scheme
FGM	female genital mutilation
FOI	Freedom of Information
FRD	Family Reunion Directive
GRETA	Group of Experts on Action against Trafficking in Human Beings
GREVIO	Group of Experts on Action against Violence against Women and Domestic Violence
IACtHR	Inter-American Court of Human Rights
IRCC	Immigration, Refugees and Citizenship Canada
MS	Member States
MVDAC	Migrant Victims of Domestic Abuse Concession
NGO	non-governmental organisation
NHS	National Health Service
NRM	National Referral Mechanism
PTSD	post-traumatic stress disorder
RGD	reasonable grounds decision
TCN	third-country national
TFEU	Treaty on the Functioning of the European Union
US	United States
VAW	violence against women
VTS	Victim of Human Trafficking or Slavery

PART I

DISCRIMINATION, VIOLENCE, AND COMPOUNDED DISADVANTAGE

1

Introduction: Setting Precedent—Migrant Women and the Law

1.1 Introduction

> When I got my spouse visa, how come I didn't get any information at that time? . . . Had I known at that time I would have gone to somebody sooner about what I could do. . . . I didn't know anything, I only had what he was telling me. . . . When I used to ask him about my visa, he would say that 'only I can do it and I'm not going to do it.' And I couldn't ask too much because it would just cause a fight.[1]

> They know I don't have paper now. They can exploit me. I have to work long and earn less money. They shouted at me if they are not happy. They know I won't say anything. I can do nothing now because I lost my paper. I'm hidden now. I'm afraid of losing jobs.[2]

These women are describing a particular predicament: being made dependent for their migration status, and all the rights that flow from it, on people who are violent towards them. The first woman was a victim of domestic violence perpetrated by her husband. The second was harassed and exploited by her employers. Both women experienced particular forms of discriminatory violence. Both were migrants in the UK.

Migration status is the personal status that attaches to migrants by virtue of their position as subjects of immigration law.[3] The type of migration status a person

[1] 'Rashida', a migrant partner quoted in Halliki Voolma, '"I Must Be Silent Because of Residency": Barriers to Escaping Domestic Violence in the Context of Insecure Immigration Status in England and Sweden' (2018) 24 Violence Against Women 1830, 1844.

[2] An overseas domestic worker quoted in Joyce Jiang, *A Special Vulnerability: Migrant Domestic Workers Enslaved by The Non-Renewable Overseas Domestic Worker Visa in the UK* (Report for The Voice of Domestic Workers, London, 2019) 10. Throughout this book, I draw on peer-reviewed, academic research and research produced by and with non-governmental organisations (NGOs). I do so for two reasons. First, to recognise victims' knowledge and standing. Secondly and relatedly, to acknowledge the role of feminist organisations in empowering victims/survivors and securing legal change. See further Ashwini Vasanthakumar, 'Epistemic Privilege and Victims' Duties to Resist Their Oppression' (2018) 35 Journal of Applied Philosophy 465.

[3] Immigration or migration law, broadly defined here, includes the UK's Immigration Rules, primary legislation, EU Directives, international conventions, and the decisions of tribunals, national and supranational courts, and monitoring bodies.

Violence against Women and Regimes of Exception. Catherine Briddick, Oxford University Press.
 DOI: 10.1093/9780191959899.003.0001

has will determine how long they can remain in either the UK or their European Union (EU) country of residence, whether they can remain, for example, for a few months, a few years, or permanently. A person's migration status also determines what rights they have: whether they can work, study, be accompanied by family members and access welfare benefits or healthcare. Migration status is 'at once transient and indelible', determining rights for a fixed period but also having an enduring impact, even after the 'migrant' has become a 'citizen'.[4]

The first woman quoted above was granted permission to remain as the partner of someone who was British or resident in the UK.[5] Those who hold this status may live and work in the UK, while their partner affirms that their relationship is continuing. The second woman was granted permission to remain as a domestic worker. This extremely precarious and restrictive migration status enabled her to work in her employer's household for just six months. The violence that both women were subjected to was perpetrated by those who were able to exercise power over them because of the migration status they held.

Migration statuses created by UK immigration law generally prohibit their holder from accessing certain public funds. Consequently, both women quoted above were excluded from those sources of State and other support that would have been available to British or resident women who were experiencing violence in their home and/or place of work. Partners and domestic workers are, for example, unable to access welfare benefits. One consequence of this is that women's refuges, and other emergency accommodation providers, are generally unable to shelter migrant women fleeing domestic violence or domestic servitude. Domestic workers are effectively precluded from either changing employers or challenging abusive employment practices. Finding a new job, or taking a case to an Employment Tribunal, is not usually possible during a six-month stay in the UK. Domestic workers who are undocumented, or who become so, are, in addition, generally unable to enforce their employment rights.[6] People with an insecure status may be made destitute by laws and policies which prevent them from working or accessing State support. They may also be detained and deported.[7] Individual perpetrators of domestic violence, or of labour exploitation, can and do make any number of threats against those that they victimise. Immigration law empowers perpetrators who threaten their partners or domestic workers with destitution or deportation,

[4] Mark Freedland and Cathryn Costello, 'Migrants at Work and the Division of Labour Law' in Cathryn Costello and Mark Freedland (eds), *Migrants at Work: Immigration and Vulnerability in Labour Law* (OUP 2014) 4.

[5] 'Leave to remain' in the relevant rules, referred to as 'permission to remain' here for ease of reading.

[6] Employees cannot rely on, or enforce, a contract that is 'tainted with illegality', for example where one party to the contract does not have valid permission to work in the UK. Astra Emir, *Selwyn's Law of Employment* (22nd edn, OUP 2022) 82. Domestic workers may bring claims where doing so does not involve relying on an illegal contract, in discrimination law for example. See further *Hounga v Allen* [2014] UKSC 47, [2014] 1 WLR 2889; *Okedina v Chikale* [2019] EWCA Civ 1393, [2019] WLR(D) 444.

[7] To capture the reality of forced removal, I use the term 'deportation' to cover all forms of lawful expulsion.

enabling them to make good these threats. Simultaneously, it denies those who are victimised the support that would enable them to escape violence and seek reparation for it. States, including the UK, and supranational and international organisations, including the EU and Council of Europe, have recognised that, in certain circumstances, the predicament confronted by migrant victims of violence requires a migration law response. These responses, characterised here as 'regimes of exception',[8] are departures from the conventional migration law position that a person who does not have valid permission to remain, or who no longer meets the conditions attached to that permission, should return to their country of origin, involuntarily if necessary. These regimes operate alongside, but differ from, refugee and other protections from *refoulement*. The latter are concerned with persecution and other serious harm that may occur in the future, in a person's country of origin.[9] In contrast, the regimes of exception enable some migrants, who have experienced some forms of violence, to receive a migration status in their country of residence.

In this book, I analyse the UK and European rules that create and distribute migration statuses, like those of 'partner' or 'domestic worker'. I also explore the regimes that purport to resolve the immigration situation of those who, like the partner and domestic worker introduced above, experience certain forms of interpersonal and discriminatory violence: forms of violence against women. I do so first, by establishing that gendered disadvantage and unlawful discrimination are pervasive features of migration law. Secondly, I examine a range of situations where the disadvantage, produced by migration law, interacts with an experience of violence against women in ways that are particular and injurious. I conceptualise the constellation of different experiences that arise from this interaction as compounded disadvantage, the distinguishing features of which include control and an intensified experience of violence. Thirdly, I delineate the obligations States owe migrant victims of violence under European and international human rights law. Having established that States should provide those it subjects to compounded disadvantage with an independent, rights-bestowing migration status, I evaluate six regimes of exception by reference to the extent to which this duty is discharged. This analysis, of under-examined and under-theorised rules from UK immigration law, EU law, and two Council of Europe conventions, reveals a number of common deficiencies, including their role in perpetuating discrimination against women.

A quick note on scope and terminology before I proceed any further. As I will explain, this book does not enter into broader, philosophical discussion of either

[8] With thanks to Cathryn Costello, who suggested this term.

[9] Convention relating to the Status of Refugees (adopted 28 July 1951, entered into force 22 April 1954) 189 UNTS 137, art 1A(2). See also Directive 2011/95/EU of the European Parliament and of the Council of 13 December 2011 on standards for the qualification of third-country nationals or stateless persons as beneficiaries of international protection, for a uniform status for refugees or for persons eligible for subsidiary protection, and for the content of the protection granted (recast) [2011] OJ L337/9.

the right of States to treat citizens and non-citizens differently or the relationships between concepts such as women, sex, and gender. I generally use the formulation 'sex/gender' to encompass a range of legal and other views on the definition and role of these terms in women's subordination.[10] Distinctions are drawn, and specific terms used, where particular legal instruments or scholarly works require me to do so. Essentially, in each case, I use terminology true to the source I discuss. The approach I adopt to 'women' is one that is alive to feminist theorising but meaningful in some specific legal contexts. Such contexts include national legal approaches to sex/gender, acknowledging that these are subject to challenge, change between jurisdictions, and alter over time. They also include the objects and purposes of the conventions I draw on.[11] These living instruments are generally responsive to women's differential vulnerability to violence on the basis of sex/gender and a range of other factors, including age, gender identity, migrant and refugee status, race, and sexual orientation.[12] Overall, here and throughout the book, I limit myself to making those kinds of arguments on both migration law and violence against women that could reasonably be advanced before national and international tribunals, courts, and treaty bodies.

1.2 The Problem

Before I set out how this book examines predicaments like those recounted above, it is helpful to explain why such experiences are neither exceptional nor anomalous, but the entirely predictable and, in some cases, lethal, consequence of the rules that determine status.

There are a range of migration routes that enable family members, including same-sex and opposite-sex partners, children, and parents, to join someone who is British or resident in the UK. Tens of thousands of people use these routes

[10] I adopt the same position on this point as Conaghan, who explains: 'In adopting an approach which effectively collapses the sex/gender distinction, I do not wish to imply that sex/gender is solely the product of language or discourse, that it does not also have a significant material including biological dimension which actively shapes how we apprehend and value a sexed/gendered social world. I do take the view that our access to the material and our apprehension of the biological is inevitably mediated by social and cultural understandings of the same: knowledge is never "pure" and a clear line between the material world and the ideas and concepts through which we perceive that world cannot really be drawn.' Joanne Conaghan, *Law and Gender* (OUP 2013) 23. See further Alice Edwards, *Violence Against Women under International Human Rights Law* (CUP 2011) 13–19.

[11] In line with the standard means of treaty interpretation, Vienna Convention on the Law of Treaties (adopted 23 May 1969, entered into force 27 January 1980) 1155 UNTS 331, art 31.

[12] On migration status, sexual orientation, and gender identity respectively, see *Jallow v Bulgaria* CEDAW Committee, Communication No 32/2011 UN Doc CEDAW/C/52/D/32/2011 (views adopted 23 July 2012); *ON and DP v Russian Federation* CEDAW Committee, Communication No 119/2017, UN Doc CEDAW/C/75/D/119/2017 (views adopted 24 February 2020); *Case of Vicky Hernández v Honduras (Merits, Reparations and Costs)* Inter-American Court of Human Rights Series C No 422 (26 March 2021).

each year. Over eighty thousand family-related visas were, for example, granted in 2023.[13] Most of these permission holders were, and remain, women.[14] Around twenty thousand people a year receive permission to enter the UK as overseas domestic workers.[15] The vast majority of these workers also were, and remain, women.[16] Being granted, and then holding, the migration statuses of partner or domestic worker depends on being in, and then maintaining, certain kinds of relationships (marriage or employment) with specific types of people (those who are British or living here). The Immigration Rules relating to these statuses not only make women dependent on their partner/employer and restrict their rights but also shape women's experiences of violence.

As Anita Raj and Jay Silverman explain, 'there is a hierarchy of immigrant status, and women's place in this hierarchy relates to their vulnerability to abuse'.[17] Migrant women subject to domestic violence experience 'particularly intense and chronic forms of abuse, reinforced by threats of deportation and destitution, as well as separation from their children'.[18] Abuse may involve severe physical, psychological, and sexual violence from a range of perpetrators, including a woman's extended family. While such treatment may be devastatingly common in violent relationships, the statuses held by migrant partners shape the 'particular techniques of control and forms of violence' to which women are subject.[19] The Immigration Rules that govern domestic workers' stay in the UK grant employers an 'inordinate

[13] 'There were 81,203 family-related visas granted in 2023, an increase of 72% from 2022 and the highest calendar year on record.' Home Office, 'National Statistics: Why Do People Come to the UK? For Family Reasons' (*GOV.UK*, 29 February 2024) <www.gov.uk/government/statistics/immigration-system-statistics-year-ending-december-2023/why-do-people-come-to-the-uk-for-family-reasons> accessed 20 March 2024.

[14] Of all those holding permission as family members in 2022, 61% were women, 25% were men, and 13% were children. Nuni Jorgensen and Peter William Walsh, 'Family Migration to the UK' (*Migration Observatory*, 6 October 2023) <https://migrationobservatory.ox.ac.uk/resources/briefings/family-migration-to-the-uk/> accessed 10 March 2024. See also Katharine Charsley and others, 'Marriage-Related Migration to the UK' (2012) 46 International Migration Review 861.

[15] There were 18,553 grants in 2022, for example; Home Office, 'National Statistics: Why Do People Come to the UK? To Work' (*GOV.UK*, 23 February 2023) <www.gov.uk/government/statistics/immigration-system-statistics-year-ending-december-2022/why-do-people-come-to-the-uk-to-work> accessed 23 April 2024.

[16] In 2018, a representative year in the period I review in chapter 2, 20,280 migrants were given permission to enter the UK as domestic workers, of whom 4,672 were men and 15,608 were women. UK Visas & Immigration Freedom of Information, *FOI Number 68009* (on file with the author, data extracted 27 January 2022) (9 February 2022).

[17] Anita Raj and Jay Silverman, 'Violence Against Immigrant Women: The Roles of Culture, Context, and Legal Immigrant Status on Intimate Partner Violence' (2002) 8 Violence Against Women 367, 375.

[18] Sundari Anitha, 'No Recourse, No Support: State Policy and Practice towards South Asian Women Facing Domestic Violence in the UK' (2010) 40 British Journal of Social Work 462, 473.

[19] Sundari Anitha, 'Legislating Gender Inequalities' (2011) 17 Violence Against Women 1260, 1278. See also Nughmana Mirza, 'The UK Government's Conflicting Agendas and "Harmful" Immigration Policies: Shaping South Asian Women's Experiences of Abuse and "Exit"' (2016) 36 Critical Social Policy 592; Sundari Anitha, Anupama Roy, and Harshita Yalamarty, 'Gender, Migration, and Exclusionary Citizenship Regimes: Conceptualizing Transnational Abandonment of Wives as a Form of Violence Against Women' (2018) 24 Violence Against Women 747.

level of control' over those workers' lives.[20] They also increase vulnerability to abuse and influence the form violence takes and that violence's intensity.[21] The role of migration law in constructing vulnerability to both labour exploitation and gender-based violence has been recognised by the UK's Supreme Court[22] and the Committee that monitors the Convention on the Elimination of All Forms of Discrimination against Women (CEDAW),[23] the CEDAW Committee.[24]

The UK's migration rules are not, in many respects, dissimilar to those of other common law and European States. Indeed, these countries share a tendency to adopt and reproduce routes and statuses that are increasingly precarious and conditional.[25] European States' regulation of marriage migration, and the imposition of requirements relating to a couple's residence, income, accommodation, and integration which differ 'in degree rather than kind', provide one notable example of this trend.[26] Such rules affect hundreds of thousands of people across and beyond Europe. EU citizens and their families enjoy the right of free movement under EU law.[27] Here, the EU has, in enabling citizens and their families to be mobile, resisted adopting some of the detrimental features of the statuses accorded to partners under European States' immigration laws. However, it only accords the family members of EU citizens *derivative* rights, so that these family members, like the partner quoted above, are also made dependent on another for their migration status.[28] Research on women's experiences of migration status and violence,

[20] Natalie Sedacca, 'Migrant Domestic Workers and the Right to a Private and Family Life' (2019) 37 Netherlands Quarterly of Human Rights 288, 295.

[21] KALAYAAN, 'Still Enslaved: The Migrant Domestic Workers Who Are Trapped by the Immigration Rules' (*KALAYAAN*, 2014) <www.kalayaan.org.uk/wp-content/uploads/2014/09/tied-visa-20141.pdf> accessed 22 April 2024; Virginia Mantouvalou, '"Am I Free Now?" Overseas Domestic Workers in Slavery' (2015) 42 Journal of Law and Society 329.

[22] 'In these cases, Ms Taiwo and Ms Onu had limited leave to enter on domestic workers' visas. It was the terms of those visas which made them particularly vulnerable to the mistreatment which they suffered.' *Taiwo v Olaigbe* [2016] UKSC 31, [2016] 1 WLR 2653 [24].

[23] Convention on the Elimination of All Forms of Discrimination against Women (adopted 18 December 1979, entered into force 3 September 1981) 1249 UNTS 13.

[24] UN Committee on the Elimination of Discrimination against Women, 'General Recommendation No 26 on Women Migrant Workers' (5 December 2008) UN Doc CEDAW/C/2009/WP.1/R [19]–[21].

[25] Catherine Dauvergne, *The New Politics of Immigration and the End of Settler Societies* (CUP 2016); Anna K Boucher and Justin Gest, *Crossroads: Comparative Immigration Regimes in a World of Demographic Change* (CUP 2018).

[26] Helena Wray, Agnes Agoston, and Jocelyn Hutton, 'A Family Resemblance? The Regulation of Marriage Migration in Europe' (2014) 16 European Journal of Migration and Law 209, 244.

[27] Regulation (EU) 2016/399 of the European Parliament and of the Council of 9 March 2016 on a Union Code on the rules governing the movement of persons across borders (Schengen Borders Code) (codification) [2016] OJ L77/1, art 2(5)–(6). The European Union's (EU) Member States (MS) are Austria, Belgium, Bulgaria, Croatia, Cyprus, Czech Republic, Denmark, Estonia, Finland, France, Germany, Greece, Hungary, Ireland, Italy, Latvia, Lithuania, Luxembourg, Malta, the Netherlands, Poland, Portugal, Romania, Slovakia, Slovenia, Spain, and Sweden. Iceland, Norway, and Liechtenstein are not members of the EU but are in the European Economic Area (the EEA). Those three States, along with Switzerland, are generally treated analogously with EU MS in the field of migration law. My focus here is on EU citizens and their family members.

[28] Case C–127/08 *Metock v Minister for Justice, Equality and Law Reform* [2008] ECR I–06241.

including that drawn on in the preceding paragraph, confirms that the accounts provided by the women quoted at the start of this chapter are representative of many women's experiences in the UK. A wealth of research confirms that they are also illustrative of women's experiences in a number of other jurisdictions, and under EU law.[29] In this book, I subject this treatment, migration law's treatment of women, to scrutiny.[30] To do so, I draw on intersectional approaches to disadvantage, European human rights law, and the specialist international legal regimes concerned with discrimination and violence against women.

1.3 Situating the Argument, Anticipating Objections

Writers from a range of disciplinary perspectives have charted the myriad of ways in which States' migration laws, including those of the UK, remain imbricated in structures of racialised and gendered exclusion, subordination, and violence.[31] Migration control practices, including those concerned with detention and deportation, have come under similar scrutiny.[32] I draw on feminist theorising on intersectional disadvantage and this broader literature on migration control, combining empirical research with doctrinal and normative legal analysis to argue that immigration law discriminates against women.

[29] These articles explore the position of migrant partners in the US, Canada, Australia, Sweden, and under EU law (in the UK, when the UK was still a member of the EU): Cecilia Menjívar and Olivia Salcido, 'Immigrant Women and Domestic Violence: Common Experiences in Different Countries' (2002) 16 Gender & Society 898; Rupaleem Bhuyan and Bronwyn Bragg, 'Epistemologies of Bordering: Domestic Violence Advocacy with Marriage Migrants in the Shadow of Deportation' (2021) 9 Migration Studies 159; Marie Segrave, 'Temporary Migration and Family Violence: How Perpetrators Weaponise Borders' (2021) 10 International Journal for Crime, Justice and Social Democracy 26; Voolma, '"I Must Be Silent Because of Residency"' (n 1); Charlotte O'Brien, 'Civis Capitalist Sum: Class as the New Guiding Principle of EU Free Movement Rights' (2016) 53 Common Market Law Review 937.

[30] Drawing on the language used by Baroness Hale, *Homer v Chief Constable of West Yorkshire Police* [2012] UKSC 15, [2012] 3 All ER 1287 [17].

[31] Examples that have influenced this work include Helena Wray, '"A Thing Apart": Controlling Male Family Migration to the United Kingdom' (2015) 18 Men and Masculinities 424; Helen Irving, *Citizenship, Alienage, and the Modern Constitutional State: A Gendered History* (CUP 2016); Anna Boucher, *Gender, Migration and the Global Race for Talent* (Manchester University Press 2016); Nadine El-Enany, *Bordering Britain: Law, Race and Empire* (Manchester University Press 2020); E Tendayi Achiume, 'Racial Borders' (2022) 110 The Georgetown Law Journal 445.

[32] Examples that have influenced this work include Matthew J Gibney, 'Is Deportation a Form of Forced Migration?' (2013) 32 Refugee Survey Quarterly 116; Sharon Pickering and Brandy Cochrane, 'Irregular Border-Crossing Deaths and Gender: Where, How and Why Women Die Crossing Borders' (2013) 17 Theoretical Criminology 27; Mary Bosworth, Andriani Fili, and Sharon Pickering, 'Women and Border Policing at the Edges of Europe' (2018) 44 Journal of Ethnic and Migration Studies 2182; Nira Yuval-Davis, Georgie Wemyss, and Kathryn Cassidy, 'Everyday Bordering, Belonging and the Reorientation of British Immigration Legislation' (2018) 52 Sociology 228; Luke de Noronha, 'Deportation, Racism and Multi-status Britain: Immigration Control and the Production of Race in the Present' (2019) 42 Ethnic and Racial Studies 2413; Victoria Canning, 'Degradation by Design: Women and Asylum in Northern Europe' (2019) 61 Race & Class 46.

Discrimination may be single-axis (on the grounds of sex) or intersectional (on the grounds of sex, race, and migration status). Intersectionality, whether understood 'as theory, concept, methodology, heuristic, or all four' has been an 'extraordinarily generative' field of feminist inquiry.[33] This work is rooted in feminist legal theorising on intersectionality, disadvantage, and discrimination.[34] Shreya Atrey explains that intersectionality 'illuminates the dynamic of sameness and difference in patterns of group disadvantage based on multiple identities'.[35] I adopt this approach for two main reasons. The first is epistemic, the second, emancipatory. Taking an intersectional approach sees people's multiple identities 'as a whole' and 'in their full and relevant context'.[36] Here, it recognises migrant women's identities as, for example, racialised women, family members, workers, victims or survivors of particular forms of violence, and, of course, as migrants and as women. This book aims to achieve more, however, than epistemic justice for those whose predicament it is concerned with. To draw on and paraphrase Atrey, the purpose of intersectional theorising is to recognise intersectional disadvantage and to transform it.[37] In the chapters that follow, I examine the disadvantage that *migrant* women are subject to, to establish what legal remedy would be reparative of it. Scholarship that examines how intersectional disadvantage experienced in the context of migration control might be remedied in and with *law* is necessary, but not of course sufficient, to achieve these aims.

Jurisprudential discussion of equality and discrimination law has considered what is wrong, or unjust, about discriminatory treatment, focusing, for example, on stereotyping,[38] the maintenance of oppressive power relations,[39] or the compounding of injustice.[40] Other accounts justify prohibitions on discriminatory treatment by reference to social inclusion,[41] human dignity,[42] or protecting deliberative freedoms.[43] Whichever account, or accounts, are preferred, discrimination

[33] Gail Lewis, 'Unsafe Travel: Experiencing Intersectionality and Feminist Displacements' (2013) 38 Signs 869, 869.

[34] It is significant that Kimberlé Crenshaw's foundational theorising on intersectional discrimination analysed the inability of United States (US) anti-discrimination *law* to uphold Black women's labour rights. Kimberlé Crenshaw, 'Demarginalizing the Intersection of Race and Sex: A Black Feminist Critique of Antidiscrimination Doctrine, Feminist Theory and Antiracist Politics' (1989) 1989 University of Chicago Legal Forum 139.

[35] Shreya Atrey, *Intersectional Discrimination* (OUP 2019) 77.

[36] ibid.

[37] ibid.

[38] Larry Alexander, 'What Makes Wrongful Discrimination Wrong? Biases, Preferences, Stereotypes, and Proxies' (1992) 141 University of Pennsylvania Law Review 149.

[39] Elizabeth Anderson, 'Recent Thinking about Sexual Harassment: A Review Essay' (2006) 34 Philosophy & Public Affairs 284.

[40] Deborah Hellman, 'Indirect Discrimination and the Duty to Avoid Compounding Injustice' in Hugh Collins and Tarunabh Khaitan (eds), *Foundations of Indirect Discrimination Law* (Hart 2018).

[41] Hugh Collins, 'Discrimination, Equality and Social Inclusion' (2003) 66 Modern Law Review 16.

[42] Denise G Réaume, 'Discrimination and Dignity' (2003) 63 Louisiana Law Review 645.

[43] Sophia Moreau, 'What Is Discrimination?' (2010) 38 Philosophy & Public Affairs 143; Sophia Moreau, 'In Defense of a Liberty-Based Account of Discrimination' in Deborah Hellman and Sophia Moreau (eds), *Philosophical Foundations of Discrimination Law* (OUP 2013).

law, broadly conceived, is concerned with differential treatment based on certain protected characteristics.[44] Discrimination can take a number of forms. It may be readily identifiable in differential treatment that is explicitly and directly based on a protected characteristic. It may also be found in apparently neutral rules or practices that adversely affect, without justification, members of a disadvantaged group. Overall, it is the field's concern with certain kinds of distinction that distinguishes discrimination from other kinds of injustice, and prohibitions of discrimination from other rights protections.

Prohibitions of discrimination, and guarantees of equal treatment, can be found in a range of legal instruments adopted at the national, regional, and international levels. Depending on the circumstances and jurisdiction, such prohibitions, and cases decided by reference to them, may characterise as discriminatory the non-justifiable differential distribution of migration opportunities,[45] harassment in the workplace,[46] and/or gender-based violence.[47] The intersectional disadvantage experienced by migrant women is produced, or contributed to, by rules that can be impugned as unlawfully discriminatory by reference to some of these instruments. Such an argument is distinct from those that characterise migration law and control as intrinsically sexist and racist, or as discriminatory *lato sensu*. Centrally, it is also different from arguments that identify the ways in which migration law engages other human rights, including the right to life.[48] As the following brief discussion indicates, understanding migration law's discrimination against women, in addition to its other rights-violating qualities, is necessary to capture the legal wrongs with which this work is concerned.

Women are significantly more likely than men to experience domestic violence, and if they do experience it, they are more likely to experience particular forms of it, and suffer more serious harm as a consequence.[49] Consequently, domestic violence is recognised as both discrimination and a breach of women's human rights by, amongst others, the European Court of Human Rights (ECtHR),[50] the Council

[44] For a detailed discussion of which, see Tarunabh Khaitan, *A Theory of Discrimination Law* (OUP 2015) ch 2.

[45] *Abdulaziz, Cabales and Balkandali v UK* App nos 9214/80, 9473/81, 9474/81 (ECtHR, 28 May 1985).

[46] Convention Concerning the Elimination of Violence and Harassment in the World of Work, ILO Convention No 190 (adopted 21 June 2019, entry into force 25 June 2021).

[47] UN Committee on the Elimination of Discrimination against Women, 'General Recommendation No 35 on Gender-Based Violence Against Women, Updating General Recommendation No 19' (26 July 2017) UN Doc CEDAW/C/GC/35 (CEDAW's GR 35).

[48] For a notable example, see Report of the Special Rapporteur of the Human Rights Council on Extrajudicial Summary or Arbitrary Executions, 'Unlawful Death of Refugees and Migrants' (2017) 29 International Journal of Refugee Law 668.

[49] Discussed in detail in chapter 3. See also Marianne Hester, 'Who Does What to Whom? Gender and Domestic Violence Perpetrators in English Police Records' (2013) 10 European Journal of Criminology 623.

[50] *Opuz v Turkey* App no 33401/02 (ECtHR, 9 June 2009).

of Europe,[51] and the CEDAW Committee.[52] States are required to respond to such discriminatory violence with 'due diligence': they must investigate it and provide victims with support and remedies which are both practical and effective.[53] States' failure to discharge these obligations may itself constitute unlawful discrimination.[54] The first woman quoted above was in the UK as a partner, dependent for her migration status on her violent husband. The *violence* she experienced was discriminatory violence that breached her human rights. The State, through migration laws that *increased* her vulnerability to such violence and then *intensified* her experience of it, also discriminated against her and breached her rights, contrary to both the European Convention on Human Rights (ECHR)[55] and CEDAW. Such treatment should, as a matter of law, be remedied.

Recourse to international, regional, and national prohibitions on discrimination, in conjunction with other protected rights, including to life and to a remedy, has improved the legal position of many victims of violence. To a significantly lesser extent, such prohibitions have also been relied on to challenge immigration rules that disadvantage women, or which fail to offer them effective protection from violence.[56] Different strands of jurisprudence, from the ECtHR and CEDAW Committee may, therefore, be woven together to establish what remedies would be practical, effective, and crucially reparative of migrant women's ill-treatment.

Drawing together the above, this book makes three contributions to the literature on migration, discrimination, and violence against women. First, it argues that migration law engages in unlawful discrimination on *at least* one prohibited ground: sex. The adverse and disadvantageous effects of this discrimination are unpacked and explored, particular attention being paid to the experiences of racialised women, family and labour migrants, and undocumented women. Secondly, it analyses the interaction between migration status and violence against women, establishing States' obligations to avert and remedy the compounded disadvantage that this interaction generates. Thirdly, it uses these obligations as a framework to evaluate six regimes of exception. Part I's focus on the

[51] Council of Europe Convention on Preventing and Combating Violence against Women and Domestic Violence (adopted 11 May 2011, entered into force 1 August 2014) CETS 210.

[52] CEDAW's GR 35 (n 47). See also *Ms AT v Hungary* CEDAW Committee, Communication No 2/2003, UN Doc CEDAW/C/36/D/2/2003 (views adopted 26 January 2005).

[53] Rashida Manjoo, 'State Responsibility to Act with Due Diligence in the Elimination of Violence against Women' (2013) 2 International Human Rights Law Review 240.

[54] *Opuz v Turkey* (n 50); *González ('Cotton Field') v Mexico (Preliminary Objection, Merits, Reparations, and Costs)* Inter-American Court of Human Rights Series C No 205 (16 November 2009).

[55] Convention for the Protection of Human Rights and Fundamental Freedoms (adopted 4 November 1950, entered into force 3 September 1953) ETS 5 (European Convention on Human Rights, as amended).

[56] Catherine Briddick, 'When Does Migration Law Discriminate against Women?' (2021) 115 AJIL Unbound 356; Catherine Briddick, 'Unprincipled and Unrealised: CEDAW and Discrimination Experienced in the Context of Migration Control' (2022) 22 International Journal of Discrimination and the Law 224.

wrong and its remedy provides the foundation to Part II's evaluation of national and supranational responses to violence experienced in the context of migration control. Accordingly, each regime of exception analysed in Part II is examined by reference to whether, and to what extent, it affords those who have been subjected to compounded disadvantage with a rights-protective permission to remain.

Before I explain how these contributions are made, I must acknowledge a series of practical and theoretical objections. Discrimination law comprises technical terminology and contested concepts, some of which I have already referred to and which include prohibited grounds and the possibility (or not) that differential treatment may be justified. Both immigration applications and discrimination claims require certain kinds of evidence to be gathered and presented, some of which may only be available to public authorities. Potential applicants are, therefore, likely to need publicly funded and specialist legal advice and representation. They also need to have the time, energy, knowledge, and will to take part in adversarial adjudicatory processes that are complex and lengthy. The practical and legal barriers faced by those who seek to resolve their immigration position or challenge their disadvantageous treatment are, I acknowledge, significant. For those who are experiencing or escaping violence, or who are undocumented, they may be simply insurmountable.

Rooting my examination of migration law's treatment of women in discrimination law may also raise more theoretical concerns. Nadine El-Enany argues that migration law is 'part of the colonial infrastructure that continues to dispossess former British subjects'.[57] Analogous and related arguments have been made in relation to European and EU responses to migration.[58] The scholarship undertaken here, which only scrutinises certain aspects of UK and EU migration law, risks falling 'into a liberal politics of recognition that fails to challenge the law's embodiment of colonial violence'.[59] Victoria Canning's research indicates that this objection may be extended to include other forms of violence, including that which is gender-based.[60] Linked to, but distinct from, such work are critiques of equality

[57] El-Enany, *Bordering Britain* (n 31) 221. El-Enany draws a parallel between the injustice experienced by indigenous peoples in Canada and Australia, who have to submit to 'colonial legal systems' in order to secure access to their land, and the position of those with 'ancestral, geographical and personal histories of British colonialism', who have to submit to UK immigration law.

[58] Gurminder K Bhambra, 'The Current Crisis of Europe: Refugees, Colonialism, and the Limits of Cosmopolitanism' (2017) 23 European Law Journal 395; Ida Danewid, 'White Innocence in the Black Mediterranean: Hospitality and the Erasure of History' (2017) 38 Third World Quarterly 1674; Karin de Vries and Thomas Spijkerboer, 'Race and the Regulation of International Migration. The Ongoing Impact of Colonialism in the Case Law of The European Court of Human Rights' (2021) 39 Netherlands Quarterly of Human Rights 291.

[59] El-Enany, *Bordering Britain* (n 31) 225.

[60] Victoria Canning, *Gendered Harm and Structural Violence in the British Asylum System* (Routledge 2017).

and human rights law which highlight their consistent and, indeed, persistent failure to respond to migrants' experiences of discrimination, particularly interpersonal and structural racism.[61]

In response, it may be fruitful to draw on E Tendayi Achiume's scholarship and explore the potential of migration to remedy patriarchy, as imbricated in, or distinct from, racial discrimination and colonisation.[62] I do not attempt this here. Instead, and in contrast to some of the work discussed above, I take as a starting point that it is legally permissible for States to treat citizens and non-citizens differently. Indeed, the regimes considered in this book affirm States' right to control the entry and residence rights of non-nationals. This ability is, of course, subject to those limitations within the relevant instruments that States have chosen to assume. State action within the domain of migration law and control is not immune from legal scrutiny, whether by reference to these international instruments or other legal sources. There is a flourishing literature on discrimination theory and law, and an emerging body of scholarship concerned with international, regional, and national adjudicatory bodies' application of various non-discrimination provisions to States' migration control practices.[63] This book speaks to both of these, applying insights from the former and adding to the latter an improved understanding of migration law generally, and the regimes of exception in particular. It also complements migration research that examines discrimination on other grounds, including disability, race, and age.[64] Centrally, it does not preclude the adoption of alternative theoretical or legal arguments that reveal and remedy migration law's discriminatory and violent past and present. The disadvantage that migration law produces may only be recognised and remedied through concerted and collaborative action that takes place at a number of legal and institutional sites. I offer this book as one contribution to this effort,

[61] Marie-Bénédicte Dembour, *When Humans Become Migrants: Study of the European Court of Human Rights with an Inter-American Counterpoint* (OUP 2015); Colm Ó Cinnéide, 'Why Challenging Discrimination at Borders is Challenging (and Often Futile)' (2021) 115 AJIL Unbound 362; Shreya Atrey, 'Structural Racism and Race Discrimination' (2021) 74 Current Legal Problems 1.

[62] E Tendayi Achiume, 'Migration as Decolonization' (2019) 71 Stanford Law Review 1509.

[63] On the former, in addition to work on these points already cited, see Sandra Fredman, 'Emerging from the Shadows: Substantive Equality and Article 14 of the European Convention on Human Rights' (2016) 16 Human Rights Law Review 273; Hugh Collins and Tarunabh Khaitan, *Foundations of Indirect Discrimination Law* (Hart 2018); Martha Albertson Fineman, 'Beyond Equality and Discrimination' (2020) 73 SMU Law Review Forum 51. On the latter, again, in addition to that already cited, see Antje Ellermann, 'Discrimination in Migration and Citizenship' (2020) 46 Journal of Ethnic and Migration Studies 2463; Catherine Briddick and Cathryn Costello, 'Introduction to the Symposium on Undoing Discriminatory Borders' (2021) 115 AJIL Unbound 328.

[64] Such as Ben Saul, 'Migrating to Australia with Disabilities: Non-Discrimination and the Convention on the Rights of Persons with Disabilities' (2010) 16 Australian Journal of Human Rights 63; E Tendayi Achiume, 'Race, Refugees, and International Law' in Cathryn Costello, Michelle Foster, and Jane McAdam (eds), *The Oxford Handbook of International Refugee Law* (OUP 2021); Péter D Szigeti, 'No Country for Old Men: Restrictions on the Immigration of Elderly Family Members' (2023) 68 McGill Law Journal 1.

hoping that the analysis it provides contributes to the work of academics, advocates, and decision-makers.[65]

1.4 This Book

In Part I, I establish that the State disadvantages and discriminates against migrant women, treatment which it is required to remedy. To discharge this obligation, I argue for migration status reform, including the abolition of *all* dependent migration statuses, such as those of partner and domestic worker. In the absence of such reform, I argue that migrant women who are victims of a defined form of violence, 'violence against women', should receive an independent, rights-bestowing migration status. This argument is advanced in three steps from chapter 2 to chapter 4.

Chapter 2 argues that the State's disadvantageous treatment of migrant women, treatment that includes the forced dependency and rights-restriction described above, is unlawfully discriminatory. To do so, I combine research on the number and proportion of women and men who hold particular migration statuses in the UK with doctrinal legal analysis, to establish that women are unjustifiably disadvantaged by immigration law. This disadvantage engages article 8 ECHR, the right to a private and family life, and constitutes unlawful discrimination contrary to article 14. The ever-shifting and highly complex nature of UK immigration law makes analysing particular migration rules and statuses something akin to shooting at a moving target. To ensure that chapter 2's arguments are not rendered obsolete by the next Statement of Changes to the Immigration Rules, the analysis offered captures the substance of particular migration statuses, even as the relevant rules change. I also highlight similarities between the UK's rules and those of other jurisdictions, European and non-European. The ECtHR does not currently take an intersectional approach to discrimination, although strands of its case law do show promising moves in this direction.[66] Consequently, I argue discrimination on the grounds of sex while engaging in an intersectional analysis. This is for the epistemic and emancipatory reasons discussed above and, pragmatically, to ensure the relevance of my discrimination arguments as the Court's jurisprudence develops, whether on intersectional or other lines. The chapter ends with a discussion of how the State could discharge its obligation to remedy its treatment of women, including by abolishing dependent and precarious migration statuses.

[65] Shreya Atrey, Catherine Briddick, and Michelle Foster, 'Contesting and Undoing Discriminatory Borders' (2022) 22 International Journal of Discrimination and the Law 210, 219. This Introduction draws on and develops the arguments made there.

[66] Atrey, *Intersectional Discrimination* (n 35) ch 3.

Chapter 3 advances a juridical account of violence against women, establishing the points at which five relevant international legal definitions of such violence converge, to establish what is at the heart of this legal wrong.[67] Accordingly, the 'violence against women' of this book's title is interpersonal, gender-based conduct that causes certain types of harm. Such violence is discriminatory and a breach of women's human rights. It arises from, creates, and perpetuates women's subordination. It can take many forms, including domestic violence and trafficking. Although it may be useful to describe immigration law's treatment of women as structurally violent in some contexts, doing so risks obscuring the connections between 'violence' and migration status.[68] In contrast, focusing on interpersonal violence enables the relationships and contexts that migration status particularly affects—intimate relationships, the home, and workplace—to be placed at the centre of analysis. Having defined violence against women and distinguished it from other types of wrong, chapter 3 concludes by establishing States' duties under the ECHR to prevent such violence and provide practical and effective protection from it to *all* those within their jurisdiction.

In chapter 4, I justify my arguments for the abolition of dependent migration statuses and the granting of an independent migration status to victims of violence, ethically and legally. I do so by reference to the State's role in compounding, through immigration laws that disadvantage and discriminate against women (per chapter 2), the experience of being subject to violence against women (as defined in chapter 3). Control, exclusion, a perilous migration status, and an intensified experience of violence are shown to be the distinguishing features of that compounded disadvantage.

As discussed above, the ECtHR does not, at present, take an intersectional approach to discrimination.[69] Instead, the Court uses the concept of vulnerability to capture and respond to applicants' different characteristics and experiences. This

[67] UN Committee for the Elimination of All Forms of Discrimination against Women, 'General Recommendation No 19' in 'Note by the Secretariat, Compilation of General Comments and General Recommendations Adopted by Human Rights Treaty Bodies' (29 July 1994) UN Doc HRI/GEN/1/Rev.1 [6] (as developed in CEDAW's GR 35 (n 47) [9]); Declaration on the Elimination of Violence against Women UNGA Res 48/104 (20 December 1993) art 1; Inter-American Convention on the Prevention, Punishment and Eradication of Violence against Women (adopted 9 June 1994, entered into force 5 March 1995) (1994) 33 ILM 1534, art 1; Protocol to the African Charter on Human and Peoples' Rights on the Rights of Women in Africa (adopted 11 July 2003, entered into force 25 November 2005) OAU Doc Cab/Leg/66.6, art 1(j); Istanbul Convention, art 3(a) and (d).

[68] For example, Victoria Canning, 'Corrosive Control: State-Corporate and Gendered Harm in Bordered Britain' (2020) 28 Critical Criminology 259. Canning uncovers and attributes responsibility for the harm that many migrant women experience in the UK. This process is somewhat obscured, however, by an analysis that does not differentiate between the predicaments of women who have very different rights and statuses in the UK.

[69] In *BS v Spain* App no 47159/08 (ECtHR, 24 July 2012), the Court discussed the applicant's vulnerability on the basis of her race, sex/gender, migration status, and involvement in prostitution. It did so despite having been invited by an intervener to adopt an intersectional analysis. See further Keina Yoshida, 'Towards Intersectionality in the European Court of Human Rights: The Case of *B.S. v Spain*' (2013) 21 Feminist Legal Studies 195.

jurisprudence, and Martha Albertson Fineman's theorising,[70] have prompted a number of scholars to conceptualise the disadvantage that flows from migration status as a distinct form of legally created vulnerability.[71] I justify my arguments for migration status reform and the provision of independent migration statuses to victims of violence by reference to this case law and literature. I also draw on the ECHR's and CEDAW's requirement that States provide practical and effective protection from, and reparative remedies for, violence against women. While the book's overarching legal analysis is intersectional, vulnerability is, therefore, drawn on in chapter 4 to expose the role of the State and, as we shall see, of the EU, in first producing and then compounding migrant women's disadvantage.

Part I provides the foundation for Part II's evaluation of six regimes of exception. Having woven together legal and normative analysis to establish that States should grant migrant victims of violence an independent and rights-bestowing permission to remain, I evaluate the rules developed by States, the EU, and the Council of Europe, by reference to the extent to which this duty is discharged. Drawing on Martha Minnow's writings, this analysis may be characterised as a 'feminist'[72] 'recasting project', as I 'gather' rules from different areas of law and offer a new framework for their analysis.[73] Differences between the regimes notwithstanding, their evaluation in this book is revealing both legally and ethically. In addition to illuminating each regime's individual deficiencies and discussing how these might be remedied, I examine their role in facilitating and normalising States' *denial of status* to most victims of violence. Such a response is, I argue, a markedly inapposite response to both the compounded disadvantage migrant women experience and the discrimination that gives rise to it.

In chapter 5, I examine two (and a bit) rules which require the granting of a migration status to *some* people who experience domestic violence, who are dependent on their partner, and whose relationship breaks down. The source of the first of these 'domestic violence rules' is EU law,[74] the second, UK immigration

[70] For an introduction to Fineman's work on the topic, see Martha Albertson Fineman, 'Populations, Pandemics, and Politics' (2021) 21 International Journal of Discrimination and the Law 184.

[71] Lourdes Peroni and Alexandra Timmer, 'Vulnerable Groups: The Promise of an Emerging Concept in European Human Rights Convention Law' (2013) 11 International Journal of Constitutional Law 1056; Oddný Mjöll Arnardóttir, 'The Differences that Make a Difference: Recent Developments on the Discrimination Grounds and the Margin of Appreciation under Article 14 of the European Convention on Human Rights' (2014) 14 Human Rights Law Review 647; Moritz Baumgärtel, *Demanding Rights: Europe's Supranational Courts and the Dilemma of Migrant Vulnerability* (CUP 2019); Shahrzad Fouladvand and Tony Ward, 'Human Trafficking, Vulnerability and the State' (2019) 81 Journal of Criminal Law 39.

[72] Martha Minnow, 'Adjudicating Differences: Conflicts Among Feminist Lawyers' in Marianne Hirsch and Evelyn Fox Keller (eds), *Conflicts in Feminism* (Routledge 1990); Denise G Réaume, 'What's Distinctive about Feminist Analysis of Law?: A Conceptual Analysis of Women's Exclusion from Law' (1996) 2 Legal Theory 265.

[73] Martha Minnow, 'Archetypal Legal Scholarship: A Field Guide' (2013) 63 Journal of Legal Education 65, 66.

[74] Directive 2004/38/EC of the European Parliament and of the Council of 29 April 2004 on the right of citizens of the Union and their family members to move and reside freely within the territory

law.[75] The first woman quoted above may have been entitled to an independent migration status in the UK under its domestic violence rule. The EU's domestic violence rule is available to similarly situated women who are the spouses of EU citizens resident in an EU Member State (MS) other than that citizen's 'home' State.[76]

In chapter 6, I evaluate the European trafficking 'regime', a multi-layered regime with diverse legal sources.[77] Here, I focus on rules that require States to grant residence permits to *some* victims of trafficking.[78] The second woman quoted above may have been entitled to such a permit, pursuant to provisions that incorporate various elements of the European trafficking regime into UK law.

The final two regimes I consider, in chapter 7, are those created by the Council of Europe Convention on Preventing and Combating Violence against Women and Domestic Violence (the Istanbul Convention).[79] Article 59 of this Convention imposes two distinct obligations to grant permission to remain: the first to *some* victims whose migration status is dependent on another, the second in a much broader set of circumstances.

As this chapter outline indicates, the regimes of exception that I examine differ from each other in several important respects. They are concerned with different forms of violence: domestic violence, trafficking, and/or violence against women more broadly. They have different rationales, from the protection of victims from violence to the investigation and prosecution of some of its perpetrators. Some regimes are gender-neutral, others are designed specifically for women. They also bestow different packages of rights. While some regimes offer permanent residence, or the promise of it, others provide only a very short-term permission to remain. The regimes also have different legal sources. Part II's analysis encompasses the UK's Immigration Rules, EU law, and human rights law emanating from the Council of Europe. UK immigration law is in an almost constant state of flux, its

of the Member States amending Regulation (EEC) No 1612/68 and repealing Directives 64/221/EEC, 68/360/EEC, 72/194/EEC, 73/148/EEC, 75/34/EEC, 75/35/EEC, 90/364/EEC, 90/365/EEC and 93/96/EEC [2004] OJ L 158/77, and corrigenda ([2004] OJ L 229/35, [2005] OJ L 197/34, and [2007] OJ L 204/28), art 13. This is discussed alongside a similar provision in Council Directive 2003/86/EC of 22 September 2003 on the right to family reunification [2003] OJ L251/12.

[75] Immigration Rules HC 590, Appendix Victim of Domestic Abuse.

[76] For example, the Mexican spouse of someone who was Spanish (so an EU citizen) but working in Germany (an EU MS other than their 'home' State).

[77] Including Council Directive 2004/81/EC of 29 April 2004 on the residence permit issued to third-country nationals who are victims of trafficking in human beings or who have been the subject of an action to facilitate illegal immigration, who cooperate with the competent authorities [2004] OJ L261/19; Council of Europe Convention on Action against Trafficking in Human Beings (adopted 16 May 2005, entered into force 1 February 2008) CETS 197; Directive 2011/36/EU of the European Parliament and of the Council of 5 April 2011 on preventing and combating trafficking in human beings and protecting its victims, and replacing Council Framework Decision 2002/629/JHA [2011] OJ L101/1.

[78] Residence Permits Directive, arts 6, 8; Trafficking Convention, arts 13, 14.

[79] Council of Europe Convention on Preventing and Combating Violence against Women and Domestic Violence (adopted 11 May 2011, entered into force 1 August 2014) CETS 210.

various elements and iterations determining the rights of different groups of people resident in, and seeking admission to, the UK. In contrast, the EU Directives, and the Council of Europe conventions I evaluate are, generally, subject to interpretation rather than revision. These interpretations have relevance within, across, and even beyond the EU. Although one of the regimes I consider, the trafficking regime, has been the subject of lively scholarly debate, the others have received comparatively little attention. Where these regimes have been the subject of academic inquiry, the focus has tended to be on a particular rule, or even a particular paragraph of a particular rule, and on the consequences of making comparatively limited, technical, changes to it. There is a wealth of research on migrant women's experiences of violence. The *legal* rules that both create the statuses migrant women hold, and which practitioners 'go to' when they seek to assist victims, have, however, been insufficiently scrutinised. Part II remedies this, offering a doctrinal and normative analysis of each regime's scope, as well as the rights, independence, and security that may be enjoyed by those who fall within them.

In this book, as in this Introduction, I root my analysis of migration law and gender-based violence in women's experiences of both. To do so, I draw on the cases in which NA[80] and EK[81] fought to remain in the UK.[82]

NA is from Pakistan; her husband KA is a dual national, having both Pakistani and German citizenship. Unlike the partner whose experience I started this chapter by discussing, NA's rights and status were determined by EU law (the UK being, at that time, a member of the EU). Like partners under UK immigration law she was, however, dependent on him for her migration status. KA was violent to NA and when their relationship ended, she sought permission to remain in the UK, rather than returning to Pakistan, on the basis of the EU's domestic violence rule. EK is from Tanzania; she held a domestic worker visa when she arrived in the UK. EK was trafficked for the purposes of domestic servitude, both into and then within the UK. Having escaped those who exploited her, she sought permission to remain under the trafficking regime. Part II follows NA's case first (chapter 5, considering both the EU's and UK's rules) and then EK's (chapter 6). The two women's experiences are then brought together (chapter 7) to explore whether their situations would have been different had they been decided under the Istanbul Convention.

All cases are, of course, constructed by significant others in the legal process, most notably, lawyers and adjudicators. Case law can only ever, therefore, present

80 Case C–115/15 *Secretary of State for the Home Department v NA* [2016] ECLI:EU:C:2016:487.

81 *EK (Article 4 ECHR: Anti-Trafficking Convention) Tanzania* [2013] UKUT 313 (IAC), [2013] Imm AR 895.

82 The inspiration for this approach was Martha Nussbaum's writing on capabilities. Nussbaum drew on the experiences of women she encountered in India to explore the obstacles which impeded their flourishing. This narrative method places an 'implicit emphasis on the political importance of the imagination and the emotions'. Martha C Nussbaum, *Women and Human Development: The Capabilities Approach* (CUP 2000) 15.

or represent a very partial and constructed account of a person's circumstances, perspective, and predicament. Such caveats notwithstanding, drawing on cases like those brought by NA and EK is productive for three reasons. First, while no two experiences of violence or migration are the same, these cases illuminate factors common to many women's experiences of both. I use these two specific encounters with the regimes of exception to explore predicaments shared by many women, including having a perpetrator of violence manipulate a dependent migration status. Secondly, these cases are legally significant. In NA's case, for example, the Court of Justice of the EU gave its first interpretation of the EU's domestic violence rule, one that continues to be relevant today. In EK's case, the Upper Tribunal drew on the ECHR to bolster, and give effect to, the rights afforded to victims under the trafficking regime, an interpretive move that the ECtHR has also now made.[83] Each case has, therefore, set a precedent for its regime's interpretation. Thirdly, the use of these cases as a narrative device, while offering a necessarily selective account, does some justice to the women who shaped each regime by challenging the rules that determined their status. It also focuses attention on women whose experiences of violence are compounded by rules that disadvantage and discriminate against them.

[83] *Chowdury v Greece* App no 21884/15 (ECtHR, 30 March 2017), discussed in chapter 6.

2
Probationary Wives and Precarious Workers

2.1 Introduction

In the UK, some migration statuses, such as 'indefinite leave to remain', bestow rights that are analogous to those that British people enjoy. Others, such as 'immigration bail', are insecure and extremely restrictive. Immigration law engages in the distribution of these, and an array of other migration statuses, in a way that is more complex than either a 'yes, you are entitled to a migration status' or 'no, you are not' distribution. *If* an applicant is granted permission to remain, s/he will be placed within a status-based hierarchy that is stratified by duration and rights. Indefinite leave to remain is at the top of this hierarchy. It is followed by statuses that enable people to naturalise within a relatively short period, or to be joined or accompanied by family members. Those statuses that are disadvantageous, which grant periods of leave that are short, which cannot be renewed, or which restrict their holder's right to work, are located at the bottom.

A person's position in this hierarchy will be determined, in large part, by reference to particular characteristics that they have. The criteria that immigration law explicitly uses to differentiate between non-nationals include the type of work a person does, the amount they earn, their protection needs, and the kind of familial relationship that they are in. Immigration law also differentiates on other grounds, including those that are not openly stated. Migration status runs along 'racial, coloured, national and ethnic lines, often all at the same time'.[1] The Immigration Rules exclude, either through the denial of status or the granting of those statuses that are particularly disadvantageous, those racialised people who have been subject to British colonial domination and dispossession.[2] Immigration law has, consequently, been impugned for producing racial meaning and inequality,[3] and for its structural racism.[4] From this starting point, I make two claims about contemporary migration law. First, women, particularly racialised women,

[1] Shreya Atrey, 'Structural Racism and Race Discrimination' (2021) 74 Current Legal Problems 1, 19.
[2] Drawing on Nadine El-Enany, *Bordering Britain: Law, Race and Empire* (Manchester University Press 2020).
[3] Luke de Noronha, 'Deportation, Racism and Multi-status Britain: Immigration Control and the Production of Race in the Present' (2019) 42 Ethnic and Racial Studies 2413.
[4] In the UK context, see Atrey, 'Structural Racism' (n 1). See also Cecilia Menjívar, 'The Racialization of "Illegality"' (2021) 150 Daedalus 91.

Violence against Women and Regimes of Exception. Catherine Briddick, Oxford University Press.
 DOI: 10.1093/9780191959899.003.0002

are disadvantaged by immigration law's creation and distribution of migration statuses. Secondly, this disadvantage is, at least in some cases, produced by rules that unlawfully discriminate on the grounds of sex.[5]

Some States do have provisions in their migration laws that intentionally treat women and men differently, discriminating against women by, for example, preventing their emigration in certain circumstances.[6] Rules, like those that create the statuses of partner and domestic worker introduced in chapter 1, do not, however, require women and men to meet different criteria. They are, on their face, sex/gender and race neutral, and so are frequently characterised as non-discriminatory. Christian Joppke provides a paradigmatic example of such an understanding in his examination of migration control and liberal States:

> The reduction of unfettered state interests to skill-based or economic selection epitomizes the contraction of state sovereignty in immigration policy more generally: the state may consider the individual only for what she *does*, not for what she *is*.[7]

Discrimination law prohibits direct discrimination, that is, treating one person less favourably than another because of a protected characteristic that the former has, such as their race or sexual orientation.[8] It also prohibits indirect discrimination, that is, treating a person less favourably than another through a provision, criterion, or practice, which, while not being 'directed at or against people with a particular protected characteristic' nevertheless has 'the effect of putting them at a disadvantage'.[9] While different legal and conceptual approaches have been and continue to be taken to these two forms of discrimination,[10] one thing

[5] The arguments made here were first tested in Catherine Briddick, 'Precarious Workers and Probationary Wives: How Immigration Law Discriminates Against Women' (2020) 29 Social & Legal Studies 201.

[6] Richa Shivakoti, Sophie Henderson, and Matt Withers, 'The Migration Ban Policy Cycle: A Comparative Analysis of Restrictions on the Emigration of Women Domestic Workers' (2021) 9 Comparative Migration Studies 1.

[7] Christian Joppke, *Selecting by Origin: Ethnic Migration in the Liberal State* (Harvard University Press 2005) 2.

[8] *Essop v Home Office* [2017] UKSC 27, [2017] 3 All ER 551 [1].

[9] ibid. See also *Homer v Chief Constable of West Yorkshire Police* [2012] UKSC 15, [2012] 3 All ER 1287 [17].

[10] Within the literature, one divide is between those who argue that the difference between direct and indirect discrimination is one of degree rather than kind and that both wrong people and those who maintain that indirect discrimination is not 'discrimination' and that those affected are not wronged by it (or if they are, are wronged in a different way). Scholarship that takes the former position includes Tarunabh Khaitan, *A Theory of Discrimination Law* (OUP 2015), the latter John Gardner, 'On the Ground of Her Sex(uality)' (1988) 18 Oxford Journal of Legal Studies 167. I find the former position more compelling, but the arguments advanced in this book hold, whether or not laws prohibiting indirect discrimination are justified by reference to the wrong of discriminatory treatment, sound public policy reasons, or both. For a more detailed discussion of these issues, and a potential way through them, see Deborah Hellman, 'Indirect Discrimination and the Duty to Avoid Compounding Injustice' in Hugh Collins and Tarunabh Khaitan (eds), *Foundations of Indirect Discrimination Law* (Hart 2018).

that may separate them is the potential for indirectly discriminatory treatment to be justified.[11] Treatment that does disadvantage a particular group will not, consequently, be unlawful if it is a proportionate means of achieving a legitimate aim.[12]

The use of rules that *appear* to be neutral to secure particular kinds of selection and exclusion has a long history in migration law and control, identifiable in both colonial and post-colonial migration regimes.[13] Such rules have been subject to legal challenge. In *East African Asians v UK* (1973),[14] the extension of immigration control to the citizens of independent Commonwealth countries and British dependencies who had their passports issued by the colonial, but not the UK government, was found to discriminate on the grounds of race. An appreciation of the role and prevalence of such discrimination enables us to see through what Bridget Anderson describes as the

> taken-for-grantedness of immigration controls which views them as neutral sorting mechanisms, and to consider them as a factor in shaping actions and processes, productive of certain types of relations.[15]

This chapter uses the effects-based concept of indirect discrimination to scrutinise apparently neutral rules and criteria, like those commended by Joppke, for their impact on people who share certain protected characteristics. In doing so, it builds on case law from the European Court of Human Rights (ECtHR) which has found that neutrally formulated immigration rules may be racially discriminatory,[16] and that States' prerogatives in the field of migration control are secondary to the non-discrimination obligations they have chosen to assume.[17] The extent to which such jurisprudence represents a decisive shift away from the deference the Court usually displays when States' migration controls are contested[18]

[11] Sandra Fredman, 'Direct and Indirect Discrimination: Is There Still a Divide?' in Hugh Collins and Tarunabh Khaitan (eds), *Foundations of Indirect Discrimination Law* (Hart 2018).

[12] ibid 36. See also *R (E) v Governing Body of JFS* [2009] UKSC 15, [2010] 2 AC 728 [57].

[13] Daniel Ghezelbash, 'Legal Transfers of Restrictive Immigration Laws: A Historical Perspective' (2017) 66 International and Comparative Law Quarterly 235. Antje Ellermann also argues that group-based discrimination 'remains an integral part' of migration law and policy. Antje Ellermann, 'Discrimination in Migration and Citizenship' (2020) 46 Journal of Ethnic and Migration Studies 2463, 2464.

[14] *East African Asians v UK* (1973) 3 EHRR 76.

[15] Bridget Anderson, *Us and Them?: The Dangerous Politics of Immigration Control* (OUP 2013) 70. See also Mathias Czaika and Hein De Haas, 'The Effectiveness of Immigration Policies' (2013) 39 Population and Development Review 487, 490.

[16] *Biao v Denmark* App no 38590/10 (ECtHR GC, 24 May 2016).

[17] On discrimination on the grounds of national origin and sexual orientation respectively, see *Kurić v Slovenia* App no 26828/06 (ECtHR GC, 26 June 2012); *Taddeucci and McCall v Italy* App no 51362/09 (ECtHR, 30 June 2016).

[18] On deference and migration control, see Marie-Bénédicte Dembour, *When Humans Become Migrants: Study of the European Court of Human Rights with an Inter-American Counterpoint* (OUP 2015).

is, as yet, unclear.[19] What is apparent is that these cases do offer 'a whole new range of possibilities' to challenge the racial, and other, 'underpinnings of measures, practices and provisions that so far had not been subject to scrutiny'.[20] The arguments I advance here, on the pervasiveness of migration law's discrimination against women, and what might remedy it, are but one such possibility.

The chapter proceeds as follows. In section 2.2, I introduce the legal framework that is at the heart of my analysis: the prohibition of discrimination found in article 14 of the European Convention on Human Rights (ECHR).[21] I also anticipate, and refute, two potential objections to my claim that particular sets of immigration rules discriminate against women. In section 2.3, I provide an overview of the rules that apply to certain family and labour migrants, which create, and then distribute, the migration statuses of partner, skilled labour migrant, and domestic worker. As it is 'commonplace' for statistical information to establish differential treatment,[22] I draw on Home Office statistical reports from over a decade to show that UK immigration law distributes certain migration statuses differently to men and women. Having explored 'who' is 'where' in the main family and labour migration routes, I proceed to discuss, in section 2.4, the disadvantage that these rules create. In section 2.5, I move from considering disadvantage to arguing discrimination. I consider and reject official justifications for disadvantageous facets of the rules, arguing that they are not just productive of certain types of subjects and relationships,[23] but discriminate on the grounds of sex. In section 2.6, I broaden out my analysis from the UK to other jurisdictions, revealing patterns of gendered disadvantage in migration laws across and beyond Europe. Finally, in section 2.7, I establish how the discriminatory treatment of women might be remedied. The focus of this chapter is, therefore, the ECHR's prohibition of discrimination and the UK's Immigration Rules.[24] Later, in chapter 5, I explore the applicability of some of the arguments I advance here to European Union (EU) law.

[19] For a discussion of which see Karin de Vries and Thomas Spijkerboer, 'Race and the Regulation of International Migration. The Ongoing Impact of Colonialism in the Case Law of the European Court of Human Rights' (2021) 39 Netherlands Quarterly of Human Rights 291.

[20] Mathias Möschel, 'The Strasbourg Court and Indirect Race Discrimination: Going Beyond the Education Domain' (2017) 80 Modern Law Review 121, 131.

[21] Convention for the Protection of Human Rights and Fundamental Freedoms (adopted 4 November 1950, entered into force 3 September 1953) ETS 5 (European Convention on Human Rights, as amended).

[22] *Essop v Home Office* (n 8) [28]. See also *DH v Czech Republic* App no 57325/00 (ECtHR GC, 13 November 2007).

[23] As argued, for example, in Helena Wray, *Regulating Marriage Migration into the UK: A Stranger in the Home* (Ashgate 2011); Eleonore Kofman, 'Gendered Labour Migrations in Europe and Emblematic Migratory Figures' (2012) 39 Journal of Ethnic and Migration Studies 579.

[24] The Immigration Rules are a unique form of subordinate legislation made under the Immigration Act 1971, s 3(2).

2.2 Discrimination and the ECHR

There are, as discussed in the previous chapter, a range of different theoretical accounts of the wrong of discriminatory treatment. There are also a myriad of domestic, regional, and international instruments prohibiting discrimination and protecting equality. At the centre of this book's analysis is article 14 of the ECHR, which states that:

> The enjoyment of the rights and freedoms set forth in this Convention shall be secured without discrimination on any ground such as sex, race, colour, language, religion, political or other opinion, national or social origin, association with a national minority, property, birth or other status.

Three things emerge from a first reading of this provision. First, article 14 is not free-standing; it must be relied on in conjunction with another protected right. Article 8 of the ECHR, the right to a private and family life, will be engaged in immigration cases involving marriage and other significant family relationships.[25] It will also be engaged where a person's employment and social connections are affected by a particular law or policy.[26] Those seeking to challenge a particular rule do not have to show that it violates article 8, or another right (although it may), only that the 'facts at issue fall within the ambit' of the Convention's 'rights and freedoms'.[27] Secondly, differential treatment has to be connected to a protected ground. Different systems identify different 'grounds', or characteristics, as requiring protection. The UK's Equality Act 2010, for example, only offers protection from discrimination on certain limited grounds, excluding migrant or refugee status.[28] In contrast, article 14's reference to 'other status' may be relied upon to challenge differences in treatment between individuals who are similarly situated for a range of different reasons, although different grounds attract different levels of scrutiny.[29] Thirdly, treatment may be discriminatory

[25] *Biao v Denmark* (n 16). See also *MA v Denmark* App no 6697/18 (ECtHR GC, 9 July 2021). ECHR, art 12, which protects the right to marry, may also be engaged alongside, or in addition to, art 8.

[26] *Emel Boyraz v Turkey* App no 61960/08 (ECtHR, 2 December 2014).

[27] See, among many others, *Weller v Hungary* App no 44399/05 (ECtHR, 31 March 2009) para 26. See also *Ponomaryovi v Bulgaria* App no 5335/05 (ECtHR, 21 June 2011) para 53.

[28] The protected characteristics are age, disability, gender reassignment, marriage and civil partnership, pregnancy and maternity, race, religion or belief, sex, and sexual orientation. Equality Act 2010, s 4. In *Taiwo v Olaigbe* [2016] UKSC 31, [2016] 1 WLR 2653, the Supreme Court considered discrimination on the grounds of migration status and found that it was different to discrimination on the grounds of race or nationality and not, therefore, covered by the Equality Act 2010. International legal instruments, including the Council of Europe Convention on Preventing and Combating Violence against Women and Domestic Violence (adopted 11 May 2011, entered into force 1 August 2014) CETS 210 (analysed in chapter 7), do have more extensive lists of grounds.

[29] Oddný Mjöll Arnardóttir, 'The Differences that Make a Difference: Recent Developments on the Discrimination Grounds and the Margin of Appreciation under Article 14 of the European Convention on Human Rights' (2014) 14 Human Rights Law Review 647.

even if it is not intended to differentiate between people or to disadvantage them.[30]

The Convention system does have a free-standing prohibition of discriminatory treatment which operates alongside article 14: that contained in article 1 of Protocol 12 to the ECHR.[31] At the time of writing, Protocol 12 has, however, only been ratified by twenty States. Consequently, I focus on treatment that is straightforwardly prohibited by article 14: indirect sex discrimination. As I do so, and as explained in the Introduction, I adopt an intersectional analysis that is consonant with the way that the Court currently approaches disadvantage and its jurisprudence on vulnerability.[32] Finally, as discussed above, indirect discrimination can be legally justified. A provision, criterion, or practice that adversely affects a protected group is not unlawful if the relevant distributive purpose is a legitimate one, pertaining to a public or social good, and there is a reasonable relationship of proportionality between that purpose and the criteria adopted.[33] Once differential treatment has been established, it is for the State to provide the requisite justification.[34]

Two potential objections to the arguments advanced in this chapter can be anticipated and refuted. The first is that it is simply incorrect to compare the statuses granted to partners, skilled labour migrants, and domestic workers. An objector arguing along these lines might contend that the rules that apply to domestic workers should instead be compared with those concerned with other 'low-skilled' labour migrants, such as seasonal workers.[35] The refutation of this objection lies not in a search through all the migration statuses created by immigration law, but in a consideration of the premise on which the objection rests.

Every distribution of a social good, such as that of different migration statuses, is governed by a purpose and criteria. The purpose of distributing labour migration statuses, for example, may be to benefit the national economy of the host State. The criteria that enable this distribution are the rules which determine who may enter to work and under what conditions. An argument that seeks to reject potential comparators is one that is grounded in a prior claim as to the purpose and criteria adopted for the relevant distribution: it 'is by reference to this purpose that

[30] As was the case in *DH v Czech Republic* (n 22) para 169, for example, which concerned 'unconscious racial bias'.

[31] Protocol No 12 to the Convention for the Protection of Human Rights and Fundamental Freedoms (adopted 4 November 2000, entered into force, 1 April 2005) ETS 177.

[32] Shreya Atrey, *Intersectional Discrimination* (OUP 2019) ch 3. See further Keina Yoshida, 'Towards Intersectionality in the European Court of Human Rights: The Case of *B.S. v Spain*' (2013) 21 Feminist Legal Studies 195. The Court's vulnerability jurisprudence is discussed in chapter 4.

[33] Very weighty reasons are, for example, required to justify differential treatment on, respectively, the grounds of nationality and sex. *Gaygusuz v Austria* App no 17371/90 (ECtHR, 16 September 1996) para 42; *Di Trizio v Switzerland* App no 7186/09 (ECtHR, 2 February 2016) para 82.

[34] *DH v Czech Republic* (n 22) para 180.

[35] Under the ECHR, applicants must establish that other persons in 'an analogous or relatively similar situation enjoy preferential treatment and that this distinction is discriminatory'. *Weller v Hungary* (n 27) para 27.

X is comparable to Y or not, as the case may be'.[36] Comparison may be required in some discrimination cases, but who a group may compare itself with should only be ascertained by reference to the purpose and criteria of the rule being impugned.

Hode and Abdi v UK (2012)[37] concerned UK Immigration Rules that enabled some refugees to reunite with their spouses, while denying that right to others. The case is interesting for a number of reasons. First, the ECtHR found that the applicant's position as a refugee who married *after* leaving his country was an 'other status' upon the basis of which an individual could be discriminated.[38] Secondly, when considering whether denying family reunion to refugees who married 'post flight' was discriminatory, both the State and the Court explicitly linked the purposes of the rules with the potential for the statuses they created to be compared. The UK, for example, argued that the migration statuses given to refugees could not be compared with those given to students and workers, because the government wished to encourage the latter and not the former.[39] The Court accepted that these purposes were relevant to questions of comparison and justification. However, it found that while a State could offer incentives to certain groups of migrants, the restrictions on family reunion that the applicants were subject to could not be justified.[40] In reaching this conclusion, the Court compared the migration statuses held by refugees with those of students and workers, all these groups being, in this case, 'in an analogous position' for the purposes of article 14.[41]

It is, consequently, only by bringing the purpose of the relevant distribution into view that we can ascertain who a potential comparator may be. An argument that the rules that apply to domestic workers should be compared with those that apply to another unskilled labour migration category takes as its premise that the purpose of these rules is to distribute statuses according to 'skill', and that domestic workers are 'low skilled'. If domestic work is assumed to be simply incomparable with 'skilled' work, then the State's distributive purpose and criteria, the reasons it gives for distributing migration statuses to labour migrants, and its assessment of the skill and value of different types of labour, are accepted without scrutiny. The range of potential comparators available is also narrowed, a sleight of hand that serves to diminish, or disguise, the disproportionate disadvantage that domestic workers experience.[42]

[36] Denise G Réaume, 'Dignity, Equality, and Comparison' in Deborah Hellman and Sophia Reibetanz Moreau (eds), *Philosophical Foundations of Discrimination Law* (OUP 2013) 7.

[37] *Hode and Abdi v UK* App no 22341/09 (ECtHR, 6 November 2012).

[38] ibid paras 46–48, drawing on the case of *Bah v UK* App no 56328/07 (ECtHR, 27 September 2011).

[39] *Hode and Abdi v UK* (n 37) para 36.

[40] ibid para 54.

[41] ibid para 50. For a narrow approach, albeit one that affirmed the reasoning advanced here, see *MT v Sweden* App no 22105/18 (ECtHR, 20 October 2022) paras 105–18.

[42] Drawing on Hugh Collins and Tarunabh Khaitan, 'Indirect Discrimination Law: Controversies and Critical Questions' in Hugh Collins and Tarunabh Khaitan (eds), *Foundations of Indirect Discrimination Law* (Hart 2018) 14.

Determining the purposes of an Immigration Rule is not straightforward, particularly when those rules have not been subject to challenge, so reasoning like that discussed above, in the case of *Hode and Abdi*, is not available. Determining what a 'skill' is and who might have it is also not a question of fact, but one of judgement. Later, I contend that if the State's distributive criteria are subjected to scrutiny, it becomes apparent that the rules that apply to domestic workers and partners are grounded in stereotypical understandings of women's roles and attributes. This serves two purposes. First, it may, in and of itself, establish wrongful and discriminatory treatment.[43] Secondly, and consistent with this chapter's article 14 ECHR analysis, considering the rules' purposes enables me to resolve any concerns about the comparison of domestic workers with (other?) skilled workers and to refute arguments justifying the disadvantage that those rules create. As we shall see, 'justifications' based on stereotypes do not pursue a legitimate aim and cannot, therefore, operate as justifications as a matter of law. Arguing that the statuses of partner and domestic worker are based on stereotypes may, consequently, either be sufficient to impugn the relevant rules as discriminatory or to establish discrimination by showing that women's comparative disadvantage cannot be justified. Such an approach is responsive to the critiques of Sophia Moreau and others, who have cautioned against the selection of comparators that reinforce both stereotyping and the very kinds of oppressive power relations with which discrimination law is concerned.[44] Consequently, statuses are compared with each other here because, in addition to being legally and statistically significant, as we shall see, they start to reveal patterns in immigration law's distribution of rights and restrictions.

The second potential objection to my arguments is that the discrimination law analysis undertaken should compare the number of applications *from* men and women for a particular migration status with the number of grants *to* men and women of it. An objector raising such an argument might suggest that, as more women than men apply to be partners and domestic workers, there can be no discrimination if more women than men hold that migration status.

I am concerned with the creation and distribution of different *migration statuses* and the consequences of this creation and distribution for women. This analysis is not undermined by gendered patterns in the numbers and proportions of men and women who apply for certain migration statuses; these are issues I do consider in

[43] Stereotyping is wrong because it denies people the ability to define themselves and make important decisions about their lives. Sophia R Moreau, 'The Wrongs of Unequal Treatment' (2004) 54 University of Toronto Law Journal 291. The ECtHR has, in some cases, found that where a decision is based on a stereotype no comparator is needed. *Carvalho Pinto de Sousa Morais v Portugal* App no 17484/15 (ECtHR, 25 July 2017) para 52. Comparators have also not been used in several notable cases concerning gender-based violence, including *Opuz v Turkey* App no 33401/02 (ECtHR, 9 June 2009). See further So Yeon Kim, 'Les Vulnérables: Evaluating the Vulnerability Criterion in Article 14 Cases by the European Court of Human Rights' (2021) 41 Legal Studies 617.

[44] Sophia R Moreau, 'Equality Rights and the Relevance of Comparator Groups' (2006) 5 Journal of Law and Equality 81.

section 2.5, where I evaluate justifications for differential treatment. What is relevant is whether the migration statuses the majority of whose subjects are women are (a) comparatively more disadvantageous than the migration statuses the majority of whose holders are men and/or (b) premised on stereotypes. These are the issues to which I now turn.

2.3 The Creation and Distribution of Migration Statuses

2.3.1 Changing Rules

UK immigration law is both continuously changing and extremely complicated, characteristics that reinforce each other. Almost every year since 2004, the start of the period under review, has brought a new piece of primary legislation concerned with immigration.[45] Innumerable statutory instruments and statements of changes to the Immigration Rules have accompanied these Acts.[46] The rules themselves are well over a thousand pages long, confusingly ordered, and extremely poorly drafted.[47] Changes made following the UK's departure from the EU have exacerbated a 'degree of complexity which even the Byzantine Emperors would have envied'.[48] Indeed, this complexity is such that judges who would usually seek to 'attempt a sensible interpretation' of particular rules have declined the task because of their incoherence,[49] it not being a 'proportionate use of court time' to try and 'reveal' their 'intended meaning'.[50]

Consequently, in this section, I provide a very simplified overview of the rules that apply to some family and labour migrants. I then draw on Home Office statistical information to get a sense of the proportion of men and women who are granted the statuses these rules create, including those of partner, skilled worker, and domestic worker. Space, the fluidity and complexity of immigration law, and changes to the way that the Home Office collects and publishes information

[45] For example, Asylum and Immigration (Treatment of Claimants, etc) Act 2004; Immigration, Asylum and Nationality Act 2006; UK Borders Act 2007; Criminal Justice and Immigration Act 2008; Borders, Citizenship and Immigration Act 2009; Immigration Act 2014; Immigration Act 2016; European Union (Withdrawal Agreement) Act 2020; Immigration and Social Security Co-ordination (EU Withdrawal) Act 2020; Nationality and Borders Act 2022; Illegal Migration Act 2023; Safety of Rwanda (Asylum and Immigration) Act 2024.

[46] Where 'contemporary' rules are discussed, they reflect Statement of Changes HC 590. Archived copies of the consolidated Immigration Rules as they were on the date before each statement came into effect can be accessed here: 'Archive: Immigration Rules' (*GOV.UK*) <www.gov.uk/government/collections/archive-immigration-rules> accessed 25 April 2024.

[47] Law Commission, *Simplification of the Immigration Rules: Report* (Law Com No 388, 2020) ch 1.

[48] *Pokhriyal v Secretary of State for the Home Department* [2013] EWCA Civ 1568, [2013] WLR(D) 471 [4].

[49] *Secretary of State for the Home Department and Israt Rumana Kabir* [2023] UKAITUR EA138702021 [23].

[50] ibid [21].

preclude me from always being able to correlate particular iterations of the relevant rules with information on who held the statuses they produced. The specific periods referred to in the paragraphs that follow are those of Home Office reports, with information disaggregated by sex being obtained, where necessary, through Freedom of Information requests.[51] This is neither a detailed doctrinal discussion of the Immigration Rules nor a quantitative examination of family and labour migration in the UK. Overall, the analysis offered is calibrated at a level of generality to chart, at a readable length, the substance of particular migration statuses and gendered patterns in those statuses' distribution.[52] This approach is consistent with the methodology of the ECtHR in its non-discrimination jurisprudence, in which statistical information, including from surveys, reports, and unofficial estimates, may be used to establish patterns of differential treatment.[53] Such differentials do not need to be significant, but 'persistent and relatively constant'.[54] Many of the differentials discussed here are both. Finally, here, and throughout the chapter, I use the language and terminology of either the Immigration Rules themselves, or the Home Office's statistical reports. In referring to 'wives', or to partners as 'she', for example, I highlight just one of the ways in which the State categorises migrant women.[55] As will become apparent, stereotypes based on sex, race, and sexual orientation are written into migration law and control in ways that would be considered unacceptable in other legal domains.

2.3.2 Partners

Before 1 January 2021, the rules that applied to European citizens and their family members differed from those that applied to the non-European family members of people who were British or resident in the UK.[56] I analyse these free movement

[51] Information from both Home Office statistical reports and Freedom of Information (FOI) requests involve data being taken from live operational database(s). Consequently, the numbers reported change as information is updated. Data retrieved by FOI request on an ad hoc basis (various dates in 2015, 2019, and 2022) may not, therefore, match publicly available data sets because of this and other changes in the recorded data. The reports and FOI results drawn on here are all on file with the author.

[52] This approach, which uses a single category, such as 'partner' or 'skilled worker', to capture a particular migration status, even though the precise rules that determine who is eligible for that status change over time, is consistent with that taken by the Home Office in its statistical and other reports.

[53] *DH v Czech Republic* (n 22) para 180. See also *Essop v Home Office* (n 8) [28].

[54] Case C–167/97 *R v Secretary of State for Employment, ex p Nicole Seymour-Smith and Laura Perez* [1999] ECR I–00623, para 61.

[55] The Home Office's statistical reports distinguish between people who are granted permission to remain under the rules as partners, referring to, for instance, husbands, wives, civil partners, common-law spouses (there is no such thing in law), and same-sex partners.

[56] The European Union's (EU) Member States (MS) are Austria, Belgium, Bulgaria, Croatia, Cyprus, Czech Republic, Denmark, Estonia, Finland, France, Germany, Greece, Hungary, Ireland, Italy, Latvia, Lithuania, Luxembourg, Malta, the Netherlands, Poland, Portugal, Romania, Slovakia, Slovenia, Spain, and Sweden. Iceland, Norway, and Liechtenstein are not members of the EU, but are in the European Economic Area (the EEA). Those three States, along with Switzerland, are generally treated analogously

rules and their regime of exception in chapter 5. As the UK prepared to leave the EU, arrangements were made which sought to protect the rights of European citizens and their families. The EU Settlement Scheme (EUSS) enabled many to receive settled or pre-settled status, permissions to remain of different lengths and stability, depending on their circumstances. As the deadline for most applications under the EUSS was in June 2021, it is not considered here. Research has, however, highlighted the intersectional disadvantage experienced by applicants who were single parents and/or victims of domestic violence.[57] Instead, my focus in this chapter is the rules that now apply to all family members.

As explained in the Introduction, partners, whether married/civilly partnered or not, fiancé(e)s, and proposed civil partners, children, and other dependent relatives *may* all be able to join someone who is British or settled in the UK using one of a variety of family migration routes. In each case, the person migrating for family reasons must meet certain criteria, set out in the Immigration Rules, before the relevant migration status is granted. For those who seek permission as partners, these conditions relate to the applicant (aged eighteen or over, able to speak English to a specified level), the couple's relationship (they are not related in certain ways, previous relationships have broken down, the current relationship is genuine and subsisting), and how they will live in the UK (together, permanently).[58] Applicants must also meet onerous financial requirements, in the form of a minimum income threshold, but are limited in both the sources of income and forms of evidence they are able to rely on to do this.[59] Those who meet these criteria have permission to enter and remain that lasts for around thirty months. This permission *may* be renewed, on application, for around another thirty months, after which the migrant partner may apply for indefinite leave to remain.[60] During this 'probationary period', the partner has permission to work, but may not generally access key sources of support from the State, including welfare benefits.[61] While requirements relating

with EU MS in the field of migration law. The reference to European citizens here refers to EU, EEA, and Swiss citizens.

[57] Adrienne Yong, 'A Gendered EU Settlement Scheme: Intersectional Oppression of Immigrant Women in a Post-Brexit Britain' (2022) 32 Social & Legal Studies 756.

[58] Immigration Rules HC 590, Appendix FM: Family Members E-ECP.2.1-10; E-ECP.4.1.

[59] ibid E-LTRP.3.1-3.4; Immigration Rules HC 590, Appendix FM-SE: Family Members Specified Evidence. At the time of writing this is increasing substantially in three stages, from £18,600 (from July 2012 to March 2024) to £29,000 (April 2024) to £38,700 (from late 2024 to early 2025). This latter figure is more than double the original requirement and aligns with the income level needed for skilled workers. Applicants who are unable to meet this may, in 'exceptional circumstances', be placed on a ten-year route to settlement. CJ McKinney and Melanie Gower, 'Research Briefing: Changes to Legal Migration Rules for Family and Work Visas in 2024' (*House of Commons Library*, 11 April 2024) <https://commonslibrary.parliament.uk/research-briefings/cbp-9920/> accessed 25 April 2024.

[60] Appendix FM: Family Members (n 58) D-ECP 1.1, E-ILRP 1.1, D-LTRP 1.1.

[61] Where an applicant is not made subject to the 'no recourse' requirement, because, for example, they are destitute or there are reasons relating to the welfare of a child, permission to remain will be granted but the applicant will only be able to apply for settlement after a continuous period of at least 120 months. ibid D-ECP 1.2, D-LTRP 1.2, GEN.1.11A.

to a couple's income and to the migrant partner's knowledge of English were introduced in 2012, the existence of a probationary period has been a consistent feature of the partner route. The length of this period has, however, increased, from twelve to twenty-four months in 2003, and from this to five years in 2012.[62]

It is disproportionately 'women-as-wives' who enter and then remain in the UK under the 'partner' route.[63] In each and every year from 2004 to 2017, for example, two-thirds or more of those entering the UK as partners were wives.[64] In each and every year from 2011 to 2020, significantly more 'wives' than 'husbands' settled in the UK.[65] It remains the case that women are significantly more likely than men to move to the UK to join someone who is British or resident.[66]

2.3.3 Labour Migrants

Labour migration in the UK is, for the most part, organised through a streamed or segmented system, some of which is points-based, in which permission to enter and remain is granted according to whether a labour migrant has certain skills or attributes. While the relevant rules now apply in the same way to all applicants, before 1 January 2021, European and non-European citizens were subject to different legal regimes. European citizens benefited from freedom of movement (again, discussed in chapter 5). In contrast, most non-European citizens required some form of permission to work in the UK. While changes to the rules following the UK's departure from the EU made European citizens subject to what was, for them, an entirely new set of requirements, the rules themselves were, in many significant ways, a continuation of those that preceded them.[67]

[62] For a history of the partner route, see Natasha Carver, '"For Her Protection and Benefit": The Regulation of Marriage-Related Migration to the UK' (2016) 39 Ethnic and Racial Studies 2758.

[63] Katharine Charsley and others, 'Marriage-Related Migration to the UK' (2012) 46 International Migration Review 861. Charsley and others note, first, that a tendency for women to follow men is documented in both the UK and US and, secondly, that there is also considerable variation within this pattern by nationality.

[64] In 2017, for example, 16,200 people were admitted to the UK as 'partners' of whom 11,300 were wives. Home Office, 'Immigration Statistics, Admission tables – ad_01 to ad_04_q, Table ad_03_f: Passengers given leave to enter the United Kingdom in family categories by country of nationality' from 'Why do people come to the UK? (4) For Family Reasons' (*GOV.UK*, 29 November 2018) <www.gov.uk/government/publications/immigration-statistics-year-ending-september-2018/why-do-people-come-to-the-uk-4-for-family-reasons> accessed 14 October 2022.

[65] Over twice as many. In 2019, for example, 14,327 wives whose spouse was a British citizen settled in comparison with 5,997 husbands. Home Office, 'Immigration Statistics, year ending June 2022: Settlement – Summary Tables, se_04 Grants of settlement to spouses on the basis of marriage, 2011 to 2020' from 'Statistical data set, Immigration statistics data tables, year ending June 2022' (*GOV.UK*, 25 August 2022) <www.gov.uk/government/statistical-data-sets/immigration-statistics-data-tables-year-ending-june-2022#settlement> accessed 29 April 2024.

[66] Nuni Jorgensen and Peter William Walsh, 'Family Migration to the UK' (*Migration Observatory*, 6 October 2023) <https://migrationobservatory.ox.ac.uk/resources/briefings/family-migration-to-the-uk/> accessed 10 March 2024.

[67] Manoj Dias-Abey, 'Path Dependent Policymaking in the Post-Brexit United Kingdom: What's New about the "Points-Based" Labour Migration System?' (2022) 1 European Law Open 720.

Labour migration routes currently exist for those with global talent or the ability to scale up a growing business. Routes also exist for skilled workers, creative workers, graduates, seasonal workers, and overseas domestic workers. The rules that create these statuses are becoming increasingly fragmented. Nevertheless, they operate hierarchically in terms of the rights that they bestow, creating a 'labour-migration-status-based hierarchy' within the general 'migration-status-based hierarchy'. Before 2021, many of these routes and their precursors were within an explicitly tiered points-based system, with Tier 1 at the top and Tier 5 at the bottom (and some tiers in between being effectively 'empty'). While many of these routes have changed, or changed names, their basic structure and content remain broadly similar.[68] At the top of the hierarchy are statuses, such as those of innovator founder or scale-up worker, which are granted to those considered 'highly skilled' and which confer significant rights. These include being able to be joined by family members and settle with them permanently in the UK. Those statuses that confer fewer rights, which require renewal, or which cannot be renewed, are lower down, or towards the bottom of this hierarchy. While some of these statuses, such as those that apply to skilled workers, ministers of religion, or sportspersons, do enable settlement in the UK, others, such as those that apply to creative workers and religious workers, do not. While some, such as creative workers, may apply to extend their stay and be accompanied by family members, others, such as seasonal workers, may not. While some temporary workers, seasonal workers, may return to the UK year-on-year, others, domestic workers, may not. The status at the bottom of this hierarchy remains, therefore, that given to overseas domestic workers.

The principal long-term labour migration route is that which applies to skilled workers—known as the Tier 2 (General) route under the pre-2021 system. Skilled workers, under both the pre- and post-2021 incarnations of the rules, must score 70 points to work in the UK. Points are allocated based on attributes, some of which are mandatory, while others may be met in more than one way.[69] Applicants must score 50 points by speaking English at the required level and having a 'skilled' job offered by an approved sponsor. The remaining 20 points are awarded for reaching a set minimum salary threshold, which can be lowered in certain circumstances (if the applicant is a 'new entrant' to the labour market).[70] These circumstances *do not* include enabling flexible or part-time work. Salary thresholds may not, therefore, be pro-rated to accommodate the needs of those with caring responsibilities who cannot work full-time. Most skilled workers may be accompanied or joined

[68] See further Colin Yeo, *Welcome to Britain: Fixing Our Broken Immigration System* (Biteback 2022) ch 7.

[69] Immigration Rules HC 590, Appendix Skilled Worker SW3.1–14.3A.

[70] The minimum salary to be sponsored for a Skilled Worker visa has also increased significantly, the baseline minimum rising from £26,200 to £38,700 in April 2024 (excluding NHS staff and education workers). McKinney and Gower, 'Research Briefing' (n 59).

by family members, who themselves will have permission to work in the UK. The exception to this is care workers.[71] The permission to remain that is available to family members, like that given to partners and discussed above, makes those family members dependent for their rights in the UK on the skilled worker (an issue I also return to in chapter 4). Skilled workers can change employers and employment type, extend their stay, and stay in a different category. Those who have spent five years in the UK are eligible for settlement, subject to being able to demonstrate that they continue to meet the salary threshold.[72]

In contrast, to be granted permission as a domestic worker, an applicant must have worked and lived in their employer's home for at least a year before entry to the UK.[73] Domestic workers must intend to work for that employer in the UK, and travel with them or their family. The employer and domestic worker must have agreed in writing the terms and conditions of the employment, conditions that include paying a salary that complies with the National Minimum Wage Act 1998. Domestic workers must leave the UK at the end of six months or at the same time as their employer, whichever is sooner. Domestic workers cannot extend their stay, remain on a different basis, or return to the UK (as seasonal workers can). Domestic workers cannot apply for settlement in the UK and their family members cannot join them.

From 2005 to 2020, more men than women migrated to the UK as labour migrants and men were also more likely to be at the 'top' of the labour migration hierarchy. Consistently more men than women were granted permission to remain as 'high value migrants' (formerly Tier 1 and its pre-points-based-system equivalent).[74] Overall, from 2005 to 2017 around three-quarters of those given permission to enter as skilled workers were men, the proportion starting to drop thereafter.[75]

The proportion of men and women entering as labour migrants equalises as we move 'down' through different labour migration routes, from a consideration

[71] From March 2024. Appendix Skilled Worker (n 69) SW 29.1A.

[72] ibid SW 19.1–25.2.

[73] Immigration Rules HC 590, Appendix Overseas Domestic Worker.

[74] The ratio of male/female applicants over the period was, broadly speaking, 60% male, 40% female. UK Visas & Immigration Freedom of Information, *FOI Number 52799* (on file with the author, data extracted 14 March 2019) (25 March 2019); UK Visas & Immigration Freedom of Information, *FOI Number 54189* (on file with the author, data extracted 24 June 2019) (9 July 2019); UK Visas & Immigration Freedom of Information, *FOI Number 54469* (on file with the author, data extracted 15 July 2019) (25 July 2019); UK Visas & Immigration Freedom of Information, *FOI Number 54749* (on file with the author, data extracted 30 July 2019) (13 August 2019); UK Visas & Immigration Freedom of Information, *FOI Number 68009* (on file with the author, data extracted 27 January 2022) (9 February 2022); supplementing and disaggregating by sex, Home Office, 'Entry Clearance Visas granted outside the UK, Volume 2, Table vi_06_q_w: Entry clearance visas granted by category and country of nationality: Work' from

'Immigration statistics, year ending September 2018: data tables' (*GOV.UK*, 29 November 2018) <www.gov.uk/government/statistics/immigration-statistics-year-ending-september-2018-data-tables> accessed 26 April 2024.

[75] ibid.

of those the State believes to have significant potential, or to be skilled, through to those whose skills it values less, or not at all. Around half of those given permission to enter the UK as temporary workers (formerly Tier 5 migrants and its pre-points-based system equivalent) were women between 2005 and 2020.[76] Three-quarters or more of those given permission to remain as domestic workers were women in every year from 2005 to 2019.[77] Indeed, this migration status is both gendered and racialised. The majority of those entering as domestic workers do so from the Philippines and other countries in South/South East Asia, the Middle East, and Africa.

Changes in migration patterns during and after the Covid-19 pandemic, both to the rules and to the way that the Home Office collates statistical information, make it difficult to trace these patterns post-2018/19. On rule changes, for example, particularly advantageous routes have been scrapped while others have been hollowed out, with comparatively few people applying to them. Conversely, the number of people entering the UK as seasonal workers, a highly disadvantageous route introduced in 2019, has increased, with research suggesting that the majority of those holding this status are men.[78] It also appears that more women are now applying as skilled workers than has previously been the case, in response to post-Covid and post-Brexit efforts to fill vacancies in the National Health Service and in social care.[79] It is, consequently, significant that this group cannot bring family members with them.[80] It remains the case, therefore, that for a significant period of time the route created for skilled workers was/is both the main labour migration route into the UK and one mainly benefiting men.[81] The overall pattern of more men than women migrating for work (with women as their dependants),[82] and more women than men receiving those statuses that

[76] ibid.

[77] ibid.

[78] Food & Rural Affairs Department for Environment and Home Office, 'Seasonal Workers Survey Results 2022' (*GOV.UK*, 25 January 2024) <www.gov.uk/government/publications/seasonal-workers-pilot-review/seasonal-workers-survey-results-2022> accessed 22 March 2024. For an illuminating discussion and comparison of both the seasonal worker and domestic worker routes, see Virginia Mantouvalou, 'The UK Seasonal Worker Visa' (2022) 1 European Law Open 711.

[79] *FOI Number 68009* (n 74).

[80] Care workers were added to the skilled worker route in February 2022, but from March 2024 were unable to bring dependants with them. This route is one of the reasons for the 'unusually high' migration from 2022 to 2023. Madeleine Sumption and Ben Brindle, 'The Ban on Care Workers' Family Members: What Will be the Impact?' (*Migration Observatory*, 5 April 2024) <https://migrationobservatory.ox.ac.uk/resources/commentaries/the-ban-on-care-workers-family-members-what-will-be-the-impact/> accessed 26 April 2024.

[81] This analysis is consistent with that of others, including Anderson, *Us and Them?* (n 15) ch 3. See also Joanna Hunt, 'Do the Immigration Rules Discriminate against Women Who Want to Work in the UK?' (*freemovement*, 4 April 2018) <https://freemovement.org.uk/do-the-immigration-rules-discriminate-against-women-who-want-to-work-in-the-uk/> accessed 11 November 2022; Joanna Hunt, 'Why the MAC Report Was a Let Down for Women' (*freemovement*, 6 February 2020) <https://freemovement.org.uk/comment-why-the-mac-report-was-a-letdown-for-women/> accessed 11 November 2022.

[82] Jorgensen and Walsh, 'Family Migration to the UK' (n 66).

are particularly disadvantageous (with no right to bring their dependants), also seems to have endured.[83]

2.4 Migration Status and Disadvantage

2.4.1 Restriction, Dependency, Precarity, and Violence

I have mapped significant family and labour migration routes to the UK, indicating who is where within those routes. Here, I explore how those who hold the status of partner or domestic worker may be disadvantaged by it, how immigration law produces both the probationary wives and precarious workers of this chapter's title. Drawing on arguments advanced by Bridget Anderson, I discuss this disadvantage in terms of the reduction or restriction of migrants' rights, forced dependency, and precarity.[84] I add to this a fourth disadvantage, one that emerges from research concerned with women's experience of the relevant statuses: an increased risk of violence and exploitation. These are not, of course, the only ways in which immigration law adversely affects people, nor are these forms of disadvantage distinct. Other statuses, notably including that held by seasonal workers, also disadvantage their holders in different and often significant ways. Finally, many migrants who *are* partners, or who undertake paid domestic work, do not actually hold the relevant migration status. Such people may have permission to remain on another basis, as students or visitors for example. They may also have no permission to remain at all. A discussion of the disadvantage faced by people in this position is beyond the scope of this chapter.

2.4.2 Partners

The partner route makes migrant partners, who are, it will be recalled, predominantly 'women-as-wives', financially and otherwise dependent on their British or resident 'husband'. It has been estimated that 'tens of thousands' of British and settled people have not been able to bring a partner to the UK following the introduction of the minimum income requirement in 2012.[85] Legal and other analysis of this provision has focused on the difficulties faced by women (particularly racialised

[83] Natalie Sedacca, 'Migrant Work, Gender and the Hostile Environment: A Human Rights Analysis' (2024) 53 Industrial Law Journal 63.

[84] Bridget Anderson, 'Migration, Immigration Controls and the Fashioning of Precarious Workers' (2010) 24 Work, Employment & Society 300.

[85] 'How Many People Have Been Prevented from Bringing a Partner to the UK Due to the £18,600 Minimum Income Requirement?' (*Migration Observatory*, 14 December 2018) <https://migrationobservatory.ox.ac.uk/resources/commentaries/how-many-people-have-been-prevented-from-bringing-a-partner-to-the-uk-due-to-the-18600-minimum-income-requirement/)> accessed 22 March 2024.

women) and younger people who want to *sponsor* a partner, as these groups are less likely than others to earn enough to do so.[86] These arguments have gained salience as the minimum income requirement is increased.[87] Such an analysis takes as its focus, however, the rights of the British or resident sponsor. If we consider the requirement from the perspective of a prospective entrant, then further gendered disadvantage may be identified. Not only must a couple demonstrate that they have substantial financial resources, but at the beginning of the process when, for example, the applicant is to travel to the UK with or to join her partner, it is only income from *his* employment/self-employment that is considered.[88] Dependency for those seeking permission to enter as a partner is created by disregarding a woman's own financial contributions, making her reliant on her husband's resources for the purposes of her immigration application. Preventing women from relying on earnings received outside of the UK, or anticipated UK earnings, from secured employment, for example, operates as a disincentive to those seeking permission in this category to seek work before they enter, or to maintain it in their country of origin during the application process. Indeed, during this pre-entry period, it makes more 'sense' for an applicant to support her husband to maximise his income, rather than to seek to secure her own.

Once in the UK, women can work and access healthcare but cannot apply for public funds, including welfare benefits and other sources of State support.[89] Migrant partners are, consequently, dependent for their status and all the rights that flow from it on their sponsor, a position that undermines women's autonomy, affecting decisions about their family and professional lives.[90] The extension of the probationary period and imposition of an immigration application mid-way through the five years, an application which is costly, and in which the applicant must demonstrate that all the requirements of the rules continue to be met, both reinforces dependency and renders the migrant partner's position in the UK precarious.[91] There has been a significant decrease in the proportion of partners

[86] *R (MM (Lebanon)) v Secretary of State for the Home Department* [2017] UKSC 10, [2017] 1 WLR 771; Michelle Yik Yu Wong, 'The Unequal Price of Love: A Critical Race Feminist Critique of the £18,600 Minimum Income Requirement for Family Reunification under Article 14 ECHR' (2019) 33 Journal of Immigration Asylum and Nationality Law 302.

[87] As explained in n 59. See also Nuni Jorgensen, 'Family Fortunes: The UK's New Income Requirement for Partner Visas' (*Migration Observatory*, 1 February 2024) <https://migrationobservatory.ox.ac.uk/resources/commentaries/family-fortunes-the-uks-new-income-requirement-for-partner-visas/> accessed 22 March 2024; Katharine Charsley and Helen Wray, 'Instead of Separating Thousands More Families—Rethink UK Family Migration Policies' (*Migration Mobilities Bristol*, 19 March 2024) <https://migration.bristol.ac.uk/2024/03/19/instead-of-separating-thousands-more-families-rethink-uk-family-migration-policies/> accessed 20 March 2024.

[88] This is because the partner's non-UK income cannot be taken into account unless they are already working legally in the UK. Appendix FM-SE (n 59).

[89] Discussed in detail in chapter 4.

[90] Katharine Charsley and others, *Marriage Migration and Integration* (University of Bristol, 2016).

[91] In certain, limited, circumstances, a variation of leave may be granted to enable access to public funds. Generally, though, if the rules cannot be met, a partner may either be moved to the longer and more expensive ten-year route to settlement, or have to leave the UK.

who complete the probationary period since these changes to the rules were first made in 2012, and these changes also appear to have disproportionately affected 'women-as-wives'.[92] Women's dependency on their partners is both expressive and material. A wife must ask for her husband to complete and sign a declaration confirming their relationship in order to submit *her* immigration application.[93] A husband's refusal to submit the declaration may result in his wife's loss of status, even if the marriage or relationship is continuing and all the other requirements of the rules are satisfied. Indeed, as *Balakoohi* (2012)[94] demonstrates, a letter from a husband to the Home Office stating that the relationship has ended can result in a wife's permission to remain being curtailed, *even if that husband does not tell her that he believes the relationship has ended.* Dependency also has consequences beyond status, or the loss thereof. Empirical research has identified a strong correlation between domestic violence and rules or practices that disadvantage women, and grant men control over them.[95] The dependency and precarity created by the probationary period has, consequently, been linked to both an increased vulnerability to domestic violence and an intensified experience of it (issues I return to in chapter 4).[96]

Finally, although the migration status given to partners does give the right to work, even this is effectively restricted as, in addition to the above, the probationary period also acts as a barrier to securing employment.[97] While the partner route confers benefits, its requirements are onerous, more onerous indeed than those that apply to skilled labour migrants.[98] The route also restricts rights and imposes dependency. Settlement, or the promise of it, obscures the precarity of a

[92] The proportion of people granted a family visa in 2016 who had been granted settlement five years later was 42%. This is much lower than the 2008–2011 range of 79–82%. While women were granted 71% of family visas in 2016, there was 'little difference' in the proportion of women and men who had permission to remain or who had settled in the UK by 2021; Home Office, *Migrant Journey: 2021 Report* (31 May 2022) 22.

[93] For example, UK Visas and Immigration, 'Declaration for spouses, civil partners, proposed civil partners, fiancé(e)s, and unmarried partners, Form to extend stay in the UK as the partner or dependent child of someone who is settled here or who is a refugee or under humanitarian protection, FLR (M)' (*UK Visas and Immigration*, 13 December 2018) <www.gov.uk/government/publications/apply-to-extend-stay-in-the-uk-as-a-partner-or-dependent-child-form-flrm> accessed 25 October 2022.

[94] *R (Balakoohi) v Secretary of State for the Home Department* [2012] EWHC 1439 (Admin).

[95] Lori L Heise and Andreas Kotsadam, 'Cross-national and Multilevel Correlates of Partner Violence: An Analysis of Data From Population-Based Surveys' (2015) 3 Lancet Global Health 332; Dan Anderberg and others, 'Unemployment and Domestic Violence: Theory and Evidence' (2016) 126 The Economic Journal 1947.

[96] Sundari Anitha, 'Legislating Gender Inequalities' (2011) 17 Violence Against Women 1260; Nughmana Mirza, 'The UK Government's Conflicting Agendas and "Harmful" Immigration Policies: Shaping South Asian Women's Experiences of Abuse and "Exit"' (2016) 36 Critical Social Policy 592.

[97] For female migrants who were spouses, civil and other partners, and dependants, the overall employment rate is 44%. This rises to 47% for those who become a UK citizen. Home Office, *Family Migration: Evidence and Analysis (2nd edition)* (Occasional Paper 94, 2011) 7. Some reasons for this are discussed in Nisan Z Kesete, Danielle Thom, and Heather Harvey, *Settling In* (Eaves 2015).

[98] Others have also reached this conclusion; Helena Wray, Agnes Agoston, and Jocelyn Hutton, 'A Family Resemblance? The Regulation of Marriage Migration in Europe' (2014) 16 European Journal of Migration and Law 209, 245.

route which tests the same requirements three times in five years, effectively creating the migration status of 'probationary wife'.

2.4.3 Labour Migrants

Domestic workers only, it will be recalled, have permission to remain in the UK for a very short and non-renewable period—just six months. Domestic workers have, in theory, been able to change employers, if not employment type, since 2016.[99] However, domestic workers' inability to extend or renew their leave to do this renders this ability 'meaningless' in practice.[100] Domestic workers who leave their employer may also lose their permission to remain, even if their employer has acted unlawfully or has been abusive. In some limited circumstances, where a domestic worker is recognised as a victim of trafficking or slavery, she can apply to extend her stay and may, therefore, be able to secure alternative employment.[101] However, domestic workers can lose their status and risk destitution or further violence if they do leave their employer, but where trafficking/slavery is not the abuse complained of, or where such a claim is not accepted.[102] Consequently, it remains extremely difficult for domestic workers to change employers or to challenge abuse. A domestic worker's visa may no longer have her employer's name stamped into it, as was the case, but domestic workers remain 'tied' to them in practice.

Finally, domestic workers' ability to support themselves and their families, and to maintain a private and family life, is severely affected by having to both work and live in their employer's home, without their own family members.[103] This predicament also contributes to domestic workers' increased risk of being subject to both violence and exploitation (again, discussed further in chapters 3 and 4).[104] As the

[99] 'Overseas Domestic Workers: Statement made on 7 March 2016, James Brokenshire, Minister of State for Immigration (Statement UIN HCWS583)' (*UK Parliament*, 7 March 2016) <https://questions-statements.parliament.uk/written-statements/detail/2016-03-07/hcws583> accessed 26 April 2024; Statement of Changes in Immigration Rules HC 877.

[100] 'Kalayaan Briefing on the Government Response to the Independent Review of the Overseas Domestic Worker (ODW) Visa' (*KALAYAAN*, 8 March 2016) 2 <www.kalayaan.org.uk/wp-content/uploads/2014/09/Kalayaan-briefing-on-Government-response-to-Independent-Review-of-ODW-visa.pdf> accessed 26 April 2024. See also James Ewins QC, 'Independent Review of the Overseas Domestic Workers Visa' (*GOV.UK*, 17 December 2015) <www.gov.uk/government/publications/overseas-domestic-workers-visa-independent-review> accessed 26 April 2024.

[101] Immigration Rules HC 590, Appendix Domestic Worker who is a Victim of Modern Slavery. This is also open to those who have permission to remain as private servants in diplomatic households.

[102] Or even not accepted at a particular time, see Immigration (Variation of Leave) Order 2016, SI 2016/948; Avril Sharp and Natalie Sedacca, *Dignity, Not Destitution* (Kalaayan 2019).

[103] Natalie Sedacca, 'Migrant Domestic Workers and the Right to a Private and Family Life' (2019) 37 Netherlands Quarterly of Human Rights 288.

[104] KALAYAAN, 'Still Enslaved: The Migrant Domestic Workers Who Are Trapped by the Immigration Rules' (*KALAYAAN*, 2014) <www.kalayaan.org.uk/wp-content/uploads/2014/09/tied-visa-20141.pdf> accessed 22 April 2024; Virginia Mantouvalou, '"Am I Free Now?" Overseas Domestic Workers in Slavery' (2015) 42 Journal of Law and Society 329.

UK's Supreme Court has observed, domestic workers may be 'treated disgracefully, in a way which employees who did not share their vulnerable immigration status would not have been treated'.[105]

2.5 From Disadvantage to (Unlawful?) Discrimination

2.5.1 Justification and the Margin of Appreciation

The rules that create the statuses of partner and domestic worker do not only disadvantage women, they also unlawfully discriminate against them. Summarising the jurisprudence of the ECtHR, in *R (SC) v Secretary of State for Work and Pensions* (2021),[106] Lord Reed outlined the 'general approach' to be adopted to discrimination under article 14 ECHR:

> (1) The court has established in its case law that only differences in treatment based on an identifiable characteristic, or 'status', are capable of amounting to discrimination within the meaning of article 14.
> (2) Moreover, in order for an issue to arise under article 14 there must be a difference in the treatment of persons in analogous, or relevantly similar, situations.
> (3) Such a difference of treatment is discriminatory if it has no objective and reasonable justification; in other words, if it does not pursue a legitimate aim or if there is not a reasonable relationship of proportionality between the means employed and the aim sought to be realised.
> (4) The contracting state enjoys a margin of appreciation in assessing whether and to what extent differences in otherwise similar situations justify a different treatment. The scope of this margin will vary according to the circumstances, the subject matter and the background.[107]

Following the arguments made in section 2.2, I am primarily concerned with discrimination on the grounds of sex (point (1), per Lord Reed's summary). In section 2.3, I compared the position of different kinds of family and labour migrants on the basis that it is only by bringing into view the purposes of the rules that distribute different migration statuses that we can ascertain who a potential comparator may be (point (2) above). My focus here is, therefore (3) and (4), justification and the margin of appreciation. I evaluate as justifications some of the original legislative

[105] *Taiwo v Olaigbe* (n 28) [14].
[106] *R (SC, CB and 8 children) v Secretary of State for Work and Pensions* [2021] UKSC 26, [2022] AC 223.
[107] ibid [37] (some punctuation removed for clarity).

purposes of the rules which make partners and domestic workers dependent on others, which restrict their rights, and which are precarious. In chapters 3 and 4, I consider violence, vulnerability to it, and States' obligations to respond to it. Of course, the justification analysis engaged in here is of a different order to that which would be carried out by a court. Ascertaining the purposes of immigration law is also far from straightforward, and some of the rules I consider may have several, including those that are not explicitly stated. I accept at face value, and analyse, the State's main stated explanations for the relevant rules. In doing so, I recognise that should these issues be litigated, the State is not bound to present, or to only present, these purposes as justifications.[108] Justifications that are grounded in stereotypes are identified and rejected.

When stereotypes are considered in discrimination law, it is usually in the context of a distributive criterion based on a stereotype that relates to a protected ground. For example, an employer seeking to employ an engineer who only wishes to hire men because he believes that women are not good at maths will be directly discriminating against women by relying on stereotypical understandings of men's and women's abilities. I am not suggesting that the rules considered here are discriminatory because they specify that the applicant for a particular migration status be male or female. Rather, I contend that the migration statuses of partner and domestic worker are premised on stereotypical understandings of women's roles and attributes. While I differentiate between 'dependent wives' and 'carer women' to illuminate different disadvantageous facets of the rules and the gendered assumptions that underpin them, there are, as will become apparent, significant areas of overlap between the two. Indeed, these stereotypes may be thought of as co-constitutive.

In *Konstantin Markin v Russia* (2012),[109] the ECtHR considered discrimination, stereotyping, and men's access to parental leave. The Grand Chamber was clear that:

> reference to the traditional distribution of gender roles in society cannot justify the exclusion of men, including servicemen, from the entitlement to parental leave . . . gender stereotypes, such as the perception of women as primary child-carers and men as primary breadwinners, cannot, by themselves, be considered to amount to sufficient justification for a difference in treatment.[110]

[108] Consistent with the approach taken in, for example, *R (Quila) v Secretary of State for the Home Department* [2011] UKSC 45, [2012] 1 All ER 1011; *A v Secretary of State for the Home Department* [2016] CSIH 38, [2016] SC 776. The government is, however, not confined to justifications presented in policy documents at the time that the relevant rules were adopted, *British Airways v Starmer* EAT/0306/05/SM, [2005] IRLR 863.

[109] *Konstantin Markin v Russia* App no 30078/06 (ECtHR GC, 22 March 2012).

[110] ibid para 143.

'Justifications' based on gender stereotypes do not pursue a legitimate aim and cannot, therefore, operate as justifications as a matter of law.[111] Of course, 'traditional' employment practices such as the division between 'women's' and 'men's' jobs, or the expectation that a wife will bear the greater responsibility for caring for a home and family *may* explain why a greater proportion of women than men *enter* as partners or domestic workers (or it may not—the reasons for migration are many and various).[112] The disadvantageous treatment of domestic workers cannot, however, be justified by reference to arguments which assert that women are more likely than men to be domestic workers, or that such work is unskilled 'women's work'.[113] To quote the ECtHR referring to *Konstantin Markin* in a later case, such 'general biased assumptions or prevailing social prejudice . . . do not provide sufficient justification for a difference in treatment on the ground of sex'.[114]

Whether a particular 'justification' 'justifies' differential treatment also depends on there being a reasonable relationship of proportionality between the means chosen and the aim to be realised. As discussed above, the ECtHR employs a proportionality test that varies in intensity depending on the ground at issue, in conjunction with granting a 'margin of appreciation' (point (4) of Lord Reed's summary) to States. The Court must decide if the measures designed to meet the legitimate aim are rationally connected to it, and that the means employed are no more than is necessary to accomplish them. 'Very weighty reasons' are required to justify differential treatment on the grounds of sex or of race.[115]

2.5.2 Partners: Dependent Wives

Historically, women were prevented from retaining their property, nationality, and bodily integrity following marriage, married women being considered in law as 'feme covert'. As Blackstone memorably explained:

> By marriage, the husband and wife are one person in law: that is, the very being or legal existence of the woman is suspended during the marriage, or at least is

[111] ibid. See also *Emel Boyraz v Turkey* (n 26); *Carvalho Pinto de Sousa Morais v Portugal* (n 43) paras 46, 52; Case 170/84 *Bilka-Kaufhaus GmbH v Karin Weber von Hartz* [2005] ECR 01607 (an example from EU law that supports this position).

[112] Studies have found that skilled women migrate more than men, but that 'gendered' immigration laws/policies devalue women's skills, Kofman, 'Gendered Labour Migrations' (n 23); Frédéric Docquier, B Lindsay Lowell, and Abdeslam Marfouk, 'A Gendered Assessment of Highly Skilled Emigration' (2009) 35 Population and Development Review 297.

[113] On the former, these are referred to as 'contextual factors' in *Essop v Home Office* (n 8) [26].

[114] *Biao v Denmark* (n 16) para 126.

[115] *Stec v UK* (2006) 43 EHRR 1017; *Biao v Denmark* (n 16). In contrast, where migration status and *not* sex or race is the ground at issue, the ECtHR has focused on whether a justification offered is 'not so manifestly unreasonable' as to exceed the wide margin of appreciation granted to States, *Hode and Abdi v UK* (n 37).

incorporated and consolidated into that of the husband: under whose wing, protection, and cover, she performs every thing.[116]

The laws that created couverture have now, of course, either been repealed or superseded. The Married Women's Property Act 1882 enabled some married women to own and control property independently of their husbands. In 1948, women were able to retain their British nationality following marriage, rather than being automatically denationalised.[117] Rape within marriage was criminalised following *R v R* (1991).[118] Notwithstanding these and many other changes, the stereotype of the 'dependent wife' persists, at least in part, because of the legal rules and structures that continue to give it meaning. Such rules include the Immigration Rules discussed here, which are both premised on, and reinforce, the stereotype.

According to the Home Office, the rules that apply to partners are intended to ensure that those establishing family life in the UK are 'genuine' families, able to 'integrate'.[119] The financial requirements are justified on the basis that migrant partners 'may' be financially dependent on their British or resident 'sponsor' and may, therefore, seek support from 'the taxpayer' if their partner is unable to support them.[120] This justification is directly premised on the stereotypical view that wives are the financial dependants of their husbands. It treats all migrant partners as if this were the case, even when the Home Office's own research demonstrates that it is not.[121] The strength and salience of the 'dependent wife' stereotype is also evident in the fact that the Home Office consistently presents the 'migrant spouse or partner' as an altogether different person from 'the taxpayer', as if migrant wives do not contribute to the economy, work, and pay tax. Indeed, in one document the Home Office states that those with job offers in the UK should come as labour migrants, the family route being for those who are 'capable of being independently supported by their sponsor'.[122] Wives, it seems, should not also be workers. It is also difficult to see any correlation between the purpose of the rules and these criteria. Migrant partners have 'no recourse to public funds' and so are not, generally, a 'burden' to 'the taxpayer' (these rules are subject to consideration in chapter 4). Further, if financial dependency in some instances of marriage migration is a 'problem', it is difficult to see how it is one that can be 'solved' by making

[116] William Blackstone, *Commentaries on the Laws of England: Book I: of the Rights of Persons* (OUP 2016) 284–85.

[117] See further Helen Irving, *Citizenship, Alienage, and the Modern Constitutional State: A Gendered History* (CUP 2016).

[118] *R v R* [1991] UKHL 12, [1991] 4 All ER 481.

[119] Home Office, *Family Migration: A Consultation* (July 2011) 14–16.

[120] ibid 21–23.

[121] ibid 21. According to the Home Office sample of case files, 28% of applicants were in paid employment at the time their application was made.

[122] Home Office, *Statement of Intent: Family Migration* (July 2012) 18.

all migrant partners so dependent. The justifications offered by the Home Office are either premised on gendered stereotypes or not rationally connected to the legitimate aim they purport to pursue.

The probationary period is justified by reference to the need to test the genuineness of migrant relationships and to encourage the 'integration' of the partner before settlement, purposes that are also traceable to the 'dependent wife' stereotype.[123] Migrant wives are, in this analysis, made appendages of their 'sponsor' husbands for five years. This dependency is in relation to both their status and the application process itself—recall the requirement that a husband sign his wife's immigration application. The justifications offered for these conditions also do not have a sufficiently proportionate relationship to the stated purposes of the rules. The connection between the validity of a relationship and its length is far from clear. A probationary period of five years (with an additional immigration application mid-way through) seems more suited to ascertaining the enduringness, not the genuineness, of a relationship. Similarly, stressing the need for wives to 'integrate' presupposes their separation (in the private sphere?) from wider society, a separation that the rules themselves impose and maintain.

Finally, references to migrant spouses' dependence or integration, the legitimacy of migrant women's relationships, and 'real concern' about 'sham marriages' stereotype on the basis of both sex and race.[124] In *Biao v Denmark* (2016),[125] the ECtHR was called on to decide whether or not extremely onerous 'integration requirements' were indirectly discriminatory. Denmark justified its rules by reference to the 'isolation' and 'maladjustment' of migrant spouses, as well as concerns about migrant spouses' willingness, or ability, to integrate. The Court rejected these 'justifications', concluding that they 'reflect negatively on the lifestyle of Danish nationals of non-Danish ethnic extraction'.[126] Drawing on its judgment on gender stereotypes in *Konstantin Markin*, the Grand Chamber in *Biao* reiterated that such 'biased assumptions' could not justify a difference in treatment which was, this time, on the grounds of race.[127] While the rules impugned in *Biao* are very different to those discussed here, the similarity between the UK's and Denmark's characterisation of migrant spouses is significant. The ECtHR's jurisprudence on stereotyping not only enables the UK's 'justifications' for gendered disadvantage to be dismissed as such, but it also offers the prospect of an analysis of migration law that captures the intersectional discrimination experienced by racialised women-as-wives.

[123] Home Office, *Family Migration* (n 119) 26.

[124] Home Office, *Statement of Intent* (n 122) 23–26. See further Anne-Marie D'Aoust, 'A Moral Economy of Suspicion: Love and Marriage Migration Management Practices in the United Kingdom' (2018) 36 Environment and Planning D: Society and Space 40.

[125] *Biao v Denmark* (n 16).

[126] ibid para 126.

[127] ibid para 126.

2.5.3 Overseas Domestic Workers: Carer Women

Women migrating for work are also subjected to gendered and racist stereotyping by the rules that determine their rights and status in the UK. These stereotypes concern women's natural ability to care for children and the/a family home, activities that should not generally be performed for economic reward.[128] Such activities are, almost by definition, 'unskilled'.

Feminist analyses of employment and the labour market have highlighted both the sexed/gendered stereotypes that underlie the categorisations of certain types of work, and worker, as either low/high skilled,[129] as well as the idea that 'skill' itself can be determined objectively.[130] As Anne Phillips and Barbara Taylor argue, '[s]kill definitions are saturated with sexual bias. The work of women is often deemed inferior simply because it is women who do it.'[131] A range of reasons have been advanced to account for this 'saturation'. Skill differentiation (low/high) and attribution (women/men) may be understood by contrasting the talents of women (empathy, dealing with bodily fluids, etc.) with the skills of men (reasoning, demonstrable through the holding of certain qualifications, etc.).[132] Eleonore Kofman's discussion of the unequal valorisation of certain types of knowledge/person similarly contrasts the classification of some kinds of knowledge as 'embrained' (that which is scientific, technical, or 'objective' in some way) with that which is 'embodied' (uses the body to acquire learning and perform tasks, 'subjective').[133] Such scholarship, legislation, and a raft of legal challenges notwithstanding, the 'carer woman' stereotype continues to impact upon almost every aspect of women's participation in the labour market. It contributes to the gender pay gap, the persistence of sex-segregated and gendered roles, the devaluation of caring work, and the devaluation of all work (whether caring or not) that women do.[134] It also explains domestic

[128] Drawing on LJB Hayes, *Stories of Care: A Labour of Law* (Palgrave 2017) 26.

[129] Ronnie J Steinberg, 'Social Construction of Skill: Gender, Power, and Comparable Worth' (1990) 17 Work and Occupations 449.

[130] Linda McDowell, 'Skills' in Bridget Anderson and Michael Keith (eds), *Migration: A COMPAS Anthology* (COMPAS 2014).

[131] Anne Phillips and Barbara Taylor, 'Sex and Skill: Notes towards a Feminist Economics' (1980) 6 Feminist Review 79, 79.

[132] Drawing on Jane Jenson, 'The Talents of Women, the Skills of Men: Flexible Specialization and Women' in Stephen Wood (ed), *The Transformation of Work: Skill, Flexibility and the Labour Process* (Unwin Hyman 1989).

[133] Kofman, 'Gendered Labour Migrations' (n 23) 583–84.

[134] Paula England and Nancy Folbre, 'The Cost of Caring' (1999) 561 The ANNALS of the American Academy of Political and Social Science 39; Daniel Muzio and Sharon C Bolton, 'Feminisation and Paradox: Stratification and Segmentation in Professional Contexts' (2006) 27 Irish Journal of Management 79; Christine Alksnis, Serge Desmarais, and James Curtis, 'Workforce Segregation and the Gender Wage Gap: Is "Women's" Work Valued as Highly as "Men's"?' (2008) 38 Journal of Applied Social Psychology 1416; Asaf Levanon, Paula England, and Paul Allison, 'Occupational Feminization and Pay: Assessing Causal Dynamics Using 1950–2000 US Census Data' (2009) 88 Social Forces 865; Francine D Blau and Lawrence M Kahn, The Gender Wage Gap: Extent, Trends, and Explanations (IZA Discussion Paper No 9656, Institute for the Study of Labor, January 2016); Heather M Clarke, 'Gender Stereotypes and Gender-Typed Work' in Klaus F Zimmermann (ed), *Handbook of Labor, Human Resources and Population Economics* (Springer 2020).

workers' exclusion from key employment protections, including their prolonged and discriminatory exclusion from the minimum wage.[135] As Siobhán Mullally and Clíodhna Murphy observe, the treatment of domestic workers in migration law 'reflects' the 'continuing characterization of domestic work as work like no other'.[136]

According to the Home Office, the purposes of the labour migration rules are to encourage 'the brightest and the best, those who contribute to our economy and who are really needed by the UK' to be able to remain in the UK permanently.[137] In comparison with those migrants who are really needed, domestic workers do not 'fill skills gaps' and 'those who enter in this capacity are not assessed against the economic needs of the country'.[138] That a domestic worker can only, in practice, work temporarily for one employer is justified by reference to both the unskilled nature of the work and the employer's longer term ability to recruit workers from the UK 'labour pool'.[139] The existence of the route has been justified in Parliament as follows:

> Looking at our national interest, if wealthy investors, skilled workers and others with the potential to benefit our economy were unable to be accompanied by *their* domestic staff they might not come here at all but take *their* money and skills to other countries only too keen to welcome them.[140]

As the-then Home Secretary Theresa May explained, the domestic worker route is one that allows those coming or returning to the UK to be accompanied by 'their' staff, not 'unskilled' workers to access the UK labour market.[141] If the domestic worker regime is a 'benefit' that accrues to someone other than the person whose rights are determined by it, its considerable disadvantages make 'sense'. The route changes demand structures in this part of the economy, depresses wages, and prevents domestic workers from securing other, better employment, even if they have been exploited. While there is an extent to which this argument can also be applied to (again, other?) 'skilled' labour migrants, the difference is that the relationship

[135] Natalie Sedacca, 'Domestic Workers, the "Family Worker" Exemption from Minimum Wage, and Gendered Devaluation of Women's Work' (2022) 51 Industrial Law Journal 771. See also *Puthenveettil v Alexander, George* Case Number: 2361118/2013 (15 December 2020). The approach adopted to indirect sex discrimination in this chapter is consistent with that taken by the Tribunal, although the case concerned employment, not immigration law.

[136] Siobhán Mullally and Clíodhna Murphy, 'Migrant Domestic Workers in the UK: Enacting Exclusions, Exemptions, and Rights' (2014) 36 Human Rights Quarterly 397, 417.

[137] Home Office, *Employment-related Settlement, Tier 5 and Overseas Domestic Workers: A Consultation* (June 2011) Ministerial Forward 3.

[138] ibid 29.

[139] ibid 30. These justifications concerned the pre-2016 regime. I contend that they apply equally to the post-2016 rules because the ability to change employer is only available theoretically.

[140] HL Deb 28 November 1990, vol 523, col 1052 (emphasis added).

[141] 'Written statement to Parliament, Immigration (employment-related settlement, overseas domestic workers, Tier 5 of the points-based system and visitors)—WMS by Theresa May and in the House of Lords by Lord Henley' (*GOV.UK*, 29 February 2012) <www.gov.uk/government/speeches/immigration-employment-related-settlement-overseas-domestic-workers-tier-5-of-the-points-based-system-and-visitors-wms> accessed 26 April 2024.

between them and their employers is one that is positioned as being mutually, although not symmetrically, beneficial. In contrast, the ability to bring 'their' domestic workers is a benefit that is bestowed upon, for example, the 'right' type of mobile citizen or migrant.

Justifications for disadvantage that treat those who experience it instrumentally, almost as chattels, either cannot be relied on as justifications for discriminatory treatment or, if they can be, are wholly disproportionate. There is simply no reasonable relationship of proportionality between the aim (benefiting the employer, whether themselves British or a migrant) and the means used (disadvantaging 'their' domestic workers to such a considerable extent). This is particularly the case given the myriad of alternatives the State has at its disposal, which, for example, include tax breaks or less restrictive immigration rules for the employers themselves (where appropriate). The Home Office's justification for, first, differentiating between domestic workers and all other workers and, secondly, disadvantaging the former for the benefit of their employers is comprehensible only by reference to the stereotypes discussed above. Within the migration context, this 'carer woman' stereotype also needs to be understood intersectionally, as sex, race, nationality, and class determine fitness for domestic work.[142] Domestic work, and those who do it, are deemed unskilled and without value because it is impossible to separate the classification and valorisation of particular skills, talents, or knowledge, from the usually non-white, female bodies of those who have them.

2.5.4 Stereotypes and Indirect Discrimination

While the rules that apply to partners and domestic workers do not specify that the holders of such statuses must be women, they are predicated on stereotypical understandings of marriage, the role of men and women within it, women's work, and women's skills. They are 'saturated with sexual bias'.[143] Women who hold the status of partner or domestic worker are disadvantaged, therefore, not just by the material disadvantage that these statuses produce, but also by being treated as if the stereotype were true, as if they were dependent on their husbands, or as if their work had no value. Such treatment is wrong in and of itself.[144] Men may also be disadvantaged by such stereotyping, their family life disrupted, their contributions dismissed, and their relationships interpreted as attempts to secure an immigration advantage.[145] Although such stereotypes may be subject to challenge and have

142 Atrey, 'Structural Racism' (n 1) 19–21.
143 Phillips and Taylor, 'Sex and Skill' (n 131) 79.
144 Moreau, 'The Wrongs of Unequal Treatment' (n 43).
145 Helena Wray, '"A Thing Apart": Controlling Male Family Migration to the United Kingdom' (2015) 18 Men and Masculinities 424; Betty de Hart, 'Superdads. Migrant Fathers' Right to Family Life before the European Court of Human Rights' (2015) 18 Men and Masculinities 448.

decreasing popular salience, their incorporation into the Immigration Rules accords them new significance. All women are harmed by this as the migration statuses strengthen the stereotypes, (re)making them anew.

Equality impact assessments published by the Home Office recognise, to a very limited extent, that different facets of the partner and domestic worker route may indirectly discriminate, both against women and on the grounds of race.[146] The examination of the relevant rules is, at best, cursory: '[t]o the extent that there may be indirect discrimination', 'it is considered proportionate to achieve the policy aims'.[147] The analysis engaged in here offers a different conclusion. There are no 'very weighty reasons' that justify migrant women's ill-treatment. While States may differentiate between and offer incentives to certain groups of migrants to attract them to their jurisdiction,[148] justifications for disadvantaging migrant women that rest solely on gendered and racist stereotypes do not have a legitimate aim and cannot operate as justifications as a matter of law.[149] Other explanations for facets of these two routes that create disadvantage have also been considered and rejected as disproportionate. The rules that apply to partners and domestic workers indirectly discriminate against women.

2.6 Migration Law and Discrimination against Women

I have, so far, focused on the migration statuses accorded to partners and domestic workers in the UK. If, however, we broaden our analysis and consider other jurisdictions, we see that the UK rules analysed here are far from anomalous in their disadvantageous treatment of women. The 'Europeanisation'[150] of the rules that apply to family migrants has produced a family resemblance[151] in the requirements that partners have to meet in a range of European jurisdictions. Germany, the Netherlands, and France, for example, all impose probationary periods as well as income and integration requirements. All of these, like those of the UK, have become more onerous over time.[152] The rules adopted in the Netherlands that apply to partners are justified by reference to concerns about migrant integration

[146] Home Office, *Family Migration Policy Equality Statement* (13 June 2012).
[147] ibid 7, 9.
[148] *Hode and Abdi v UK* (n 37).
[149] *Konstantin Markin v Russia* (n 109).
[150] Laura Block and Saskia Bonjour, 'Fortress Europe or Europe of Rights? The Europeanisation of Family Migration Policies in France, Germany and the Netherlands' (2013) 15 European Journal of Migration and Law 203. For an interesting discussion of 'common ground', EU law, and the family reunion rights of refugees, see *BF v Switzerland* App nos 13258/18, 15500/18, 57303/18 (ECtHR, 4 July 2023) para 98.
[151] Wray, Agoston, and Hutton, 'A Family Resemblance?' (n 98).
[152] Block and Bonjour, 'Fortress Europe' (n 150). See also Saskia Bonjour and Laura Block, 'Ethnicizing Citizenship, Questioning Membership. Explaining the Decreasing Family Migration Rights of Citizens in Europe' (2016) 20 Citizenship Studies 779.

and fraudulent relationships; they also appear to be animated by the 'dependent wife' stereotype.[153] Sweden similarly imposes a probationary period, and it too has been linked to migrant women's experiences of domestic violence.[154] Following the adoption of EU rules on family migration, rules discussed in chapter 5, most European States now impose similar income and 'integration' measures.[155] Overall, within Europe:

> States may require varying levels of income and standards of accommodation and knowledge of language and of society, to the point where the hurdle may hold very different significance, but there [are] very few examples of regulation based on a totally different model.[156]

Australia, New Zealand, and the United States (US) also have rules that impose probationary periods and require evidence of 'genuineness'.[157] The treatment of migrant partners by the US has, once again, been linked to both the 'dependent wife' stereotype and domestic violence.[158] Finally, the '[e]nduring vulnerability'[159] of migrant domestic workers at the intersection of both immigration and labour law in many jurisdictions has been the subject of both sustained scholarly analysis and criticism from the Committee that monitors the Convention on the Elimination of All Forms of Discrimination against Women (CEDAW),[160] the CEDAW Committee.[161]

[153] Betty de Hart and Saskia Bonjour, 'A Proper Wife, a Proper Marriage: Constructions of "Us" and "Them" in Dutch Family Migration Policy' (2013) 20 The European Journal of Women's Studies 61.

[154] Monica Burman, 'Immigrant Women Facing Male Partner Violence – Gender, Race and Power in Swedish Alien and Criminal Law' (2012) 2 feminists@law 1; Halliki Voolma, '"I Must Be Silent Because of Residency": Barriers to Escaping Domestic Violence in the Context of Insecure Immigration Status in England and Sweden' (2018) 24 Violence Against Women 1830.

[155] Council Directive 2003/86/EC of 22 September 2003 on the right to family reunification [2003] OJ L251/12; European Migration Network (EMN), *Family Reunification of Third-Country Nationals in the EU plus Norway: National Report* (Migrapol EMN, Doc 382, 2017).

[156] Wray, Agoston, and Hutton, 'A Family Resemblance?' (n 98) 244.

[157] Ana Borges Jelinic, 'Australia's Family Violence Provisions in Migration Law: A Comparative Study' (2020) 21 Flinders Law Journal 259. See also Marie Segrave, 'Temporary Migration and Family Violence: How Perpetrators Weaponise Borders' (2021) 10 International Journal for Crime, Justice and Social Democracy 26.

[158] Janet M Calvo, 'Spouse-Based Immigration Laws: The Legacies of Coverture' (1991) 28 San Diego Law Review 593; Cecilia Menjívar and Olivia Salcido, 'Immigrant Women and Domestic Violence: Common Experiences in Different Countries' (2002) 16 Gender & Society 898; Sabrina Balgamwalla, 'Bride and Prejudice: How US Immigration Law Discriminates Against Spousal Visa Holders' (2014) 29 Berkeley Journal of Gender, Law & Justice 25.

[159] Clíodhna Murphy, 'The Enduring Vulnerability of Migrant Domestic Workers in Europe' (2013) 62 International and Comparative Law Quarterly 599.

[160] Convention on the Elimination of All Forms of Discrimination against Women (CEDAW) (adopted 18 December 1979, entered into force 3 September 1981) 1249 UNTS 13.

[161] Judy Fudge, 'The Precarious Migrant Status and Precarious Employment: The Paradox of International Rights for Migrant Workers' (2012) 34 Comparative Labor Law & Policy Journal 95; UN Committee on the Elimination of Discrimination against Women, 'General Recommendation No 26 on Women Migrant Workers' (5 December 2008) UN Doc CEDAW/C/2009/WP.1/R (CEDAW's GR 26).

The rules that determine the status of partners and domestic workers in the UK have been shown to disadvantage and discriminate against women. This brief survey of the literature on other, primarily European, jurisdictions supports the broader claim that migration law disadvantages a significant proportion of the women whose status it determines. Such disadvantage may also be the product of unlawful discrimination against women (on the grounds of sex and, potentially, intersectionally). Of course, not all migrant women are disadvantaged or discriminated against, either in the UK or elsewhere. For those that are, however, the consequences of this treatment may be significant and long-lasting.

2.7 Pre-emptive Migration Status Reform

Different parts of the Immigration Rules have been challenged both in the UK and before the ECtHR on the grounds that they are discriminatory and breach migrants' rights. Such challenges, where successful, have either compelled the State to grant, or resulted in the State granting, individuals or groups permission to enter or remain and caused it to change certain rules, or even to abandon them altogether. The State may not only be required to end discriminatory practices when they are challenged in court. As Sandra Fredman explains, the prohibition on indirect discrimination includes a duty to take 'pre-emptive action to address a pattern of disparate impact, even in the absence of litigation'.[162] It will be recalled that the State can justify disadvantageous treatment by demonstrating that there is no other, or no less disadvantageous, means of achieving the relevant legitimate aim. The corollary of this, Fredman contends, is that in order to successfully defend itself from discrimination claims, the relevant duty-bearer must consider and review how it achieves its aims and, if necessary, change the means it adopts to do so.[163] This argument is reinforced, in the case of public authorities like the Home Office, by obligations imposed by the Equality Act 2010 which require them to have 'due regard' to the need to eliminate discrimination and advance equality.[164] Although the partner and domestic worker routes have not (yet) been challenged in court on the basis of the arguments advanced here, the State should, following Fredman's analysis, take pre-emptive action to address the patterns of disadvantage I have identified.

Space precludes a detailed discussion of the migration statuses that could emerge from a reviewed and reformed non-discriminatory system of migration rules and policies. This chapter's analysis of the partner and domestic worker

[162] Sandra Fredman, 'Addressing Disparate Impact: Indirect Discrimination and the Public Sector Equality Duty' (2014) 43 Industrial Law Journal 349, 349.
[163] ibid.
[164] Equality Act 2010, s 149.

routes suggests, however, some key changes to the current Immigration Rules. In advancing these arguments, I start from the position that migration status reform should level up, not level down.[165] Some scholars argue that levelling down is a permissible response to discrimination. Such a course may be the 'unavoidable price we must pay to optimize the range of opportunities to which members of protected groups have access'.[166] Levelling down would be an inapposite and, indeed, potentially unlawful response to the disadvantage identified here, which is produced by rules that engage a range of human rights. Giving *all* labour migrants, including those considered skilled or highly skilled, a short(er) period of permission to remain in the UK, or one which provides few(er) rights may, at first glance, appear to reduce or eliminate sex discrimination. However, it would fail to provide migrants with effective protection from violence and exploitation, contrary to the ECHR.[167] As I explain in the next chapter, such a move could also perpetuate the rules' unlawful discrimination by failing to protect women from gender-based violence.[168]

So, what might pre-emptive migration status reform entail? As dependency on another is a key source of migrant women's disadvantage, dependent migration statuses should be abolished and replaced by those that are wholly independent of any family or other relationship. In the context of family migration, this would involve granting the migrant partner of someone who is British or resident in the UK permanent residence, either when they enter or when the relevant application is granted. Such a move would abolish the probationary period. One of the central justifications for the dependency imposed on partners is, as discussed, the need to test the 'genuineness' of a relationship. Those concerned to ensure that this route is not 'abused' might argue that instead of granting migrant wives a wholly independent migration status, the disadvantage the current probationary period causes could be ameliorated by its reduction. This approach has been advocated by the Council of Europe's Parliamentary Assembly, which has recommended migrant spouses/partners be given an independent migration status in their country of residence after one year.[169] However, as Immigration, Refugees and Citizenship Canada (IRCC) has recognised, even a comparatively short probationary period (referred to as conditional permanent residence) can produce significant disadvantage:

> [A] sponsored spouse or partner can be vulnerable for many reasons, including gender, age, official language proficiency, isolation and financial dependence,

165 The position that rules that produce disadvantage in the migration statuses disproportionately held by women should be changed to ensure that no one is so disadvantaged (levelling up), rather than extended to the migration statuses the majority of whose holders are men (levelling down).

166 Khaitan, *A Theory of Discrimination Law* (n 10) 133.

167 *Rantsev v Cyprus and Russia* (2010) 51 EHRR 1.

168 *Opuz v Turkey* (n 43) paras 191, 199–202.

169 Council of Europe, Parliamentary Assembly 'Protecting Migrant Women in the Labour Market' Resolution 1811 (2011).

> and that these factors can create an imbalance between the sponsor and their spouse or partner. It was further assessed that the conditional permanent residence two-year co-habitation requirement could compound these vulnerabilities in situations of domestic abuse. Noting that women made up a majority (70%) of affected individuals who submitted requests to IRCC for an exception to the condition on the basis of abuse or neglect, IRCC assessed that this regulatory requirement may potentially result in vulnerable spouses and partners remaining in abusive relationships out of fear of losing their permanent resident status in Canada.[170]

Canada's conditional permanent residence requirement was, consequently, repealed in 2017.[171] If the 'genuineness' of a relationship is to be tested, then this must be done proportionately, without reference to either the 'dependent wife' or other gendered and racialised stereotypes. One alternative approach, which would not assume or enforce dependency, might be to ask couples for evidence of commitment from a broad array of sources, including but not limited to evidence of co-habitation, communication, visits, and mutual material, or other, support.[172]

It will be recalled that domestic workers have a dependent, precarious, and generally non-renewable migration status, designed for the benefit of their employer. Precarity is another key source of migrant women's disadvantage. It is created by statuses that are temporary and have onerous or repeatedly tested conditions attached to them. Pre-emptive migration status reform should, therefore, ensure that domestic workers also receive an independent migration status, but one that is for a non-temporary period and is renewable. This status should also bestow rights comparable to those enjoyed by other labour migrants, including the right to be accompanied by family members. Unlike the migration status that must be accorded to the partners of those who are British or resident in the UK, such a status would not have to bestow permanent residence on its holder to meet these requirements.

170 Immigration, Refugees and Citizenship Canada, '2017 Annual Report to Parliament on Immigration' (*Government of Canada/Gouvermement du Canada*, 1 November 2017) <www.canada.ca/en/immigration-refugees-citizenship/corporate/publications-manuals/annual-report-parliament-immigration-2017.html#section4> accessed 27 April 2024. On the impact of conditional permanent residence, see Rupaleem Bhuyan and Bronwyn Bragg, 'Epistemologies of Bordering: Domestic Violence Advocacy with Marriage Migrants in the Shadow of Deportation' (2021) 9 Migration Studies 159.

171 'Canada Gazette, Part I, Volume 150, Number 44: Regulations Amending the Immigration and Refugee Protection Regulations' (*Government of Canada/Gouvermement du Canada*, 29 October 2016) <www.gazette.gc.ca/rp-pr/p1/2016/2016-10-29/html/reg1-eng.html> accessed 27 April 2024; Immigration, Refugees and Citizenship Canada, 'Notice—Government of Canada Eliminates Conditional Permanent Residence' (*Government of Canada/Gouvermement du Canada*, 28 April 2017) <www.canada.ca/en/immigration-refugees-citizenship/news/notices/elminating-conditional-pr.html> accessed 3 February 2023.

172 Such requirements would have to be calibrated to be capable of being satisfied by couples from a broad range of cultural and religious communities and backgrounds, see further Katharine Charsley and Michaela Benson, 'Marriages of Convenience, and Inconvenient Marriages: Regulating Spousal Migration to Britain' (2012) 26 Journal of Immigration Asylum and Nationality Law 10.

Finally, although this chapter focuses on the migrant partners of those who are British or resident in the UK, the arguments made here may also be applied to the partners of labour migrants. Here, the migration status granted would, like that given to labour migrants themselves, not need to be permanent but independent and rights-bestowing.

Treating different kinds of migrants differently is legally permissible, and, indeed, may be required in some circumstances. Such treatment should not, however, be rooted in sexist or other discriminatory stereotypes which valorise some skills and attributes and denigrate others. Arguing that domestic workers should receive a migration status that is more akin to that currently given to labour migrants the State considers 'skilled' than those it considers 'unskilled' raises two related questions. First, can the current system's differentiation between domestic work and other types of labour migration be maintained? Secondly, is a non-discriminatory labour migration system that distinguishes on the basis of 'skill' possible?

Following this chapter's discussion of sex and skill, I would answer the first question in the negative. The UK's treatment of domestic workers seems comprehensible only when considered by reference to the gendered stereotypes discussed above. If labour migrants are to be differentiated between, and some given greater rights than others (even within the framework outlined here, in which no migrant can be given a precarious status), domestic work should be both valued and regulated in a manner that is analogous with other types of employment. This brings us to the second question, the answer to which is not so straightforward and which, thankfully, I do not need to resolve here to make my arguments for pre-emptive migration status reform. I remain to be convinced that it is possible for the State to differentiate between labour migrants on the basis of skill without stereotyping or otherwise discriminating.[173] However, as Anna Boucher's multi-jurisdictional and gendered analysis of skilled labour migration rules indicates, some countries, like Denmark and Canada, perform better in terms of 'gender awareness' than others, such as Austria, Australia, and the UK.[174] One reason such countries do so is that they undertake regular gender audits of their immigration rules. It may not be necessary, therefore, to abandon wholly a skills-based labour migration system in order to remedy some, or all, of the disadvantage and discrimination that women experience. It may be enough if all labour migrants considered low(er) skilled are granted, per this section's argument, an independent, rights-bestowing status, and that any differentiation between those considered low/high skilled is justified by reference to rules that are regularly subject to gender-informed scrutiny.

[173] See further Desiree Lim, 'The Indirect Gender Discrimination of Skill-Selective Immigration Policies' (2019) 22 Critical Review of International Social and Political Philosophy 906.

[174] Anna Boucher, *Gender, Migration and the Global Race for Talent* (Manchester University Press 2016) ch 2.

This section has suggested reforms to the rules that, absent justification, disadvantage and discriminate against women. Additional support for these arguments can also be found in CEDAW Committee recommendations which require States to ensure that their visa schemes do not indirectly discriminate.[175] According to the Committee, this may entail revising rules that disproportionately disadvantage women, like those that make partners and particular types of labour migrants dependent on another.[176] In the two chapters that follow, I provide further justification for, and add detail to, this section's sketch of the kinds of reform necessary to remedy immigration law's discrimination against women.

2.8 Conclusion

Jean-Baptiste Farcy argues that legal prohibitions of discrimination, and protections of equality, are 'an unfulfilled promise' in the context of migration law and control, the imperatives driving the two bodies of law seeming 'irreconcilable'.[177] There are many similarities between Farcy's arguments and my own. Farcy's article, like this chapter, charts the stratification, precarity, and exclusion produced by rules that determine admission and stay. Farcy considers the potential for skill-based selection, or minimum income requirements, to adversely affect women and others who share different protected characteristics. Farcy also explains that applying prohibitions on indirect discrimination to such requirements is not straightforward, because of difficulties in selecting comparators and evaluating justifications.

In this chapter, I have outlined who sits where in the main labour and family migration routes. The statistical discussion and doctrinal analysis engaged in here is at a high level of generality, capturing broad patterns in the creation and distribution of rights and disadvantage within immigration law's highly complex and differentiated status-based hierarchy. Notwithstanding these and other caveats, immigration law's creation and distribution of migration statuses disadvantages and discriminates against women, particularly racialised women. The State should reform these rules and the migration statuses they produce, whether or not its treatment of women is subject to legal challenge. The abolition of dependent migration statuses, and the refashioning of migration status more broadly to ensure that no migrant's position is precarious, would go some way towards discharging this obligation. While Farcy captures the elusiveness of equality in the migration

[175] CEDAW's GR 26 (n 161) [26(a)].

[176] UN Committee on the Elimination of Discrimination against Women, 'General Recommendation No 38 on Trafficking in Women and Girls in the Context of Global Migration' (20 November 2020) UN Doc CEDAW/C/GC/38 [58]–[60].

[177] Jean-Baptiste Farcy, 'Equality in Immigration Law: An Impossible Quest?' (2020) 20 Human Rights Law Review 725, 725–26.

context, this analysis has offered solutions to some of the problems he identifies.[178] On comparison, for example, I have argued that it is only by bringing the purposes of the relevant rules into view that we can establish who potential comparators may be. In doing so, I show that the rules that apply to partners and domestic workers are grounded in gendered and racialised stereotypes. This may be sufficient to establish discrimination in and of itself, and to show that women's comparative disadvantage cannot be justified.

Finally, this book is being written against the backdrop of significant change to legal rules, administrative practices, and migration patterns following Britain's departure from the EU, the global coronavirus pandemic, and a raft of populist legislation (the latter being discussed further in Part II). It is, as yet, unclear whether, how, and to what extent these and other changes have shifted the gendered patterns described here. However, if comparative disadvantage between different kinds of labour migration status becomes harder to establish, the arguments made in this chapter could be developed to include differences *between* skilled labour migrants in different occupations.[179] Relevant here would be a discussion of the removal of some migrants' right to bring family members with them and the inability of (increasing) salary thresholds to be pro-rated. The discussion of stereotyping and discrimination also becomes more significant. Finally, this chapter has not considered the legal implications of the increased risk of violence that women on the partner and domestic worker routes experience. I remedy this in the chapters that follow.

[178] ibid 743.

[179] 78% of nurses sponsored as skilled workers were female, compared to 25% of IT professionals in 2018/19, Home Office, *Equality Impact Assessment of the Points-Based Immigration System* (2022) 51. This pattern may have persisted and, indeed, become more significant as the number of care workers in the UK has increased.

3
Violence against Women

3.1 Introduction

In *Opuz v Turkey* (2009),[1] the European Court of Human Rights (ECtHR) was called on to establish States' obligations to protect women from both violence and discrimination. The applicant, Mrs Nahide Opuz, was physically and psychologically abused by her husband for a number of years. This violence culminated in Opuz's husband murdering her mother. Opuz and her mother had reported numerous assaults, threats to kill, and incidents of harassment to the authorities. They did not receive the assistance and protection they needed, from either the police or the courts. Opuz sought, therefore, to hold Turkey responsible for failing to protect her and her mother from domestic violence. In its judgment, the ECtHR first considered the applicant's, and her mother's, rights to life and to be free from torture, inhuman, and degrading treatment. It identified breaches of articles 2 and 3 of the European Convention on Human Rights (ECHR)[2] in relation to the State's response to both women's ill-treatment. The positive or 'due diligence' obligations owed by States generally to those within their jurisdiction, and, specifically, to victims of violence, are discussed in the second half of this chapter. For the moment, I am concerned with the more limited questions of, first, how the ECtHR conceptualises the violence women experience, and secondly, how its approach to such violence accords with that of other regional and international courts and regimes.[3]

In considering the nature of the violence Opuz and her mother were subject to, the Court took as its starting point its general, article 14, non-discrimination jurisprudence.[4] It quickly, however, turned to other 'specialised legal instruments and the decisions of international legal bodies on the question of *violence against women*'[5] to

[1] *Opuz v Turkey* App no 33401/02 (ECtHR, 9 June 2009).

[2] Convention for the Protection of Human Rights and Fundamental Freedoms (adopted 4 November 1950, entered into force 3 September 1953) ETS 5 (European Convention on Human Rights, as amended).

[3] I have applied some of the arguments advanced here to refugee law, see Catherine Briddick, 'Resisting Domestic Violence' (2024) 36 International Journal of Refugee Law 106.

[4] *Opuz v Turkey* (n 1) para 183. In doing so, the Court quotes at length from *DH v Czech Republic* App no 57325/00 (ECtHR GC, 13 November 2007).

[5] *Opuz v Turkey* (n 1) para 185 (emphasis added).

Violence against Women and Regimes of Exception. Catherine Briddick, Oxford University Press.
 DOI: 10.1093/9780191959899.003.0003

> clarify the scope of a Convention provision that more conventional means of interpretation have not enabled it to establish with a sufficient degree of certainty.[6]

The Court then reviewed the Convention on the Elimination of all Forms of Discrimination against Women (CEDAW),[7] the CEDAW Committee's General Recommendation No 19 on Violence against Women (GR 19),[8] the Inter-American Convention on the Prevention, Punishment and Eradication of Violence against Women (the Convention of Belém do Pará),[9] and a case decided with reference to it, *Maria da Penha v Brazil* (2001).[10] It drew on these to offer, or affirm, two assessments of the meaning of discrimination in the context of domestic violence. First, that violence against women, including domestic violence, is itself a form of discrimination against women.[11] Secondly:

> the State's failure to protect women against domestic violence breaches their right to equal protection of the law and that this failure does not need to be intentional.[12]

The Court went on to find that Turkey had also violated article 14 of the Convention (in conjunction with articles 2 and 3). It justified its conclusions here on the grounds that:

> Bearing in mind its finding above that the general and discriminatory judicial passivity in Turkey, albeit unintentional, mainly affected women, the Court considers that the violence suffered by the applicant and her mother may be regarded as gender-based violence which is a form of discrimination against women.[13]

In addition to being confused, the Court's reasoning in this part of the judgment contradicts the analysis of violence and discrimination it offered just paragraphs before. The domestic violence experienced is, this time, gender-based violence *because* the judiciary's unintentional, but nonetheless (indirectly?) discriminatory

[6] ibid para 184.

[7] Convention on the Elimination of All Forms of Discrimination against Women (CEDAW) (adopted 18 December 1979, entered into force 3 September 1981) 1249 UNTS 13.

[8] UN Committee for the Elimination of All Forms of Discrimination against Women, 'General Recommendation No 19' in 'Note by the Secretariat, Compilation of General Comments and General Recommendations Adopted by Human Rights Treaty Bodies' (29 July 1994) UN Doc HRI/GEN/1/Rev.1 (CEDAW's GR 19).

[9] Inter-American Convention on the Prevention, Punishment and Eradication of Violence against Women (adopted 9 June 1994, entered into force 5 March 1995) (1994) 33 ILM 1534 (Convention of Belém do Pará).

[10] *Maria da Penha Maia Fernandes v Brazil* Report No 54/01 (Inter-American Commission on Human Rights, 16 April 2001).

[11] *Opuz v Turkey* (n 1) para 187.

[12] ibid para 191.

[13] ibid para 200.

attitudes created a 'climate that was conducive' to it.[14] The gendered nature of the violence *itself* and, centrally, its role in establishing and maintaining control over women, is not considered.[15] Instead, the Court engages article 14 by referring to the State's unresponsiveness to a form of violence that 'mainly' affects women.[16]

The opacity of the Court's reasoning may, in part, stem from the lengths it goes to to avoid concluding that the authorities intentionally discriminated against women, and particularly Kurdish women, when denying them protection.[17] The central problem is, however, that the Court is not dealing with one but two distinct forms of discrimination, each of which is prohibited by its own legal framework. The first of these is violence against women itself, of which domestic violence is but one particular subset. Drawing on and following CEDAW article 1 and GR 19, such violence is understood by the ECtHR in this case to *be* discrimination against women.[18] The Court does not, however, explain how domestic violence-as-discrimination fits within its article 14 jurisprudence when, for example, the actors responsible for it may be private individuals, and when such violence occurs in a greater variety of contexts than those discrimination law is usually concerned with, including the home.

The second form of discrimination identified is the State's failure to protect women, notably Kurdish women, from violence.[19] Here, the Court is concerned with the non-violent inaction of the 'usual' discrimination law duty-bearers: the police and courts. This discrimination is straightforwardly prohibited by article 14, whether or not it is intentional. Following the legal framework set out in chapter 2, it involves non-justifiable differential treatment on the basis of sex, alone or in conjunction with other grounds, including race and national origin.[20] The Court did not have to determine whether or not domestic violence *is* violence against women, or whether or not such violence *is also* discrimination, to find that Turkey had discriminated against women and intersectionally in its failure to *respond to it*.[21] It could simply draw on its own jurisprudence on indirect discrimination, which enables applicants to provide statistical and other evidence to prove differential treatment.[22] Having done so, however, the Court should have explained with greater

[14] ibid para 198.

[15] Shazia Choudhry and Jonathan Herring, 'Opuz v Turkey' in Loveday Hodson and Troy Lavers (eds), *Feminist Judgments in International Law* (Hart 2019) 254.

[16] *Opuz v Turkey* (n 1) paras 198, 200.

[17] The Court's reluctance on this point is surprising given (1) the evidence it cites on domestic violence in Turkey and the authorities' response to it, and (2) its reliance on *Maria da Penha Maia Fernandes v Brazil* (n 10). *Opuz v Turkey* (n 1) paras 91–105, 192–202.

[18] *Opuz v Turkey* (n 1) paras 185–87.

[19] ibid paras 191, 199–202.

[20] Again, following *DH v Czech Republic* (n 4). *Opuz v Turkey* (n 1) para 183.

[21] Discrimination could be established if, for example, the State failed to respond to *women's* experiences of violence that were gender neutral/indiscriminate. In contrast, CEDAW's GR 19's (n 8) 'violence against women is discrimination' position was necessary to enable CEDAW (and the broader United Nations) to respond to it. Alice Edwards, *Violence Against Women under International Human Rights Law* (CUP 2011) 183–90.

[22] *Opuz v Turkey* (n 1) para 183.

clarity its reasoning on what violence against women is, and when such violence, as distinct from States' response to it, is discrimination contrary to article 14.[23]

Opuz v Turkey remains a landmark judgment in the field of women's rights.[24] The issues it left unresolved have, however, given rise to a jurisprudence in which article 14 is applied inconsistently in domestic violence cases, some judges requiring applicants to meet a particularly high threshold of systematic ill-treatment.[25] In *Bălşan v Romania* (2017),[26] *Tkhelidze v Georgia* (2021),[27] and *A and B v Georgia* (2022),[28] for example, both the domestic violence experienced and the States' response to it were characterised as discrimination against women.[29] In contrast, in two other cases involving fatal domestic violence, *Y v Bulgaria* (2022)[30] and *Landi v Italy* (2022),[31] the violence was discussed in the context of discrimination against women, but no violation of article 14 was found on the basis that the applicants had not established discriminatory attitudes or general passivity on the part of the authorities.[32] Finally, in *AE v Bulgaria* (2023),[33] it was accepted, on the basis of statistical information, that domestic violence disproportionally affected women, such disproportionality creating an obligation to ensure that the State takes 'remedial measures' 'to ensure that women can fully enjoy human rights and freedoms on an equal footing with men'.[34] The subsequent article 14 violation was found not in relation to the violence, but the State's failure to respond to a situation of which they were aware (reasoning I return to in Part II).[35] As will be recalled from chapter 2, indirect discrimination does not require discriminatory intent, systematic ill-treatment, or passivity (although these may be present), but unjustifiable differential treatment that can be linked to a protected ground (or grounds).

[23] For a 'feminist judgment' that does this, see Choudhry and Herring, 'Opuz v Turkey' (n 15).

[24] See the discussion in Sandra Fredman, 'Emerging from the Shadows: Substantive Equality and Article 14 of the European Convention on Human Rights' (2016) 16 Human Rights Law Review 273.

[25] *Talpis v Italy* App no 41237/14 (ECtHR, 2 March 2017) (compare the judgment with the Partly Concurring, Partly Dissenting Opinion of Judge Eicke, paras 13, 19, Partly Dissenting Opinion of Judge Spano, para 18). See further Lourdes Peroni, 'Talpis v. Italy: Elements to Show an Article 14 Violation in Domestic Violence Cases' (*Strasbourg Observers*, 19 April 2017) <https://strasbourgobservers.com/2017/04/19/talpis-v-italy-elements-to-show-an-article-14-violation-in-domestic-violence-cases/#more-3628> accessed 24 June 2019.

[26] *Bălşan v Romania* App no 49645/09 (ECtHR, 23 May 2017).

[27] *Tkhelidze v Georgia* App no 33056/17 (ECtHR, 8 July 2021). Notably, this case concerned a 'systemic failure', para 57.

[28] *A and B v Georgia* App no 73975/16 (ECtHR, 10 February 2022).

[29] For example, *Bălşan v Romania* (n 26) paras 79, 85–88.

[30] *Y v Bulgaria* App no 9077/18 (ECtHR, 22 March 2022).

[31] *Landi v Italy* App no 10929/19 (ECtHR, 7 April 2022). See further Lorena Sosa, 'The Istanbul Convention in the Context of Feminist Claims' in Johanna Niemi, Lourdes Peroni, and Vladislava Stoyanova (eds), *International Law and Violence Against Women: Europe and the Istanbul Convention* (2020) 35.

[32] For example, *Y v Bulgaria* (n 30) paras 122, 131–32.

[33] *AE v Bulgaria* App no 53891/20 (ECtHR, 23 May 2023).

[34] ibid para 119.

[35] The Court did, in its analysis, refer to domestic violence as a form of violence against women, yet this was not the basis on which the violation was found. ibid paras 116, 122–23. This case is discussed further in chapter 7.

The Court's uncertainty as to when violent conduct is discrimination, or discrimination contrary to article 14, may also explain why it has *never* applied article 14 to cases involving trafficking and, more broadly, the different approach it takes to violence experienced both in and out of the migration control context.[36]

The Court's failure in *Opuz* to define, and then explain, the relationship between the two forms of discrimination it discusses, one violent, the other not, is indicative of a broader lack of conceptual and legal clarity as to the nature of violence against women, and the place of its prohibition within the general and specialist human rights frameworks concerned with discrimination. I started this book with quotes from two migrant women who described a particular predicament: being made dependent for their migration status, and all the rights that flow from it, on people who were violent towards them. The first woman, a migrant spouse, was a victim of domestic violence perpetrated by her husband. The second, a domestic worker, was demeaned and exploited by her employers. I stated that both women experienced forms of a particular kind of violence: violence against women. Explaining and delineating the type of violence I am concerned with is, therefore, necessary to set the foundations for the arguments I advance on the obligations States owe migrant women who have experienced it (in chapter 4) and the extent to which these obligations are discharged (Part II's evaluation of the regimes of exception). To do so, I advance a juridical account of violence against women, establishing the points at which five central international legal instruments' definitions converge to establish what is at the core of this legal wrong. Accordingly, the 'violence against women' of this book's title is interpersonal, gender-based conduct that causes certain types of harm. Such violence *is* discriminatory, a cause and consequence of women's subordination. In the sections that follow, I justify and explain this definitional approach, applying it to both domestic violence and trafficking. This enables me to establish States' obligations under the ECHR to victims of such violence within their jurisdiction.

3.2 A Juridical Account

3.2.1 Explanations, Demarcations, and Caveats

'Violence against women' is a term of art, used to denote a particular type of unjustifiable violence and a particular kind of wrong. Like 'persecution' in refugee law, the phrase 'violence against women' has definitions in international human rights law that are, or may be, different from the phrase's ordinary meaning, and

[36] Described as a 'territorial bias' in Janna Wessels, 'The Boundaries of Universality—Migrant Women and Domestic Violence Before the Strasbourg Court' (2019) 37 Netherlands Quarterly of Human Rights 336.

usage within other disciplines. As with ‘persecution’, academics and practitioners debate what the term includes, and what it excludes. The complexity of this debate is increased, and differences between legal instruments and academic approaches are obscured, when phrases including ‘violence against women’, ‘gender-based violence’, and ‘gender-based violence against women’, are used interchangeably, and without explanation.[37] The same is true for key constitutive terms, such as ‘women’, ‘sex’, and ‘gender’. Here, I briefly explain my approach to each of these and explain the value of establishing violence against women’s focal meaning *in international law.*

For many, the ‘concept and category of woman is the necessary point of departure for any feminist theory and feminist politics’.[38] Yet feminist writing on sex and gender has called into question the underpinnings and, indeed, the very viability of that category.[39] As Mari Mikkola explains, such theorising generates a series of both semantic and ontological questions.[40] What are feminists talking about when they talk about ‘women’?[41] ‘How should we understand the category of women that is meant to undergird feminist political solidarity, if there are no necessary and sufficient conceptual conditions underlying our gender talk?’[42] Feminists may be left to articulate political claims in the name of ‘women’, while simultaneously debating the concept.[43] Others, including Alice Walker who introduces some of her writing as ‘womanist prose’, found that the category was denied to them:

> It is, apparently, inconvenient, if not downright mind straining, for white women scholars to think of black women *as women*, perhaps because ‘woman’ (like ‘man’ among white males) is a name they are claiming for themselves, and themselves alone. Racism decrees that if they are now women . . . then black women must, perforce, be something else.[44]

[37] Human rights instruments/bodies tend to use the term ‘violence against women’ while ‘gender-based violence’ is more frequently referred to in the jurisprudence, guidelines, and statements of the broader UN. Edwards, *Violence Against Women* (n 21) 20.

[38] Linda Alcoff, ‘Cultural Feminism versus Post-Structuralism: The Identity Crisis in Feminist Theory’ (1988) 13 Signs 405, 405.

[39] See further Judith Butler, *Undoing Gender* (Routledge 2004); Martha C Nussbaum, ‘The Professor of Parody’ (*The New Republic*, 22 February 1999) <https://newrepublic.com/article/150687/professor-parody> accessed 23 September 2020; Kathryn McNeilly, ‘Gendered Violence and International Human Rights: Thinking Non-discrimination Beyond the Sex Binary’ (2014) 22 Feminist Legal Studies 263.

[40] Mari Mikkola, *The Wrong of Injustice: Dehumanization and its Role in Feminist Philosophy* (OUP 2016) ch 2.

[41] ibid 27–28.

[42] ibid 27–28. See also Joan Wallach Scott, ‘Gender: Still a Useful Category of Analysis?’’ (2010) 225 Diogenes 7.

[43] Linda Martín Alcoff, *Visible Identities: Race, Gender, and the Self* (OUP 2006) ch 6.

[44] Alice Walker, ‘One Child of One’s Own: A Meaningful Digression Within the Work(s)’ in *In Search of Our Mothers’ Gardens: Womanist Prose* (Phoenix 2005) 376.

Writing about women in international law generates a series of separate, but related, questions and objections. 'Is', asks Hilary Charlesworth, 'the pervasive devaluation of women's lives enough to link women in the effort to add a gender dimension to international human rights?'[45] If it is, how might this dimension be added? CEDAW, often referred to simply as 'the Women's Convention', has attracted criticism for its asymmetrical concern with 'discrimination against women'. Darren Rosenbaum has argued that this focus reinforces a 'binary that must be dismantled to achieve change'.[46] Diane Otto contends that the Convention's 'protective responses' 're-entrench[] women's inequality, rather than fundamentally challenging it'.[47] In a slightly different vein, Julie Goldscheid argues that adopting a 'woman-specific frame erases the experiences' of others who have experienced gendered discrimination and violence, including men.[48] A range of alternative approaches have been offered in place of those that, like CEDAW, theoretically and legally, centre women's lives and experiences. Such approaches include 'contextualized gender-neutrality',[49] unsexing CEDAW,[50] or otherwise interpreting it to respond to all forms of sexed/gendered discrimination.[51]

This book makes claims about migrant women's rights *legal* rights. Consequently, I do not enter into philosophical discussion of sex and/or gender, other than to acknowledge, very briefly with the preceding paragraphs, some of the questions and contestation that those who do have addressed in their work. The arguments I make on the duties States owe migrant women in different contexts do, however, rely on being able to interpret particular legal instruments and, consequently, to delineate certain sets of obligations. Establishing violence against women's focal meaning *in international law* is necessary to determine how legal responses to a particular kind of wrong should be evaluated, and how the predicament of being subject to such violence, and to migration control, might be remedied. The approach I adopt to both 'women' and 'violence' is one that is therefore informed by feminist theorising but drawn from, and relevant to, some specific legal contexts. These include national and regional legal frameworks, understanding that these evolve while differing from and influencing each other.[52] Also relevant are regional

[45] Quoted and discussed in Rebecca J Cook, 'Women's International Human Rights Law: The Way Forward' in Rebecca J Cook (ed), *Human Rights of Women: National and International Perspectives* (University of Pennsylvania Press 2012) 5. See further Hilary Charlesworth, 'What Are "Women's International Human Rights?"' in Rebecca J Cook (ed), *Human Rights of Women: National and International Perspectives* (University of Pennsylvania Press 2012).

[46] Darren Rosenblum, 'Unsex CEDAW, Or What's Wrong with Women's Rights' (2011) 20 Columbia Journal of Gender and Law 98, 104.

[47] Dianne Otto, 'Queering Gender [Identity] in International Law' (2015) 33 Nordic Journal of Human Rights 299, 302–03.

[48] Julie Goldscheid, 'Gender Neutrality, the "Violence against Women" Frame, and Transformative Reform' (2014) 82 UMKC Law Review 623, 635.

[49] ibid.

[50] Rosenblum, 'Unsex CEDAW' (n 46).

[51] Otto, 'Queering Gender' (n 47).

[52] Case law from the UK on sex, gender, and marriage has, for example, influenced, while remaining distinct from, the approach to these adopted in other common law jurisdictions. Sharon Cowan,

human rights protections and the specialist legal regimes concerned with discrimination against women.

The CEDAW Committee understands that the discrimination women face 'based on sex and gender is inextricably linked with other factors that affect women, such as race, ethnicity, religion or belief, health, status, age, class, caste and sexual orientation and gender identity'.[53] Consequently, the Committee has affirmed that intersectionality is a 'basic concept' for understanding States' obligations under the Convention.[54] Violations of the Convention have thus been found where States have failed to respond to the violence and discrimination experienced by migrant, refugee, and lesbian women.[55] The Inter-American Court of Human Rights has drawn on the CEDAW Committee's work when applying the Convention of Belém do Pará's provisions on gender-based violence to that experienced by trans women.[56] Finally, and as will be discussed in more detail in chapter 7, the Council of Europe Convention on Preventing and Combating Violence against Women and Domestic Violence (the Istanbul Convention)[57] protects victims from discrimination on a range of grounds, including, sex, gender, language, race, religion, sexual orientation, gender identity, disability, and migrant

'"Gender is No Substitute for Sex": A Comparative Human Rights Analysis of the Legal Regulation of Sexual Identity' (2005) 13 Feminist Legal Studies 67. The legal position in the UK, set out in the Gender Recognition Act 2004 and Equality Act 2010, was developed in response to the ECtHR's decision in *Goodwin v UK* App no 28957/95 (ECtHR, 11 July 2002) and the House of Lords' judgment in *Bellinger v Bellinger* [2003] UKHL 21, [2003] 2 AC 467.

[53] UN Committee on the Elimination of Discrimination against Women, 'General Recommendation No 28 on the Core Obligations of States Parties under Article 2 of the Convention on the Elimination of All Forms of Discrimination against Women' (19 December 2010) UN Doc CEDAW/C/2010/47/GC.2 [18] (CEDAW's GR 28). In addition to acknowledging that women may be discriminated against on the ground of gender identity, the Committee has made recommendations to States in support of the rights of trans and intersex people. Christine Chinkin and Marsha A Freeman, 'Introduction' in Marsha A Freeman, Christine Chinkin, and Beate Rudolf (eds), *The UN Convention on the Elimination of All Forms of Discrimination against Women: A Commentary* (OUP 2012) 14–16; UN Committee on the Elimination of Discrimination against Women, 'Concluding Observations on the Eighth Periodic Report of the United Kingdom of Great Britain and Northern Ireland' UN Doc CEDAW/C/GBR/CO/8 (14 March 2019) [16](c).

[54] CEDAW's GR 28 (n 53) [18].

[55] Respectively, *Jallow v Bulgaria* CEDAW Committee, Communication No 32/2011, UN Doc CEDAW/C/52/D/32/2011 (views adopted 23 July 2012); *RSAA v Denmark* CEDAW Committee, Communication No 86/2015, UN Doc CEDAW/C/73/D/86/2015 (views adopted 15 July 2019); *ON and DP v Russian Federation* CEDAW Committee, Communication No 119/2017, UN Doc CEDAW/C/75/D/119/2017 (views adopted 24 February 2020).

[56] *Case of Vicky Hernández v Honduras (Merits, Reparations and Costs)* Inter-American Court of Human Rights Series C No 422 (26 March 2021) para 133. Here, the Court focused on the purpose of the Convention: the 'eradication' of gender-based violence, a 'phenomenon which is structurally rooted in our societies'. ibid para 134. Doing so required, once again, taking an intersectional approach, one that understood that Vicky Hernández's particular vulnerability to gender-based violence was informed by her gender identity, her involvement in prostitution, her HIV+ status, and her advocacy for trans women's rights. ibid paras 135–36.

[57] Council of Europe Convention on Preventing and Combating Violence against Women and Domestic Violence (adopted 11 May 2011, entered into force 1 August 2014) CETS 210 (Istanbul Convention).

or refugee status.[58] It also encourages States to provide the Convention's domestic violence protections to all victims, including men and boys.[59] Contrary to some of the critiques introduced above, regimes which focus on discrimination and violence against women have neither erased identities and experiences nor denied protection.[60] Indeed, they have shown themselves able to both illuminate and respond to intersectional violence and discrimination.[61] The mobilisation of these specialist regimes, in conjunction with other instruments which protect rights and prohibit discrimination on multiple and intersecting grounds, ensure that they remain a vital, but not by any means the only, response to gendered violence and inequality.[62]

3.2.2 Instruments and Elements: Violence against Women in International Law

There are five main international legal definitions of violence against women.[63] These can be found in CEDAW's GR 19[64] and 35,[65] the UN Declaration on the

[58] ibid art 4(3).

[59] ibid art 2(2).

[60] Consonant with Rikki Holtmaat, 'The CEDAW: A Holistic Approach to Women's Equality and Freedom' in Anne Hellum and Henriette Sinding Aasen (eds), *Women's Human Rights: CEDAW in International, Regional and National Law* (CUP 2013); Jonathan Herring, 'The Istanbul Convention: Is Domestic Abuse Violence Against Women?' in Gillian Douglas, Mervyn Murch, and Victoria Stephens (eds), *International and National Perspectives on Child and Family Law: Essays in Honour of Nigel Lowe* (Insentia 2018). But see Rosenblum, 'Unsex CEDAW' (n 46) and Goldscheid, 'Gender Neutrality' (n 48).

[61] Drawing on Shreya Atrey, 'Lifting as We Climb: Recognising Intersectional Gender Violence in Law' (2015) 5 Oñati Socio-Legal Series 1512. This is not to downplay justified criticism of their jurisprudence. Lorena PA Sosa, 'Inter-American Case Law on *Femicide*: Obscuring Intersections?' (2017) 35 Netherlands Quarterly of Human Rights 85; Shreya Atrey, 'From Progress to Transformation, An Intersectional Response to Martha Nussbaum' (2018) 40 Human Rights Quarterly 859.

[62] See, for example, UN Committee against Torture, 'General Comment No 2 (2007) on the Implementation of Article 2 by States Parties' (24 January 2008) UN Doc CAT/C/GC/2 [21]. Other relevant instruments include, of course, the International Convention on the Elimination of All Forms of Racial Discrimination (adopted 21 December 1965, entered into force 4 January 1969) 660 UNTS 195; Convention on the Rights of Persons with Disabilities (adopted 13 May 2006, entered into force 3 May 2008) 2515 UNTS 3.

[63] Not considered here, because it does not contain a definition of violence against women, is a sixth regional approach, the Declaration on the Elimination of Violence against Women in the ASEAN Region (13 June 2004) 2004 ASEAN DS 253.

[64] CEDAW's GR 19 (n 8) [6]: 'The Convention in article 1 defines discrimination against women. The definition of discrimination includes gender-based violence, that is, violence that is directed against a woman because she is a woman or that affects women disproportionately. It includes acts that inflict physical, mental or sexual harm or suffering, threats of such acts, coercion and other deprivations of liberty.'

[65] UN Committee on the Elimination of Discrimination against Women, 'General Recommendation No 35 on Gender-Based Violence Against Women, Updating General Recommendation No 19' (26 July 2017) UN Doc CEDAW/C/GC/35 [9] (CEDAW's GR 35): 'The concept of "violence against women", as defined in general recommendation No.19 and other international instruments and documents ... places an emphasis on the fact that such violence is gender based. Accordingly, in the present recommendation, the term "gender-based violence against women" is used as a more precise term that makes explicit the gendered causes and impacts of the violence.'

Elimination of Violence against Women (DEVAW),[66] the Convention of Belém do Pará,[67] the Protocol to the African Charter on Human and Peoples' Rights on the Rights of Women in Africa (the Maputo Protocol),[68] and the Istanbul Convention.[69] Significant numbers of States have ratified these instruments. As the above discussion of *Opuz* demonstrates, their definitions have influenced the jurisprudence of regional courts and human rights bodies. Depending on the instrument and jurisdiction, these definitions may also have a direct bearing on relevant national and European Union (EU) law. This is particularly the case following the EU's partial accession to the Istanbul Convention and the culmination of efforts to adopt a Directive on violence against women (both discussed in Part II).[70] Consequently, the points at which different elements of these definitions converge represent a weak international consensus as to the nature of this form of violence.[71] These points of convergence also provide an uncontentious foundation to this book's claims that certain conduct is 'violence against women'. Drawing on these instruments and elements, violence against women is interpersonal, gender-based conduct that causes certain types of harm.[72] Such violence is, in and of itself, discrimination against women and a violation of women's human rights.

[66] Declaration on the Elimination of Violence against Women UNGA Res 48/104 (20 December 1993) art 1: '[T]he term "violence against women" means any act of gender-based violence that results in, or is likely to result in, physical, sexual or psychological harm or suffering to women, including threats of such acts, coercion or arbitrary deprivation of liberty, whether occurring in public or in private life.' See also Intensification of Efforts to Eliminate All Forms of Violence against Women UNGA GA Res 61/143 (30 January 2007).

[67] Convention of Belém do Pará, art 1: '[V]iolence against women shall be understood as any act or conduct, based on gender, which causes death or physical, sexual or psychological harm or suffering to women, whether in the public or the private sphere.' Per art 2, this definition includes physical, sexual, and psychological violence.

[68] Protocol to the African Charter on Human and Peoples' Rights on the Rights of Women in Africa (adopted 11 July 2003, entered into force 25 November 2005) OAU Doc Cab/Leg/66.6 art 1(j): '"Violence against women" means all acts perpetrated against women which cause or could cause them physical, sexual, psychological, and economic harm, including the threat to take such acts; or to undertake the imposition of arbitrary restrictions on or deprivation of fundamental freedoms in private or public life in peace time and during situations of armed conflicts or of war.'

[69] Istanbul Convention, art 3(a): '"[V]iolence against women" is understood as a violation of human rights and a form of discrimination against women and shall mean all acts of gender-based violence that result in, or are likely to result in, physical, sexual, psychological or economic harm or suffering to women, including threats of such acts, coercion or arbitrary deprivation of liberty, whether occurring in public or in private life.' ibid art 3(d): '"gender-based violence against women" shall mean violence that is directed against a woman because she is a woman or that affects women disproportionately.'

[70] Directive (EU) 2024/1385 of the European Parliament and of the Council of 14 May 2024 on combating violence against women and domestic violence [2024] OJ L2024/1385, art 2(a) which draws on Istanbul Convention, art 3(a) and (d). See further European Commission, 'Proposal for a Directive of the European Parliament and of the Council on Combating Violence against Women and Domestic Violence' COM(2022) 105 final, 8 March 2022.

[71] Following the standard means of treaty interpretation, Vienna Convention on the Law of Treaties (adopted 23 May 1969, entered into force 27 January 1980) 1155 UNTS 331, art 31.

[72] For a similar approach, one which identifies as 'common elements' that the violence causes certain kinds of harm and is based on gender, see Ekaterina Yahyaoui Krivenko, 'The Role and Impact of Soft Law on the Emergence of the Prohibition of Violence against Women within the Context of the CEDAW' in Stéphanie Lagoutte, Thomas Gammeltoft-Hansen, and John Cerone (eds), *Tracing the Roles of Soft Law in Human Rights* (OUP 2016).

All the legal instruments considered here define violence against women in terms of acts or conduct that cause certain types of harm. This harm may be physical, psychological, sexual, and/or economic in nature. Such harmful conduct may cause injury and have fatal outcomes, including homicide and suicide.[73] Consistent with four of the five definitions, the exception potentially being the Convention of Belém do Pará, threats of harmful acts are included in my account of violence against women.[74] Similarly included are acts that have the potential to cause harm, whether or not it materialises. Although all the legal instruments are silent on the question of omissions, omissions are characterised as conduct and are also included here, again, where they give rise, or have the potential to give rise, to relevant harm. Failing to seek medical assistance, a common feature in the abuse of women with disabilities, for example, is an omission which may cause significant physical harm.[75] As Martha Nussbaum observes, many forms of behaviour which are not obviously violent, such as the under-nutrition of girls (an omission) or the non-consensual publishing of private images (an act), should be understood to be so.[76] This is because such behaviour has 'the same crippling effects'—produces the same harms and has the same impact on women's physical and mental integrity—as direct physical violence does.[77]

The inclusion of economic harm in both the Maputo Protocol and Istanbul Convention has been interpreted as being consistent with a broader approach to violence against women, one which encompasses structural violence.[78] Structural violence is the indirect, harmful, coercive, discriminatory, and/or unjust conduct of institutions and social structures.[79] The system that determines women's eligibility for international protection in the UK has, for example, been characterised as structurally violent.[80] Interpersonal violence is, in contrast, the violence that one or more individuals perpetrates against another. Perpetrators may be actors linked to the State, such as police officers or border guards.[81] They may also be

[73] For a discussion of these harms, see World Health Organization, 'Violence Against Women' (*World Health Organization*, 25 March 2024) <www.who.int/news-room/fact-sheets/detail/violence-against-women> accessed 30 April 2024.

[74] Anthony P Ewing, 'Establishing State Responsibility for Private Acts of Violence against Women under the American Convention on Human Rights' (1995) 26 Columbia Human Rights Law Review 751. Of course, a broader, non-literal, interpretative approach could be taken to the definition, in line with the Convention's purpose.

[75] The World Health Organization also includes deprivation and neglect within their typology of 'violence', Etienne G Krug and others, *World Report on Violence and Health* (World Health Organization 2002) 6-7.

[76] Martha C Nussbaum, 'Women's Bodies: Violence, Security, Capabilities' (2005) 6 Journal of Human Development 167, 167. The first example given is Nussbaum's own, the second is mine.

[77] ibid 168.

[78] For example, Edwards, *Violence Against Women* (n 21) 25.

[79] Drawing on, Johan Galtung, 'Violence, Peace, and Peace Research' (1969) 6 Journal of Peace Research 167.

[80] Victoria Canning, *Gendered Harm and Structural Violence in the British Asylum System* (Routledge 2017).

[81] They may, therefore, be part of broader 'violent' or 'unjust' structures, in addition to, or as well as being a perpetrator of interpersonal violence. The two forms of violence, structural and interpersonal, may be distinct but overlapping in many contexts and circumstances.

private individuals, a woman's partner or employer, for example, or a person unknown to her.

In limiting my account of violence against women to interpersonal violence, I am not seeking to undermine the scholarly value and practical efficacy of characterising some forms of inequality, or injustice, as violent in nature. Such an approach is rejected here for two main reasons.[82] First, it risks conflating related but fundamentally different legal wrongs. In chapter 2, I argued that the differential distribution of certain migration statuses unlawfully discriminated against women. This treatment may be included in accounts of violence against women which encompass structural violence but it is excluded from my own. Such disadvantageous and discriminatory conduct is, however, as that chapter argues, a distinct legal wrong which requires a remedy. Characterising migration law as unlawfully discriminatory is, consequently, sufficient to found both a normative and legal attack upon it. Indeed, describing unequal or unjust treatment as violence may have the opposite effect to the one intended, devaluing other kinds of ethical and legal wrongs by implying that they are less 'requiring of a response' than those that are violent in nature. Secondly, a focus on interpersonal, rather than structural, violence enables the relationships and contexts that migration status particularly affects—family relationships, the home, and the workplace—to be placed at the centre of analysis. In chapter 2, I also discussed empirical research on migrant women's increased vulnerability to particular forms of violence, implicating rules which make women dependent on a partner or employer in this increased risk. An understanding of the difference that migration status makes to a woman's extant risk of being subject to violence, and to its experience, may be obscured by the adoption of a definitional approach to 'violence' that also encompasses the distribution of migration statuses.

The violence I am concerned with is, consequently, interpersonal conduct that causes harm. That it is a woman who experiences such violence is necessary, but not sufficient, to render it 'violence against women'. Consonant with CEDAW's GR 19 and 35, the Istanbul Convention, and the Convention of Belém do Pará, such conduct must also be gender-based. This does not require evidence of direct or individual discriminatory intent. Violence will be gender-based where it is directed at a woman because she is a woman, and/or where it affects women disproportionately. This position is narrower than that adopted by one of the instruments, the Maputo Protocol, which encompasses *any* violence that women experience. Alice Edwards endorses the Maputo approach, asserting that it enables women to be protected from violence in situations, such as armed conflict, where women are at a greater risk than men but where the harm is nevertheless 'more easily' described

[82] A third, and more pragmatic reason for excluding structural violence, is that such an approach is in line with the 'ordinary' meaning of the term 'violence' and is, therefore, more likely to be satisfying to the practitioners and policymakers I seek to engage.

as 'random, generalised, or indiscriminate'.[83] This argument may be straightforwardly refuted. If research establishes that forms of violence *characterised* as indiscriminate *actually* affect women disproportionately, in their prevalence, form, or impact, then it is that erroneous characterisation that should be changed. To employ a phrase often used by feminist activists, violence against women is both a cause and consequence of women's inequality. It is, to draw on the preambles of three of the instruments, a manifestation of historically unequal power relations and one of the mechanisms by which women are subordinated.[84] To focus on violence which is gender-based is to recognise, and respond to, that violence's constitutive role in patriarchy. As Michelle Madden Dempsey explains:

> The point of view I adopt in what follows is an explicitly *feminist* point of view; one which assumes that at least some of the salient features of women's condition are best understood by reference to patriarchy. This point of view does not deny that a variety of other considerations, including other intersecting structural inequalities, are also relevant to a fully illuminated account of women's condition. Rather, it merely shines one particular light on this issue, so as to illuminate an admittedly partial yet nonetheless salient aspect of women's condition.[85]

Finally, limiting my account to that violence which is gender-based is not an argument that such violence is *only* gender-based. As the jurisprudence of the CEDAW Committee and Inter-American Court discussed above indicate, violence may be, and indeed usually is, determined by sex/gender in conjunction with a range of other characteristics and identities.[86]

3.2.3 Applying the Definition

Migrant women who experience domestic violence, who are trafficked, or who have experienced other forms of violence against women may have recourse to one, or more, of the regimes of exception which I evaluate in Part II. Although different conceptual approaches to domestic violence or trafficking may be taken, specific legal definitions of these are relied on here to discuss, very briefly, how the account developed above may be applied. First, though, some more caveats. In stating that domestic violence, or trafficking, can and should be categorised as

[83] Edwards, *Violence Against Women* (n 21) 24.

[84] Drawing on the preambles of DEVAW, Convention of Belém do Pará, and Istanbul Convention. See also CEDAW's GR 35 (n 65) [19].

[85] Michelle Madden Dempsey, *Prosecuting Domestic Violence: A Philosophical Analysis* (OUP 2009) 135.

[86] See also Atrey, 'Lifting as We Climb' (n 61); Lorena Sosa, *Intersectionality in the Human Rights Legal Framework on Violence against Women: At the Centre or the Margins?* (CUP 2017).

forms of violence against women under certain circumstances, I am not arguing that they can or should *only* be understood in these terms. Domestic violence that occurs within same-sex relationships, for example, may or may not fall within my account.[87] Conduct that meets or falls within legal definitions of trafficking, the formulation of which are contested, as chapter 6 explains, must be gender-based if it is also to be considered violence against women. Violence, as a general phenomenon, can take many forms, and so will present the elements identified above to a greater or lesser extent, if at all.

Domestic violence is defined in the Istanbul Convention as:

> all acts of physical, sexual, psychological or economic violence that occur within the family or domestic unit or between former or current spouses or partners, whether or not the perpetrator shares or has shared the same residence with the victim.[88]

Such violence, occurring within a particular set of relationships, is interpersonal conduct that entails the infliction of certain kinds of harm. Contrary to accounts that present domestic violence in gender-neutral terms, such violence is usually gendered.[89] Women are significantly more likely than men to experience domestic violence and, when they do, are more negatively affected by it, and by particular forms of it.[90] Research on domestic violence has also consistently emphasised the attempt or desire of male perpetrators to coerce, control, and dominate their female victims.[91] Domestic violence has, therefore, been linked to women's inequality. Inequality within individual relationships, and within society more broadly, is correlated with both a greater individual risk of experiencing domestic violence, and higher societal levels of it.[92]

87 For an analysis of power and violence in lesbian relations that highlights its gendered nature, see Claire M Renzetti, *Violent Betrayal: Partner Abuse in Lesbian Relationships* (Sage 1992).

88 Istanbul Convention, art 3(b).

89 Herring, 'The Istanbul Convention' (n 60), drawing on Madden Dempsey, *Prosecuting Domestic Violence* (n 85) ch 6.

90 Worldwide, almost one third (27%) of women aged fifteen to forty-nine years who have been in a relationship report that they have been subjected to some form of physical and/or sexual violence by their intimate partner. World Health Organization, *Violence against Women Prevalence Estimates, 2018: Global, Regional and National Prevalence Estimates for Intimate Partner Violence against Women and Global and Regional Prevalence Estimates for Non-Partner Sexual Violence against Women* (World Health Organization 9 March 2021) 20 <www.who.int/publications/i/item/9789240022256> accessed 30 April 2024. See also Marianne Hester, 'Who Does What to Whom? Gender and Domestic Violence Perpetrators in English Police Records' (2013) 10 European Journal of Criminology 623; European Union Agency for Fundamental Rights, *Violence Against Women: An EU-Wide Survey: Main Results Report* (Publications Office of the European Union 2014).

91 Michael P Johnson, 'Conflict and Control: Gender Symmetry and Asymmetry in Domestic Violence' (2006) 12 Violence Against Women 1003; Evan Stark, *Coercive Control: The Entrapment of Women in Personal Life* (OUP 2007); Marieh Tanha and others, 'Sex Differences in Intimate Partner Violence and the Use of Coercive Control as a Motivational Factor for Intimate Partner Violence' (2010) 25 Journal of Interpersonal Violence 1836.

92 Emma Fulu and others, *Why Do Some Men Use Violence Against Women and How Can We Prevent It? Quantitative Findings from the United Nations Multi-Country Study on Men and Violence in Asia*

While conducting empirical and other research on trafficking is challenging, there is an evidence base which can be drawn on to argue that conduct that falls within the trafficking definition may also be characterised as violence against women.[93] Trafficking is defined in European law as:

> the recruitment, transportation, transfer, harbouring or receipt of persons, by means of the threat or use of force or other forms of coercion, of abduction, of fraud, of deception, of the abuse of power or of a position of vulnerability or of the giving or receiving of payments or benefits to achieve the consent of a person having control over another person, for the purpose of exploitation.[94]

As I will explain in Part II, the particular wrong captured by this definition is not exploitation itself but a process that may, or may not, lead to it. This process overall, and particularly the 'means' element, usually entails interpersonal conduct that causes a range of harms.[95] Such conduct is highly likely to include physical and sexual violence, isolation, forced or coerced use of drugs/alcohol, and economic exploitation.[96] Trafficking is, therefore, correlated with serious mental and physical ill-health, including depression, post-traumatic stress disorder, and physical pain.[97] Notwithstanding difficulties assessing the prevalence and scale of trafficking, in Europe women and girls are more likely to be trafficked, and are also more likely to be trafficked for particular kinds of exploitation, including sexual exploitation and domestic servitude.[98] Inequalities, including those based on race,

and the Pacific (UNDP, UNFPA, UN Women, and UNV 2013); Lori L Heise and Andreas Kotsadam, 'Cross-national and Multilevel Correlates of Partner Violence: An Analysis of Data From Population-Based Surveys' (2015) 3 Lancet Global Health 332; Dan Anderberg and others, 'Unemployment and Domestic Violence: Theory and Evidence' (2016) 126 The Economic Journal 1947; World Health Organization, *Violence against Women* (n 90).

[93] On the challenges, see Mary Bosworth, Carolyn Hoyle and Michelle Madden Dempsey, 'Researching Trafficked Women: On Institutional Resistance and the Limits to Feminist Reflexivity' (2011) 17 Qualitative Inquiry 769.

[94] Council of Europe Convention on Action against Trafficking in Human Beings (adopted 16 May 2005, entered into force 1 February 2008) CETS 197, art 4(a) (Trafficking Convention), chosen because this instrument is analysed in Part II.

[95] For a theoretical approach that understands trafficking as a multi-staged process of cumulative harm, see Cathy Zimmerman, Mazeda Hossain, and Charlotte Watts, 'Human Trafficking and Health: A Conceptual Model to Inform Policy, Intervention and Research' (2011) 73 Soc Sci Med 327.

[96] Physical or sexual violence while in the trafficking situation was reported by 95% of women taking part in the study; 71% reported experiencing both. Cathy Zimmerman and others, *Stolen Smiles: The Physical and Psychological Health Consequences of Women and Adolescents Trafficked in Europe* (The London School of Hygiene & Tropical Medicine 2006) 2.

[97] ibid. See also Cathy Zimmerman and Heidi Stöckl, *Human Trafficking* (World Health Organization, WHO/RHR/1242, 2012); Ligia Kiss and others, 'Health of Men, Women, and Children in Post-Trafficking Services in Cambodia, Thailand, and Vietnam: An Observational Cross-sectional Study' (2015) 3 The Lancet Global Health 154; Sukran Altun and others, 'Mental Health and Human Trafficking: Responding to Survivors' Needs' (2017) 14 BJPsych International 21.

[98] In 2022, 63% of registered victims of trafficking in human beings in the EU were women or girls, these women and girls being subjected to gendered exploitation. 'Trafficking in Human Beings

age, and sexual orientation, interact with and reinforce each other, as stereotypes concerning some women's roles and attributes shape their vulnerability to different forms of exploitation.[99]

It will be recalled that the jurisprudence of the ECtHR is unclear on whether particular forms of violence against women, in addition to engaging rights, such as the right to be free from inhuman and degrading treatment, or to a family life, are also, in and of themselves, discrimination, or discrimination contrary to article 14.[100] In contrast, and as the ECtHR observed in *Opuz,* the CEDAW Committee has authoritatively defined such violence as discrimination against women. The Committee's jurisprudence, GR 19, and subsequent recommendations, situate both domestic violence and trafficking firmly within the Convention's non-discrimination framework.[101] My focus on interpersonal, gender-based conduct, whether perpetrated by State actors or private individuals, is consonant with CEDAW's prohibition of discrimination in both the public *and* private domains.[102] It is also consistent with the obligations that CEDAW imposes on States to eliminate discrimination and ensure the advancement of women in all spheres of life. This approach, and its crossing of the public/private divide has, in addition, been adopted by other treaty bodies and UN organs, as well as by the Inter-American and European systems in their jurisprudence and violence against women-specific conventions.[103] Finally, my approach follows the broad conception of discrimination offered in chapter 1, which drew on theoretical discussion of the field to understand discrimination law as being concerned with differential treatment based on certain protected characteristics. The arguments advanced in the chapters that follow do not depend on determining the particular question

Statistics' (*eurostat*, January 2024) <https://ec.europa.eu/eurostat/statistics-explained/index.php?title=Trafficking_in_human_beings_statistics> accessed 30 April 2024. See also Sylvia Walby and others, *Study on the Gender Dimension of Trafficking in Human Beings* (Publications Office of the European Union 2016).

99 See, for example, the discussion in Laura María Agustín, 'A Migrant World of Services' in Sarah van Walsum and Thomas Spijkerboer (eds), *Women and Immigration Law: New Variations on Classical Feminist Themes* (Routledge Cavendish 2006).

100 On the relationship between domestic violence and ECHR arts 3 and 8, see Ronagh JA McQuigg, 'The European Court of Human Rights and Domestic Violence: *Volodina v. Russia*' (2021) 10 International Human Rights Law Review 155.

101 CEDAW's GR 19 (n 8); CEDAW's GR 35 (n 65); UN Committee on the Elimination of Discrimination against Women, 'General Recommendation No 38 on Trafficking in Women and Girls in the Context of Global Migration' (20 November 2020) UN Doc CEDAW/C/GC/38. For arguments against this 'soft' law approach, see Rashida Manjoo and Jackie Jones, *The Legal Protection of Women From Violence: Normative Gaps in International Law* (Routledge 2019).

102 CEDAW, arts 1 and 2(e). The latter requires States to take all appropriate measures to eliminate discrimination against women by any person, organisation, or enterprise.

103 Convention of Belém do Pará, art 6; *González ('Cotton Field') v Mexico (Preliminary Objection, Merits, Reparations, and Costs)* Inter-American Court of Human Rights Series C No 205 (16 November 2009) paras 390–402; Istanbul Convention, arts 1(b), 2(1), and 3(a). The outlier again here is, therefore, the Maputo Protocol.

of whether or not specific forms of violence against women are sometimes, or always, *discrimination as prohibited by the ECHR*. The theoretical discussion and research offered here could, however, be drawn on to resolve the Court's sometimes contradictory jurisprudence on this point, and to characterise such violence as discrimination that falls squarely within the ambit of article 14. I return to this issue in Part II.

3.3 From Violence to Obligations and Remedies

3.3.1 States' Obligations in Relation to Violence against Women

In *Aydin v Turkey* (1997),[104] the rape and ill-treatment of Mrs Şükran Aydin by State security forces was found to breach the prohibition of torture set out in article 3 of the ECHR. Human rights law does not just prohibit States from directly violating a protected right, as occurred in Aydin's case, it also imposes positive or 'due diligence' obligations on them to *respond* appropriately to violence, whether or not it is attributable to the State.[105] It is for this reason that the State's failure to respond to the violence perpetrated against Nahide Opuz and her mother by a private actor (the applicant's husband/ex-husband) was found to violate articles 2 and 3 of the ECHR.

Broadly speaking, there are two categories, or levels, at which due diligence obligations operate. At the structural or systemic level are general obligations owed by the State to all those within the jurisdiction. At the individual level are specific obligations owed to identifiable people, or to particular groups of people.[106] A full consideration of States' positive obligations under the ECHR is well beyond the scope of this chapter and book.[107] Here, certain key obligations are mapped to establish how States should respond to violence against women.

[104] *Aydin v Turkey* App no 23178/94 (ECtHR, 25 September 1997).

[105] Such obligations have been found to be inherent in protected rights and have also been justified by reference to States' obligations to secure rights within their jurisdictions and provide effective remedies (arts 1 and 13 ECHR). For example, *MC v Bulgaria* App no 39272/98 (ECtHR, 4 December 2003) [149]. The ECtHR has referred to, but not adopted, the terminology of 'due diligence' (used by the CEDAW Committee, the Inter-American Commission and Court, and now the Istanbul Convention) when considering States' positive obligations. As space precludes me from examining how these institutions/instruments differ in their definitions of and approaches to positive obligations/due diligence, the terms are used interchangeably here. See further Vladislava Stoyanova, 'Due Diligence versus Positive Obligations: Critical Reflections on the Council of Europe Convention on Violence Against Women' in Johanna Niemi, Lourdes Peroni, and Vladislava Stoyanova (eds), *International Law and Violence against Women: Europe and the Istanbul Convention* (Routledge 2020).

[106] Adapted from Rashida Manjoo, 'State Responsibility to Act with Due Diligence in the Elimination of Violence against Women' (2013) 2 International Human Rights Law Review 240, 262. A similar distinction is drawn in Clare McGlynn, 'Rape, Torture and the European Convention on Human Rights' (2009) 58 International & Comparative Law Quarterly 565, 592–93.

[107] For which, see Vladislava Stoyanova, *Positive Obligations under the European Convention on Human Rights: Within and Beyond Boundaries* (OUP 2023).

At the structural level, States are required to put in place laws, processes, and policies to address the 'root causes' of rights violations and to prevent and deter them. If and when violations occur, States should identify perpetrators, hold them to account, and ensure appropriate reparation to their victims. States should, therefore, criminalise under appropriate labels, conduct that falls within the ambit of protected rights.[108] Criminal offences must be effectively investigated and, where appropriate, prosecuted.[109] To be effective, an investigation should be prompt, pursued with diligence, and not terminated by statutory limitation (where delays are due to State inaction).[110] States must ensure that their judicial systems are functioning, responsive, and independent.[111] Such systems should be able to impose and enforce on perpetrators proportionate sanctions capable of deterring them, and others, from committing further acts of violence.[112] Positive obligations do not just arise in relation to a State's criminal justice system. Civil restraining and protective orders must be available and accessible.[113] States should have effective child protection procedures,[114] robust employment laws, and appropriately responsive welfare benefits systems.[115] States' immigration rules should also offer 'practical and effective' protection from violence, trafficking, and exploitation.[116] Where 'structural and systematic dysfunction' in a State's legal system gives rise to violations of the Convention, the Court may provide detailed information on the general measures to be adopted to remedy this.[117]

In addition to these systemic obligations, States are also required to offer victims or potential victims of violence 'effective measures of prevention, protection, punishment and reparation'.[118] Following *Osman v UK* (1988),[119] a State is required to take 'preventative operational measures' where it knows, or ought to know, that a particular individual faces a 'real and immediate risk' to life.[120] Preventative measures can take many forms and must be responsive to the individual's circumstances and predicament. Where a person may be removed from a harmful situation, such as one in which trafficking is alleged, investigations must be undertaken 'as a matter of urgency' to enable this.[121] Allegations of domestic violence should be responded

[108] *MC v Bulgaria* (n 105) para 166; *CN v UK* (2013) 56 EHRR 24.
[109] *MC v Bulgaria* (n 105) paras 166–85.
[110] *MS v Italy* App no 32715/19 (ECtHR, 7 July 2022).
[111] *Opuz v Turkey* (n 1) para 200.
[112] *TI v Greece* App no 40311/10 (ECtHR, 18 July 2019); *EG v Moldova* App no 37882/13 (ECtHR, 13 April 2021).
[113] *ES v Slovakia* App no 8227/04 (ECtHR, 15 September 2009).
[114] *Z v UK* App no 29392/95 (ECtHR GC, 10 May 2001) paras 73–74.
[115] *JD and A v UK* App nos 32949/17 and 34614/17 (ECtHR, 24 October 2019).
[116] *Rantsev v Cyprus and Russia* (2010) 51 EHRR 1.
[117] *Tunikova v Russia* App nos 55974/16, 53118/17, 27484/18, and 28011/19 (ECtHR, 14 December 2021) paras 146–59.
[118] Manjoo, 'State Responsibility' (n 106) 245.
[119] *Osman v UK* App no 23452/94 (ECtHR GC, 28 October 1998).
[120] ibid para 116.
[121] *Rantsev v Cyprus and Russia* (n 116) para 288.

to immediately, including with 'an autonomous, proactive and comprehensive risk assessment' that takes into account the dynamics and potential escalation of such violence.[122] States must take into account the intersectional disadvantage (my terminology) or 'special vulnerability' (the Court's, as will be explained in chapter 4) that particular victims may be subject to on the basis of, for example, their age, sex/gender, race, or migration status.[123] Account must also be taken of the dynamics of different kinds of violence, and of the recurrence of successive episodes of it within a particular family.[124] As with other positive obligations, such measures are not limited to those available to criminal justice agencies and may include, for example, public law child protection procedures.[125]

Although it is not discussed in these terms by the ECtHR, protection from *refoulement*, from return to a situation where a person's life or freedom is threatened, could be considered a preventative operational measure. Whether or not the harm feared is anticipated to materialise in the State's own jurisdiction or, as in *refoulement* cases, the country of return, the obligation to the relevant individual is triggered in comparable circumstances: where she/he faces a 'real and immediate risk',[126] or a 'real risk',[127] of serious harm contrary to articles 2 or 3 of the ECHR.[128] It should be noted at this juncture that an individual may be protected from removal but not, under the ECHR *alone*, be granted a migration status.[129] Finally, where appropriate, the effects on a person of past violence should be considered in any later legal proceedings.[130]

The positive obligations outlined briefly here should ensure that women are protected from violence, but that when it does occur, those responsible are identified and held to account. Where States fail to discharge these obligations, victims of violence are entitled to an effective remedy, pursuant to article 13 of the ECHR. This right is broader than the right to, for example, have the criminal conduct of a perpetrator of domestic violence investigated by the police. It requires an examination of the State's failure to conduct such an investigation, a harm that is linked to, but separate from, the original violation. Şükran Aydin, for example, argued that Turkey had also breached her article 3 rights by failing to properly investigate her

[122] *Kurt v Austria* App no 62903/15 (ECtHR GC, 15 June 2021) para 190.

[123] *BS v Spain* App no 47159/08 (ECtHR, 24 July 2012) paras 57, 62; *Kurt v Austria* (n 122) para 163; *JI v Croatia* App no 35898/16 (ECtHR, 8 September 2022) para 97.

[124] *Kurt v Austria* (n 122).

[125] *Z v UK* (n 114).

[126] *Osman v UK* (n 119) para 116.

[127] *MSS v Belgium and Greece* [2011] 53 EHRR 28, para 365.

[128] Or, in *refoulement* cases, the 'flagrant breach' of another protected right, *EM (Lebanon) v SSHD* [2008] UKHL 64, [2009] 1 AC 1198. States would, however, have to take 'positive operational measures' to prevent the breach of Convention rights before the 'flagrant breach' test is reached.

[129] *Hayaati Ahmed Ali v The Netherlands* App no 26494/09 (ECtHR, 24 January 2012) para 19. In Part II, I explain how positive obligations under the ECHR, in conjunction with the requirements imposed on States by the regimes of exception, *may* yield short-term regularisation.

[130] *AI v Italy* App no 70896/17 (ECtHR, 1 April 2021). In relation to non-punishment, *VCL and AN v UK* App nos 77587/12 and 74603/12 (ECtHR, 16 February 2021).

detention and torture, and by subjecting her to repeated virginity tests.[131] Rather than considering this complaint separately under article 3, the Court found that the whole investigation was ineffective and in breach of article 13.[132]

To be effective, a remedy must be capable of enforcing the substance of a protected right by granting appropriate relief.[133] Once again, civil remedies are included.[134] The right to a remedy may also require a State to pay compensation to a victim, for both pecuniary and non-pecuniary damage.[135] Article 13 does not, however, oblige States to provide victims with any *specific* remedy. In relation to immigration matters, the ECtHR has declined to find that, to be effective, a remedy should prevent a migrant from being removed from a particular jurisdiction (where deportation does not expose the individual to a risk of harm, and where no other rights are engaged).[136] Instead, it is sufficient if the person concerned is able to challenge the relevant decision through an independent and impartial procedure.[137] Article 13 may protect from deportation in situations where removing the victim of violence would prevent her from taking part in criminal proceedings. This is because such proceedings will only be effective if the victim is involved 'to the extent necessary to safeguard their legitimate interests'.[138]

Finally, positive obligations, both structural and owed to individuals, must be discharged on a non-discriminatory basis. Whether or not the ECtHR characterises a particular form of violence as discriminatory, as discussed above, States' *response* to violence against women must not itself discriminate, directly or indirectly, intentionally or otherwise. Indeed, however violence is characterised, where it disproportionately affects women, States must provide a remedy to ensure their equal treatment before the law.[139]

3.3.2 States' Obligations to Migrant Women

Migration law disadvantages women, according them those statuses which enforce dependency, which are precarious and restrictive, and which increase

[131] *Aydin v Turkey* (n 104) paras 76, 88, and 107.

[132] ibid paras 103–09. While the Court's evaluation of the investigation was thorough, it failed to recognise that the virginity tests were themselves violence and discrimination against women that breached the applicant's art 3 rights.

[133] ibid.

[134] *IP v Moldova* App no 33708/12 (ECtHR, 28 April 2015).

[135] ECHR, art 41 allows the Court to order a State to afford 'just satisfaction' 'if necessary' to the injured party where a Convention right(s) has been violated for which only partial reparation can be made.

[136] *De Souza Ribeiro v France* App no 22689/07 (ECtHR GC, 13 December 2012). See also Michael Reiertsen, *Effective Remedies and the European Court of Human Rights* (CUP 2022) 180–85.

[137] In addition to the references above in n 136, see *Khlaifia v Italy* App no 16483/12 (ECtHR GC, 15 December 2016).

[138] *CN v UK* (n 108) para 69; see also *Chowdury v Greece* App no 21884/15 (ECtHR, 30 March 2017) paras 116–28.

[139] *AE v Bulgaria* (n 33) paras 119–22.

vulnerability to violence and exploitation. Much of this violence and exploitation will, per the above account, be violence against women.[140] In increasing women's vulnerability to such violence, these rules may discriminate against women and breach States' positive obligations under the ECHR. In *Rantsev v Cyprus and Russia* (2010),[141] the ECtHR was called on to consider these issues in the context of trafficking. While trafficking is not explicitly prohibited by the ECHR, the Court in *Rantsev* ruled that it nonetheless fell within the Convention's scope.[142]

Oxana Rantseva was a 21-year-old woman who travelled from Russia to Cyprus in 2001, and who died shortly afterwards. Ms Rantseva's migration status was governed by Cyprus's 'artiste' visa scheme, a scheme which made her dependent on her employer and subjected her to several, significant, rights restrictions.[143] In Ms Rantseva's case, these restrictions resulted in her being detained and then returned by the police, just hours before she died, to an employer she had sought to leave.

The ECtHR held that the artiste regime violated the positive obligations of article 4 of the ECHR, as it did not afford sufficient protection from trafficking and exploitation.[144] It also found that the State's failure to effectively investigate Ms Rantseva's death breached article 2.[145] In reaching these conclusions, the ECtHR found that an obligation on an employer to notify the authorities if their employee leaves was 'a legitimate measure to allow the authorities to monitor the compliance of immigrants'.[146] However, requiring employers to provide financial guarantees for their employees, and employees to sign separate bonds, were 'particularly troubling' and 'of equal concern'.[147]

Notably absent from the Court's reasoning is a legal response to its finding that the vast majority of those holding artiste visas were women. The scheme disadvantaged women, restricting their rights and increasing their vulnerability to violence.[148] The Court could have found indirect discrimination on the grounds of sex (ideally in conjunction with race and national origin) simply by drawing on its *Opuz* arguments on *responding* to violence.[149] It also could have done so on the basis that Rantseva may have been subject to interpersonal, gender-based conduct

[140] Much but not all.
[141] *Rantsev v Cyprus and Russia* (n 116).
[142] ibid paras 272–82. See further Jean Allain, '*Rantsev v Cyprus and Russia*: The European Court of Human Rights and Trafficking as Slavery' (2010) 10 Human Rights Law Review 546.
[143] *Rantsev v Cyprus and Russia* (n 116) paras 291–93.
[144] ibid paras 292–93.
[145] ibid paras 234–42.
[146] ibid para 292.
[147] ibid para 292.
[148] ibid para 291, where the Court cites evidence that, pursuant to the scheme, 'thousands of young foreign women' had entered Cyprus and 'were exploited by their employers under cruel living and working conditions'.
[149] This argument is also made in Alexandra Timmer, 'Toward an Anti-Stereotyping Approach for the European Court of Human Rights' (2011) 11 Human Rights Law Review 707.

that caused her a range of harms. It did neither, a failure that it has yet to correct in its trafficking jurisprudence.

While the Court's analysis of migration law in *Rantsev v Cyprus and Russia* is partial and incomplete, what is provided may, in conjunction with its reasoning in *Opuz*, be relied on to support chapter 2's migration status reform arguments. The dependency imposed by the domestic worker route, for example, appears comparable to that which the ECtHR impugned in *Rantsev*. While domestic workers in the UK are now theoretically able to change employers, in practice they cannot do so because they are unable to renew, or extend, their permission to remain (other than in certain cases of trafficking/slavery). The 2016 change to the Immigration Rules that enabled this followed the 'Ewins Review', a government-commissioned, independent review of the older (post-2012 rules) which 'tied' domestic workers to their employers.[150] The review recommended that, to prevent abuse and exploitation, domestic workers should be given both the right to change employers *and* to renew their visas, for a period of up to two-and-a-half years.[151] The right to change employer would only be meaningful, the review concluded, if *all* domestic workers could extend their leave to do so. Tellingly, this is very similar to the 'reformed' domestic worker migration status sketched in chapter 2, which was also independent, non-temporary, and renewable. In failing to implement fully the review's recommendations, the UK is, however, affording domestic workers less protection from violence than it has repeatedly been advised to provide.[152] The post-2016 rules continue, therefore, to maintain domestic workers' dependent and precarious position. They discriminate against women, including by failing to offer effective protection from violence, in violation of articles 3, 4, and 14 (and potentially 2) of the ECHR.[153]

3.4 Conclusion

This chapter has examined two forms of discrimination against women, and the different, but complementary and connected, legal regimes that respond to it. The first form of discrimination is violence against women itself. I identified the points

[150] James Ewins QC, 'Independent Review of the Overseas Domestic Workers Visa' (*GOV.UK*, 17 December 2015) <www.gov.uk/government/publications/overseas-domestic-workers-visa-independent-review> accessed 26 April 2024.

[151] ibid 34–35.

[152] The full implementation of the review has, for example, been recommended by the monitoring body of the Trafficking Convention. Group of Experts on Action Against Trafficking in Human Beings (GRETA), *Report Concerning the Implementation of the Council of Europe Convention on Action against Trafficking in Human Beings by the United Kingdom, Second Evaluation Round* (GRETA(2016)21, 7 October 2016); Group of Experts on Action Against Trafficking in Human Beings (GRETA), *Evaluation Report: United Kingdom* (GRETA(2021)12, 20 October 2021).

[153] For a similar and broader argument, see Natalie Sedacca, 'Migrant Work, Gender and the Hostile Environment: A Human Rights Analysis' (2024) 53 Industrial Law Journal 63.

at which five specialist legal instruments' definitions of such violence converge, to establish an international consensus as to the nature of this legal wrong. Violence against women is, according to this account, interpersonal and gender-based conduct that causes certain kinds of harm. Domestic violence and trafficking were examined using this approach and found to be forms of violence against women.

This chapter has also delineated some of the positive obligations European States have to ensure that all women are afforded practical and effective protection from violence. In charting these obligations, I highlighted another form of discrimination: States' failure to respond to violence against women with due diligence. Having concluded by discussing States' responsibilities in the field of migration law, I can proceed to analyse rules that subject migrant women to a particular, compounded form of disadvantage.

4
The Wrong and Its Remedy

4.1 Introduction

In chapter 2, I explained that women are disadvantaged by immigration law's distribution of migration statuses and that the rules responsible for this distribution are, sometimes at least, unlawfully discriminatory. In chapter 3, I argued that women are at risk of, and experience, particular forms of interpersonal and discriminatory violence: violence against women. Here, I capture a series of distinct scenarios where law and violence interact in particular, injurious ways, to produce a qualitatively different experience of both.[1] Over thirty years have passed since Kimberlé Crenshaw analysed the 'double subordination' experienced by migrant women of colour who were subject to domestic violence.[2] 'Compounded disadvantage' is, to draw on and paraphrase Crenshaw, the term I use to explain the difference that migration status makes to an experience of violence against women.[3]

The European Court of Human Rights (ECtHR) uses the concept of vulnerability to respond to applicants' different characteristics and experiences. This strand of its non-discrimination jurisprudence, in conjunction with Martha Albertson Fineman's theorising,[4] has been relied on by scholars who have sought to understand the disadvantage that flows from migration status as a distinct form of legally created vulnerability. In the first part of this chapter, I justify my analytical approach, one that is rooted in this jurisprudence and theorising, and which reveals the role of the State in first producing, and then compounding, migrant

[1] In advancing this argument I am not asserting the primacy of these experiences over others. As the previous two chapters have discussed, women's experiences of both migration status and violence are influenced by a range of factors. A focus on compounded disadvantage, however, reveals how these two phenomena interact, within a range of intersecting and co-constituting inequalities.

[2] Kimberle Crenshaw, 'Mapping the Margins: Intersectionality, Identity Politics, and Violence against Women of Color' (1991) 43 Stanford Law Review 1241, 1247.

[3] ibid 1299. See also Deborah Hellman, 'Indirect Discrimination and the Duty to Avoid Compounding Injustice' in Hugh Collins and Tarunabh Khaitan (eds), *Foundations of Indirect Discrimination Law* (Hart 2018).

[4] Notably, Martha Albertson Fineman, 'The Vulnerable Subject: Anchoring Equality in the Human Condition' (2008) 20 Yale Journal of Law and Feminism 1; Martha Albertson Fineman, 'The Vulnerable Subject and the Responsive State' (2010) 60 Emory Law Journal 251; Martha Albertson Fineman, 'Beyond Identities: The Limits of an Anti-Discrimination Approach to Equality' (2012) 92 Boston University Law Review 1713; Martha Albertson Fineman, 'Equality and Difference—The Restrained State' (2015) 66 Alabama Law Review 609; Martha Albertson Fineman, 'Vulnerability and Inevitable Inequality' (2017) 4 Oslo Law Review 133; Martha Albertson Fineman, 'Beyond Equality and Discrimination' (2020) 73 SMU Law Review Forum 51.

Violence against Women and Regimes of Exception. Catherine Briddick, Oxford University Press.
© Catherine Briddick 2025. DOI: 10.1093/9780191959899.003.0004

women's disadvantage. I then explain the circumstances which give rise to compounded disadvantage and draw on empirical research to trace its features. Finally, I bring to a conclusion arguments made in the previous two chapters, arguments concerning migration status reform and due diligence responses to violence against women, to explore how compounded disadvantage could be remedied. Establishing both the nature of compounded disadvantage and what is or may be reparative of it, provides the foundation for Part II's evaluation of the legal rules which currently determine victims' migration statuses, the regimes of exception.

4.2 The Wrong: Compounding Disadvantage

4.2.1 Anchoring Compounded Disadvantage: Intersectionality and Vulnerability

There is a wealth of research, theoretical and empirical, that has sought to capture the particular predicament of being subject to violence and to migration control. Much of this work either draws on, or has been significantly influenced by, Crenshaw's intersectionality thesis. Crenshaw used the term 'intersectionality' to critique 'but for' conceptions of equality that 'condition us to think about subordination as disadvantage occurring along a single categorical axis'.[5] Such thinking, she contends, 'erases Black women' by 'limiting inquiry to the experiences of otherwise-privileged members of the group'.[6] In the work quoted at the start of this chapter, Crenshaw analyses from this perspective a US immigration rule that enables some women who have experienced domestic violence to receive a migration status. This domestic violence rule is a regime of exception, like those considered in Part II. It enables some migrant victims of a certain form of violence to receive an independent migration status in their country of residence, when otherwise they might be compelled to return to their country of origin. Crenshaw explains that language barriers and limited access to resources may make the requirements of the US rule particularly hard to meet for 'immigrant women of color'.[7] While focusing on race and gender, grounds recognised by discrimination law, Crenshaw argues that such an intersectional analysis should consider a range of identities and characteristics.[8] Work focused on migration and violence in the UK has sought to do just this. One of Sundari Anitha's studies of domestic violence highlights the intersection between immigration control and inequalities based on

[5] Kimberle Crenshaw, 'Demarginalizing the Intersection of Race and Sex: A Black Feminist Critique of Antidiscrimination Doctrine, Feminist Theory and Antiracist Politics' (1989) 1989 University of Chicago Legal Forum 139, 140.
[6] ibid 140.
[7] Crenshaw, 'Mapping the Margins' (n 2) 1248–49.
[8] ibid 1244–45, particularly the comments at nn 8 and 9.

culture, gender, class, and race.[9] Aisha Gill and Kaveri Sharma argue that migrant women face a 'quadruple whammy' of marginalisation as a result of their immigration status, gender, ethnicity, and experiences of abuse.[10] Similar approaches and conclusions have been reached in research that compares migrant women's experiences of violence in the UK with those of women in other European jurisdictions.[11]

One potential criticism of this work is its authors' delineation of ever more complex sub-groups at the expense of a focus on the relationships of domination and subordination that determine them—the latter being referred to as structural intersectionality.[12] Sumi Cho, Kimberlé Crenshaw, and Leslie McCall describe this as the 'et cetera problem'.[13] One example they give of 'more narrowly circumscribed demands for inclusion' is 'battered immigrant women'.[14] Intersectionality has been an extremely influential field of feminist inquiry, in part because of contestation about the concept's meaning, interpretation, or most productive application.[15] What is under-appreciated about Crenshaw's own work is her use of intersectionality to destabilise, rather than delineate, different identity categories. Intersectionality is, for Crenshaw, a 'provisional concept', one that acts to bridge contemporary politics and postmodern theorising by 'tracing' categories, such as race and gender, 'to their intersections' in order to 'disrupt' them.[16]

In *BS v Spain* (2012),[17] the ECtHR was invited to engage in an intersectional analysis of discrimination experienced on more than one ground. The Court did not do so, instead choosing to discuss the applicant's 'vulnerability' as an African woman involved in prostitution.[18] The ECtHR has maintained this approach. In *JI v Croatia* (2022),[19] for example, the Court declined to find that the applicant, a Roma woman who had been subject to prolonged domestic and sexual violence, had been discriminated against by the authorities who had failed abjectly to protect

[9] Sundari Anitha, 'Legislating Gender Inequalities' (2011) 17 Violence Against Women 1260.

[10] Aisha Gill and Kaveri Sharma, 'Response and Responsibility: Domestic Violence and Marriage Migration in The UK' in Sarah van Walsum and Thomas Spijkerboer (eds), *Women and Immigration Law: New Variations on Classical Feminist Themes* (Routledge Cavendish 2007) 189.

[11] For example, Monica Burman, 'Immigrant Women Facing Male Partner Violence—Gender, Race and Power in Swedish Alien and Criminal Law' (2012) 2 feminists@law 1.

[12] Sumi Cho, Kimberlé Crenshaw, and Leslie McCall, 'Toward a Field of Intersectionality Studies: Theory, Applications, and Praxis' (2013) 38 Signs 785.

[13] ibid 787.

[14] ibid 791.

[15] For example, Cho, Crenshaw, and McCall, 'Intersectionality Studies' (n 12); Gail Lewis, 'Unsafe Travel: Experiencing Intersectionality and Feminist Displacements' (2013) 38 Signs 869; Kathryn Cassidy, Nira Yuval-Davis, and Georgie Wemyss, 'Intersectional Border(ing)s' (2018) 66 Political Geography 139. Cho, Crenshaw, and McCall discuss 'structural intersectionality' (which emphasises structural inequalities, rather than 'categories, identities and subjectivities') and 'political intersectionality' (which involves contesting inequality). In contrast, Cassidy, Yuval-Davis, and Wemyss compare 'situated intersectionality' with intersectional approaches that see different power relationships/inequalities as 'additive', 'cross-cutting', or 'interlocking'.

[16] Crenshaw, 'Mapping the Margins' (n 2) 1244–45, n 9.

[17] *BS v Spain* App no 47159/08 (ECtHR, 24 July 2012).

[18] ibid paras 57, 62.

[19] *JI v Croatia* App no 35898/16 (ECtHR, 8 September 2022).

her.[20] Instead, when finding a violation of article 3 of the European Convention on Human Rights (ECHR),[21] the Court took into account her 'particular vulnerability on account of her sex, ethnic origin and past traumas'.[22]

The Court has not defined 'vulnerability' or explained how it relates to the grounds protected by article 14, the prohibition of discrimination set out in the ECHR. It has, however, characterised as 'vulnerable' Roma/Gypsies,[23] people with learning disabilities,[24] people who are HIV+,[25] asylum seekers,[26] women who have experienced domestic violence,[27] and children in families with one parent.[28] Some of these decisions, including those concerned with Roma/Gypsies, are justified by reference to the group being a minority and having been subjected to sustained discrimination and exclusion.[29] Asylum seekers and children in single-parent households are, for different reasons, considered inherently vulnerable.[30] Consequently, Oddný Mjöll Arnardóttir concludes her review of this jurisprudence with the observation that:

> the Court's application of the concept of vulnerability is diverse and multifaceted. It seems sometimes relational in character but sometimes essentialist; it sometimes focuses on group identities, but sometimes on otherwise precarious situations; and it sometimes enables a reaction to intersectional situations, while sometimes being used outside that context.[31]

This 'vulnerable groups' jurisprudence of the ECtHR has been analysed by scholars from theoretical perspectives rooted in both intersectionality and vulnerability. The former have welcomed the Court's more robust use of article 14 to respond to

[20] ibid para 97. The discrimination arguments were held by the Court to have been unsubstantiated, either in relation to the facts of the case or by statistical information. This case provides further support for chapter 3's analysis of the Court's lack of clarity on the relationship between violence and discrimination against women.

[21] Convention for the Protection of Human Rights and Fundamental Freedoms (adopted 4 November 1950, entered into force 3 September 1953) ETS 5 (European Convention on Human Rights, as amended) (ECHR).

[22] *JI v Croatia* (n 19) para 97.

[23] *Chapman v UK* App no 27238/95 (ECtHR, 18 January 2001) (the first 'vulnerability' case); *DH v Czech Republic* App no 57325/00 (ECtHR GC, 13 November 2007); *Oršuš v Croatia* App no 15766/03 (ECtHR GC, 16 March 2010).

[24] *Alajos Kiss v Hungary* App no 38832/06 (ECtHR, 20 May 2010).

[25] *Kiyutin v Russia* App no 2700/10 (ECtHR, 10 March 2011).

[26] *MSS v Belgium and Greece* [2011] 53 EHRR 28.

[27] *Talpis v Italy* App no 41237/14 (ECtHR, 2 March 2017); *JI v Croatia* (n 19).

[28] *Yocheva and Ganeva v Bulgaria* App nos 18592/15 and 43863/15 (ECtHR, 11 May 2021).

[29] *DH v Czech Republic* (n 23) para 182: '[t]he Court notes that as a result of their turbulent history and constant uprooting the Roma have become a specific type of disadvantaged and vulnerable minority'. See also *Kiyutin v Russia* (n 25) para 48.

[30] *MSS v Belgium and Greece* (n 26) para 251; *Yocheva and Ganeva v Bulgaria* (n 28) paras 92, 108.

[31] Oddný Mjöll Arnardóttir, 'Vulnerability under Article 14 of the European Convention on Human Rights' (2017) 4 Oslo Law Review 150, 169.

lived experiences of intersectional discrimination.[32] The latter has sought to trace connections between the Court's approach and Martha Fineman's 'account of the human condition as one of universal and continuous vulnerability'.[33]

Embodiment, as Fineman has observed, 'carries with it the ever-present possibility of harm, injury and misfortune from mildly adverse to catastrophically devastating events, whether accidental, intentional, or otherwise'.[34] There are two 'relevant forms of individual difference' in Fineman's approach to vulnerability, 'those that arise because we are *embodied* beings and those that arise because we are social beings *embedded* in social institutions and relationships'.[35] Vulnerability to violence, and the experience of it, will be shaped by embodied/personal and embedded/societal factors including, for example, a woman's age, health, and ability to access medical care.

While connecting the ECtHR's 'vulnerable groups' jurisprudence and Fineman's work may appear attractive, the very brief introduction provided to both here indicates that the two share terminology but little else. Fineman's universal and continuous, if variable, vulnerability, is at odds with the Court's designation of only *some* people and groups as being so. In addition to highlighting inconsistencies within the ECtHR's reasoning, scholars have drawn on Fineman's work to criticise the Court for locating the cause of people's ill-treatment with them and for stigmatising further the groups concerned.[36] Others have critiqued both Fineman's theorising *and* the Court's approach. On the former, Fineman developed her thinking on vulnerability in part, at least, as a response to a particular context: formal approaches to non-discrimination in the US which are predicated on very limited State action or engagement. Its applicability to the legal framework created by the Council of Europe cannot, therefore, be assumed. On the latter, Ekaterina Yahyaoui Krivenko asserts that refugees in particular have not benefited from the Court's jurisprudence on *migrant* vulnerability.[37] Rather, the gains of comparatively few applicants have been undermined by the introduction of arbitrary and invidious categories of deservingness.[38] Interestingly, the Inter-American Court of Human Rights (IACtHR) has also characterised migrants in

[32] Keina Yoshida, 'Towards Intersectionality in the European Court of Human Rights: The Case of *B.S. v Spain*' (2013) 21 Feminist Legal Studies 195; Shreya Atrey, *Intersectional Discrimination* (OUP 2019) 133–34.

[33] Fineman, 'Vulnerability and Inevitable Inequality' (n 4) 134.

[34] Fineman, 'The Vulnerable Subject: Anchoring Equality in the Human Condition' (n 4) 9.

[35] Fineman, 'Vulnerability and Inevitable Inequality' (n 4) 143.

[36] Lourdes Peroni and Alexandra Timmer, 'Vulnerable Groups: The Promise of an Emerging Concept in European Human Rights Convention Law' (2013) 11 International Journal of Constitutional Law 1056; So Yeon Kim, 'Les Vulnérables: Evaluating the Vulnerability Criterion in Article 14 Cases by the European Court of Human Rights' (2021) 41 Legal Studies 617.

[37] Ekaterina Yahyaoui Krivenko, 'Reassessing the Relationship between Equality and Vulnerability in relation to Refugees and Asylum Seekers in the ECtHR: The *MSS* Case 10 Years On' (2022) 34 International Journal of Refugee Law 192.

[38] ibid.

different contexts as 'vulnerable'.[39] Like the ECtHR, it too has been criticised for doing so at the expense of a substantive engagement with the policies that create or increase migrants' vulnerability.[40]

The Explanatory Report to the Council of Europe Convention on Preventing and Combating Violence against Women and Domestic Violence (the Istanbul Convention)[41] also provides an account of *migrant* women's vulnerability.[42] The Report explains that perpetrators of violence often target migrant women:

> because they know that they are less likely to be able to defend themselves, or seek prosecution of the perpetrator and other forms of reparation, because of their situation.[43]

Such statements, along with the Convention itself, have been scrutinised for their contribution to gendered and racialised stereotyping that defines migrant women 'exclusively by their intrinsic diminished capacity to protect themselves'.[44] While compelling, such accounts do not fully engage with the Report's location of migrant women's vulnerability in 'their situation'.[45] It is migration status and the control it gives to perpetrators that militates against women 'defending themselves'.[46] Migration status is also the reason why migrant women are 'particularly vulnerable to gender-based violence' and face 'difficulties and structural barriers in overcoming violence'.[47] That a woman's migration status may be determinative of her 'situation' is acknowledged later in the Report:

[39] Notably in *Juridical Condition and Rights of the Undocumented Migrants* Advisory Opinion OC-18, Inter-American Court of Human Rights Series A No 18 (17 September 2003); *Case of the Girls Yean and Bosico v Dominican Republic* (Preliminary Objections, Merits, Reparations and Costs) Inter-American Court of Human Rights Series C No 130 (8 September 2005).

[40] *Vélez Loor v Panama* (Preliminary Objections, Merits, Reparations and Costs) Inter-American Court of Human Rights Series C No 218 (23 November 2010) as discussed by Marie-Bénédicte Dembour, *When Humans Become Migrants: Study of the European Court of Human Rights with an Inter-American Counterpoint* (OUP 2015) ch 11.

[41] Council of Europe Convention on Preventing and Combating Violence against Women and Domestic Violence (adopted 11 May 2011, entered into force 1 August 2014) CETS 210 (Istanbul Convention).

[42] The approach adopted by the Istanbul Convention departs in several respects from that taken by the ECtHR. Lisa Grans, 'The Impact of Vulnerability on State Obligations in Criminal Proceedings on Domestic Violence: Interpreting the Istanbul Convention and the European Convention on Human Rights' (2023) Women & Criminal Justice, 1–16 <https://doi.org/10.1080/08974454.2023.2296624> accessed 2 May 2024.

[43] Council of Europe, *Explanatory Report to the Council of Europe Convention on Preventing and Combating Violence against Women and Domestic Violence* (CETS No 210) (2011) [87]. Others considered vulnerable are those with disabilities, pregnant women, lesbian women, and the homeless.

[44] Lourdes Peroni, 'Violence Against Migrant Women: The Istanbul Convention Through a Postcolonial Feminist Lens' (2016) 24 Feminist Legal Studies 49, 63.

[45] Council of Europe, *Explanatory Report* (n 43) [87].

[46] ibid [87].

[47] ibid [298].

> [F]ear of deportation or loss of residence status is a very powerful tool used by perpetrators to prevent victims of violence against women and domestic violence from seeking help from authorities . . . As a result, many victims whose residence status is dependant on that of the perpetrator stay in relationships where they are forced to endure situations of abuse and violence for long periods of time.[48]

What is not acknowledged, however, is that it is the Convention's *Parties* that have created this 'very powerful tool'.[49] Compounded disadvantage, the production and experience of which are discussed in the sections that follow, arises from vulnerability that is embodied and embedded. Crucially, and as the ECtHR has partially recognised, it also arises from vulnerability that is legally constructed and imposed.[50]

According to Fineman, the counterpoint to vulnerability is resilience, such resilience being provided by 'assets' which enable people to 'address and confront misfortune'.[51] A family may be an asset, as may be a functioning criminal justice system, a good job, a religious faith, or a course of medical treatment. Fineman argues that many of the assets that provide us with resilience can only exist through State action.[52] A recognition of vulnerability gives rise, therefore, to 'a duty for the state to actively assume broad societal responsibility in regard to ensuring equality for citizens and *others to whom it owes some obligation*'.[53] States may discharge this responsibility by acting directly, by providing a funded health system, for example. They may also so do indirectly, by granting status to religious institutions and ensuring that they act in accordance with particular values, such as non-discrimination.

Notwithstanding the criticisms discussed above, and however the ECtHR reaches its determination of a group's vulnerability, doing so has had some positive effects. One is to narrow the margin of appreciation accorded to the respondent

[48] ibid [301].

[49] ibid [301].

[50] *MSS v Belgium and Greece* (n 26) paras 233, 251, and 259; *Chowdury v Greece* App no 21884/15 (ECtHR, 30 March 2017) paras 95–97; *Zoletic v Azerbaijan* App no 20116/12 (ECtHR, 7 October 2021) para 166. See also Bridget Anderson, 'Mobilizing Migrants, Making Citizens: Migrant Domestic Workers as Political Agents' (2009) 33 Ethnic and Racial Studies 60; Shahrzad Fouladvand and Tony Ward, 'Human Trafficking, Vulnerability and the State' (2019) 81 Journal of Criminal Law 39; Fulvia Staiano, 'Protection beyond Victimisation: The Significance of the Istanbul Convention for Migrant Women' in Johanna Niemi, Lourdes Peroni, and Vladislava Stoyanova (eds), *International Law and Violence against Women: Europe and the Istanbul Convention* (Routledge 2020). But see Moritz Baumgärtel, 'Facing the Challenge of Migratory Vulnerability in the European Court of Human Rights' (2020) 38 Netherlands Quarterly of Human Rights 12. Baumgärtel's conceptualisation of 'migratory vulnerability' acknowledges, but does not give adequate weight to, the role of immigration law in producing disadvantage (in comparison with the political and social processes considered).

[51] Fineman, 'The Vulnerable Subject and the Responsive State' (n 4) 269.

[52] ibid 269–72.

[53] ibid 256 (emphasis added).

State and to require it to provide weighty reasons for differential treatment.[54] Another effect is to impose obligations on States, who may be compelled to give special consideration and protection to the group in question.[55] Finally, the threshold for the level of severity required to constitute a violation of physical and mental integrity may be lowered.[56] Many of Fineman's 'assets', and their provision, can be mapped onto States' positive or due diligence obligations to people within their jurisdiction generally, and to victims of violence specifically. States may, in the creation and distribution of migration statuses, generate or amplify vulnerability to different forms of harm. They may also, as will be explained, deny migrants access to those State-supported assets that provide resilience to it. Yet, the *responsive* State should ethically (drawing on Fineman) and legally (following the ECtHR jurisprudence) provide and support the provision of those assets which afford resilience to vulnerability.

The arguments that follow on compounded disadvantage bring the sometimes complementary, sometimes competing, and often contradictory strands of literature on vulnerability and intersectionality into conversation with each other. This is, perhaps, less ambitious than it seems. Fineman does argue that 'it is not multiple *identities* that intersect to produce compounded inequalities' but 'systems of power and privilege that interact to produce webs of advantages and disadvantages'.[57] This phrasing is not, however, very far from that used by Cho, Crenshaw, and McCall in their discussion of the use of *structural* intersectionality to 'excavate and expose multilayered structures of power and domination'.[58] My argument here, that migration status and violence interact to produce compounded disadvantage, enables me to contend that States have certain ethical and legal duties to remedy vulnerability that they have, at least in part, created. It is also consonant with my overarching theoretical perspective (intersectionality) and pragmatic approach (limiting myself to those arguments that could be made before a court). It is rooted in the jurisprudence as it is now, cognisant that assertions of vulnerability should not be a substitute for a substantive equality analysis, and building on those moves within the case law that do start to respond to intersectional discrimination.[59]

[54] *Alajos Kiss v Hungary* (n 24) para 42.

[55] *Oršuš v Croatia* (n 23) para 148; *Horváth and Kiss v Hungary* App no 11146/11 (ECtHR, 29 January 2013) para 116; see further Barbara Havelková, 'Judicial Scepticism of Discrimination at the ECtHR' in Hugh Collins and Tarunabh Khaitan (eds), *Foundations of Indirect Discrimination Law* (Hart 2018).

[56] Grans, 'The Impact of Vulnerability' (n 42).

[57] Fineman, 'The Vulnerable Subject: Anchoring Equality in the Human Condition' (n 4) 16.

[58] Cho, Crenshaw, and McCall, 'Intersectionality Studies' (n 12) 804. See also the text accompanying n 16.

[59] Drawing on and heeding Krivenko, 'Reassessing the Relationship' (n 37).

4.2.2 The Interaction between Migration Status and Violence

As discussed in the previous chapter, women are at risk of and experience a particular type of violence: violence against women. Such violence is interpersonal and discriminatory. It enables and results from women's gendered subordination. Compounded disadvantage arises when migration status and this violence interact. Here, I sketch *how* this interaction occurs. This enables me to explain, in the next section, *why* this interaction produces compounded disadvantage, and what such disadvantage entails.

Compounded disadvantage will *always* arise where a woman who experiences violence is *dependent for her migration status on the person who is violent towards her*. Compounded disadvantage is, therefore, experienced by a woman with permission to remain as a partner whose husband perpetrates domestic violence against her. This is the case whether or not her husband is British, settled, or is himself a migrant in the UK. Compounded disadvantage is also experienced by a domestic worker whose employer sexually harasses her. The nature and extent of the disadvantage experienced will, of course, vary, depending on a range of factors, including the severity of that violence, the assets available to the person concerned, and the type of migration status held.

Compounded disadvantage *may or may not* arise when a woman is *not dependent* on the person who is violent towards her for her migration status. A woman who is a student and who experiences domestic violence from her partner may experience compounded disadvantage if, for example, her studies are affected by it, as her status depends on her attendance and course progression. A skilled worker who is sexually harassed by her employer may similarly experience compounded disadvantage. Again, any disadvantage experienced will vary. A skilled labour migrant may have assets that provide resilience that students do not, including an independent income. Compounded disadvantage may not arise where there is sufficient distance between the experience of violence and the migration status held, where, for example, harassment from a neighbour does not interfere with a labour migrant's employment because she is able to change her accommodation without difficulty.

Finally, where there is *no interaction* between a woman's migration status and her experience of violence, there is no compounded disadvantage. This would be the case where, for example, the woman concerned is a citizen or permanent resident who has been living in the UK.[60]

[60] Indeed, women who are entitled to permanent residence in more than one country because, for example, they are dual nationals, may be comparatively advantaged by having access to assets that provide resilience to violence in two jurisdictions. British or resident women returning to the UK to escape violence experienced in another country may, however, be precluded from accessing certain sources of State support. In the latter case the interaction between migration status and violence will give rise to compounded disadvantage.

Having set out how migration status and an experience of violence may interact to produce compounded disadvantage, I can now chart its contours. The section that follows explores the first scenario described above, where the perpetrator of violence is the person on whom a woman depends for her migration status.

4.2.3 The Facets of Compounded Disadvantage

While migration status and violence may interact to produce a constellation of different experiences, what is shared and what are, therefore, the defining features of compounded disadvantage are control, exclusion, and an intensified experience of violence.

Turning first to control. The migration status given to the partners of those who are British or resident here, in which the same requirements are tested three times in five years, gives a perpetrator of violence who has control over that status three opportunities to exercise it. Similar control may be exercised over the dependant of a skilled labour migrant. A violent husband may, for example, refuse to support his wife's immigration application, even while their relationship is 'subsisting'. Perpetrators may use immigration processes to 'exert pressure' on their spouse/partner,[61] renewals of passports, or of permission to remain, being manipulated as a source of coercive control.[62] A migrant partner may be, at any time, just one letter away from having her leave curtailed, as cases like *Balakoohi* (2012)[63] (discussed in chapter 2) demonstrate. If the victim does not know about the curtailment decision, or does not challenge it in time, she may become undocumented. Challenging such decisions is also far from straightforward. In *R (on the application of AT)* (2017),[64] HHJ Kerr found that the Home Office had applied a 'double standard' when considering the evidence provided by an abusive partner that his relationship had ended: '[o]ne is left with the uncomfortable feeling that the man's evidence counted for more than the woman's.'[65] Tellingly, the Home Office has itself acknowledged the interaction between the migration statuses accorded to partners and any coercive control they may be subject to.[66] The Domestic Abuse Commissioner for England and Wales has gone further, arguing for the recognition

[61] Nughmana Mirza, 'The UK Government's Conflicting Agendas and "Harmful" Immigration Policies: Shaping South Asian Women's Experiences of Abuse and "Exit"' (2016) 36 Critical Social Policy 592, 602.

[62] ibid; Rebecca Gail Dudley, 'Domestic Abuse and Women with "No Recourse to Public Funds": The State's Role in Shaping and Reinforcing Coercive Control' (2017) 6 Families, Relationships and Societies 201.

[63] *R (Balakoohi) v Secretary of State for the Home Department* [2012] EWHC 1439 (Admin).

[64] *R (AT) v Secretary of State for the Home Department* [2017] EWHC 2589 (Admin), [2018] Imm AR 483.

[65] ibid [101].

[66] Home Office, *Controlling or Coercive Behaviour: Statutory Guidance Framework* (5 April 2023).

of 'immigration abuse', the use of a victim's insecure immigration status to exert further power and control over her.[67]

The permission to remain given to domestic workers also accords their employers an extraordinary level of control over those workers' lives.[68] As the 'Ewins Review' (introduced in chapter 3) explains, many domestic workers' economic position is one of 'relative desperation'; their migration status 'rests solely on their employer's professed want/need of them'.[69] The employer who understands this 'special vulnerability'[70] and threatens 'their' domestic worker with destitution or loss of status should she ask to receive payment for work done can, therefore, make good these threats.[71]

Such control is very difficult to escape. Partners cannot simply change relationships, although some may be able to remain in the UK on a different basis. Domestic workers may theoretically be able to change employers, but doing so in practice will require an extension of leave beyond the grant of six months. This *may* be possible where the worker is recognised as a victim of slavery or trafficking.[72] Meeting the required legal and evidential standards is, however, extremely difficult.[73] As a consequence, domestic workers may either be unable to apply for the extension of leave or, if they are able to apply, may be denied it. They may also only be recognised as a victim after their original permission to remain has expired, something that has significant consequences in terms of rights and support.[74] All of these scenarios expose domestic workers to still further financial and other hardship. Finally, some victims of domestic violence and trafficking may be able to access a regime of exception and receive an independent migration status in the UK. To foreshadow the arguments advanced in Part II, however, only a small proportion of those subject to compounded disadvantage are able to benefit from these regimes. Potentially *the* defining feature of compounded disadvantage is, therefore,

[67] 'Identifying and naming immigration abuse is vital in ensuring that national and local policy makers and frontline practitioners are equipped to identify and respond appropriately to victims and survivors.' Domestic Abuse Commissioner for England and Wales, *Safety before Status: Improving Pathways to Support for Migrant Victims of Domestic Abuse* (2021) 5.

[68] Natalie Sedacca, 'Migrant Domestic Workers and the Right to a Private and Family Life' (2019) 37 Netherlands Quarterly of Human Rights 288, 295.

[69] James Ewins QC, 'Independent Review of the Overseas Domestic Workers Visa' (*GOV.UK*, 17 December 2015) [29]–[30] < www.gov.uk/government/publications/overseas-domestic-workers-visa-independent-review> accessed 26 April 2024.

[70] ibid [30].

[71] See further *Puthenveettil v Alexander, George* Case Number: 2361118/2013 (15 December 2020); Judy Fudge and Kendra Strauss, 'Migrants, Unfree Labour, and the Legal Construction of Domestic Servitude: Migrant Domestic Workers in the UK' in Cathryn Costello and Mark Freedland (eds), *Migrants at Work: Immigration and Vulnerability in Labour Law* (OUP 2014).

[72] As explained in chapter 2 and discussed in chapter 3, Immigration Rules HC 590, Appendix Domestic Worker who is a Victim of Modern Slavery. This provision is a response to violence experienced in the context of migration control, but one that involves extending stay under the same broad conditions rather than granting status. It is not, consequently, analysed here as a regime of exception. Doing so elsewhere, may, however, be illuminating.

[73] Avril Sharp and Natalie Sedacca, *Dignity, Not Destitution* (Kalaayan 2019).

[74] Per the Immigration (Variation of Leave) Order 2016, SI 2016/948.

the control that perpetrators of violence are able to exercise over the women they victimise. Dependent migration statuses grant perpetrators access to the coercive power of the State, providing them with the means to manipulate status and increase their victim's vulnerability to a range of significant harms.

Exclusion is the second feature, or facet, of compounded disadvantage. In the UK, assets that provide resilience to violence, to use Fineman's terminology, may be delivered directly by the State, through the National Health Service (NHS) or the justice system, or indirectly, through specialist organisations such as women's refuges.[75] A British or resident woman made homeless by domestic violence may, for example, be placed in emergency accommodation by her local authority. Alternatively, she may secure her own accommodation or go into a women's refuge. In the latter case, the refuge may be an independent charity, but accessing its services (or, for example, accessing accommodation in the private or not-for-profit sectors) usually depends on being eligible for either benefits or support from the local authority. Financial support from the State is, therefore, an asset that provides women with the means to separate from, and live independently of, a perpetrator of violence.

As discussed in chapter 2, different migration statuses place different restrictions on their holders' rights, including in relation to work and financial support. Those who are subject to immigration control are not generally entitled to receive benefits, their permission to remain being subject to the condition that they have no recourse to public funds.[76] Migrants are also generally excluded from receiving support from their local authority, including in relation to housing and homelessness assistance. The relevant rules are extremely complicated and have been frequently litigated.[77] Generally, though, where a woman *has* some form of permission to remain, support will *only* be provided if she has children that require it and/or has care needs that arise *not* from destitution but from some form of ill-health.[78] Those *without* permission are only entitled to support where it is necessary to prevent a breach of their ECHR-protected rights, a test that is very difficult to meet.[79] This remains the case even when a woman's lack of status is linked to

[75] There are, of course, a number of sources of resilience to violence that are not provided by the State. These include a woman's savings and social capital, as well as her ability to access support from friends or religious institutions. Whether or not an individual woman is affected by the exclusions listed here and to what extent, will, therefore, vary.

[76] Immigration and Asylum Act 1999, s 115. See also Immigration Rules HC 590, Introduction for the definition of 'public funds'.

[77] For example, *R (AB) v Secretary of State for the Home Department* [2022] EWHC 1524 (Admin), [2022] WLR(D) 282. It is possible to apply to have the condition lifted in some circumstances. Home Office, *Permitting access to public funds* (Version 2, 3 May 2024). See also 'NRPF Network' (*NRPF Network*) <www.nrpfnetwork.org.uk> accessed 4 May 2024.

[78] Families with a child 'in need' may be eligible for assistance under the Children Act 1989, s 17. An adult with care needs may be eligible for assistance under the Care Act 2014. Different but analogous provisions apply in Wales, Scotland, and Northern Ireland.

[79] Nationality Immigration and Asylum Act 2002, s 54 and sch 3. Particularly relevant here is the right to be free from inhuman and degrading treatment.

the violence she has been subject to, where, for example, an abusive husband takes his wife's passport. The underfunding of local authorities, in conjunction with the complexity of these rules, also yields poor and sometimes indefensible decision-making. Reports abound of cases where support is denied, (non-abusive) mothers threatened with the removal of their children, or support provided to children only, leaving their mothers 'starved'.[80] While NHS treatment is not classed as a public fund for immigration purposes, a person's migration status will affect whether or not they have to pay for medical treatment.[81] The law in this area is, once again, extremely complicated. These exclusions constitute and operate alongside those of the hostile environment: a more extensive and pervasive array of restrictions that impact upon a person's ability to rent accommodation, work, or open a bank account.[82] The relevant rules, ostensibly aimed at those who do not have permission to remain, negatively affect both migrants *and* citizens, particularly those from racialised groups.[83]

There are no general legal restrictions on migrants' use of either the civil or criminal justice systems. However, these systems' ability to respond to violence and exploitation experienced in the context of migration control is extremely limited. Domestic workers who want to enforce their labour rights at an Employment Tribunal may be legally or practically unable to do so.[84] Violence against women is already underreported, the police's response to racialised women being the subject of critical scrutiny.[85] Migrant women may be further deterred from seeking

[80] Described in Sundari Anitha, 'No Recourse, No Support: State Policy and Practice towards South Asian Women Facing Domestic Violence in the UK' (2010) 40 British Journal of Social Work 462, 471.

[81] National Health Service (Charges to Overseas Visitors) (Amendment) Regulations 2017, SI 2017/756. See further Rayah Feldman, 'Maternity Care for Undocumented Migrant Women: The Impact of Charging for Maternity Care' (2016) 24 British Journal of Midwifery 52.

[82] Implemented through the Immigration Act 2014 and Immigration Act 2016. For an analysis of which, see Melanie Griffiths and Colin Yeo, 'The UK's Hostile Environment: Deputising Immigration Control' (2021) 41 Critical Social Policy 521; Sheona York, 'The "Hostile Environment"—How Home Office Immigration Policies and Practices Create and Perpetuate Illegality' (2018) 32 Journal of Immigration Asylum and Nationality Law 363.

[83] Nira Yuval-Davis, Georgie Wemyss, and Kathryn Cassidy, 'Everyday Bordering, Belonging and the Reorientation of British Immigration Legislation' (2018) 52 Sociology 228. See also Amelia Gentleman, *The Windrush Betrayal: Exposing the Hostile Environment* (Faber 2019).

[84] Taking a case to an Employment Tribunal takes longer than the six months a domestic worker has in the UK. On the challenges faced by similarly disadvantaged workers, see Catherine Barnard, Amy Ludlow, and Sarah Fraser Butlin, 'Beyond Employment Tribunals: Enforcement of Employment Rights by EU-8 Migrant Workers' (2018) 47 Industrial Law Journal 226. Domestic workers who become undocumented are also generally unable to enforce their employment rights. Employees cannot rely on, or enforce, a contract that is 'tainted with illegality', for example where one party to the contract does not have valid permission to work in the UK, Astra Emir, *Selwyn's Law of Employment* (22nd edn, OUP 2022) 82. However, claims for protection can be made where doing so does not involve relying on any illegal contract. This means that a person who is undocumented may be able to bring a discrimination claim. *Hounga v Allen* [2014] UKSC 47, [2014] 1 WLR 2889. See also *Okedina v Chikale* [2019] EWCA Civ 1393, [2019] WLR (D) 444, in which a successful claim for unpaid wages was brought by a domestic worker on the specific facts that she was unaware of her status.

[85] Aisha K Gill and Karen Harrison, 'Police Responses to Intimate Partner Sexual Violence in South Asian Communities' (2016) 10 Policing 446.

help because they fear that, if they did so, they would either be denied it or be arrested themselves. Crucially, such fears are entirely justified.[86] Well over two thousand *victims* of crimes, including those relating to domestic violence and sexual exploitation, were reported to immigration enforcement between 2020 and 2022.[87] Finally, alongside all of these exclusions are those barriers that women may face due to the language they speak, their health or disability status, and their caring responsibilities. Women with children who do want to return to their country of origin may not have their partner's permission to take their children with them. Those who wish to remain, or who have no choice but to do so, face making both themselves and their children destitute. Racism, both interpersonal and institutional, is also a key element in the denial of services and support.[88] The 'no recourse' rules and associated exclusions may cause migrants considerable hardship, denying someone who has lost their job or home the means to support and accommodate themselves. Taken cumulatively, their effect on victims of violence is profound and may even be deadly.[89] Those fleeing violence in their home may be denied the safety of a women's refuge. Those who want to leave an abusive employer may be unable to secure alternative work, safe accommodation, or financial support.[90] Perpetrators may also use these exclusions to intimidate their victims, threatening them with destitution to prevent them from leaving abusive situations.

Finally, the violence itself. Anitha ends one of her studies with the conclusion that:

[86] 'There is also clear evidence in some of the victim case examples we've seen that the police do sometimes prioritise immigration enforcement.' Her Majesty's Inspectorate of Constabulary and Fire and Rescue Services, College of Policing and Independent Office for Police Conduct, *Safe to Share? Liberty and Southall Black Sisters' Super-Complaint on Policing and Immigration status* (17 December 2020) 10.

[87] Nicole Jacobs, 'Letter to Rt Hon Robert Jenrick MP, Minister of State for Immigration' (Domestic Abuse Commissioner for England and Wales, 8 July 2023) <https://domesticabusecommissioner.uk/wp-content/uploads/2023/07/Domestic-Abuse-Commissioner-to-the-Minister-for-Immigration-_-The-Governments-response-to-Safety-Before-Status-The-Solutions-_-8th-July-2023.pdf> accessed 19 March 2024.

[88] Khatidja Chantler, 'Independence, Dependency and Interdependence: Struggles and Resistances of Minoritized Women Within and on Leaving Violent Relationships' (2006) 82 Feminist Review 27; Monica McWilliams, Priyamvada Nellum Rose Yarnell, and Molly Churchill, 'Forced Dependency and Legal Barriers: Implications of the UK's Immigration and Social Security Policies for Minoritized Women Living in Abusive Intimate Relationships in Northern Ireland' (2015) 5 Oñati Socio-Legal Series 1536. On the broader point of barriers, see Sofia Strid, Sylvia Walby, and Jo Armstrong, 'Intersectionality and Multiple Inequalities: Visibility in British Policy on Violence Against Women' (2013) 20 Social Politics 558.

[89] Sheffield Safer and Sustainable Communities Partnership, *Learning from Domestic Homicide Review (DHR): Adult D* (January 2014), which concerned the murder of Adult D by her former partner in front of their/his child(ren): 'The Review has identified that after Adult D fled the home there were gaps in service responses, and finds that these were due not only to her status as an A2 migrant; and to the lack of knowledge and understanding of staff about her rights as an A2 migrant fleeing domestic violence; but most importantly, to deficits in the systems available to ensure she was provided with her rights in law and the resources for refuge, support and safety which would be provided to a UK national in similar circumstances.'

[90] Natalie Sedacca, 'Migrant Work, Gender and the Hostile Environment: A Human Rights Analysis' (2024) 53 Industrial Law Journal 63.

> women with insecure immigration status face intensified forms of domestic violence as well as specific patterns of abuse that can be attributed to the imbalance of power between the perpetrators and the women, an imbalance created by the immigration laws which leave them with very few viable alternatives, thus reinforcing the patriarchal structures within their communities.[91]

The abuse Anitha describes includes severe physical, psychological, and sexual violence from a range of perpetrators, including a woman's partner and extended family. Victims report being beaten, imprisoned, and forced to engage in non-consensual sexual activity. They may also be denied reproductive autonomy, or access to their earned income and basic goods, including food, appropriate clothes, and a place to sleep. While such conduct may be identifiable in many cases of domestic violence and labour exploitation, migration status shapes 'particular techniques' and 'forms' of abuse, notably the above in conjunction with threats of destitution and deportation.[92] Children are also victims of such abuse. In one account Anitha analyses, a woman describes holding her baby while being beaten by her husband; she was also repeatedly threatened with deportation by other family members.[93] Migrant domestic workers recount analogous experiences, with labour exploitation, physical, verbal, and sexual abuse being accompanied, once again, by threats of destitution and deportation.[94] The State does not only increase vulnerability to violence and exploitation: by stripping women of key sources of resilience, it both intensifies violence and makes it harder to escape.[95]

While the legal position discussed here is that of the UK, parallel regimes and experiences are discussed in work relating to a range of jurisdictions. States across the European Union (EU) have rules which impose dependency on migrant spouses/partners, and which preclude them from sources of State support. These rules and exclusions have been criticised for both generating illegality and denying victims safety.[96] The 'uncertainty of women's immigration status' in the UK and

[91] Anitha, 'Legislating Gender Inequalities' (n 9) 1278–79.

[92] ibid 1278. See also Sundari Anitha, Anupama Roy, and Harshita Yalamarty, 'Gender, Migration, and Exclusionary Citizenship Regimes: Conceptualizing Transnational Abandonment of Wives as a Form of Violence Against Women' (2018) 24 Violence Against Women 747.

[93] Anitha, 'Legislating Gender Inequalities' (n 9) 1274.

[94] Virginia Mantouvalou, '"Am I Free Now?" Overseas Domestic Workers in Slavery' (2015) 42 Journal of Law and Society 329; Joyce Jiang, *A Special Vulnerability: Migrant Domestic Workers Enslaved by The Non-Renewable Overseas Domestic Worker Visa in the UK* (Report for The Voice of Domestic Workers, London, 2019); Natalie Sedacca, 'Domestic Workers, the "Family Worker" Exemption from Minimum Wage, and Gendered Devaluation of Women's Work' (2022) 51 Industrial Law Journal 771.

[95] See further Yvonne Amanor-Boadu and others, 'Immigrant and Nonimmigrant Women: Factors That Predict Leaving an Abusive Relationship' (2012) 18 Violence Against Women 611.

[96] OpCit Research London and others, *Access to Shelters of Undocumented Migrant Women Fleeing Domestic Violence: The Legal and Practical Situation in the Member States* (Directorate General for Internal Policies, Policy Department C: Citizens' Rights and Constitutional Affairs, European Union, 2013).

in Sweden 'compounds the control that perpetrators wield over them'.[97] Research on US immigration law recounts, with striking similarity and regularity, women's experiences of control, exclusion, and victimisation.[98] Finally, Marie Segrave describes compellingly how perpetrators 'weaponise' migration statuses granted under Australian immigration law, using them to dominate and coerce those they abuse.[99] Control of migration status is also a feature of the European jurisprudence relating to labour exploitation.[100]

As those assets which, Fineman argues, the responsive State should provide may be mapped onto the positive obligations States owe within their jurisdictions, so may the different facets of compounded disadvantage be used to chart States' failure to discharge those obligations to victims of violence. States, it will be recalled from chapter 3, have positive obligations to ensure that their laws and policies offer practical and effective protection from violence and exploitation. To bring that chapter's analysis of the ECHR together with that advanced here, the ECtHR has, in its post-*Opuz v Turkey* (2009)[101] jurisprudence, discussed these obligations in terms of applicants' vulnerability to (further) violence and the responsibilities States have to respond to it. In *Talpis v Italy* (2017),[102] the ECtHR found:

> that children and other vulnerable individuals—into which category fall victims of domestic violence—in particular are entitled to State protection, in the form of effective deterrence, against such serious breaches of personal integrity.[103]

Such effective protection involves providing support to enable victims to recover, including that which responds to victims' 'psychological, physical and material

[97] Halliki Voolma, '"I Must Be Silent Because of Residency": Barriers to Escaping Domestic Violence in the Context of Insecure Immigration Status in England and Sweden' (2018) 24 Violence Against Women 1830, 1836.

[98] Janet M Calvo, 'Spouse-Based Immigration Laws: The Legacies of Coverture' (1991) 28 San Diego Law Review 593; Anita Raj and Jay Silverman, 'Violence Against Immigrant Women: The Roles of Culture, Context, and Legal Immigrant Status on Intimate Partner Violence' (2002) 8 Violence Against Women 367; Cecilia Menjívar and Olivia Salcido, 'Immigrant Women and Domestic Violence: Common Experiences in Different Countries' (2002) 16 Gender & Society 898; Sabrina Balgamwalla, 'Bride and Prejudice: How US Immigration Law Discriminates Against Spousal Visa Holders' (2014) 29 Berkeley Journal of Gender, Law & Justice 25; Edna Erez, 'Migration/Immigration, Domestic Violence and the Justice System' (2002) 26 International Journal of Comparative and Applied Criminal Justice 277; Radha Vishnuvajjala, 'Insecure Communities: How an Immigration Enforcement Program Encourages Battered Women to Stay Silent' (2012) 32 Boston College Journal of Law & Social Justice 185; Deisy Del Real, 'Toxic Ties: The Reproduction of Legal Violence within Mixed-Status Intimate Partners, Relatives, and Friends' (2019) 53 International Migration Review 548.

[99] Marie Segrave, 'Temporary Migration and Family Violence: How Perpetrators Weaponise Borders' (2021) 10 International Journal for Crime, Justice and Social Democracy 26. See also Stefani Vasil, '"I Came Here, and it Got Worse Day by Day": Examining the Intersections Between Migrant Precarity and Family Violence Among Women with Insecure Migration Status in Australia' (2023) <https://journals.sagepub.com/doi/abs/10.1177/10778012231159414> accessed 4 May 2024.

[100] *Siliadin v France* (2006) 43 EHRR 16; *CN v UK* (2013) 56 EHRR 24.

[101] *Opuz v Turkey* App no 33401/02 (ECtHR, 9 June 2009).

[102] *Talpis v Italy* (n 27).

[103] ibid para 99.

situation'.[104] Yet the effectiveness of criminal investigations will be compromised if migrant women are deterred from cooperating with the police because they correctly fear deportation or destitution.[105] A State's ability to take preventative operational measures to protect may also be hampered by exclusions which deny women access to refuges and other places of safety.[106] The effective protection required of immigration rules that determine the rights and status of different kinds of worker will be undermined by provisions that enable a perpetrator to exercise control over the person they victimise.[107] An experience of compounded disadvantage could, depending on the circumstances, involve violations of the right to be free from torture, inhuman, and degrading treatment; to be free from slavery, forced labour, and servitude; and the right to respect for private and family life (per articles 3, 4, and 8 of the ECHR). It may also involve violations of the right to life (article 2 of the ECHR). Following the arguments made in chapter 3, article 14 may also be engaged, by both the violence itself and by States' failure to respond to it.[108]

4.3 The Remedy: An Independent Migration Status

4.3.1 Pre-emptive Migration Status Reform

I have woven together ethical and legal approaches to vulnerability, the embodied, the embedded, the constructed, and the imposed, to argue that migrant women subject to violence experience a compounded disadvantage that States are obliged to remedy. In this, the final section of this chapter and of Part I, I consider how this might be achieved.

First, the account of compounded disadvantage advanced here lends further support to my arguments, started in chapter 2, for migration status reform. Such reform, it will be recalled, would require the abolition of all dependent migration statuses. It would entail the granting of immediate permanent residence to the migrant partners of British citizens/residents. It would also involve providing an independent, renewable, rights-bestowing status to other partners and to domestic workers.

[104] ibid para 115. The State's failure to provide that support was found to breach its positive obligations under arts 2, 3, and 14 ECHR.

[105] Drawing on *Paul and Audrey Edwards v UK* App no 46477/9 (ECtHR, 14 March 2002).

[106] Drawing on *Osman v UK* App no 87/1997/871/1083 (ECtHR, 28 Oct 1988); *CN v UK* (n 100) (on States' obligations to take appropriate measures within the scope of their powers to remove an individual from a situation or risk of violence).

[107] Drawing on *Rantsev v Cyprus and Russia* (2010) 51 EHRR 1.

[108] On States' obligations to respond to violence that disproportionally affects women, see *AE v Bulgaria* App no 53891/20 (ECtHR, 23 May 2023).

Turning first to those with permission to remain as the partner of someone who is British or resident in the UK. The abolition of the probationary period and a grant instead of permanent residence would both decrease a migrant partner's vulnerability to violence and release them from the control that intensifies it. Permanent residence is justified because these partners are on a route to settlement and should not be compelled to choose between that and safety. Interestingly, similar arguments to these were advanced by the Canadian government to justify the decision, discussed in chapter 2, to abolish their equivalent of the probationary period, 'conditional permanent residence':

> On balance, the program integrity benefits of conditional permanent residence have not been shown to outweigh the potential risks to vulnerable sponsored spouses and partners subject to the two-year cohabitation requirement...
>
> ... the proposed repeal of conditional permanent residence recognizes that the majority of relationships are genuine, and the majority of applications are made in good faith. Eliminating conditional permanent residence would facilitate family reunification, remove the potential increased vulnerability faced by abused and neglected spouses and partners, and support the Government's commitment to combatting gender-based violence.[109]

Granting an independent status to *these* partners would not, however, prevent all those who *are* partners from experiencing compounded disadvantage. The partners of labour migrants should also receive an independent status. This need not be permanent and could mirror, in duration, rights, and renewability, the permission given to the labour migrant. In section 4.2.2, I gave the example of a woman who experienced domestic violence and whose permission to remain *as a student* was jeopardised as a result. This is precisely what happened in *OB* (2016).[110] Here, the woman concerned became an overstayer, because her violent husband manipulated her migration status.[111] Ensuring that *no* migration status is precarious, because of its temporariness, or because it has onerous or repeatedly

[109] 'Canada Gazette, Part I, Volume 150, Number 44: Regulations Amending the Immigration and Refugee Protection Regulations' (*Government of Canada/Gouvermement du Canada*, 29 October 2016) <www.gazette.gc.ca/rp-pr/p1/2016/2016-10-29/html/reg1-eng.html> accessed 27 April 2024. See also Immigration, Refugees and Citizenship Canada, 'Notice—Government of Canada Eliminates Conditional Permanent Residence' (*Government of Canada/Gouvermement du Canada*, 28 April 2017) <www.canada.ca/en/immigration-refugees-citizenship/news/notices/elminating-conditional-pr.html> accessed 3 February 2023; Immigration, Refugees and Citizenship Canada, '2017 Annual Report to Parliament on Immigration' (*Government of Canada/Gouvermement du Canada*, 1 November 2017) <www.canada.ca/en/immigration-refugees-citizenship/corporate/publications-manuals/annual-report-parliament-immigration-2017.html#section4> accessed 27 April 2024. On the impact of conditional permanent residence, see Rupaleem Bhuyan and Bronwyn Bragg, 'Epistemologies of Bordering: Domestic Violence Advocacy with Marriage Migrants in the Shadow of Deportation' (2021) 9 Migration Studies 159.

[110] *Secretary of State for the Home Department v OB* [2016] Appeal Number IA/27725/2014.

[111] ibid [4].

tested conditions attached to it, will help ensure that this does not occur. Such arguments also apply to domestic workers. The abolition of dependent and precarious migration statuses, in practice as well as in law, would not only decrease vulnerability to exploitation but would also affect its nature and reduce its severity.[112] It would, in short, ensure that statuses given to the partners of labour migrants, students, and domestic workers offer effective protection by enabling their holders to end relationships, suspend/renew their studies, or secure alternative, safe employment.

Finally, States are permitted to impose restrictions on migrants' ability to access the full range of services provided by the State.[113] Such restrictions should not however, per Fineman's theorising and my account of States' positive and other ECHR obligations, operate to deny women protection from violence. Nor should they result in a failure to respond to violence that disproportionately affects women.[114] Key rights, such as access to healthcare or to safe accommodation, should not be restricted. As recommended by the Committee that monitors the Convention on the Elimination of All Forms of Discrimination against Women (CEDAW),[115] the CEDAW Committee, restrictive immigration laws that discourage women from reporting violence should be repealed.[116] States should also ensure that legal proceedings, protective support measures, and services should be accessible to all women, irrespective of migration status. Some migrants could be required to demonstrate that they can maintain and accommodate themselves without recourse to public funds before arriving. Once within the jurisdiction, a 'firewall' should exist between 'the enforcement of immigration law, on the one hand, and the protection of general human rights, on the other'.[117] Access to public funds secures both effective protection from violence and the means to recover from it. Without such a

[112] Research conducted on the pre-2016 rules for domestic workers found that those who were 'tied' to their employers were twice as likely to report being physically abused and more likely to be confined to the 'family' home than those admitted under the pre-2012 rules. KALAYAAN, 'Still Enslaved: The Migrant Domestic Workers who are Trapped by the Immigration Rules' (*KALAYAAN*, 2014) <www.kalayaan.org.uk/wp-content/uploads/2014/09/tied-visa-20141.pdf> accessed 22 April 2024.

[113] *Bah v UK* App no 56328/07 (ECtHR, 27 September 2011).

[114] *AE v Bulgaria* (n 108).

[115] Convention on the Elimination of All Forms of Discrimination against Women (adopted 18 December 1979, entered into force 3 September 1981) 1249 UNTS 13 (CEDAW).

[116] UN Committee on the Elimination of Discrimination against Women, 'General Recommendation No 35 on Gender-Based Violence Against Women, Updating General Recommendation No 19' (26 July 2017) UN Doc CEDAW/C/GC/35 [29(c)(iii)], [31(b)]. Within the UK context, see further UN Committee on the Elimination of Discrimination against Women, 'Concluding Observations on the Eighth Periodic Report of the United Kingdom of Great Britain and Northern Ireland' (14 March 2019) UN Doc CEDAW/C/GBR/CO/8.

[117] Joseph H Carens, *The Ethics of Immigration* (OUP 2013) 133–34. See also UN Human Rights Council, 'The Impact of Migration on Migrant Women and Girls: a Gender Perspective, Report of the Special Rapporteur on the Human Rights of Migrants' (15 April 2019) UN Doc A/HRC/41/38 [66]. In relation to the UK context specifically, see Domestic Abuse Commissioner for England and Wales, *Safety before Status* (n 67); Women and Equalities Committee, *So-Called Honour-Based Abuse: Sixth Report of Session 2022–23* (HC 831, 19 July 2023) paras 58–59.

separation 'the disciplinary and punitive reach of immigration controls functions as a limit to the claiming of rights'.[118]

4.3.2 A Reparative Response to Compounded Disadvantage

Gendered disadvantage and discrimination are pervasive features of migration law. They intersect, are informed by, and co-constitute disadvantage and discrimination that relates to a range of protected grounds, including race. The reimagining of immigration law that I started in chapter 2 is offered in response to particular facets of family and labour migration rules that enforce dependency and restrict rights. It has also been justified by reference to States' obligations to provide effective protection from violence and the theorising and jurisprudence on vulnerability discussed here. The reforms I suggest are, of necessity, partial and very briefly sketched. They may remedy some of the discrimination experienced by migrant women but be insufficient to respond to the broader patterns of exclusion and dispossession discussed in chapter 1. They do not, however, seem likely to be realised any time soon. Indeed, in the UK and elsewhere, the trend appears to be towards the adoption of family and labour migration routes which are more precarious and contingent, and which place more barriers between the migrant and either permanent residence or citizenship.[119] The 'family resemblance' in European States' approach to marriage migration and the ever more onerous demands made of families were also discussed in chapter 2.[120] Similarly, States, including the UK, are increasing their reliance on highly precarious seasonal and temporary labour migration routes, rather than those that place migrants on a route to long-term residence.[121] What obligations might States have in these, distinctly non-ideal, circumstances? What remedies are those now subject to discrimination and disadvantage entitled to?

As discussed in chapter 3, States' positive obligations in relation to violence and the right to a remedy can prevent or delay removal in certain circumstances. On the latter, to be effective, a remedy must be capable of enforcing the substance of protected rights by granting appropriate relief.[122] This does not, following current

[118] Siobhán Mullally and Clíodhna Murphy, 'Migrant Domestic Workers in the UK: Enacting Exclusions, Exemptions, and Rights' (2014) 36 Human Rights Quarterly 397, 414.

[119] Catherine Dauvergne, *The New Politics of Immigration and the End of Settler Societies* (CUP 2016); Anna K Boucher and Justin Gest, *Crossroads: Comparative Immigration Regimes in a World of Demographic Change* (CUP 2018).

[120] Helena Wray, Agnes Agoston, and Jocelyn Hutton, 'A Family Resemblance? The Regulation of Marriage Migration in Europe' (2014) 16 European Journal of Migration and Law 209.

[121] Virginia Mantouvalou, 'The UK Seasonal Worker Visa' (2022) 1 European Law Open 711; Vladimir Bogoeski and Francesco Costamagna, 'Law and the Production of Precarious Work in Europe: An Introduction' (2022) 1 European Law Open 660.

[122] *Aydin v Turkey* App no 23178/94 (ECtHR, 25 September 1997).

ECtHR jurisprudence, require a migration status to be granted to someone who cannot be so removed.[123] The right to a remedy may, for example, prevent deportation where removing a victim of crime would prevent her from taking part in its investigation or prosecution. Such protection would, however, be for a comparatively short period of time and conditional on cooperation with the relevant authorities. It would not necessarily grant a victim other rights, such as access to the labour market. Under the ECHR, therefore, victims of compounded disadvantage may only be entitled to short-term non-removal for particular purposes, potentially without status or rights.

In international law, an action is considered reparative of a wrong when it involves restitution (to restore the pre-violation status quo), compensation (eg the payment of damages), and satisfaction (eg the acknowledgement of wrongdoing, guarantees of non-repetition).[124] In the sphere of human rights protection, Ruth Rubio-Marín and Clara Sandoval contend that because violence against women occurs in the context of structural discrimination, to be reparative a remedy must transform that context:

> Arguably, the law would be wrong if, discarding alternative options, it simply sought to return women to the *status quo ante*, when doing so entails perpetuating conditions of discrimination, violence, and poverty—which were often at the root of the violence and which accounted for the specific and compounded form of harm that women experienced.[125]

Rubio-Marín and Sandoval root this argument in the jurisprudence of the IACtHR, particularly *González et al ('Cotton Field') v Mexico* (2009),[126] a case concerned with the abduction, sexual abuse, and murder of three women: Ms Laura Berenice Ramos Monárrez, Ms Claudia Ivette González, and Ms Esmeralda Herrera Monreal. Here, the Court found that reparations made

[123] As will be recalled from chapter 3, to be effective under the ECHR, a remedy must be capable of enforcing the substance of the relevant protected right by granting those who seek access to it appropriate relief. ibid paras 103–07. States are not, however, required to provide a residence permit. *Hayaati Ahmed Ali v The Netherlands* App no 26494/09 (ECtHR, 24 January 2012); *De Souza Ribeiro v France* App no 22689/07 (ECtHR GC, 13 December 2012). The relationship between migration status, positive obligations, and the regimes of exception will be discussed further in Part II.

[124] UNGA Res 56/83 'Responsibility of States for Internationally Wrongful Acts' (12 December 2001) UN Doc A/RES/56/83, arts 34–37. Notably this relates to States' interactions with other States. See further James Crawford and Simon Olleson, 'The Character and Forms of International Responsibility' in Malcolm D Evans (ed), *International Law* (5th edn, CUP 2018).

[125] Ruth Rubio-Marín and Clara Sandoval, 'Engendering the Reparations Jurisprudence of the Inter-American Court of Human Rights: The Promise of the *Cotton Field* Judgment' (2011) 33 Human Rights Quarterly 1062, 1070. See also Carla Ferstman, 'Reparations for Sexual and Other Gender-Based Violence' in *Gender Perspectives on Torture: Law and Practice* (Center for Human Rights & Humanitarian Law 2018).

[126] *González ('Cotton Field') v Mexico (Preliminary Objection, Merits, Reparations, and Costs)* Inter-American Court of Human Rights Series C No 205 (16 November 2009).

> must be designed to change this situation, so that their effect is not only of restitution, but also rectification. In this regard, re-establishment of the same structural context of violence and discrimination is not acceptable.[127]

It is illuminating to briefly contrast the remedies available to migrant victims of violence under the ECHR against these standards. Non-removal, without status, or with one that is temporary, precarious, and rights-restrictive, does not provide a victim with restitution, compensation, or satisfaction. Although it may enable someone to take part in relevant legal proceedings, it may also expose them to the risk of further violence and exploitation. Removal itself may also appear to involve the relatively benign re-establishment of the status quo but it can also entail (often prolonged) detention, (sometimes extreme) violence, and family separation. Indeed, non-deportation followed by forced migration, in the form of forced removal, is more likely to enforce than to alleviate compounded disadvantage.[128] It also proves correct the threats that perpetrators of violence make against those they victimise: 'if you seek to leave (this relationship or employment) you risk destitution and deportation.' To draw on and paraphrase Rubio-Marín and Sandoval, the 'remedy' of delayed involuntary removal may perpetuate the 'conditions of discrimination, violence, and poverty' which account 'for the specific and compounded form of harm'[129] migrant women experience. It is not, therefore, reparative of compounded disadvantage.

In contrast, granting permanent residence to the migrant partners of British citizens/residents, and an independent, rights-bestowing status to other victims of violence, would be transformative, enabling women to leave a violent situation and access the support they need to recover from it. While permanent residence may be appropriate for those on a route to settlement, for others, including the partners of labour migrants and domestic workers, three years' permission to remain with the possibility of extension and/or naturalisation (an analogous status to that given to refugees in the EU) could be sufficient.[130] Such statuses would reduce vulnerability to further violence and offer effective protection from it. They would guarantee compounded disadvantage's non-repetition. They would also enable victims to engage meaningfully with criminal or other legal proceedings against their perpetrator, including for lost wages, compensation, or in relation to children. Finally, these statuses would offer some element of compensation to a victim

[127] ibid para 450.

[128] Drawing on Matthew J Gibney, 'Is Deportation a Form of Forced Migration?' (2013) 32 Refugee Survey Quarterly 116.

[129] Rubio-Marín and Sandoval, 'Engendering' (n 125) 1070.

[130] Directive 2011/95/EU of the European Parliament and of the Council of 13 December 2011 on standards for the qualification of third-country nationals or stateless persons as beneficiaries of international protection, for a uniform status for refugees or for persons eligible for subsidiary protection, and for the content of the protection granted (recast) [2011] OJ L337/9, art 24 (Qualification Directive (recast)).

of compounded disadvantage, enabling her to establish herself in her country of residence securely and independently of her abuser. Of course, the provision of such statuses would not preclude a State from encouraging, or even assisting, a migrant to return 'home' voluntarily, through a resettlement programme, for example. Its provision would, however, ensure that any such return was indeed truly voluntary.

An independent, non-temporary, rights-bestowing migration status has all the hallmarks, therefore, of a response to compounded disadvantage that is effective *and* reparative. Notably, similar arguments and recommendations to States have been made by others, including the UN's Special Rapporteurs on trafficking and violence against women.[131] According to the CEDAW Committee, States should pass non-discriminatory residency regulations, including to 'allow for the legal stay of a woman who flees her abusive employer or spouse'.[132] Migrant victims of violence should also be granted 'all necessary benefits', including, where necessary, a migration status, reintegration, and support services.[133]

4.4 Conclusion

This chapter has argued for migration status reform, including the abolition of dependent statuses. It has also argued for migrant victims of violence to be granted an independent, rights-bestowing migration status. These arguments have been justified ethically and legally by reference to the State's role in compounding, through immigration laws that discriminate against women, the disadvantage experienced by victims of violence against women. The distinguishing features of such compounded disadvantage are control, exclusion, and an intensified experience of violence. The ethical foundations to the obligations identified have been provided by theorising on vulnerability and resilience, particularly that of Martha Fineman. The ECHR's prohibition of discrimination, jurisprudence on vulnerability and on effective protection, have been relied on to provide their legal foundation. Finally, I drew on gender-sensitive approaches to remedies and CEDAW Committee recommendations, to contend that an independent, rights-bestowing migration

[131] UN Human Rights Council, 'Report of the Special Rapporteur on Violence against Women, its Causes and Consequences, Rashida Manjo' (19 April 2010) UN Doc A/HRC/14/22; UNGA, 'Trafficking in Persons, Especially Women and Children, Note by the Secretary-General' (9 August 2011) UN Doc A/66/283, [16], [41], see also draft principle 9(b)(i).

[132] UN Committee on the Elimination of Discrimination against Women, 'General Recommendation No 26 on Women Migrant Workers' (5 December 2008) UN Doc CEDAW/C/2009/WP.1/R [26(f)]; see also UN Committee on the Elimination of Discrimination against Women 'General Recommendation No 38 on Trafficking in Women and Girls in the Context of Global Migration' (20 November 2020) UN Doc CEDAW/C/GC/38 [25], [89]–[92] (discussed further in chapter 6).

[133] *Zheng v The Netherlands* Communication No 15/2007 (14 November 2008) UN Doc CEDAW/C/42/D/15/2007 dissenting opinion of Committee members Mary Shanthi Dairiam, Violeta Neubauer, and Silvia Pimentel (the majority finding the trafficking complaint inadmissible) [8.7].

status offers both effective protection from, and a reparative remedy for, compounded disadvantage. The regimes of exception considered in Part II are, consequently, evaluated by reference to the extent to which they provide such a remedy.

The regimes of exception are migration law responses to violence experienced in the context of migration control. They have different legal sources and bestow different packages of rights. They operate alongside, but differ from, refugee and other protections from *refoulement*. The latter are future-oriented, concerned with persecution and other serious harm that may materialise in a person's country of origin.[134] In contrast, the regimes of exception grant status on the basis of past violence, usually experienced in the country of residence. That States and others have developed or adopted such regimes may be taken as a tacit, or even explicit, recognition of some of the arguments made here. The UK has, for example, a rule that enables *some* migrant victims of domestic violence to receive permanent residence if their relationship has broken down because of domestic violence.[135] This rule is accompanied by a concession that enables *some* victims to receive public funds or other, limited, support.[136] Both the rule and concession are frequently justified on the basis that, again, *a limited number* of victims of domestic violence should not have to choose between safety and settlement.[137] The EU's own domestic violence rule,[138] as well as the UK's, will be analysed in chapter 5. Chapter 6 then moves on to evaluate provisions that enable some victims of trafficking to receive a residence permit.[139] Chapter 7 concludes with a consideration of the Istanbul Convention's article 59, which contains two regimes designed to respond to violence against women.

[134] Convention relating to the Status of Refugees (adopted 28 July 1951, entered into force 22 April 1954) 189 UNTS 137, art 1A(2). See also Qualification Directive (recast).

[135] Immigration Rules HC 590, Appendix Victim of Domestic Abuse.

[136] Home Office, *Migrant Victims of Domestic Abuse Concession (formerly the destitute domestic violence concession (DDVC))* (Version 4, 4 April 2024).

[137] Home Office, *Migrant Victims of Domestic Abuse: Review Findings* (2020) para 31, which confirms that some victims of domestic violence have a 'reasonable expectation' of settlement and should receive it.

[138] Directive 2004/38/EC of the European Parliament and of the Council of 29 April 2004 on the right of citizens of the Union and their family members to move and reside freely within the territory of the Member States amending Regulation (EEC) No 1612/68 and repealing Directives 64/221/EEC, 68/360/EEC, 72/194/EEC, 73/148/EEC, 75/34/EEC, 75/35/EEC, 90/364/EEC, 90/365/EEC and 93/96/EEC [2004] OJ L 158/77, and corrigenda ([2004] OJ L 229/35, [2005] OJ L 197/34, and [2007] OJ L 204/28), art 13. This is discussed alongside a similar provision in Council Directive 2003/86/EC of 22 September 2003 on the right to family reunification [2003] OJ L251/12.

[139] Council Directive 2004/81/EC of 29 April 2004 on the residence permit issued to third-country nationals who are victims of trafficking in human beings or who have been the subject of an action to facilitate illegal immigration, who cooperate with the competent authorities [2004] OJ L261/19, arts 6, 8; Council of Europe Convention on Action against Trafficking in Human Beings (adopted 16 May 2005, entered into force 1 February 2008) CETS 197, arts 13, 14.

PART II
SIX REGIMES OF EXCEPTION

5
Domestic Violence Rules Compared

5.1 Introduction

This chapter is the first of three to evaluate the rules, characterised in this book as regimes of exception, that States and the European Union (EU) have created to respond to certain forms of violence experienced in the context of migration control. In this and the chapters that follow, selected regimes are evaluated by reference to the extent to which they provide a reparative remedy for compounded disadvantage and the discrimination that is imbricated in it. Here, I focus on two rules which require either the relevant EU Member State (MS) or the UK to grant permission to remain to some victims of domestic violence whose relationship with their spouse or partner has broken down. The legal source of the first of these 'domestic violence rules', article 13(2)(c) of the Citizens' Directive,[1] is EU law, while the source of the second, Appendix Victim of Domestic Abuse, is UK immigration law.[2] These rules operate alongside human rights protections, including, where relevant, those provided by the Charter of Fundamental Rights of the European Union (the CFREU or Charter)[3] and the European Convention on Human Rights (ECHR).[4] The rights of migrant victims of domestic violence may also be determined by refugee law,[5] as well as by other relevant prohibitions on *refoulement*.[6] Finally, the Council of Europe Convention on Preventing and Combating Violence against Women and Domestic Violence (the Istanbul Convention)[7] may likewise

[1] Directive 2004/38/EC of the European Parliament and of the Council of 29 April 2004 on the right of citizens of the Union and their family members to move and reside freely within the territory of the Member States amending Regulation (EEC) No 1612/68 and repealing Directives 64/221/EEC, 68/360/EEC, 72/194/EEC, 73/148/EEC, 75/34/EEC, 75/35/EEC, 90/364/EEC, 90/365/EEC and 93/96/EEC [2004] OJ L 158/77, and corrigenda ([2004] OJ L 229/35, [2005] OJ L 197/34, and [2007] OJ L 204/28) (Citizens' Directive).

[2] Immigration Rules HC 590, Appendix Victim of Domestic Abuse.

[3] Charter of Fundamental Rights of the European Union [2007] OJ C303/01 (CFREU).

[4] Convention for the Protection of Human Rights and Fundamental Freedoms (adopted 4 November 1950, entered into force 3 September 1953) ETS 5 (European Convention on Human Rights, as amended) (ECHR).

[5] Including pursuant to the Convention relating to the Status of Refugees (adopted 28 July 1951, entered into force 22 April 1954) 189 UNTS 137. See further Catherine Briddick, 'Resisting Domestic Violence' (2024) 36 International Journal of Refugee Law 106.

[6] Including that provided by Convention on the Elimination of All Forms of Discrimination against Women (adopted 18 December 1979, entered into force 3 September 1981) 1249 UNTS 13. See further Catherine Briddick, 'Unprincipled and Unrealised: CEDAW and Discrimination Experienced in the Context of Migration Control' (2022) 22 International Journal of Discrimination and the Law 224.

[7] Council of Europe Convention on Preventing and Combating Violence against Women and Domestic Violence (adopted 11 May 2011, entered into force 1 August 2014) CETS 210.

Violence against Women and Regimes of Exception. Catherine Briddick, Oxford University Press.
 DOI: 10.1093/9780191959899.003.0005

afford important protections, including by interacting with both EU law and relevant national law. The Istanbul Convention defines domestic violence as:

> all acts of physical, sexual, psychological or economic violence that occur within the family or domestic unit or between former or current spouses or partners, whether or not the perpetrator shares or has shared the same residence with the victim.[8]

The Convention then establishes a series of preventative and protective responses to both violence against women and domestic violence, including two regimes of exception, these operating alongside a prohibition on *refoulement*. The EU's and UK's troubled engagement with the Istanbul Convention as a whole, and these regimes in particular, is considered in chapter 7.

To evaluate the domestic violence regimes of exception, I draw on the legal case that NA, first introduced in chapter 1, fought for permanent residence in the UK.[9] At the time that NA's case was decided, the UK was a member of the EU. NA's case was the first case of the Court of Justice of the EU (CJEU) on the EU's domestic violence rule.

NA was from Pakistan. Under EU law, countries that are not members of the EU, or countries whose citizens do not enjoy the EU right to freedom of movement, are 'third countries'.[10] At the relevant time, NA was, therefore, a third-country national (TCN). NA's husband KA was a dual national, being a citizen of both Pakistan (a third country) and Germany (an EU MS). The migration status of TCN women may be determined by EU law when they are the family member of a particular type of EU Citizen, their rights depending on and deriving from those that their EU Citizen family member enjoys. NA's ability to remain in the UK was, therefore, determined primarily by EU law. KA was violent to NA throughout their relationship. When KA abandoned her and their child, NA sought to live permanently in the UK. Her attempt to do so was unsuccessful and, as her case proceeded through the UK courts, a reference was made to the CJEU. As will become apparent, that Court's decision in NA's case did more to enable

[8] ibid art 3(b).

[9] Case C-115/15 *Secretary of State for the Home Department v NA* [2016] ECLI:EU:C:2016:487 (*NA (CJEU Judgment)*).

[10] Regulation (EU) 2016/399 of the European Parliament and of the Council of 9 March 2016 on a Union Code on the rules governing the movement of persons across borders (Schengen Borders Code) (codification) [2016] OJ L77/1, art 2(5)–(6). The European Union's (EU) Member States are Austria, Belgium, Bulgaria, Croatia, Cyprus, Czech Republic, Denmark, Estonia, Finland, France, Germany, Greece, Hungary, Ireland, Italy, Latvia, Lithuania, Luxembourg, Malta, the Netherlands, Poland, Portugal, Romania, Slovakia, Slovenia, Spain, and Sweden. My focus here is on EU Citizens and their family members. Iceland, Norway, and Liechtenstein are not members of the EU, but are in the European Economic Area (the EEA). Those three States, along with Switzerland, are generally treated analogously with EU MS in the field of migration law.

domestic violence than it did to combat it, an outcome that has only partially been remedied.[11]

The analysis proceeds as follows. First, I introduce the EU Directives that determine the rights and status of TCN family members, introducing their provisions on relationship breakdown and domestic violence. I then provide the legal context to, and chart the progression of, NA's case to the CJEU. The ability of article 13(2)(c) to provide a reparative response to compounded disadvantage is discussed through a critical evaluation of the CJEU's judgment in both her case and one that followed it, *X v Belgian State* (2021).[12] The final section of the chapter moves from the EU to the UK, exploring the latter's domestic violence rule and a policy that relates to it, the Migrant Victims of Domestic Abuse Concession (MVDAC).[13] I discuss discrimination law challenges to the UK's provisions, before using NA's situation to analyse the UK's response to compounded disadvantage.

5.2 Freedom to Move, But for Whom?

Although the rights of some TCNs in the EU have been the subject of sustained academic attention, the position of those who derive their status from their family relationships has received considerably less. The position of *former* family members, almost none.[14] This chapter speaks to this gap in the literature, picking up chapter 2's arguments on status and disadvantage to demonstrate the relevance of Part I's analysis to women whose experiences of violence and migration are shaped by EU law. This is an important move, empirically and legally, given the number of people whose rights are determined by EU law and its broader influence on European and other States' migration laws and policies.[15]

[11] Catherine Briddick, 'Combatting or Enabling Domestic Violence? Evaluating the Residence Rights of Migrant Victims of Domestic Violence in Europe' (2020) 69 International and Comparative Law Quarterly 1013. Some of the analysis of the case presented here is developed from this piece.

[12] Case C-930/19 *X v Belgian State* [2021] ECLI:EU:C:2021:657.

[13] Home Office, *Migrant Victims of Domestic Abuse Concession (formerly the destitute domestic violence concession (DDVC))* (Version 4, 4 April 2024) (Home Office, *MVDAC*).

[14] I have been able to identify just five substantive articles on the EU's domestic violence rule, in addition to my own. These are: Adam Weiss, 'Transnational Families in Crisis: An Analysis of the Domestic Violence Rule in E.U. Free Movement Law' (2009) 30 Michigan Journal of International Law 841; Helen Oosterom-Staples, 'Residence Rights for Caring Parents Who Are Also Victims of Domestic Violence' (2017) 19 European Journal of Migration and Law 396; Vladislava Stoyanova, 'On the Bride's Side? Victims of Domestic Violence and their Residence Rights under EU and Council of Europe Law' (2019) 37 Netherlands Quarterly of Human Rights 311; Francesca Strumia, 'Speaking Too Little, Yet Saying Too Much. The Wrong Signals about EU Values: *X. v. Belgian State*' (2022) 59 Common Market Law Review 1195; Judit Villena Rodó, 'A Preliminary Analysis of the Intersection Between Domestic Violence, Coercive Control and Migration Statuses in Ireland and Spain' (2022) 9 Deusto Journal of Human Rights 13.

[15] For an interesting discussion on 'common ground', EU law, and the family reunion rights of refugees in Europe, see *BF v Switzerland* App nos 13258/18, 15500/18, 57303/18 (ECtHR, 4 July 2023) para 98.

Two parallel legal regimes determine the rights and status of TCN family members.[16] At the heart of this chapter's analysis is the EU's Citizens' Directive.[17] As its name suggests, this Directive governs those who are the family member of certain kinds of EU Citizen, including TCNs. The Family Reunion Directive (FRD),[18] in contrast, sets minimum standards for MS' treatment of TCNs and their family members.[19]

EU Citizens have the right to have their family members accompany or join them if they move from one EU MS to another.[20] This applies whether or not that family member is an EU Citizen or a TCN.[21] EU Citizens and their families who enter another MS have, under the Directive, an initial right of residence for up to three months.[22] Subject to conditions, after three months EU Citizens who are economically active in particular ways have an extended right of residence; their family members enjoy the same.[23] Those considered economically active include workers, self-employed people, self-sufficient people, and students.[24] Some statuses may be retained in certain circumstances enabling, for example, workers who lose their employment to undertake vocational training or to seek work.[25] After five years' residence in accordance with the Directive, EU Citizens and their family members have the right of permanent residence.[26]

The Citizens' Directive defines 'family member' expansively, those falling within its definition also being able to join an EU Citizen in a greater variety of different circumstances than under either the FRD or UK immigration law.[27] Family members do not have to meet conditions that relate to accommodation or a family's finances, nor do they have to reapply and demonstrate that they continue to meet

[16] There are other regimes that apply to certain categories of TCN; these are not considered here.

[17] For a detailed discussion of which, see Elspeth Guild, Steve Peers, and Jonathan Tomkin, *The EU Citizenship Directive: A Commentary* (2nd edn, OUP 2019).

[18] Council Directive 2003/86/EC of 22 September 2003 on the right to family reunification [2003] OJ L251/12 (FRD).

[19] For a detailed discussion of which, see Steve Peers and others, 'Family Reunion' in Steve Peers and others (eds), *EU Immigration and Asylum Law (Text and Commentary): Second Revised Edition* (2nd edn, Brill | Nijhof 2012).

[20] Citizens' Directive. See also Case C-200/02 *Zhu and Chen* [2004] ECR I-09925.

[21] Note the FRD's art 3(3), which confirms that this Directive 'shall not apply to members of the family of a Union citizen'.

[22] Citizens' Directive, art 6.

[23] ibid art 7(1)–(2).

[24] ibid art 7(1)–(2). These conditions include not becoming a burden on the social assistance programmes of a particular MS and, for those who are not workers or self-employed, having comprehensive sickness insurance.

[25] ibid art 7(3).

[26] ibid art 16.

[27] ibid arts 2 and 3, compared with the FRD, art 4. The former covers spouses/registered partners; dependent relatives in the ascending line (parents, parents-in-law); relatives in the descending line who are under the age of twenty-one or still dependent on their parents; durable partners; and extended family relationships which involve the provision of care. The latter only provides reunion rights to spouses and minor children (with derogations that relate to children over twelve and fifteen years old). MS are given latitude over the stay of dependent parents, adult unmarried children, and durable partners.

the Directive's requirements. EU Citizens and their family members who reside in another MS on the basis of the Citizens' Directive also have a general right, albeit one that is being eroded, to receive the same treatment as that accorded to MS' own nationals.[28] The TCN family member of, for example, an EU Citizen worker would not, consequently, have been subject to the exclusions and 'no recourse' rules described in chapter 4. The rights of families to migrate or reunite are qualified rights which may be limited by the EU and MS permissibly in a range of different circumstances.[29] Notably, the Citizens' Directive's limitations are considerably less restrictive than those that apply to family members under either the FRD or many MS' own immigration rules.[30] Finally, the Directive offers different forms of protection to spouses and *registered* partners, whether same-sex or opposite-sex.[31] These apply in the event of the death or departure of the TCN's EU Citizen family member (article 12) or their relationship breakdown (article 13).[32] The latter of these, article 13, specifically refers to domestic violence:

> (2) Without prejudice to the second subparagraph, divorce, annulment of marriage or termination of the registered partnership referred to in point 2(b) of Article 2 shall not entail loss of the right of residence of a Union Citizen's family members who are not nationals of a Member State where: . . .
>
> (c) this is warranted by particularly difficult circumstances, such as having been a victim of domestic violence while the marriage or registered partnership was subsisting; . . .
>
> Before acquiring the right of permanent residence, the right of residence of the persons concerned shall remain subject to the requirement that they are able to show that they are workers or self-employed persons or that they have sufficient resources for themselves and their family members not to become a burden on the social assistance system of the host Member State during their period of residence and have comprehensive sickness insurance cover in the host Member State, or that they are members of the family, already constituted in the host Member State, of a person satisfying these requirements. 'Sufficient resources' shall be as defined in Article 8(4).[33]

[28] Citizens' Directive, art 24. On its erosion, see Charlotte O'Brien, 'The ECJ Sacrifices EU Citizenship in Vain: *Commission v. United Kingdom*' (2017) 54 Common Market Law Review 209.

[29] Pursuant to obligations under, ECHR, art 8; CFREU, arts 7 and 52.

[30] Citizens' Directive, arts 27–33. Restrictions on the right of free movement and residence are permitted on limited grounds, including public policy, public security, or public health.

[31] On same-sex marriages and free movement, see C–673/16 *Coman v Inspectoratul General pentru Imigrări and Ministerul Afacerilor Interne* [2018] ECLI:EU:C:2018:385.

[32] Citizens' Directive, art 13(1) and (2) state that the rule is for the benefit of those whose marriage or registered partnership is terminated. Art 13(1) provides that for the EU Citizen family members of EU Citizens, relationship breakdown 'shall not affect the right of residence of his/her family members who are nationals of a Member State'.

[33] Citizens' Directive, art 13 (edited for clarity).

Notably, this provision does not require the perpetrator of violence to be the person on whom the TCN is dependent for her migration status. Women who experience violence from other family members can rely on the rule if its requirements are met. The violence also does not have to have caused the relationship to break down, the duration of the marriage or registered partnership itself also being irrelevant. Article 18 of the Directive complements article 13(2), the former enabling TCNs who retain their rights pursuant to the latter to acquire permanent residence after five years. One can think of these provisions together as passing to the TCN spouse or registered partner, when 'particularly difficult circumstances' arise, both an independent route to permanent residence *and* the requirement to be economically active in particular ways.

The CJEU has, historically at least, defended and developed the rights of both EU Citizens and their family members.[34] Yet rights that appear to pertain to EU Citizenship generally continue to attach only to certain kinds of EU Citizens. These include those who move from one MS to another and/or those who engage in certain kinds of economic activity. The rights of residence given to those who are not *considered* to be economically active, or who are not self-sufficient, are much more limited. EU Citizenship is not, therefore, a 'fundamental status'[35] but a 'patchwork of personhoods'.[36] Gender, race, sexual orientation, and class all inform the type of EU Citizen who is, in fact, able to benefit from the rights that citizenship bestows.[37] This has negatively affected women who, for example, care for dependent relatives, but whose care work is not recognised as 'work'.[38] It has also affected pregnant EU Citizen women who were initially excluded from 'worker' status in some circumstances. While this has been partially remedied, significant issues remain. These include the length of time a woman's worker status is protected for, how long she has to return to work or find another job, and how her status may be impacted by, for instance, any illness or disability that she or her child experiences.[39] In contrast, a TCN woman whose care work enabled the economic activity of her EU Citizen family member did have her residence rights protected.[40] Similarly protected is the

[34] See, for example, Case C–85/96 *Martínez Sala v Freistaat Bayern* [1998] ECR I–02691, in which the non-economically active applicant was able to receive a benefit on the same basis as the citizens of the MS in which she lived.

[35] Citizens' Directive, recital 3.

[36] Charlotte O'Brien, '"I trade, therefore I am": Legal Personhood in the European Union' (2013) 50 Common Market Law Review 1643, 1643.

[37] Dimitry Kochenov, '*Ius Tractum* of Many Faces: European Citizenship and the Difficult Relationship between Status and Rights' (2009) 15 Columbia Journal of European Law 169; Cristina Juverdeanu, 'The Different Gears of EU Citizenship' (2021) 47 Journal of Ethnic and Migration Studies 1596.

[38] Compare, for example, Case C–77/95 *Züchner v Handelskrankenkasse (Ersatzkasse) Bremen* [1996] ECR I–05689 with Case 196/87 *Steymann v Staatssecretaris van Justitie* [1988] ECR 6159.

[39] C–507/12 *Jessy Saint Prix v Secretary of State for the Work and Pensions* [2014] ECLI:EU:C:2014:2007; Nicole Busby, 'Crumbs of Comfort: Pregnancy and the Status of "Worker" under EU Law's Free Movement Provisions' (2015) 44 Industrial Law Journal 134.

[40] Case C–60/00 *Carpenter v Secretary of State for the Home Department* [2002] ECR I–06279.

worker status of those who are temporarily prevented from working because of illness or industrial accident.[41] What is afforded by EU Citizenship is, consequently, a form of 'market citizenship'.[42]

Turning to the FRD, this Directive sets minimum standards for MS' treatment of TCNs who have 'reasonable prospects of obtaining the right of permanent residence' and who hold a residence permit issued by a MS which is valid for one year or more.[43] While more favourable rules can and do exist alongside those of the Directive, the FRD has been credited with contributing to a restrictive turn in States' family migration rules.[44] At the heart of the Directive is the obligation on MS to authorise the stay of certain family members, provided certain conditions are met.[45] The CJEU has held that this requirement imposes specific obligations on MS, obligations that correspond to defined individual rights.[46] In contrast to the Citizens' Directive, however, the FRD delineates a range of conditions that *may* be imposed by MS on TCN family members.[47] These and other restrictions should be interpreted strictly.[48] Conditions may relate to a TCN sponsor's resources and accommodation, and the family member's ability to integrate. The FRD also contains a number of significant derogations, including a provision that enables States to require a sponsor to have resided there for two years (and in some cases longer) before a family member may join them.[49] Family members able to reunite in an EU MS must be given 'every facility' to obtain the necessary permissions and then be granted a renewable residence permit of at least one year.[50] Subject to some restrictions, family members are given the right to access education, employment, self-employment, and training on the same basis as their sponsor.[51] Family members are, during this period, dependent on their TCN sponsor for their rights in the relevant EU MS. After five years' residence, a spouse, partner, or child (who has reached the age of majority) is entitled to receive an autonomous residence permit.[52] Such permits may also be granted to other family members, in certain circumstances.[53] If, however, the TCN sponsor's residence comes to an end and the

[41] Citizens' Directive, art 7(3)(a).
[42] For a timely discussion of which, see Cristina Juverdeanu, 'The EU Market Citizenship Paradigm: Embraced or Abandoned?' (2022) 44 Journal of European Integration 1011 and the books reviewed therein.
[43] FRD, art 3(1). The Directive also has rules that apply to refugees and their families; these are not considered here.
[44] Laura Block and Saskia Bonjour, 'Fortress Europe or Europe of Rights? The Europeanisation of Family Migration Policies in France, Germany and the Netherlands' (2013) 15 European Journal of Migration and Law 203.
[45] FRD, art 4.
[46] Case C-578/08 *Chakroun v Minister van Buitenlandse Zaken* [2010] ECR I-01839; Case C-153/14 *Minister van Buitenlandse Zaken v K and A* [2015] ECLI:EU:C:2015:453.
[47] FRD, arts 6–7.
[48] *Chakroun v Minister van Buitenlandse Zaken* (n 46).
[49] FRD, art 8.
[50] ibid art 13.
[51] ibid art 14.
[52] ibid art 15(1), although again, this may be limited.
[53] ibid art 15(2).

family member does not have an autonomous right of residence, States may withdraw or refuse to renew their residence permit.[54]

In contrast to the Citizens' Directive, the FRD does not contain any explicit reference to domestic violence. It does, however, contain a provision that may benefit some of its victims.[55] Article 15(3) states that:

> In the event of widowhood, divorce, separation, or death of first-degree relatives in the direct ascending or descending line, an autonomous residence permit may be issued, upon application, if required, to persons who have entered by virtue of family reunification. Member States shall lay down provisions ensuring the granting of an autonomous residence permit in the event of particularly difficult circumstances.

No reference is made in this provision to the economic activity of either the TCN sponsor or their family member.

The family members of EU Citizens appear to be advantageously placed in comparison with those whose rights and status are determined by the FRD and/or European States' own immigration laws.[56] The CJEU has, for example, required States to enable the TCN family members of EU Citizens to enter their territories, to give permission to remain to TCN spouses, and to grant residence rights (and the right to work) to the TCN parents of EU Citizen children.[57] The nature and extent of the rights accorded to TCN family members has, therefore, developed in concert with those granted to EU Citizens. Yet, it is evident from the structure of the Citizens' Directive that TCN rights remain predicated on the Citizen's right of residence.[58] The jurisprudence confirms this. The presence of a TCN wife in an EU MS is permitted and protected where it enables her husband to exercise the rights that attach to *his* citizenship. As the Court stated in *Metock* (2008):

> [I]f Union citizens were not allowed to lead a normal family life in the host Member State, the exercise of the freedoms they are guaranteed by the Treaty would be seriously obstructed.[59]

[54] ibid art 16(3).

[55] European Commission, 'Communication from the Commission to the European Parliament and the Council on guidance for application of Directive 2003/86/EC on the right to family reunification' (COM(2014) 210 final, 3 April 2014) point 5(3).

[56] Compared, for example, with the rules discussed in chapter 2. See also Helen Oosterom-Staples, 'The Family Reunification Directive: A Tool Preserving Member State Interest or Conducive to Family Unity?' in Anneliese Baldaccini, Elspeth Guild, and Helen Toner (eds), *Whose Freedom, Security and Justice? EU Immigration and Asylum Law and Policy* (Bloomsbury 2007).

[57] Case C–459/99 *MRAX v Belgian State* [2002] ECR I–06591; *Carpenter v Secretary of State for the Home Department* (n 40); Case C–503/03 *Commission v Spain* [2006] ECR I–01097; Case C–34/09 *Ruiz Zambrano v Office national de l'emploi* [2011] ECR I–01177.

[58] For example, Citizens' Directive, art 23.

[59] Case C–127/08 *Metock v Minister for Justice, Equality and Law Reform* [2008] ECR I–06241, para 62.

This reasoning was affirmed in *Iida v Stadt Ulm* (2012).[60] Here, the Court explained that rights conferred on TCNs are not autonomous rights to be enjoyed by '*those* nationals' but rights derived from the EU Citizen's freedoms.[61] As family members' rights are derivative they, like partners under the FRD or those subject to UK immigration law, are *made dependent* on another for their migration status and all the rights that flow from it.

The statuses fashioned by the Citizens' Directive and FRD are complex and fragmented. Status-based hierarches are created, like those in States' national migration laws, but these hierarchies generate disadvantage for both EU Citizens *and* TCNs. EU Citizen women are, for example, disadvantaged by a citizenship status which has not shaken off its market origins. The FRD's requirements on resources, accommodation, and integration may constitute indirect discrimination, both on the grounds of sex and intersectionally.[62] TCN family members are also disadvantaged by being made dependent on another for their rights and status. Here, the nature of any resulting deprivations will depend on whether or not their family member is themselves an EU Citizen or a TCN. In the case of the regime created by the Citizen's Directive, for instance, family members are made the adjuncts of EU Citizens and their economic activity. As will become apparent in the discussion that follows, the requirement to be so active may even pass to them in particular circumstances.

5.3 NA's Fight for Residence: Timing

5.3.1 NA's Case and Compounded Disadvantage

NA, it will be recalled, was a TCN who came to the UK as the family member of an EU Citizen worker.[63] NA was from Pakistan. KA was a dual national, being a citizen of both Germany and Pakistan. NA and KA married in September 2003 and moved to the UK in March 2004. KA was economically active as required by the

[60] Case C–40/11 *Iida v Stadt Ulm* [2012] ECLI:EU:C:2012:691.

[61] ibid para 67 (emphasis added). See further Sara Iglesias Sánchez, 'Fundamental Rights Protection for Third Country Nationals and Citizens of the Union: Principles for Enhancing Coherence' (2013) 15 European Journal of Migration and Law 137.

[62] Indeed, it is notable how many references concerning integration requirements have been brought in relation to women and minor children. For a discussion of the jurisprudence, see Patrycja Dąbrowska-Kłosińska, 'The Right to Family Reunion vs Integration Conditions for Third-Country Nationals: The CJEU's Approach and the Road Not Taken' (2018) 20 European Journal of Migration and Law 251.

[63] For the facts of NA's case, see Case C–115/15 *Secretary of State for the Home Department v NA* [2016] ECLI:EU:C:2016:259, Opinion of AG Wathelet, paras 11–23 (*NA (AG Opinion)*); *Ahmed (Amos; Zambrano; reg 15A(3)(c) 2006 EEA Regs)* [2013] UKUT 00089 (IAC); Bojana Asanovic, *Note on SSHD v NA Pakistan, C-115/15, AIRE Centre Intervening* (Resources for Members, Immigration Law Practitioners' Association, 28 July 2016).

Citizens' Directive, being, at various times, either employed or self-employed. The couple had two daughters, MA (born in 2005) and IA (born 2007). Both daughters were German. KA was violent to NA throughout their relationship. In October 2006, following an assault on NA who was at that time pregnant, and which involved the police, KA left the 'family home' and, two months later, the UK for Pakistan. Almost immediately after his return, KA wrote to the Home Office asking them to cancel NA's residence permit and to be informed when they had done so. In March 2007, KA purported to divorce NA by a *talaq* (an Islamic divorce) issued in Karachi, Pakistan. NA began divorce proceedings in the UK in September 2008. The decree absolute was issued in August 2009 and NA was granted sole custody of their two children. From January 2009 and September 2010 respectively, MA and IA attended school in the UK. Both NA's divorce and the entry of her children into school occurred *after* her EU Citizen husband had departed from the UK.

NA applied for permanent residence in the UK, relying in part on the domestic violence rule. Her application was rejected.

It will be recalled that under article 13(2) divorce 'shall not *entail loss of the right of residence*' (emphasis added) where 'this is warranted by particularly difficult circumstances'. The applicant also has to show that at the relevant point in time 'they are workers or self-employed persons'. There are thus two main elements to the rule: one that relates to timing, the other that relates to economic activity. NA's case concerned the first. The second does not appear to have been an issue, as NA was self-employed for a period following her divorce. On one interpretation, that adopted by the UK's Home Office, the rule protected a *current right of residence* at the point the relationship legally ended. For an applicant to have had such a right, she must be deriving it from her (soon to be former) EU Citizen partner (who must themselves be in the relevant MS in accordance with EU law). NA appealed against the decision to refuse her permanent residence and her case progressed through the appellate courts in the UK until the Court of Appeal referred four questions to the CJEU for a preliminary ruling.[64] One of these questions concerned how the domestic violence rule should be interpreted when the EU Citizen, on whom a TCN depended for the residence right she sought to retain, left the country *before* that right could be protected.

The nature and extent of NA's dependency on KA may be illustrated by reference to *Diatta* (1985),[65] a case which pre-dates the Citizens' Directive and concerned the rights of a TCN who was separated from her EU Citizen husband. The Court held that, in such situations, TCNs *only* have residence rights *while* their EU Citizen spouse is economically active in the country of residence and until the marriage is ended by divorce. Following *Diatta*, when a marriage ends or, as in

[64] *NA v Secretary of State for the Home Department* [2014] EWCA Civ 995, [2014] 7 WLUK 691; *Secretary of State for the Home Department v NA (Pakistan)* [2015] EWCA Civ 140, [2015] 2 WLUK 800.

[65] Case C–267/83 *Diatta v Land Berlin* [1985] ECR 00567.

NA's case, the EU Citizen departs, such derivative rights are lost. Article 13 of the EU Citizens' Directive was adopted to respond to the rights lacuna highlighted by the *Diatta* decision, putting 'safeguards' in place which should enable a TCN to retain her derived rights, including where domestic violence has occurred.[66] As a recital to the Directive explains:

> Family members should be legally safeguarded in the event of the death of the Union Citizen, divorce, annulment of marriage or termination of a registered partnership. With due regard for family life and human dignity, and in certain conditions to guard against abuse, measures should therefore be taken to ensure that in such circumstances family members already residing within the territory of the host Member State retain their right of residence exclusively on a personal basis.[67]

However, when called to rule on this issue again, in *Singh and Others* (2015),[68] the CJEU confirmed the *Diatta* position that where divorce occurs *after* departure, the TCN family member has no derivative rights to retain. Neither *Diatta* nor *Singh and Others* concerned domestic violence. If, however, the Court applied its reasoning in these cases to NA's predicament, her residence rights would be extinguished by KA's departure. This connection between residence rights and perpetrator conduct is significant because KA, like many abusive partners, sought to use NA's migration status as a source of control over her. It is telling that KA not only wrote to the Home Office to request that they cancel her residence permit, but that he also wanted to be informed when they had done so. That KA sought both NA's return to Pakistan and knowledge of when this might occur indicates that, had she been compelled to leave, she might have been at risk of further violence there—an issue I return to in chapter 8's Conclusion. This is not, however, the only way in which an EU Citizen could exercise control over their family member's status. A perpetrator of violence could threaten to depart from a MS, could stop working or being economically active, or could threaten to do so. Victims may also be deterred from reporting offences to the police. A victim may lose their residence rights if, for example, an abusive partner's work was affected by criminal proceedings, or if a perpetrator of violence was imprisoned.[69]

Finally, TCNs who, pre-Brexit, *had* a right of residence in the UK under EU law were able to work, to access welfare benefits and housing services, as well as

[66] European Commission, 'Proposal for a European Parliament and Council Directive on the right of citizens of the Union and their family members to move and reside freely within the territory of the Member State' (COM(2001) 257 final, 23 May 2001) 15 (European Commission, Proposal).

[67] Citizens' Directive, recital 15. The recitals set out the reasons for the relevant legislative act and its provisions.

[68] Case C-218/14 *Singh v Minister for Justice and Equality* [2015] ECLI:EU:C:2015:476.

[69] Time spent in prison is not legal residence under EU law, Case C-378/12 *Onuekwere v Secretary of State for the Home Department* [2014] ECLI:EU:C:2014:13.

services provided by local authorities and the NHS. These all enabled a victim of violence to support themselves financially, and to either maintain, or secure, alternative accommodation, including, if necessary, in a woman's refuge. TCN family members, or former TCN family members, who *did not* have an EU right of residence required permission to remain under immigration law and were, therefore, subject to the full panoply of 'no recourse' rules chapter 4 describes. These rules have had devastating, even lethal consequences for victims of violence.[70] They may also have affected the healthcare, financial, or other support that NA sought or received. Indeed, the Advocate General refers to NA being 'denied' key benefits because of her status.[71] While NA was able to maintain self-employment for a period following the breakdown of her relationship, we simply do not know what impact these exclusions and her precarity of status had, either on her or on her children.

5.3.2 The Judgment

In this, its first judgment on the EU's domestic violence rule, the Court devoted just one paragraph to NA's experience of abuse. The phrasing it adopts is significant:

> The marital relationship deteriorated subsequently. NA was the victim of domestic violence on a number of occasions.[72]

The Court does not attribute to KA, the EU Citizen, responsibility for this violence. Other key details are also omitted, including those that relate to KA's conduct before and after his departure from the UK. Similarly absent is a discussion of domestic violence or of discrimination. This partial account of NA's circumstances sets the stage for a decision that denies NA, and others in her predicament, an independent and secure migration status:

> Article 13(2)(c) of Directive 2004/38 must be interpreted as meaning that a third-country national, who is divorced from a Union Citizen at whose hands she has been the victim of domestic violence during the marriage, cannot rely on the retention of her right of residence in the host Member State, on the basis of that provision, where the commencement of divorce proceedings post-dates the departure of the Union Citizen spouse from that Member State.[73]

[70] Sheffield Safer and Sustainable Communities Partnership, *Learning from Domestic Homicide Review (DHR): Adult D* (January 2014). See also Charlotte O'Brien, 'The Pillory, the Precipice and the Slippery Slope: The Profound Effects of the UK's Legal Reform Programme Targeting EU Migrants' (2015) 37 Journal of Social Welfare and Family Law 111.
[71] *NA (AG Opinion)* (n 63) para 30.
[72] *NA (CJEU Judgment)* (n 9) para 16.
[73] ibid para 51.

Three other questions were asked of the CJEU in NA's case. These concerned rights that NA might have as the carer of EU Citizen children and those children's rights in the UK. Confirming the judgment of the UK's Upper Tribunal,[74] the CJEU found that NA had a right of residence under Regulation (EEC) No 1612/68,[75] on the basis that KA's children had the right to continue their education here.[76] Such a right is purely instrumental. The Court drew on the '(admittedly latently patriarchal) notion of the "primary caregiver"'[77] to regularise NA's position while her children attended school. Here, I focus on three interpretative moves made by the CJEU to justify its narrow interpretation of the domestic violence rule, contrasting these with the more rights-protective approach taken by the Advocate General.[78]

First, the Court starts from the premise that it can, and indeed ought to, transpose its reasoning in *Singh and Others* to NA's case.[79] TCN victims of violence should, following this logic, either divorce as soon as their relationship breaks down or leave.[80] By contrast, Advocate General Wathelet also refers to *Singh and Others*, but distinguishes it from cases involving domestic violence where victims may, he opines, be deterred or prevented from taking action to preserve their legal position because they fear the perpetrator of violence, because that perpetrator manipulates their migration status, or because they are simply worn down by their experiences.[81] The Advocate General is also alive to the fact that perpetrators of violence may seek to evade criminal penalties by departing from the country in which they committed offences, thereby 'effectively depriving' their spouse of their residence rights.[82]

Secondly, in reasoning that supports the characterisation of the EU's domestic violence rule as a 'regime of exception', the Court frames article 13(2)(c) as a 'derogation' from the general position that it is EU Citizens, not TCNs, who have rights of entry and residence in other MS.[83] This approach, which understands the rule as a provision relevant only in 'exceptional cases', provides further justification for denuding its protective capacity.[84] In contrast, Advocate General Wathelet starts

[74] *Ahmed (Amos; Zambrano; reg 15A(3)(c) 2006 EEA Regs)* (n 63).
[75] Regulation (EEC) No 1612/68 of the Council of 15 October 1968 on freedom of movement for workers within the Community [1968] OJ L257/2.
[76] ibid art 12. *NA (CJEU Judgment)* (n 9) paras 52–68.
[77] Cathryn Costello, *The Human Rights of Migrants and Refugees in European Law* (OUP 2016) 163. Costello made this observation in relation to cases like *Carpenter v Secretary of State for the Home Department* (n 40). NA's case provides a further example of this trend.
[78] For a full analysis of the case, see Catherine Briddick, 'Secretary of State for the Home Department v NA' (2016) 30 Journal of Immigration Asylum and Nationality Law 368.
[79] *NA (CJEU Judgment)* (n 9) para 37.
[80] Francesca Strumia, 'Divorce Immediately, or Leave. Rights of Third Country Nationals and Family Protection in the Context of EU Citizens' Free Movement: *Kuldip Singh and Others*' (2016) 53 Common Market Law Review 1373.
[81] *NA (AG Opinion)* (n 63) para 70.
[82] ibid para 72.
[83] *NA (CJEU Judgment)* (n 9) para 41.
[84] ibid para 42.

his analysis by acknowledging the precarity of NA's status and the exclusions that flow from it:

> After all . . . the Court's answers to the various questions put to it will determine whether NA is eligible for certain social security benefits and special non-contributory benefits which she is currently denied because of the restriction of the rights conferred by a right of residence based on Article 8 ECHR. A right of residence based directly on EU law would at the very least be such as to afford NA an increased level of legal certainty.[85]

The Court then moves to interpret article 13(2)(c) by reference to article 12, which, it may be recalled, concerns EU Citizens' departure. The fact that this provision does not enable rights to be retained provides the Court with its third justification for denying rights to NA.[86] That the EU Citizens' Directive has a general provision for cases which involve departure does not tell us anything, however, about the specific provision it has on domestic violence. These are not presented hierarchically, so the EU legislature has not indicated which provision should take precedence should more than one apply. Indeed, in the absence of such an indication, one might argue that the correct interpretative approach would be to treat the specialist rule as having precedence over the rule of more general application. Once again, the Court's approach departs significantly from the Advocate General's. Having addressed the domestic violence element of NA's case directly, the Advocate General opines that adopting a restrictive interpretation of article 13(2)(c) would be 'manifestly contrary' to the provision's protective objective.[87] He concludes:

> If the fact of being a victim of an act of domestic violence was regarded by the EU legislature as a ground for converting a derived right into an individual right, the recognition of such a right cannot depend exclusively on whether the perpetrator of those acts chooses to remain in the territory of the host Member State.[88]

It is telling that, when declining to follow the Advocate General's opinion, the Court failed to engage with, or even acknowledge, any of the domestic violence-specific arguments he made.

The Court does, at one point, refer to the Commission proposals which resulted in adoption of article 13(2)(c), recalling that its purpose was:

85 *NA (AG Opinion)* (n 63) para 30.
86 *NA (CJEU Judgment)* (n 9) paras 43–44.
87 *NA (AG Opinion)* (n 63) para 73.
88 ibid para 76.

> to offer certain legal safeguards to third-country nationals whose right of residence was dependent on a family relationship by marriage and who could therefore be open to blackmail accompanied by threats of divorce, and that safeguards were necessary only in the event of final divorce, since, in the event of *de facto* separation, the right of residence of a spouse who is a third-country national is not at all affected.[89]

The Court takes from this, however, that rights only require protection on divorce *and not departure*, because before a couple legally end their marriage, the TCN's rights do not require safeguarding.[90] This is very troubling. The Court was hearing NA's case precisely because she could not have ended her violent marriage before her partner's sudden departure.

NA legally divorces KA, she obtains sole custody of her children (presumably as a protection from potential abduction), she sets herself up as self-employed and maintains that employment. She resists first her husband's, and then the Home Office's, attempts to remove her from the UK. Yet, in eyes of the Court, NA is simply the primary carer of EU Citizens.[91] NA sought the stability provided by an independent and permanent right of residence. What she received from the CJEU was another precarious status, valid only during and dependent on her children's schooling. This 'positive outcome' to NA's case came ten years after KA left the UK, ten years during which her and her children's residence may have been in doubt, and during which she may have been excluded from support.[92] If NA as the survivor of domestic violence is absent from the Court's reasoning, so too is NA as the bearer of human rights. The Court simply did not engage with CFREU rights relevant to her situation, including the right to equality before the law (article 20), to be protected from discrimination, including on the grounds of sex (article 21), and to equality between men and women (article 23). The CJEU's jurisdiction to give preliminary rulings rests on its ability to, amongst other things, ensure EU law's compatibility with the CFREU.[93] Yet, when faced with ambiguity in its domestic violence rule, the CJEU failed to respond to, or even to acknowledge, the discrimination that NA had experienced.[94]

[89] *NA (CJEU Judgment)* (n 9) para 47.

[90] ibid paras 48–51.

[91] The possibility that NA might have obtained permanent residence on other grounds was raised by the Commission and confirmed by the Advocate General but not discussed by the Court. See Briddick, 'Secretary of State for the Home Department v NA' (n 78) for a discussion of this point.

[92] In *Ahmed (Amos; Zambrano; reg 15A(3)(c) 2006 EEA Regs)* (n 63) the Upper Tribunal found that NA could not be removed from the UK as to do so would be a disproportionate interference with her and her children's right to a private and family life. This decision may have offered NA a route to a permanent residence in the UK, but subject to a number of restrictions. We do not know what form of permission to remain NA eventually received.

[93] Joined Cases C–391/16, 77/17, and 78/17 *M v Ministerstvo vnitra* [2019] EU:C:2019:403, para 71.

[94] Such arguments were made on NA's behalf. Indeed, *Opuz v Turkey* App no 33401/02 (ECtHR, 9 June 2009) (which found that domestic violence was a form of discrimination against women, see chapter 3) was referred to in the domestic litigation, *Ahmed (Amos; Zambrano; reg 15A(3)(c) 2006 EEA*

Article 13(2)(c), as interpreted by the CJEU in NA's case, failed to provide a reparative response to the compounded disadvantage experienced by TCNs who were unable, for a variety of practical and/or legal reasons, to initiate divorce proceedings at the 'right' time.[95] In drawing this conclusion, it should be recalled that the factual matrix of NA's case was not unusual. Indeed, NA's circumstances appear to be almost exactly those that this rule was designed to address.[96] The judgment had significant implications for TCN victims of violence across the EU, implications that the Court was not unaware of. The CJEU had received arguments on the potential for perpetrators of violence to 'abuse', to draw on concerns expressed by the UK's Court of Appeal, their citizenship rights and exercise control over their partner.[97] Yet the CJEU made a decision that disadvantaged TCNs knowing, because the Advocate General had told them, that doing so enabled migration statuses granted under EU law to be manipulated by perpetrators of violence, including transnationally. To return to the language the Court used in *Metock*, 'normal family life'[98] in the EU following *NA* comprised the right to take your family with you when you moved and to abandon them, whichever was convenient. This did not have to be the outcome of the reference made in *NA*, as the Advocate General's opinion and a case that followed, *X v Belgian State* (2021),[99] demonstrate.

5.4 *X v Belgian State*: Economic Activity

If the decision in *NA* provided a 'shameful'[100] and, as we shall see, short-term answer to one set of questions concerning the domestic violence rule, it left unresolved a series of other issues. What would, for example, be the situation of a similarly situated TCN who did not have children (or EU Citizen children or children in education)? What would happen to a TCN who was not economically active at the right time or in the right way? It was this latter issue that came before

Regs) (n 63) [17]. In Case C–400/10 *J McB v LE* [2010] ECR I–08965, the CJEU held that a Regulation must be interpreted to ensure the protection of CFREU rights. The Court also reiterated that the meaning and scope of rights protected by the CFREU are the same as those protected by the ECHR.

[95] See *Baigazieva v Secretary of State for the Home Department* [2018] EWCA Civ 1088 for a discussion of when the relevant conditions of art 13(2) need to be met, as distinct from when rights are retained.

[96] European Commission, Proposal (n 66) 14–15.

[97] *NA v Secretary of State for the Home Department* (n 64) [21]. The Court of Appeal noted that there was considerable force in the arguments made that art 13(2) should be construed purposefully, so as to avoid potential abuse by EU Citizens in cases involving domestic violence or contested proceedings relating to children.

[98] *Metock v Minister for Justice* (n 59) para 62.

[99] *X v Belgian State* (n 12).

[100] Steve Peers, 'Domestic Violence and Free Movement of EU Citizens: A Shameful CJEU Ruling' (*EU Law Analysis*, 25 July 2016) <http://eulawanalysis.blogspot.co.uk/2016/07/domestic-violence-and-free-movement-of.html> accessed 2 August 2016.

the Court in *X v Belgian State*. Once again, my focus here is on the judgment's approach to both domestic violence and discrimination.[101]

In September 2010, X, an Algerian national, married a French national in Algeria. He travelled to Belgium to join his wife in February 2012. The couple had a daughter who was French. X, like NA, had permission to remain in an EU MS as the TCN family member of an EU Citizen. X's relationship ended in spring 2015 when domestic violence forced him to leave the family home. X's wife and daughter subsequently left Belgium for France. X's right of residence was, consequently, 'terminated' in March 2016. X challenged this decision and sought to remain in Belgium on the basis of the Citizens' Directive's domestic violence rule. In December 2017, X's application to retain his rights was refused because although he was in a 'difficult situation', 'he had not adduced evidence that he had sufficient resources to support himself'.[102] X appealed against this decision, the case generating a reference to the CJEU. X also initiated divorce proceedings in July 2018, the divorce being pronounced that same month.

As the Court notes, at the time that X sought to retain his rights as a victim of domestic violence, he met neither the timing nor the economic activity elements of the rule. Indeed, the divorce took place nearly three years *after* X's wife and daughter had left Belgium. The reference to the CJEU, however, concerned X's ability to support himself and whether or not the different treatment of TCNs in this regard under the Citizens' Directive, in comparison with the FRD, was discrimination contrary to articles 20 and 21 of the CFREU (on equality before the law and non-discrimination respectively).[103] The Court answered this question in the negative. TCN victims of domestic violence whose status was determined by the Citizens' Directive were not being treated unequally because their situation was simply not comparable to that of TCN victims whose status was determined by the FRD.[104] To reach this decision, the CJEU drew on one of the interpretative moves it used in *NA*, reiterating that Court's framing of the domestic violence rule as a 'derogation' from the usual EU law position on TCNs, one relevant only in 'exceptional cases'.[105] Notably, however, this framing justified a restrictive approach not to the timing of divorce but to the equality and non-discrimination analysis of the two rules before it.

On timing, the CJEU departed from its *NA* position on divorce and departure. Adopting the arguments made by Advocate General Wathelet in *NA* on precarity and control of status, the Court overturned its previous decision on this point, finding that rights could indeed be retained where divorce proceedings are initiated 'within a reasonable period following such departure'.[106] The nearly three

[101] A detailed analysis of the case being provided in Strumia, 'Speaking Too Little' (n 14).
[102] *X v Belgian State* (n 12) para 18.
[103] ibid para 20.
[104] ibid para 90.
[105] ibid paras 34–35.
[106] ibid para 43.

years that X took to end his marriage, did not, however, appear to the Court to represent such a period.[107]

On the CFREU, the CJEU drew on its case law on discrimination between EU Citizens and TCNs, to find that article 21 could not apply to differences of treatment between TCNs.[108] The Court then moved to article 20 and affirmed that those in 'comparable situations should not be treated differently and that different situations should not be treated in the same way, unless such different treatment is objectively justified'.[109] However, the CJEU found that while the Directives did indeed 'share the objective of ensuring protection for family members who are victims of domestic violence', they related to different fields, had different subject matters, and different objectives.[110] It is notable how, when unpacking these differences, the Court robustly affirms TCNs' position as dependent and derivative rights-holders. While acknowledging the aims of the Citizens' Directive's domestic violence rule and related provisions, the Court remains adamant that:

> those objectives of protection and integration are secondary to the primary objective of that directive, which is to promote the freedom of movement of Union citizens.[111]

In contrast, the FRD seeks to ensure the 'efficient management of migration flows'.[112]

Finally, the Court concludes that the regimes also differ in respect of the discretion given to MS with regard to their implementation domestically, such discretion being very limited in the case of the Citizens' Directive and much broader in relation to the FRD.[113] The Court draws on this to argue that any difference of treatment that victims are or may be subject to in relation to economic activity stems not from the Directives themselves, but the choices made by EU MS pursuant to that discretion.[114]

Following *NA* and *X*, a TCN victim of domestic violence may be able to secure an independent right of residence under the Citizens' Directive in the following circumstances. The EU Citizen spouse or registered partner must reside, or have resided, in the relevant EU MS in accordance with the Directive, being economically active as a worker or self-employed person, for example. While the

[107] ibid para 45.
[108] ibid paras 51–54, drawing on Joined Cases C-22/08 and 23/08 *Vatsouras and Koupatantze* [2009] EU:C:2009:344.
[109] *X v Belgian State* (n 12) para 57.
[110] ibid para 89.
[111] ibid para 82.
[112] ibid para 75.
[113] ibid paras 84–88.
[114] ibid para 89. The Court exaggerates this difference, as explained in Strumia, 'Speaking Too Little' (n 14).

TCN does now have a period in which to reflect on their position if their spouse or partner leaves the jurisdiction, they should nevertheless start divorce proceedings promptly.[115] Lastly, the TCN partner must also be economically active (or the family member of someone else who is).[116] This economic activity must be maintained for the requisite period if the TCN wishes to secure permanent residence. This requirement initially appears justifiable as the Directive requires no more of TCNs that it does of EU Citizens, the benefits of Citizenship accruing only to those who are economically active in particular ways (or, again, the family member of someone who is). A closer look at the discrimination argument made in *X* offers a different perspective on this, however.

The discrimination that the Court is being confronted with in *X v Belgian State* is discrimination on the grounds of migration status. TCNs whose rights are determined by one regime have to satisfy more onerous conditions than TCNs whose status is determined by another. As explained in chapter 2, an argument that seeks to reject potential comparators is one that is grounded in a prior claim as to the purpose and criteria adopted for the relevant distribution.[117] Recall *Hode & Abdi v UK* (2012),[118] an article 14 ECHR case on this point. At issue was a UK immigration rule that denied family reunion to the post-flight spouses of refugees. The UK argued that the migration statuses given to refugees could not be compared with those given to students and workers, as it wished to encourage the latter of these groups and not the former. The European Court of Human Rights (ECtHR) took a different view, finding refugees, students, and workers to be comparable as they were in a 'relatively similar situation'.[119]

An argument to the effect that the rules that apply to the family members of Citizens cannot be compared with those that apply to the family members of TCNs accepts without scrutiny the purposes set out above concerning the *rights* of EU Citizens versus the *control* of TCNs. Yet these are, to an extent at least, purposes which the CJEU itself manufactures through the 'unnecessary emphasis' it places on the 'distinction between the domains of Union citizenship law and of EU immigration law'.[120] This emphasis is used to obscure what the rules share: the protection of TCN residence rights in certain difficult, but relatively similar, situations. The comparator/equality assessment that the Court engages in is, therefore, one that is both artificial and denuded, inconsistent with its own case law and the broader international framework on discrimination in which that jurisprudence is imbricated.[121]

[115] Divorce (and divorce at a particular time) remains a 'gateway' requirement to the rule; this is particularly problematic in jurisdictions where the ability to divorce is restricted.

[116] Per the references to Citizens' Directive, art 7, in art 13.

[117] See further Denise G Réaume, 'Dignity, Equality, and Comparison' in Deborah Hellman and Sophia Reibetanz Moreau (eds), *Philosophical Foundations of Discrimination Law* (OUP 2013) 7.

[118] *Hode and Abdi v UK* App no 22341/09 (ECtHR, 6 November 2012), discussed in chapter 2.

[119] ibid para 50.

[120] Strumia, 'Speaking Too Little' (n 14) 1202.

[121] ibid 1211–12.

When I first wrote about NA's case, I drew on Joseph HH Weiler's critique of the then ECJ for defining what it means to be a citizen by reference to what it means to be an outsider; the former a rights-holder, the 'other' someone who can be stripped of her rights.[122] I argued that the CJEU's judgment in *NA* demonstrated the continued relevance of this analysis and criticised the Court's instrumentalisation of TCNs.[123] By adopting the Advocate General's Opinion in *NA*, the Court in *X v Belgian State* 'corrects' its overly restrictive interpretation of the rule. The CJEU's revised position on divorce and departure enables more TCN victims of violence to receive an independent migration status in the EU MS in which they have made their home. For them, a more secure or even permanent status (and with it the right to work, to claim benefits, or access other forms of State support) may be reparative of compounded disadvantage. However, the CJEU's equality analysis affirmed Citizens' rights at the expense of TCNs', continuing the latter's instrumentalisation and exclusion, both legally and from the EU's broader political community.

Finally, in chapter 2 I argued that some migration statuses, like those of partner or domestic worker, were based on stereotypes. Similar, but not analogous observations may be made here about EU Citizenship and the Directive's transfer, from the Citizen to the TCN, of the requirement to be economically active. First, the conception of citizenship that undergirds the Court's analysis is one that is informed by, and reflects, gendered stereotypes. As Charlotte O'Brien explains:

> Free movement and equal treatment are arguably the core citizenship rights, yet are asymmetrically enjoyed, according to an economic profile which is not gender neutral and prevents women from feeling the full protection of EU citizen status.[124]

Secondly, TCNs who obtain an autonomous right of residence through the domestic violence rule receive with it the requirement to be economically active in accordance with this gendered conception of labour. What is being provided here are the rights that accrue to *market citizenship*, to enter the workforce, and to be an economic actor. Such rights may be of little use to those whose caring responsibilities are not considered to be 'work' or who need time to recover from the violence they were subject to. *X v Belgian State* affirms the enduring nature of the disadvantage that EU Citizenship, in its current semi-market, semi-rights-based incarnation, generates for both Citizens and TCNs. The gendered and racialised stereotypes that animate the Court's approach to citizenship and economic

[122] Joseph HH Weiler, 'Thou Shalt Not Oppress a Stranger: On the Judicial Protection of the Human Rights of Non-EC Nationals—A Critique' (1992) 3 European Journal of International Law 65.

[123] Briddick, 'Combatting or Enabling Domestic Violence?' (n 11). Notably, arguments made here were referred to in Case C–930/19 *X v Belgian State* [2021] ECLI:EU:C:2021:225, Opinion of AG Szpunar, para 51.

[124] O'Brien, '"I trade, therefore I am"' (n 36) 1671.

activity, in relation to work, caring, and violence, may negatively affect both women and men including, potentially, X himself.[125] However, among migrant couples in abusive relationships, there would appear to be a relationship of inverse proportionality between the severity of abuse experienced and the TCN's ability to support themselves.[126] If this is correct, the Citizens' Directive's rule becomes less effective as the vulnerability of the individual it purports to protect increases, disadvantaging and potentially discriminating against women.

5.5 The UK's Domestic Violence Regime

5.5.1 A Concession and a Rule

This section shifts focus from the EU to the UK. It will be recalled that partners, whether same-sex or opposite-sex, married/civilly partnered or not, *may* all be able to join someone who is a British citizen, who is resident, or who is working in the UK. As I explained in chapter 2, different rules apply in different circumstances, but all the relevant provisions make the migrant partner dependent on another for their rights and status. Those who are the partners of people who are British or resident in the UK are dependent on them for the five years of their 'probationary period'. The partners of labour migrants may travel with them or join them in the UK, but they are also dependent for their migration status on the continuance of their relationship and the labour migrant's own compliance with the rules.

The UK's domestic violence regime of exception has two connected elements. The first is the MVDAC.[127] This concession, a policy existing outside the Immigration Rules, enables certain partners whose relationship has broken down because of domestic violence to receive a three-month independent permission to remain.

The second element of the regime, which can be found in the Immigration Rules' Appendix Victims of Domestic Abuse, provides for victims to receive indefinite leave to remain where certain conditions are met. At the heart of these is the requirement that:

> The relationship between the applicant and their partner must have broken down permanently as a result of domestic abuse.[128]

[125] See, for example, chapter 2's discussion of *Konstantin Markin v Russia* App no 30078/06 (ECtHR GC, 22 March 2012). On race, citizenship, and disadvantage, see Theodora Kostakopoulou, *Co-Creating European Citizenship: Policy Review* (European Commission, 2013) 26–28.

[126] Weiss, 'Transnational Families' (n 14) 874.

[127] Home Office, *MVDAC* (n 13).

[128] Appendix Victim of Domestic Abuse (n 2) VDA 4.2.

At first glance, this combination of concession and rule appears to offer a reparative response to compounded disadvantage, the regime providing victims with, first, short-term regularisation to secure support and, secondly, a route to permanent residence. This is not, however, what this concession and rule deliver.

Eligibility for the MVDAC is limited to those who have, or were last granted, a dependent permission to remain on one of a range of immigration routes. Included are the partners of those who are British or resident in the UK, of some European citizens,[129] of those with refugee protection, of members of HM Armed Forces, of labour migrants, and of students.[130] In contrast to the EU law provisions discussed above, those eligible include spouses, civil partners, and durable partners. Permission to remain under the MVDAC will be granted where the person's relationship has broken down due to domestic violence and they require a short, independent period of stay, with the ability to apply for public funds.[131]

The MVDAC is, on paper at least, open to those with a broader range of migration statuses than was the case with the Destitute Domestic Violence Concession (the DDVC),[132] the scheme which preceded it. There are, nonetheless, many migrants subject to compounded disadvantage who are unable to apply under the MVDAC.[133] Excluded are those granted permission as students or workers, for whom compounded disadvantage may arise where studies or employment are affected by violence. Those with permission as fiancé(e)s or proposed civil partners are ineligible for assistance, as are victims with no permission to remain. Also excluded are those who are the partners of those who are British or settled here, but who do not have permission in this capacity, as well as the partners of visitors.

As an applicant to the MVDAC is declaring that their relationship has broken down, their previous permission, held as a partner, will be varied to permission granted under the concession.[134] However, permission granted under the MVDAC cannot be extended (unless a valid application is made under, for example, the domestic violence rule). This means that those granted permission under the MVDAC can work and can access welfare benefits and support services, but have *just three months* to either regularise their position or leave the UK.

[129] The reference to European citizens here refers to EU, EEA, and Swiss citizens (n 10). See also Adrienne Yong, 'A Gendered EU Settlement Scheme: Intersectional Oppression of Immigrant Women in a Post-Brexit Britain' (2022) 32 Social & Legal Studies 756.

[130] Home Office, *MVDAC* (n 13) 6.

[131] ibid.

[132] The Destitute Domestic Violence Concession (DDVC, sometimes also referred to as DDV Concession) was only available to those who had permission as the spouse or partner of someone who was British or settled here. Home Office, *Destitute Domestic Violence (DDV) Concession* (5 February 2018).

[133] The 'Support for Migrant Victims Scheme', a trial scheme that was subsequently extended until 2025, may assist some of those excluded from the concession. It enables selected voluntary organisations to provide short-term support to a small number of migrant victims of gender-based violence.

[134] Home Office, *MVDAC* (n 13) 10–11. If a person is refused under this concession they have no right of appeal, no right to an administrative review, and no automatic right to have the refusal reconsidered.

The domestic violence rule provides victims with permanent residence in the UK, if certain conditions are met.[135] This independent, secure migration status offers a reparative response to compounded disadvantage. This rule differs from its EU counterpart in a number of key respects. First, like the concession, it is open to those granted permission as partners in a broad range of relationships, including durable relationships (whether same-sex or opposite-sex), which are excluded from the EU's rules. Secondly, and as intimated above, the domestic violence experienced has to be the *cause* of the relationship breakdown and this breakdown must be permanent. While the rule itself does not specify the kinds of evidence that an applicant must provide on this point, relevant guidance refers to protective orders, criminal convictions and cautions, and supporting letters from domestic violence support organisations.[136] Thirdly, the rule can be relied on at the point of relationship breakdown, not when the relationship ends as a matter of law. Fourthly, a person does not have to be in the UK to benefit from the rule. Applications can be made by those subject to transnational abandonment, enabling them to return to and then secure settlement in the UK.[137] Fifthly, those who meet the criteria receive a secure migration status immediately. Finally, the rule does not require anything of the applicant in terms of their financial position. Indeed, the MVDAC and associated guidance on application fees and welfare benefits assumes that many victims will be destitute and require support.

Centrally, however, the definition of partner under the domestic violence *rule* is significantly narrower than that of the *concession*. The rule's primary beneficiary group remains those granted permission as the partner of someone who is British or resident in the UK.[138] While this has been broadened to, for example, include the partners of refugees and of some European citizens, those who are the partners of workers or students are excluded from the rule's ambit.[139] These beneficiaries of the MVDAC will, in practice, be required to leave the UK once their three-month permission to remain has expired.[140] The guidance is clear that victims

[135] Appendix Victim of Domestic Abuse (n 2) VDA 4.2, VDA 9.1–10.2.

[136] Such guidance being subject to review by the Courts where it operates to undermine the effectiveness of the rule. *JL (Domestic violence: evidence and procedure) India* [2006] UKAIT 58.

[137] Appendix Victim of Domestic Abuse (n 2) VDA 4.3. See further Sundari Anitha, Harshita Yalamarty, and Anupama Roy, 'Changing Nature and Emerging Patterns of Domestic Violence in Global Contexts: Dowry Abuse and the Transnational Abandonment of Wives in India' (2018) 69 Women's Studies International Forum 67.

[138] Appendix Victim of Domestic Abuse (n 2) VDA 4.1 (a).

[139] Ibid VDA 4.1 (a), (aa), and (b).

[140] Unless, for example, another application can be made, including for international protection. The challenges of switching from one migration status to another are discussed in chapter 2. Here, this would be complicated further by the fact that a person would be switching from having permission to remain granted outside of the Immigration Rules. For pertinent examples of the kinds of situations where destitution and deportation may result from an application to the concession, see the case studies discussed in Home Office, 'Evaluating the Support for Migrant Victims (SMV) Pilot: Findings from a Process Evaluation' (*GOV.UK*, 4 August 2023) <www.gov.uk/government/publications/evaluating-the-support-for-migrant-victims-smv-pilot/evaluating-the-support-for-migrant-victims-smv-pilot-findings-from-a-process-evaluation> accessed 4 August 2023.

who do not do so will be overstayers, unable to access public funds, and at risk of removal.[141]

5.5.2 A Concession and a Rule Subject to Challenge and Change

Applications made under the domestic violence rule which are refused can be reviewed administratively. Refusals may also be appealed (in cases also involving human rights claims) or challenged via judicial review proceedings.[142] As will become apparent, the scrutiny of tribunals and courts has shaped the rule and concession discussed above, with discrimination law challenges being at the heart of their evolution. Relevant here is the ECtHR's article 14 jurisprudence on both sex and migration status, the former being potentially engaged by both the violence experienced and States' response to it.

In *A v Secretary of State for the Home Department* (2016),[143] the Inner House upheld a challenge to the domestic violence rule brought by the wife of a refugee who was, at that time, excluded from it even though domestic violence had caused her relationship to break down. As the case involved a discrimination challenge to the rule's scope, the Court was not concerned with whether the State *should* provide a migration status to victims of violence, but rather that, if it did so, the rule's beneficiary group was properly delineated. First, the Court affirmed that as women are 'significantly' more likely than men to be victims of domestic violence, an overly restrictive approach to eligibility would be indirectly discriminatory to women.[144] Secondly, the Court identified the measure's legitimate aim: the provision of an independent migration status to victims of domestic violence who had a reasonable expectation of making their lives in the UK.[145] Thirdly, the Court found that the rule's differential treatment of those granted permission as the spouses or partners of refugees could not be justified.[146] Here, the Court concluded that refugee spouses could be compared to the spouses of British Citizens or residents, but *not* to the spouses of workers and others:

> A person admitted to the country as a student or for work is very clearly someone admitted on a limited and temporary basis, entirely at the discretion of the state. The status of refugee, as has been pointed out, is declaratory. Once it has been determined to exist the state has no discretion, in terms of its international and

[141] Home Office, *MVDAC* (n 13) 10.
[142] *R (AT) v Secretary of State for the Home Department* [2017] EWHC 2589 (Admin), [2018] Imm AR 483.
[143] *A v Secretary of State for the Home Department* [2016] CSIH 38, [2016] SC 776.
[144] ibid [79].
[145] ibid [80].
[146] ibid [82].

> humanitarian obligations, but must grant asylum. The worker or student enters the country by choice; the refugee out of necessity. The circumstances in which refugee status may be lost are extremely limited, and can in no reasonable way be compared to the situation applying to a worker or student. Once refugee status is acknowledged, international obligations require the state to facilitate assimilation and naturalisation, again a situation quite different from that of a worker or student.[147]

This reasoning cannot be faulted for its recognition of the declaratory nature of refugee status and the obligations on States which flow from it. However, the judgment partially accepts the justification offered by the Home Office and endorses the rule's denial of status to victims whose position in the UK is deemed, by people other than the migrants concerned, 'temporary'. The Inner House in *A v Secretary of State for the Home Department* ensured the rule's expansion to the spouses and partners of refugees in reasoning that reinforced the exclusion of many women who may reasonably expect to have their life and home in the UK. While the purposes of the relevant rules were different, it is notable that the Court's approach here differs from that of the ECtHR in *Hode and Abdi* where these migration statuses were found comparable.[148]

R (on the application of FA (Sudan)) (2021)[149] concerned the spouse of someone who was British, but who did not have permission in this capacity. Indeed, the legal basis for the applicant's arrival and stay in the UK was unclear and contested. FA and her British spouse had two children. She left the family home before the birth of her second child, seeking the assistance of the DDVC (the forerunner to the MVDAC). She was denied it. A judicial review and appeal against its refusal followed, which, amongst other things, argued indirect discrimination on the grounds of sex, motherhood, and migration status.[150] The Court of Appeal acknowledged the 'unfortunate reality' that most victims of domestic violence are women.[151] It then engaged in tortuous reasoning to remain blind to the consequences of this for any delineation of the rule's scope, opining that, contrary to the approach in *A v Secretary of State for the Home Department*, the rule would only discriminate if more men than women benefited from it.[152] The Court then dismissed the appeal by finding that any differential treatment that did arise was justified by reference to the concession's 'underlying rationale',[153] to ensure that:

[147] ibid [66].
[148] *Hode and Abdi v UK* (n 118) para 50.
[149] *R (FA (Sudan))* [2021] EWCA Civ 59, [2021] 4 WLR 22.
[150] ibid [27], [35].
[151] ibid [44].
[152] ibid [44].
[153] ibid [48].

> a person *whose application for settlement* in the UK is dependent on her spouse or partner should not feel compelled to stay in an abusive relationship for that reason. Otherwise there is a danger that the immigration system itself will contribute to an injustice, because the victim of domestic violence may be exploited by her abuser precisely because her ability to apply for settlement will be jeopardised if she is no longer living with the abusive partner.[154]

R (on the application of AM) (2022)[155] was brought by a victim of spousal abandonment who was, again at that time, also unable to apply under the domestic violence rule. This challenge was slightly different from the others, in that it concerned geographical location (in or out of the UK), rather than sex or migration status. It was also 'unusual' in that there was no 'aim' to exclude those victims outside the UK, it was 'simply that the Defendant has not addressed her mind to the issue'.[156] This differential treatment could not, therefore, be justified.

Finally, *R (on the application of SWP)* (2023)[157] concerned the wife of a skilled worker. The case involved severe domestic and sexual violence, including one incident, interrupted by the couple's son, in which the perpetrator of violence, WP, attempted to suffocate the applicant while sexually abusing her.[158] Consonant with the account of compounded disadvantage provided in chapter 4, SWP felt unable to seek assistance from the authorities because:

> her husband specifically threatened that if she left him, she would be deported from the UK because her immigration status was dependent upon his.[159]

SWP sought the support offered by the DDVC, seeking to regularise her status using the domestic violence rule. The application and a subsequent claim for judicial review was dismissed, the judge who did so noting that:

> SWP is now living in difficult circumstances because she is neither able to work nor have recourse to public funds. She does receive minimal support of £77 for food and other basic necessities, despite her 'nil recourse' status. That is all that stands between her and destitution at present, unless she were to leave this country. Z is being provided with education at school. SWP wishes to teach and is currently doing volunteer work full-time at Z's school.
>
> She is very reluctant to return to WP but says she would consider this as a last resort, for her son's sake, rather than return to India where, she says, she would be

[154] ibid [46] (emphasis added).
[155] *R (AM) v Secretary of State for the Home Department* [2022] EWHC 2591, [2023] 1 WLR 732.
[156] ibid [74].
[157] *R (SWP) v Secretary of State for the Home Department* [2023] EWCA Civ 439, [2023] 4 WLR 37.
[158] ibid [18].
[159] ibid [16].

unable to provide Z with a good education, as it is too expensive. She hopes that this judicial review will enable her to obtain access to state benefits and, eventually, that she will be able to settle here with Z independently of WP and work as a teacher.[160]

The central discrimination argument made in this case concerned migration status.[161] The Court of Appeal upheld SWP's exclusion from the concession, proving true the threats her husband had made. The difference of treatment between SWP and other migrant victims of domestic violence, whether on a route to settlement or not, was rejected. A wide margin of appreciation was to be afforded in cases such as these, which involve economic or polycentric issues.[162]

These cases cumulatively disclose a lack of clarity on the relationship between violence against women and the ambit of the concession and rule. The analysis provided by the Inner House in *A v Secretary of State for the Home Department* on violence and indirect discrimination against women is replaced by confusion in *R (on the application of FA (Sudan))* (2021) and silence in the cases that followed. Relatedly, settlement is used to both identify comparators and justify differential treatment, these different elements of the analysis being effectively collapsed into, and reinforcing, each other.[163]

According to the ECtHR, differential treatment on the grounds of sex, a suspect discrimination law ground, must be justified by very weighty reasons.[164] In contrast, differential treatment on the grounds of migration status, not a suspect ground, is subject to a wide margin of appreciation.[165] Of concern here is whether or not the distinction drawn is manifestly without reasonable foundation.[166] In these cases, the Court's failure to understand the relationship between gendered violence and the rule's scope has produced a corresponding failure to provide the required level of scrutiny. In *R (on the application of FA (Sudan))*, for example, the rationale of the rule, settlement, 'justifies', in two short sentences, distinctions based on both migration status and sex.[167] If, however, adjudicators built on the reasoning set out in *A*, any proffered justification, in relation to settlement for example, would have to be sufficiently weighty. This is significant, because settlement itself is frequently used as a proxy to discuss and dismiss control over status in situations where victims may indeed have a reasonable expectation of making their lives in the UK.[168] SWP had such an expectation. She sought protection and an

[160] ibid [22] (paragraph numbers within the quote omitted for clarity).
[161] ibid [23], [42].
[162] ibid [49]–[50].
[163] ibid [60].
[164] *Stec v UK* (2006) 43 EHRR 1017, para 52.
[165] *Hode and Abdi v UK* (n 118) paras 39, 45, and 52.
[166] *R (FA (Sudan))* (n 149) [37]–[38].
[167] ibid [48].
[168] Following the reasoning in *A v Secretary of State for the Home Department* (n 143), *R (FA (Sudan))* (n 149), and as occurred in *R (SWP) v Secretary of State for the Home Department* (n 157). Per the

independent migration status. Doing so made her destitute and placed her at risk of deportation. The compounded disadvantage she was subject to was reinforced and, contrary to one of the identified purposes of the rule, she was forced to choose between safety and status. A higher level of scrutiny could enable this to be unpicked and the State's justification for denying her access to the rule assessed in its correct legal context: States' obligations to provide effective protection from violence.

5.5.3 Encountering the UK's Domestic Violence Rule: NA's Case Reimagined

Here, I return to NA's situation, reimagining it to explore what might have happened had she sought to rely on the UK's domestic violence rule and the MVDAC. Doing so provides insight into this regime's response to compounded disadvantage.

If NA had been the partner of someone who was British or settled here (rather than of an EU Citizen) she would, it appears, have been able to benefit from both the MVDAC and the domestic violence rule. NA was subject to domestic violence and that violence caused her relationship to permanently break down, as could be evidenced by the police's involvement and KA's subsequent departure from the family home. KA's location and economic activity (or lack thereof) would not impact upon NA's ability to apply for protection. Nor would it matter whether or not NA was economically active or able to financially support herself and their children. Indeed, the MVDAC would provide a secure foundation for her economic activity and/or enable her to receive public funds, including welfare benefits and housing support.

What if NA had a migration status that was dependent on someone who themselves needed permission to remain? If NA were the dependant of a skilled labour migrant, an analogous position to the one that she actually had, she would be eligible for three months of support under the MVDAC, but excluded from the domestic violence rule. If NA sought assistance via the concession, once the relevant three months had expired, she would be subject to the full panoply of exclusions discussed earlier, at risk of both detention and deportation. She would be in a similar position to that actually faced by SWP, who received short-term support before being compelled to either secure status on another basis or leave the UK.

The comparative simplicity of the MVDAC and UK's domestic violence rule, combined with the fact that the latter bestows permanent residence *on those eligible for it*, enables this regime to provide a reparative response to some victims'

arguments made in chapter 4, whether or not someone is on a route to settlement may be relevant in determining what kind of status they should receive from a regime of exception, but not their ability to access it.

experience of compounded disadvantage. Those eligible for the concession and accompanying rule are, however, only a small proportion of those who experience domestic violence and whose migration status may be affected by it. As NA's reimagined UK case illustrates, for some victims of domestic violence, seeking support under the MVDAC may, in practice, accelerate their loss of status and involuntary departure from the UK. Strikingly, this is even the case for women who are in fact the partners of those who are British or resident in the UK, but who do not have permission on this basis because of the violence to which they were subject.

5.6 Conclusion

This chapter has examined two domestic violence regimes of exception, considering the extent to which they provide a reparative remedy for compounded disadvantage. Migration status, disadvantage, and discrimination were discussed first in the context of EU free movement law. Here, the focus was on article 13(2)(c) of the Citizens' Directive and its ability to provide an independent and rights-bestowing status to TCN victims of domestic violence. The analysis then focused on the UK and a concession and rule that have developed in response to both political contestation and legal challenge.

Domestic violence is both a cause and a consequence of women's inequality, and the EU, which aims to eliminate such inequality,[169] has consequently committed 'to combat all kinds of domestic violence'.[170] Notwithstanding these strong legal foundations, the EU's emergence as an actor in the field of violence against women has been slow, piecemeal, and unsteady.[171] It was not, for example, until the adoption of a Directive and Regulation on protective orders, in 2011 and 2013 respectively, that measures adopted by the EU could be relied on by victims themselves.[172] EU initiatives have also been criticised for failing to recognise the discriminatory nature of violence against women and focusing instead on particular 'culturised' forms of it as experienced and/or perpetrated by non-European 'outsiders'.[173]

[169] Consolidated Version of the Treaty on the Functioning of the European Union [2012] OJ C326/47, art 8, see also arts 10 and 19(1).

[170] ibid, Declaration on Article 8 of the Treaty on the Functioning of the European Union.

[171] For a more positive assessment, see Matthias Möschel, 'The European Union's Actions in the Domain of Combating Gender-Based Violence' in Elena Brodeală, Ivana Jelić, and Silvia Şuteu (eds), *Violence Against Women under European Human Rights Law: From Supranational Standards to National Realities* (Edward Elgar 2024).

[172] Directive 2011/99/EU of the European Parliament and of the Council of 13 December 2011 on the European protection order [2011] OJ L338/2; Regulation (EU) No 606/2013 of the European Parliament and of the Council of 12 June 2013 on mutual recognition of protection measures in civil matters [2013] OJ L181/4.

[173] Celeste Montoya and Lise Rolandsen Agustín, 'The Othering of Domestic Violence: The EU and Cultural Framings of Violence against Women' (2013) 20 Social Politics 534. Contrast this with Shazia Choudhry, 'Towards a Transformative Conceptualisation of Violence Against Women—A Critical Frame Analysis of Council of Europe Discourse on Violence Against Women' (2016) 79 Modern Law Review 406.

It is, therefore, a profound disappointment that when the CJEU was given the opportunity to vindicate *women's* rights in *NA*, it failed to do so. The restrictive interpretation of an already restrictive rule had profound implications for victims of domestic violence across the EU who were unable to divorce at the 'right' time. The correction provided by *X* has significantly improved the position of those who are abandoned by the person on whom they depend for their status. The Court's affirmation of the rule's economic activity requirement, however, places the remedy it provides out of the reach of many. Indeed, the more vulnerable a victim is, the less likely it is that they will be able to either retain their rights or secure permanent residence. The EU has now adopted a Directive on violence against women.[174] With its criminalisation of female genital mutilation (FGM) and forced marriage, but silence on consent and rape, the Directive offers further evidence of the EU's 'othering' of both certain forms of violence and certain kinds of women.[175] A new and specific provision on access to shelters regardless of migration status may, however, improve the position of TCN victims of violence and is to be welcomed, even as the Directive leaves unaddressed one of the causes of their vulnerability to compounded disadvantage.[176]

Decades of feminist activism and strategic litigation have shaped and expanded the UK's response to violence experienced in the context of migration control. These strategies have yielded successes, of which the MVDAC is itself one. Litigation has, however, failed to subject the rule's restrictive scope to the correct level of scrutiny in discrimination law. Consequently, a regime that is potentially reparative of the compounded disadvantage experienced by some women subject to domestic violence continues to exclude many from its purview, with potentially devastating consequences.

The limited scope of each regime and the failure of the CJEU in particular to engage with the substantive legal issues that arose from NA's experience of domestic violence adds impetus to calls for both the EU and UK to ratify, *in full*, the Istanbul Convention. Article 59 of the Istanbul Convention provides for autonomous or renewable rights of residence to be granted to some migrant victims of violence against women. As we shall see, this provision draws on, but is significantly more expansive than, the EU's domestic violence rule. In chapter 7, I return to NA's case to evaluate article 59. In doing so, I reveal the potential of this Convention to provide reparative responses to the disadvantage generated by both EU and UK law.

[174] Directive (EU) 2024/1385 of the European Parliament and of the Council of 14 May 2024 on combating violence against women and domestic violence [2024] OJ L2024/1385 (Violence against Women Directive).

[175] On attempts to harmonise the rape definition, see Dilken Çelebi, Lisa Marie Koop, and Leokadia Melchior, 'Germany Blocks Europe-Wide Protection of Women Against Violence' (*VerfBlog*, 17 January 2024) <https://verfassungsblog.de/germany-blocks-europe-wide-protection-of-women-against-violence/> accessed 8 June 2024.

[176] Violence against Women Directive, art 30(3).

6
Regime of Exception or Regime of Readmission?

6.1 Introduction

This chapter is the second of three to focus on the regimes of exception. Here, I analyse rules that require either the UK or a European Union (EU) Member State (MS) to regularise the stay of some victims of trafficking—to grant them a residence permit. My focus is the Council of Europe Convention on Action against Trafficking in Human Beings (the Trafficking Convention).[1] I also consider the EU's Residence Permits Directive[2] and Trafficking Directive.[3] Some trafficked women may, of course, be recognised as refugees or protected from *refoulement* where returning them to their countries of origin would expose them to a real risk of persecution or other serious harm.[4] The European trafficking regime, like both the EU's and UK's domestic violence rules, operates alongside these protections, as well as States' obligations under human rights law, including the European Convention on Human Rights (ECHR)[5] and the Charter of Fundamental Rights of the European Union (the CFREU or Charter).[6]

[1] Council of Europe Convention on Action against Trafficking in Human Beings (adopted 16 May 2005, entered into force 1 February 2008) CETS 197.

[2] Council Directive 2004/81/EC of 29 April 2004 on the residence permit issued to third-country nationals who are victims of trafficking in human beings or who have been the subject of an action to facilitate illegal immigration, who cooperate with the competent authorities [2004] OJ L261/19.

[3] Directive 2011/36/EU of the European Parliament and of the Council of 5 April 2011 on preventing and combating trafficking in human beings and protecting its victims, and replacing Council Framework Decision 2002/629/JHA [2011] OJ L101/1.

[4] Pursuant to the Convention relating to the Status of Refugees (adopted 28 July 1951, entered into force 22 April 1954) 189 UNTS 137 and within the EU, Directive 2011/95/EU of the European Parliament and of the Council of 13 December 2011 on standards for the qualification of third-country nationals or stateless persons as beneficiaries of international protection, for a uniform status for refugees or for persons eligible for subsidiary protection, and for the content of the protection granted (recast) [2011] OJ L337/9. The legal and evidential requirements that those seeking refugee recognition must meet renders the protection these instruments offer unobtainable in all but a minority of cases. Satvinder S Juss, 'Recognizing Refugee Status for Victims of Trafficking and the Myth of Progress' (2015) 34 Refugee Survey Quarterly 107; Catherine Briddick and Vladislava Stoyanova, 'Human Trafficking and Refugees' in Cathryn Costello, Michelle Foster, and Jane McAdam (eds), *The Oxford Handbook of International Refugee Law* (OUP 2021).

[5] Convention for the Protection of Human Rights and Fundamental Freedoms (adopted 4 November 1950, entered into force 3 September 1953) ETS 5 (European Convention on Human Rights, as amended) (ECHR).

[6] Charter of Fundamental Rights of the European Union [2007] OJ C303/01 (CFREU).

Violence against Women and Regimes of Exception. Catherine Briddick, Oxford University Press.
 DOI: 10.1093/9780191959899.003.0006

Following the arguments I advanced in Part I, the regimes analysed here are examined by reference to whether, and to what extent, they afford those who have been subjected to compounded disadvantage a rights-protective permission to remain. I start by charting the development of the European trafficking regime, examining its content and the UK's shifting engagement with it. As I do so, I explain that the regime establishes victims' return, involuntarily if necessary, to be the default means by which a trafficking case is resolved. To analyse the Trafficking Convention's ability to offer a reparative response to compounded disadvantage, I draw on the legal proceedings that EK fought to remain in the UK.[7] I also use EK's case to examine relevant provisions in EU law. EK was, it may be recalled from chapter 1, from Tanzania. She entered the UK on a domestic worker visa but was trafficked into, and then within, the jurisdiction. Unlike NA (from the previous chapter), EK's reliance on the Trafficking Convention, in conjunction with the ECHR, did yield a positive result—she was granted permission to remain in the UK.

The Trafficking Convention defines trafficking as:

> the recruitment, transportation, transfer, harbouring or receipt of persons, by means of the threat or use of force or other forms of coercion, of abduction, of fraud, of deception, of the abuse of power or of a position of vulnerability or of the giving or receiving of payments or benefits to achieve the consent of a person having control over another person, for the purpose of exploitation.[8]

There are three elements to this definition. One, an action that relates to a person and their movement in some way: their recruitment, transfer, or receipt. Two, this movement is achieved through certain means: the use of force or the abuse of a position of vulnerability. Three, this action and these means are for a purpose: exploitation. The wrong that trafficking is concerned with is, therefore, a particular form of coerced, involuntary, or forced movement. This movement does not have to be across an international border, nor does the intended exploitation have to have occurred for the definition to apply. A person may have a migratory project, they may intend to leave their country and work in another, and yet they may nonetheless be trafficked. As in EK's case, this could be because a person is deceived as to the exploitative nature of their 'employment'. Consonant with the arguments made in chapter 3, and subject to the caveats detailed there, I understand some instances of trafficking to entail violence against women. A number of human rights are engaged in such cases, including the right to be free from slavery, servitude, and

[7] *EK (Article 4 ECHR: Anti-Trafficking Convention) Tanzania* [2013] UKUT 313 (IAC), [2013] Imm AR 895. EK is Elizabeth Kawogo. I refer to her as EK here in line with the approach taken by the domestic courts.

[8] Trafficking Convention, art 4(a).

forced labour, and the prohibition of discrimination.[9] Adopting such an approach does not denote uncritical endorsement of the way that trafficking is deployed in political debate or the legal regimes that have emerged to 'fight' it. It simply posits the existence of conduct that falls within both the trafficking definition and the conceptual account of violence against women I advance, grounding this chapter's evaluation of the European trafficking regime, per the legal and normative framework set out in Part I, in the latter.

Unlike the domestic violence rules considered in the previous chapter, the European trafficking regime, and international legal responses to trafficking more broadly, have been the subject of sustained and critical scholarly attention. Some of this attention has, to coin a phrase, generated more heat than light. It is helpful, therefore, to situate this chapter within the broader scholarly research and, in doing so, to foreshadow some of the arguments advanced in the pages that follow.

At the risk of oversimplification, one can identify within the literature concerned with international legal responses to trafficking two broadly sceptical approaches. The first is concerned with the 'significant collateral human rights damage' done by providing a 'context for developed states to pursue a border control agenda under the cover of promoting human rights'.[10] Relevant legal instruments, such work explains, approach trafficking 'first and foremost [as] a matter of criminality and an assault on state security and sovereignty'.[11] Measures adopted pursuant to anti-trafficking instruments empower States to 'protect' 'victims' through deterrence policies and the enforcement of border control—deportation.[12] They also make it harder for refugees to access jurisdictions that are safe, pushing people into ever more dangerous and deadly journeys and containing them in situations where grave human rights violations occur.[13] These instruments obscure the role of States in creating and compounding vulnerability to exploitation.[14] Associated

[9] Trafficking was brought within the ambit of ECHR, art 4 in *Rantsev v Cyprus and Russia* (2010) 51 EHRR 1; see also CFREU, art 5(3). As discussed in chapter 3, art 14 ECHR is not relied on in trafficking cases.

[10] James C Hathaway, 'The Human Rights Quagmire of "Human Trafficking" ' (2008–09) 49 Virginia Journal of International Law 1, 26.

[11] Audrey Macklin, 'Dancing across Borders: "Exotic Dancers", Trafficking, and Canadian Immigration Policy' (2003) 37 International Migration Review 464, 492.

[12] Bridget Anderson, 'Trafficking' in Elena Fiddian-Qasmiyeh and others (eds), *The Oxford Handbook of Refugee and Forced Migration Studies* (OUP 2014) 364–65.

[13] In relation to just one cause of this, carrier sanctions, see Tilman Rodenhäuser, 'Another Brick in the Wall: Carrier Sanctions and the Privatization of Immigration Control' (2014) 26 International Journal of Refugee Law 223. See also Thomas Gammeltoft-Hansen and James C Hathaway, '*Non-Refoulement* in a World of Cooperative Deterrence' (2015) 53 Columbia Journal of Transnational Law 235; United Nations Support Mission in Libya, *Desperate and Dangerous: Report on the Human Rights Situation of Migrants and Refugees in Libya* (Office of the High Commissioner for Human Rights, 20 December 2018).

[14] Consonant with the arguments made in chapter 3. See also Bridget Anderson and Rutvica Andrijasevic, 'Sex, Slaves and Citizens: The Politics of Anti-Trafficking' (2008) 40 Soundings 135; Judy Fudge and Kendra Strauss, 'Migrants, Unfree Labour, and the Legal Construction of Domestic Servitude: Migrant Domestic Workers in the UK' in Cathryn Costello and Mark Freedland (eds), *Migrants at Work: Immigration and Vulnerability in Labour Law* (OUP 2014); Shahrzad Fouladvand and Tony Ward, 'Human Trafficking, Vulnerability and the State' (2019) 81 Journal of Criminal Law 39.

anti-trafficking rhetoric also both victimises and eroticises certain racialised women.[15] Notably absent from the regime are either substantive rights for victims, to regularisation for example, or concrete measures that would improve their protection through, for instance, robust labour market regulation.[16] Not only does the regime provide States with the means to return victims of trafficking, by associating them with transnational organised crime, it also renders victims 'invisible' as refugees.[17]

Criminal law and migration control-based approaches to trafficking have not gone unchallenged, even if their dominance has not been displaced. Consequently, the second sceptical strand within the scholarship engages with its potential to protect forced or coerced migrants from (further) harm. Those working in this vein would echo much of the above, acknowledging that the 'true driving force' behind international efforts to respond to trafficking is States' concerns with migration and security.[18] The difference is, therefore, one of focus and emphasis, rather than substance. Such analysis seeks to situate the regime within the broader international human rights law framework.[19] It does so through a focus on victims' rights, States' responsibilities, and work promoting the provision of *unconditional* support to trafficked persons. It also ensures that the rhetorical use that 'ideal' victimhood is put to by States and others does not deflect attention from trafficked women's real and diverse experiences of violence and exploitation.[20]

My analysis of the trafficking regime draws inspiration from both critiques but seeks to advance the latter by paying close attention to the development of co-extensive obligations, obligations in the Trafficking Convention and the ECHR that operate alongside and interact with each other. My premise is that the

[15] Jo Doezema, 'Loose Women or Lost Women? The Re-Emergence of the Myth of White Slavery in Contemporary Discourses of Trafficking in Women' (1999) 18 Gender Issues 23; Rutvica Andrijasevic, 'Beautiful Dead Bodies: Gender, Migration and Representation in Anti-Trafficking Campaigns' (2007) 86 Feminist Review 24; Sally Engle Merry and Vibhuti Ramachandran, 'The Limits of Consent: Sex Trafficking and the Problem of International Paternalism' in Michael N Barnett (ed), *Paternalism Beyond Borders* (CUP 2016).

[16] Suzanne Egan, 'Protecting the Victims of Trafficking: Problems and Prospects' (2008) 1 European Human Rights Law Review 106; Janie A Chuang, 'Exploitation Creep and the Unmaking of Human Trafficking Law' (2014) 108 The American Journal of International Law 609.

[17] Susan Kneebone, 'The Refugee–Trafficking Nexus: Making Good (The) Connections' (2010) 29 Refugee Survey Quarterly 137, 139. In addition to the references at n 4, see also Anna Dorevitch and Michelle Foster, 'Obstacles on the Road to Protection: Assessing the Treatment of Sex-Trafficking Victims under Australia's Migration and Refugee Law' (2008) 9 Melbourne Journal of International Law 1; Udara Jayasinghe and Sasha Baglay, 'Protecting Victims of Human Trafficking Within a "Non-Refoulement" Framework: Is Complementary Protection an Effective Alternative in Canada and Australia?' (2011) 3 International Journal of Refugee Law 489.

[18] Anne Gallagher, 'Human Rights and the New UN Protocols on Trafficking and Migrant Smuggling: A Preliminary Analysis' (2001) 23 Human Rights Quarterly 975, 976.

[19] Anne T Gallagher, *The International Law of Human Trafficking* (CUP 2010).

[20] Drawing on Carolyn Hoyle, Mary Bosworth, and Michelle Dempsey, 'Labelling the Victims of Sex Trafficking: Exploring the Borderland between Rhetoric and Reality' (2011) 20 Social & Legal Studies 313.

'ideological capture' of feminist and rights-based approaches to trafficking is not yet complete.[21] To hold otherwise is to cede the field.

6.2 The European Trafficking Regime

6.2.1 Rights, Residence Permits, and Return: An Overview

In essence, the trafficking regime creates a process whereby victims of trafficking, having been identified as such by a 'competent authority', may be granted, in certain circumstances, first a period of reflection and/or recovery and secondly a residence permit. How someone is identified as a victim, and the rights that accrue to them on this basis, depend on whether their status is determined by EU law, the Trafficking Convention, or both.[22] This chapter examines the granting of residence permits under article 8 of the EU Residence Permits Directive and article 14 of the Trafficking Convention. These obligations have quite different legal sources: EU law on the one hand, human rights law emanating from the Council of Europe on the other. Consequently, they also have quite different means of implementation or incorporation, and of enforcement. MS must transpose EU Directives into their domestic law.[23] Directives may also have direct effect, enabling victims and their legal representatives to rely on them where domestic implementing measures are unclear, incorrect, or otherwise lacking in some way.[24] Individuals may, therefore, enforce the rights the relevant Directive provides before national courts and, if necessary, the CJEU—as NA attempted with the EU's domestic violence rule. In contrast, how a State Party to the Council of Europe's Trafficking Convention meets its legal obligations will vary and depend on issues including how that State's domestic legal order interacts with international law and what steps it has taken on or before ratification. An individual who seeks to enforce her rights under the Convention can only do so if national law provides for this. There is no supranational 'trafficking court'. Instead, the Convention is monitored by the Group of Experts on Action against Trafficking in Human Beings (GRETA).[25] Notwithstanding these

[21] Siobhán Mullally, 'Migration, Gender, and the Limits of Rights' in Ruth Rubio-Marín (ed), *Human Rights and Immigration* (OUP 2014) 175. Mullally also highlights the 'normative re-emergence of protective categories' that 'do little to enhance women's autonomy, agency, or equality' but which are relied on to justify the 'coercive interventions' of States. ibid 146.

[22] All members of the Council of Europe, forty-six States, have ratified the Trafficking Convention as have two non-member States: Belarus and Israel. While the Convention applies to all victims of trafficking, the EU Directives only apply to third-country national victims; see further n 44 and its accompanying text.

[23] On the failure of one State to do so, see Case C-266/08 *Commission of the European Communities v Kingdom of Spain* [2009] ECLI:EU:C:2009:311.

[24] Following Case 26/62 *Van Gend en Loos v Netherlands Inland Revenue Administration* [1963] ECR 1.

[25] Trafficking Convention, arts 36–38. The Committee of the Parties may then draw on GRETA reports and recommendations to engage with States on their compliance with the Convention.

and an array of other differences, the granting of residence permits to victims operates as a narrow exception, and one that is usually only temporary, to both the EU's and Council of Europe's default position of 'return or be removed'.

One can trace the contemporary origins of the European trafficking regime to the UN Convention against Transnational Organized Crime[26] and its Protocol.[27] It was from the latter, for example, that the European regime's definition of trafficking, set out above, was drawn.[28] The UN Trafficking Protocol is 'in substance very much an instrument of criminal law *as opposed to* human rights law'.[29] States have criminalised trafficking, as required by the Protocol, and have been enthusiastic about doing so.[30] Indeed, there is a pronounced tendency to over-criminalise through the adoption of more expansive definitions domestically in order to facilitate prosecutions.[31] In contrast, States are only encouraged to protect victims' 'privacy and identity' '[i]n appropriate cases and to the extent possible'.[32] States are also only required to '*endeavour* to provide for the physical safety of victims of trafficking' *within* their territory.[33] It is telling that the only clear obligations on States that concern victims arise in relation to their role as witnesses in criminal proceedings. States 'shall ensure', for example, that victims are given information on court proceedings and assistance to enable their views to be considered.[34]

The immigration position of victims of trafficking is dealt with in articles 7 and 8 of the Protocol. Article 7 briefly encourages States to 'consider' adopting measures to permit victims of trafficking to remain in their territory, taking into account 'humanitarian and compassionate factors'. In contrast, article 8 delineates detailed obligations on the 'repatriation' of victims. States in which the trafficked person last had a right of permanent residence are to 'facilitate and accept' their return.[35] They are also to assist in verifying the identity of a trafficked person, and to facilitate

[26] United Nations Convention against Transnational Organized Crime (adopted 15 November 2000, entered into force 29 September 2003) 2225 UNTS 209.

[27] Protocol to Prevent, Suppress and Punish Trafficking in Persons, Especially Women and Children, supplementing the United Nations Convention against Transnational Organised Crime (adopted 15 November 2000, entered into force 25 December 2003) 2237 UNTS 319 (UN Trafficking Protocol). For analysis that takes a longer view, see Jean Allain, *Slavery in International Law: Of Human Exploitation and Trafficking* (Brill 2013).

[28] Compare Trafficking Convention, art 4(a) with UN Trafficking Protocol, art 3(a).

[29] Jean Allain, 'No Effective Trafficking Definition Exists: Domestic Implementation of the Palermo Protocol' (2014) 7 Albany Government Law Review 111, 121 (emphasis added).

[30] UN Trafficking Protocol, art 5.

[31] Including by intentionally omitting the 'means element', for example in Belgium and Israel. Soumya Silver, 'Twenty Years After the Passage of the Palermo Protocol: Identifying Common Flaws in Defining Trafficking through the First Global Study of Domestic Anti-Trafficking Laws' (2021) 40 Yale Law & Policy Review 336.

[32] UN Trafficking Protocol, art 6(1).

[33] ibid art 6(5) (emphasis added). See also art 6(3), which invites States to 'consider' implementing support services for victims.

[34] ibid art 6(2).

[35] ibid art 8(1). An interesting requirement, as States are not usually obliged to admit former permanent residents.

re-documentation.[36] Overall then, the Protocol's provisions on victims' safety are of a lower standard than that required by human rights law, where States must respond to violence with due diligence and offer protection that is practical and effective.[37] The Protocol also establishes victims' involuntary return as the default means of resolving a trafficking case,[38] its drafters having rejected a proposal that required any repatriation to be both safe and voluntary.[39]

Both the EU and the Council of Europe replicated the UN Trafficking Protocol's migration control and criminal law-based approach to trafficking, but to differing extents.[40] While, for example, the 2002 EU Framework Decision[41] required MS to criminalise certain trafficking-related activities, victims were offered 'protection and assistance' only insofar as these arose through, or resulted from, criminal proceedings.[42] The Framework Decision did not address the immigration position of victims, the EU legal order not doing so until the adoption of the Residence Permits Directive.

The Residence Permits Directive explicitly links the provision of a short-term residence permit to the need to 'tackle illegal immigration at source' by incentivising victims to cooperate in criminal proceedings.[43] There is no explicit provision in the Directive that requires MS to identify victims of trafficking. Indeed, the wording of article 3(1), which refers to third-country nationals (TCNs)[44] who are, or have been, *victims of offences*, implies that the identification of *victims of trafficking* is inherently linked to criminal justice processes. Victims are then provided with 'information' and a 'reflection period' in order to decide whether they wish to cooperate with the authorities.[45] The duration and start of such a period are determined by MS' national law. In the Netherlands, for instance, the maximum reflection period granted is three months, a period that may not be extended.[46]

[36] ibid art 8(3)–(4).

[37] As discussed in detail in chapter 3.

[38] UN Trafficking Protocol, art 8(2); while a return is 'preferably voluntary', it does not have to be so.

[39] Hathaway, 'The Human Rights Quagmire' (n 10) 3.

[40] A similar, but not identical approach was taken in ASEAN Convention against Trafficking in Persons, especially Women and Children (adopted 21 November 2015, entered into force 8 March 2016). See further Ranyta Yusran, 'The ASEAN Convention Against Trafficking in Persons: A Preliminary Assessment' (2018) 8 Asian Journal of International Law 258.

[41] Council Framework Decision of 19 July 2002 on combating trafficking in human beings (2002/629/JHA) [2002] OJ L203/1.

[42] ibid, arts 1–3 and 7. Indeed, the assistance offered by art 7 (to adult victims) is that criminal offences be investigated whether or not the trafficked person has reported those offences to the relevant authorities.

[43] Residence Permits Directive, recitals 2, 9, 11, and art 1.

[44] Under EU law, countries that are not members of the EU, or countries whose citizens do not enjoy the EU right to freedom of movement, are 'third countries'. Regulation (EU) 2016/399 of the European Parliament and of the Council of 9 March 2016 on a Union Code on the rules governing the movement of persons across borders (Schengen Borders Code) (codification) [2016] OJ L77/1, art 2(5)–(6).

[45] Residence Permits Directive, arts 5 and 6. The reflection period does not, in and of itself, create any entitlement to residence.

[46] Case C-66/21 *OTE v Staatssecretaris van Justitie en Veiligheid* [2022] ECLI:EU:C:2022:809, paras 20–22.

As with the UN Trafficking Protocol, the Residence Permits Directive demands less of MS than is required by human rights law. Before the granting of any permit, for example, MS are only required to 'take due account of the safety and protection needs' of those who have been trafficked.[47] The special needs of victims, including 'the most vulnerable' victims, are to be attended to, with psychological assistance available 'where appropriate' and 'if provided by national law'.[48]

Article 8(1) of the Directive then states:

> After the expiry of the reflection period, or earlier if the competent authorities are of the view that the third-country national concerned has already fulfilled the criterion set out in subparagraph (b), Member States shall consider:
> (a) the opportunity presented by prolonging his/her stay on its territory for the investigations or the judicial proceedings, and
> (b) whether he/she has shown a clear intention to cooperate and
> (c) whether he/she has severed all relations with those suspected of acts that might be included among the offences referred to in Article 2(b) and (c).

Permits are to be valid for six months and may be renewed. Being granted such a permit is, however, contingent on first, there being criminal proceedings against any suspected trafficker(s) and secondly, the victim cooperating with those proceedings. This near-complete conditionality renders any assistance that is provided of 'dubious worth' to those it purports to benefit.[49]

In contrast, the Council of Europe's Trafficking Convention requires States to identify victims using independent, collaborative procedures.[50] The benefits granted to those identified are not dependent on cooperating with criminal proceedings. They include protection from discrimination, protection of private life, and the provision of material support to assist physical, psychological, and social recovery.[51] States are also required to establish compensation mechanisms and to protect victims from punishment for any involvement in trafficking-related criminal activities.[52] Pursuant to article 13, where there are 'reasonable grounds' for believing that a person has been trafficked, they are to be accorded a 'recovery and reflection period' of at least thirty days. After this, under article 14(1):

> Each Party shall issue a renewable residence permit to victims, in one or other of the two following situations or in both:

[47] Residence Permits Directive, art 7(2).
[48] ibid art 7(1).
[49] Egan, 'Protecting the Victims' (n 16) 111.
[50] Trafficking Convention, art 10.
[51] ibid arts 3, 11, and 12.
[52] ibid arts 15 and 26.

(a) the competent authority considers that their stay is necessary owing to their personal situation;
(b) the competent authority considers that their stay is necessary for the purpose of their co-operation with the competent authorities in investigation or criminal proceedings.

Following the above, States are not *required* to provide permits in *both* of these sets of circumstances. States will be complying with the Convention where, for example, they *only* grant residence permits to victims who are cooperating with criminal proceedings per article 14(1)(b), and not to those who are not so cooperating but who nevertheless wish to remain in their country of residence for personal reasons per article 14(1)(a).

Within the EU legal order, the Residence Permits Directive was followed by the Trafficking Directive, the latter replacing the Framework Decision.[53] Although the Trafficking Directive does not engage with the residence status of victims, one can nevertheless identify a shift of emphasis.[54] The recitals position trafficking as both a crime and a serious violation of human rights, referring to the CFREU in so doing.[55] As the CFREU also prohibits trafficking, it and the Directive are mutually reinforcing—the Directive giving effect to one of the Charter's fundamental rights, the Charter tilting the Directive towards a more rights-based approach. Trafficking is recognised as a gender-specific phenomenon that requires, where appropriate, a gender-specific or sensitive response.[56] Although the Directive does not address the question of *how* victims are to be identified, in language that echoes that of the Council of Europe's Convention, assistance and support, including safe accommodation and psychological assistance, 'shall' be provided to victims.[57] MS 'shall' also 'ensure' that victims have access to legal assistance and representation, as well as to existing compensation schemes.[58]

Overall, the rights that follow recognition as a victim of trafficking under EU law are more limited than those that follow from recognition as a victim under the Council of Europe's Trafficking Convention.[59] One example is

[53] Trafficking Directive, art 21.
[54] While the Trafficking Directive requires States to provide support unconditionally to victims, this requirement is 'without prejudice' to relevant provisions in either the Residence Permits Directive or 'similar national rules'. Trafficking Directive, art 11(3).
[55] Trafficking Directive, recitals 1, 4, and 7. The recitals set out the reasons for the relevant legislative act and its provisions. The Directive was adopted under Consolidated Version of the Treaty on the Functioning of the European Union [2012] OJ C326/47, arts 82(2) and 83(1) and so has judicial co-operation and criminal-law-based approaches to trafficking as its focus.
[56] Trafficking Directive, recital 3 and art 1.
[57] ibid art 11.
[58] ibid arts 12 and 17.
[59] For a detailed consideration of States' obligations, see Vladislava Stoyanova, *Human Trafficking and Slavery Reconsidered: Conceptual Limits and States' Positive Obligations in European Law* (CUP 2017).

illustrative: non-punishment. Here, the relevant protective provision of the Convention is broader than that of the Directive. While the former focuses on protecting victims from prosecution where crimes were committed because the trafficking victim lacked autonomy, the latter requires that any offence be a 'direct consequence' of a trafficking situation.[60]

In order to benefit from the protections offered by the European trafficking regime, the trafficked person has to be physically present in the host State. Yet 'the mere recognition' of an individual as a victim does *not* usually yield this result, under either EU law or the Trafficking Convention.[61] Indeed, the involuntary return of a trafficking victim to their country of origin or residence is the 'standard resolution' to their case.[62] The European Commission understands that conditionality, in residence permits and, therefore, in rights, is not 'fully coherent' with a human rights-based approach to trafficking.[63] Yet it is not proposing to remedy this, even though, in its proposal for an amended Directive, it is responding to other protection gaps, including on victim identification.[64] The position is slightly better under the Council of Europe's Trafficking Convention, in terms of the provision of assistance that is not conditional on cooperation with criminal proceedings and through some protections for those facing return. Nonetheless, the starting point remains that while return 'shall preferably be voluntary', it does not have to be so.[65] Following the UN Trafficking Protocol, the Convention also requires 'receiving States' to verify the identity and migration status of victims, to re-document them, and to facilitate return 'without undue or unreasonable delay'.[66] '[D]ue regard' is, however, to be given to the 'rights, safety and dignity' of the trafficked person, by both the State into which she was trafficked and the State to which she is returned.[67] These requirements were pertinent to EK's case, as we shall see. States are also obliged to establish repatriation programmes that avoid re-victimisation and which assist victims' reintegration.[68] Where residence permits are granted, if they

[60] Trafficking Convention, art 26, which refers to compulsion, compared with Trafficking Directive art 8.

[61] Stoyanova, *Human Trafficking and Slavery Reconsidered* (n 59) 443.

[62] ibid 133, in addition to the arguments made here.

[63] European Commission, 'Commission Staff Working Document Evaluation of the Proposal for a Directive of the European Parliament and of the Council amending Directive 2011/36/EU on preventing and combating trafficking in human beings and protecting its victims' (SWD(2022) 427 final, 19 December 2022) 50–51 (European Commission, Evaluation). See further Alice Bosma and Conny Rijken, 'Key Challenges in the Combat of Human Trafficking: Evaluating the EU Trafficking Strategy and EU Trafficking Directive' (2016) 7 New Journal of European Criminal Law 315.

[64] European Commission, 'Proposal for a Directive of the European Parliament and of the Council amending Directive 2011/36/EU on preventing and combating trafficking in human beings and protecting its victims' (COM(2022) 732 final, 19 December 2022). The proposals also broaden the definition of trafficking and enhance criminal-law-based responses to it. At the time of writing, the proposed Directive was awaiting adoption by the European Parliament and Council.

[65] Trafficking Convention, art 16(2).

[66] ibid art 16(1), (3)–(4).

[67] ibid art 16(1).

[68] ibid art 16(5)–(6).

are granted, they provide only a temporary stay on removal. As the Explanatory Report to the Convention explains, the '*[i]mmediate* return' of victims is 'unsatisfactory' because those who are so returned are unlikely to provide the authorities with information.[69]

In sketching the European trafficking regime, one can identify a move away from the UN Protocol's criminal law and migration control approach to one that is (comparatively) more rights-based. The former continues, however, to dominate, so much so that any theoretical advances made in relation to victims' 'rights' are in danger of being denuded, in practice, by the removal of those victims from the very States which have undertaken to uphold them. This tension is explored further in the sections that follow.

6.2.2 The UK's Engagement with and Disengagement from the European Regime

The international legal framework discussed in the previous section developed incrementally, and broadly consistently, along the lines I have described. In contrast, the UK's response to the protection of those who have been trafficked has not so much developed, as staggered. The UK has sometimes engaged with the European regime, sometimes disengaged, sometimes offered protection to victims, and more recently, has sought to strip it away. Opposition to immigration has been central to the breakthrough of populist leaders and politics, such opposition taking the form of animus towards European migration and in calls for religion- and race-based restrictions on movement.[70] The UK's erratic and contradictory approach to trafficking offers an almost paradigmatic illustration of the impact of a particular kind of populist politics on migration law and policy. Here, a combination of anti-trafficking rhetoric and allegations of victims' incredibility have been used to justify some of the most draconian legislation on the statute book: the Illegal Migration Act 2023 and the Safety of Rwanda (Asylum and Immigration) Act 2024. The use that trafficking was put to when this legislation was passed seems to confirm the fears of the first group of trafficking sceptics, discussed above. Yet something more is happening here. The UK discourse has shifted from one that 'protects' victims, by returning them 'home', to one that justifies deportation on the basis that those who have been trafficked, and who (consequently?) travel irregularly to the UK, pose some kind of threat.[71] This section provides a broad overview

[69] Council of Europe, *Explanatory Report to the Council of Europe Convention on Action against Trafficking in Human Beings* (CETS No 197) (2005) [181] (emphasis added).
[70] Christian Joppke, 'Immigration in the Populist Crucible: Comparing Brexit and Trump' (2020) 8 Comparative Migration Studies 49.
[71] Home Office, 'Illegal Migration Bill: Modern Slavery Factsheet' (20 July 2023) <www.gov.uk/government/publications/illegal-migration-bill-factsheets/illegal-migration-bill-modern-slavery-factsheet> accessed 11 May 2024.

of the UK's position. As with chapter 2, the analysis proceeds at a relatively high level of generality to capture the substance of relevant rules and processes as they change over time. The sections that follow focus on EK's case, using it to examine both the European trafficking regime and legislative developments in the UK.

The UK is primarily a dualist jurisdiction: it differentiates between national and international law and requires the incorporation of the latter into the former to be domestically enforceable.[72] The UK ratified the Council of Europe Trafficking Convention on 17 December 2008; it came into force in the jurisdiction on 1 April 2009. A combination of policy and legislation purports to give effect to the UK's obligations under the Convention, including through the creation of a National Referral Mechanism (NRM) for victims. In relation to EU law, the UK, when itself a MS, did not opt in to the Residence Permits Directive. The UK did not initially take part in the adoption of the Trafficking Directive but did opt in later.[73] Accordingly, the UK was required to implement its provisions from 6 April 2013 until 31 December 2020.[74]

Consonant with the criminal law-based approach discussed above, the UK's first substantive response to trafficking was to define and criminalise it. Legislation was amended and specific offences were created, all of which were consolidated in the Modern Slavery Act 2015.[75] The Act also created an Independent Anti-Slavery Commissioner and put in place a series of protection measures for victims.[76]

Parallel to these developments was the creation of the NRM.[77] The NRM is a three-stage process, now underpinned by legislation and statutory guidance,[78] which purports to identity, and then offer protection to, victims of 'modern slavery'.[79]

[72] For a detailed discussion, see Lord Lloyd-Jones, 'International Law before United Kingdom Courts: A Quiet Revolution' (2022) 71 International and Comparative Law Quarterly 503.

[73] Commission Decision of 14 October 2011 on the request by the United Kingdom to accept Directive 2011/36/EU of the European Parliament and of the Council on preventing and combating trafficking in human beings and protecting its victims, and replacing Council Framework Decision 2002/629/JHA [2011] OJ L271/49.

[74] For a discussion of the rights of trafficked persons following the UK's withdrawal from the EU, see Alison Harvey, *Human Trafficking and Article 2 of the Ireland/Northern Ireland Protocol* (Northern Ireland Human Rights Commission 2022).

[75] Modern Slavery Act 2015, ss 1–4 (offences). The UK's approach to victimhood is one that is derived from this criminalisation: a person is a victim of trafficking where they are the victim of an offence that the UK government has described as trafficking. See further Virginia Mantouvalou, 'The UK Modern Slavery Act 2015 Three Years On' (2018) 81 Modern Law Review 1017.

[76] Modern Slavery Act 2015, pt 4 (Independent Anti-Slavery Commissioner), pt 5 (protection of victims through the provision of a defence for victims who commit offences, the provision of special measures in criminal proceedings, the provision of civil legal aid, and the imposition of a duty to notify).

[77] The National Referral Mechanism (NRM) for victims of trafficking was first established in 2009, as part of the UK's ratification of the Trafficking Convention. It was later extended to cover all victims of modern slavery.

[78] Home Office, *Modern Slavery: Statutory Guidance for England and Wales (under s49 of the Modern Slavery Act 2015) and Non-Statutory Guidance for Scotland and Northern Ireland (version 3.8)* (22 February 2024).

[79] Modern slavery being defined as trafficking, slavery, servitude, forced or compulsory labour. See further Slavery and Human Trafficking (Definition of Victim) Regulations 2022, SI 2022/877.

Potential victims are identified by designated 'first responders'[80] who, with the (adult) victim's consent, refer their cases to a 'Competent Authority'.[81] The Competent Authority is responsible for deciding whether or not there are 'reasonable grounds' for believing that the individual concerned is a victim of trafficking or, if not, another form of modern slavery.[82] Following section 61 of the Nationality and Borders Act 2022, an individual who receives a positive reasonable grounds decision (RGD) is granted a period of recovery of (at least) thirty days. The Nationality and Borders Act 2022 reduced this period from forty-five days, a change characterised as a 'regressive measure' by Special Procedures of the UN Human Rights Council.[83] During this shortened period, a victim cannot be removed from the UK and is entitled to limited support, including accommodation and financial assistance.[84] During or at the end of this time, the Competent Authority has to make a conclusive grounds decision (CGD), to decide whether or not there are 'conclusive grounds' for believing that the individual is a victim of trafficking or another form of modern slavery.[85]

Victims whose migration status in the UK is insecure and who have a positive conclusive grounds decision *may* be granted 'Temporary Permission to stay as a Victim of Human Trafficking or Slavery', referred to here as 'VTS permission'. However, the bases on which permission may be granted, now set out in the Nationality and Borders Act 2022 section 65(2), do not appear to map onto *both* limbs of the Trafficking Convention's article 14. The former may preclude the granting of a residence permit to someone whose stay cannot be linked directly to their recovery from harm (eg where it arises from the needs of family members).[86]

[80] First responders include local authorities, police forces, certain parts of the Home Office, the Gangmasters and Labour Abuse Authority, and specialist NGOs such as the Refugee Council and Kalayaan. Different rules apply when the victim is a child.

[81] There are two Competent Authorities, the Single Competent Authority and the Immigration Enforcement Competent Authority. The latter is tasked with making decisions about foreign national offenders and about those whose protection claims are considered inadmissible, who are in detention and facing removal. The former deals with all other cases.

[82] Home Office, *Modern Slavery: Statutory Guidance* (n 78) 63–64, 133.

[83] 'The Nationality and Borders Bill and its compliance with the State's obligations under international law', Joint letter of the Mandates of the Special Rapporteur on trafficking in persons, especially women and children; the Special Rapporteur on the human rights of migrants; the Special Rapporteur on contemporary forms of slavery, including its causes and consequences and the Special Rapporteur on the promotion and protection of human rights and fundamental freedoms while countering terrorism (OL GBR 11/2021, 5 November 2021) 7.

[84] Through the Modern Slavery Victim Care Contract. The extremely low level of financial support provided, even in comparison with the support given to asylum seekers, has been the subject of litigation, *R (K and AM) v Secretary of State for the Home Department* [2018] EWHC 2951, [2019] 4 WLR 92; *R (MD and EH) v Secretary of State for the Home Department* [2021] EWHC 1370, [2021] WLR (D) 300.

[85] Home Office, *Modern Slavery: Statutory Guidance* (n 78) 63–64, 154.

[86] Compare Trafficking Convention, art 14(1)(a) with Nationality and Borders Act 2022, s 65(2)(a). See further Joint Committee on Human Rights, *Legislative Scrutiny: Nationality and Borders Bill (Part 5)—Modern Slavery (Eleventh Report of Session 2021–22)* (HC 964, HL Paper 135, 21 December 2021) [86]–[87].

Such an approach would not be in breach the Convention—recall that States are required to provide permits in just one of the two sets of circumstances listed (co-operation and/*or* personal circumstances).[87] This limited basis for granting permission, along with the reduced recovery period, are two examples of the UK's curtailment of victims' rights.

VTS permission may be granted for twelve months to enable someone to seek compensation in respect of their exploitation.[88] It may be granted for thirty months to assist a person to recover from harm or to enable them to cooperate in criminal proceedings.[89] Those with VTS permission can apply for welfare benefits and housing assistance, receive medical treatment, and access the labour market.[90] Positive CGDs do not, however, usually result in such short-term regularisation. Between 2014 and 2016, just 384 conclusively identified victims were granted discretionary leave to remain, the forerunner to VTS permission.[91] Those not granted VTS permission may be required to leave the UK if they cannot remain on another legal basis, or are not seeking permission through, for example, a claim for international protection.

Finally, there is no right of appeal against an adverse RGD or CGD, although these decisions can be reconsidered by the Home Office. Judicial review proceedings do enable reasonable or conclusive grounds decisions to be scrutinised to ensure that they are made lawfully, in accordance with those policies that give effect to the UK's obligations under the Trafficking Convention.[92] Indeed, relevant guidance 'must be construed so far as possible to give effect' to the UK's obligations under the Trafficking Convention (and EU law, when it was applicable).[93] Decisions also have to be made rationally, taking into account evidence provided by experts.[94] Decisions that are unlawful or irrational may be quashed and orders for them to

[87] On this, it is interesting to note the point made in Home Office, *Temporary Permission to Stay Considerations for Victims of Human Trafficking or Slavery* (8 June 2023) 8: 'From the date of this guidance the Secretary of State will grant VTS in the circumstances described in Article 14(1)(b) as mirrored in s65(2)(c) of the Nationality and Borders Act 2022 (NAB Act). The Secretary of State will also grant VTS in compliance with section 65 of the NAB Act. This is not because she considers that, other than s65(2)(c) as discussed above, this is required by ECAT (or any other international obligations), but because she has been bound to do so by Parliament as a matter of domestic law.' Thank you to Alison Harvey who drew this to my attention.

[88] Immigration Rules HC 590, Appendix Temporary Permission to Stay for Victims of Human Trafficking or Slavery, VTS 5.1.

[89] ibid VTS 5.1.

[90] ibid VTS 5.2.

[91] 'Immigration: Question for Home Office (UIN 68451, tabled on 20 March 2017, answered on 30 March 2017)' (*UK Parliament*) <https://questions-statements.parliament.uk/written-questions/detail/2017-03-20/68451> accessed 30 October 2023. It is possible that some of those who were not granted permission as victims of trafficking did receive other statuses (eg were recognised as refugees).

[92] *R (Atamewan) v Secretary of State for the Home Department* [2013] EWHC 2727, [2014] 1 WLR 1959; *R (PK (Ghana)) v Secretary of State for the Home Department* [2018] EWCA Civ 98, [2018] 1 WLR 3955 (in which EK's case is cited with approval).

[93] *MN and IXU v Secretary of State for the Home Department* [2020] EWCA Civ 1746, [2021] 1 WLR 1956 [85].

[94] *R (AB) v Secretary of State for the Home Department* [2015] EWHC 1490 (Admin).

be reconsidered made. In practice, many of those who seek protection as a victim of trafficking do so through both the NRM and asylum process. Consequently, the question of whether or not a person is a victim of trafficking may also arise in immigration or asylum adjudication, where a person appeals against a negative asylum decision or on human rights grounds.[95] In such circumstances, tribunals may make their own decision as to whether or not a person has been trafficked.

The Illegal Migration Act 2023 seeks to make a series of significant changes to the above. It requires the Secretary of State to 'make arrangements' for certain people's removal 'as soon as is reasonably practicable'—a duty to deport.[96] This duty applies to any person who has arrived in the UK irregularly, after 20 July 2023, without permission, and not 'directly' from a country in which their life and liberty are threatened.[97] This duty to deport is accompanied by a requirement to disregard claims and a power to detain. Consequently, it applies regardless of whether a person makes a claim for international protection, as a victim of slavery or trafficking, or for judicial review.[98] Such claims must be declared inadmissible without being assessed.[99] The Illegal Migration Act 2023 also significantly expands the Secretary of State's detention powers. Those subject to the duty to deport may be held as long as 'reasonably necessary'.[100] The ability to challenge decisions, either to deport or to detain, is limited. Even where a challenge to the duty to remove is successful, it does not enable the granting of a protection status or the rights contingent on it. At the time of writing, the main bulk of the Act's provisions are not in force.

Central to the Illegal Migration Act 2023 and the legislation it builds on is the deportation of those subject to its provisions to a safe third country. In *R (on the application of AAA (Syria) and Others)* (2023),[101] the UK's Supreme Court held that the Secretary of State's policy to remove protection seekers to the jurisdiction it had identified for these purposes, Rwanda, was unlawful because that country was not, in fact, safe.[102] In a move that has significant consequences for the UK's 'collaborative constitution',[103] this decision was met with the enactment of legislation requiring decision-makers to 'conclusively' treat Rwanda as safe.[104] The Safety

[95] See further *MS (Pakistan) v Secretary of State for the Home Department* [2020] UKSC 9, [2020] 1 WLR 1373.

[96] Illegal Migration Act 2023, ss 2 and 6.

[97] ibid s 2(2)–(6). See also s 2(11)(d) in relation to victims of trafficking and slavery.

[98] ibid s 5(1), on children see s 4, for whom there is a power, rather than a duty, to deport.

[99] ibid s 5.

[100] ibid s 12.

[101] *R (AAA (Syria)) v Secretary of State for the Home Department* [2023] UKSC 42, [2023] 1 WLR 4433.

[102] ibid [105]. See further Catherine Briddick and Cathryn Costello, 'Supreme Judgecraft: Non-Refoulement and the End of the UK-Rwanda "deal"?' (*VerfBlog*, 20 November 2023) <https://verfassungsblog.de/supreme-judgecraft/> accessed 23 November 2023; Catherine Briddick, 'When Treaties are Forbidden' (*VerfBlog*, 29 February 2024) <https://verfassungsblog.de/when-treaties-are-forbidden/> accessed 29 March 2024.

[103] Drawing on Aileen Kavanagh, *The Collaborative Constitution* (CUP 2023).

[104] Safety of Rwanda (Asylum and Immigration) Act 2024, s 2.

of Rwanda (Asylum and Immigration) Act 2024 also dis-applies key sections of the Human Rights Act 1998 and precludes courts and tribunals from having regard to interim measures indicated by the European Court of Human Rights (ECtHR).[105] At the time of writing, it seems unlikely that any removals to Rwanda will take place.[106]

The Illegal Migration Act 2023 is significant because of its explicit repudiation of the UK's international obligations to refugees, victims of trafficking, and others in need of international protection. In the words of two UN High Commissioners, it 'extinguishes' access to asylum for those who, fleeing persecution and other serious violations of human rights, are compelled to travel irregularly.[107] It also strips victims of trafficking and slavery of the already very limited protections described above. Section 22 of the Illegal Migration Act 2023 provides for the 'disapplication' of those provisions, outlined above, which provide for a recovery period and VTS permission. This 'disapplication' will enable the deportation of recognised trafficking victims.[108] It also enables any permission to remain that has been granted to a victim to be revoked.[109] A very narrow exception is created for some victims who cooperate with criminal investigations.[110] Even here, however, the Secretary of State is to assume that, unless 'compelling circumstances' require it, it is *not* necessary for victims to remain in the UK.[111] The Secretary of State is also required to consider 'any significant risk of serious harm to members of the public which is posed by that person'.[112] According to the Explanatory Notes, these changes involve the extension of certain public order disqualifications provided for by the Nationality and Borders Act 2023.[113] This means that disqualifications from assistance, applied to, for example, some foreign national offenders, are being extended to *all* those victims of trafficking for whom the duty to deport applies. This extraordinary change is justified on the basis of:

> a number of factors including the pressure placed on public services, the large number of irregular arrivals and the loss of life caused by arrivals from illegal and dangerous journeys, including via small boat Channel crossings.[114]

[105] ibid ss 3 and 5.

[106] For a summary of the position at the time of writing, see James Goddard, 'Illegal Migration: Dealing with Inadmissible Asylum Applications' (*UK Parliament*, 3 May 2024) <https://lordslibrary.parliament.uk/illegal-migration-dealing-with-inadmissible-asylum-applications/> accessed 11 May 2024.

[107] 'UK Illegal Migration Bill: UN Refugee Agency and UN Human Rights Office warn of profound impact on human rights and international refugee protection system' (*UNHCR*, 18 July 2023) <https://www.unhcr.org/uk/news/press-releases/uk-illegal-migration-bill-un-refugee-agency-and-un-human-rights-office-warn> accessed 31 October 2023.

[108] Illegal Migration Act 2023, s 22(1)–(2).

[109] ibid s 22(9).

[110] ibid s 22(3)–(4).

[111] ibid s 22(5).

[112] ibid s 22(3)(c).

[113] Nationality and Borders Act 2022, s 63(2).

[114] Explanatory Notes: Illegal Migration Act 2023 [147].

GRETA has expressed 'deep concern' that, if brought into force, these provisions would deny victims of trafficking the support they are entitled to under the Trafficking Convention.[115] This legislation does more than that, however, as with one legal and linguistic move, recognised victims of trafficking cease to be bearers of (albeit very limited) rights and are recast instead as threats to public order.[116]

6.3 EK's Fight for Residence: Residence as Reparation

EK, a Tanzanian national, worked as a domestic servant for her first trafficker, Mrs Alibhai, in Dar-es-Salaam for two years before accompanying her to the UK in July 2006 on a domestic worker visa. Having been trafficked into the UK, EK was later re-trafficked within the jurisdiction. EK's case was summarised by the Upper Tribunal as follows:

> 26. . . . The appellant was tricked into accompanying Mrs Alibhai on a false pretence and was left in the United Kingdom with Mrs Alibhai's parents, Mr and Mrs Dhanji. She was required to work for them attending to all domestic duties and cooking all meals. She worked from 7am until around 10.30 at night. She was fed only stale food, scraps or leftovers and was required to sleep on a thin mattress on the kitchen floor, although there was an unused spare bedroom in the house. The mattress had to be rolled up each night and kept outside in a garage. The appellant received no wages from the Dhanji family and was only allowed out of their house to attend church on Sundays. The appellant's passport was kept by the Dhanji family. Although she asked to be allowed to return to Tanzania on a number of occasions she was told that she could not do so until at least July 2007. The appellant was on occasions unwell whilst living in the Dhanji household but was required to work nevertheless. She was told that there was no one she could complain to about her conditions and that if she went to the police to complain they would not help her.
>
> 27. In the summer of 2007, with the assistance of a lady she had met at church, the appellant ran away from the Dhanjis leaving all of her possessions behind. She was given accommodation at the house of a Mrs Miriam Kilumanga. After some time, and with the assistance of the Tanzanian Embassy, she recovered her passport from the Dhanjis. She then realised that her original visa had only been

[115] '"UK's Illegal Migration Bill should be reviewed to ensure it complies with the anti-trafficking convention', says Council of Europe Expert Group on Trafficking' (*Council of Europe*, 29 March 2023) <www.coe.int/en/web/anti-human-trafficking/-/-uk-s-illegal-migration-bill-should-be-reviewed-to-ensure-it-complies-with-the-anti-trafficking-convention-says-council-of-europe-expert-group-on-trafficking> accessed 31 October 2023.

[116] For a judicial analysis of these provisions and their diminution of trafficking victims' rights, see *In re NIHRC* [2024] NIKB 35 [150]–[158].

> for a duration of 6 months and had now expired. Conditions at the Kilumanga household were little better than before. The appellant was manipulated by Mrs Kilumanga and required to work as a domestic worker for her. Again she was often required to sleep on a mattress on the floor. By early 2008 the appellant was aware that the poor health she had suffered from at the Dhanji household was worsening. She asked Mrs Kilumanga for help and was told that it was difficult for her to get medical attention without paying for it, as she did not have a visa. The appellant had no money. By the latter half of 2008 the appellant was aware of having real difficulties in breathing and sleeping on her left side. Her breathing was noticeably noisy. In September of 2008 she was taken by Mrs Kilumanga to see a solicitor in connection with her claim against the Dhanjis. Mrs Kilumanga interpreted for the appellant as she could speak very little English. The appellant understood the solicitor to have observed that she needed to go to a hospital or see a doctor. On her return home Mrs Kilumanga again insisted that it was very difficult for the appellant to obtain medical assistance as she did not have the correct paperwork. By early October 2008 the appellant was so ill that she was eventually taken to hospital as an emergency by Mrs Kilumanga and was admitted for a two week period. On her return to the Kilumanga household she was again put to work, despite her physically weak condition. She continued to attend for hospital appointments until July 2009. In March 2010, with the assistance of the organisation known as Kalayaan, the appellant was able to leave the Kilumanga household and was given accommodation by the Poppy Project. By this time her health was very poor.[117]

EK became involved with Kalayaan in (around) March 2009 when they arranged for her to attend English classes.[118] Kalayaan, a non-governmental organisation (NGO) and 'first responder', referred EK into the NRM in May 2010, at which point she also made a claim for asylum.[119] In doing so, she explained that she feared retribution and violence. On 25 November 2010, EK received a positive CGD.[120] On 26 November, just one day later, the Home Office refused EK's claim for asylum[121] and denied her permission to remain—a residence permit.[122] The refusal letter EK received did not engage with the UK's obligations under either the Trafficking Convention or the ECHR.[123] In July 2010, the Secretary of State issued removal directions against EK. She sought to challenge this decision

[117] *EK (Article 4 ECHR: Anti-Trafficking Convention) Tanzania* (n 7) [26]–[27].
[118] ibid [32].
[119] ibid [32].
[120] ibid [60].
[121] ibid [65]. Consonant with the analysis referenced at n 4 and n 17, this part of EK's appeal was characterised as 'a less easy fit' with the relevant refugee jurisprudence. *EK v Secretary of State for the Home Department* AA/16743/2010 (27 February 2012) [5].
[122] *EK (Article 4 ECHR: Anti-Trafficking Convention) Tanzania* (n 7) [65].
[123] ibid [65]–[66].

in the First-tier Tribunal (Asylum and Immigration) but was unsuccessful.[124] EK appealed, arguing that the Tribunal had erred in its approach to the relevant law, an argument that the Upper Tribunal accepted in part on 27 February 2012 ('the error of law determination').[125] The Upper Tribunal finally adjudicated on the trafficking elements of EK's case on 13 March 2013.[126]

EK did not only take legal action to seek to resolve her immigration position, she also initiated proceedings against the Dhanjis in an Employment Tribunal (ET). In August 2008, the ET awarded her £58,585 in recognition of the injury she had suffered and for her unpaid wages.[127] This award was not enforced because the Dhanjis were in receipt of welfare benefits.[128] Finally, EK also reported the Dhanjis' conduct to the police. They failed to adequately investigate her ill-treatment. EK made an application to the ECtHR in relation to this failure. This was struck out when the UK offered to pay EK damages and accepted, per chapter 3's discussion of positive obligations, that:

> the relevant authorities could have done more to investigate the applicant's situation with a view to possible criminal prosecution and conviction of those involved in her domestic servitude in the United Kingdom. This amounted to a procedural violation of article 4 of the Convention.[129]

EK entered the UK under British immigration law as a domestic worker. The rules that determined EK's migration status were a previous iteration of those discussed in chapter 2.[130] While restrictive, these rules did enable domestic workers to change employers and, crucially, to extend their permission to remain. That EK did not do either of these is attributable to the conduct of those responsible for her ill-treatment *in conjunction* with the Home Office's failure to follow the correct procedure for granting her permission to enter.

According to the policy that applied at the time EK sought entry to the UK, when determining a domestic worker's application, the entrance clearance officer should interview the applicant alone to ensure that they wish to travel and that they understand and consent to the conditions of their employment.[131] Those granted permission as domestic workers should then be given written information, in a

[124] ibid [1].
[125] *EK v Secretary of State for the Home Department* (n 121).
[126] *EK (Article 4 ECHR: Anti-Trafficking Convention) Tanzania* (n 7).
[127] *EK v Secretary of State for the Home Department* (n 121) [33].
[128] ibid [33].
[129] *Kawogo v UK* App no 56921/09 (ECtHR, 3 September 2013) 4.
[130] The post-2012 route is the subject of chapter 2. See further Siobhán Mullally and Clíodhna Murphy, 'Migrant Domestic Workers in the UK: Enacting Exclusions, Exemptions, and Rights' (2014) 36 Human Rights Quarterly 397.
[131] Home Office, *Immigration Directorates' Instructions* Chapter 5 *Section 12: Domestic Workers in Private Households* (December 2006) [3.2]; *EK (Article 4 ECHR: Anti-Trafficking Convention) Tanzania* (n 7) [24].

language they understand, about their migration status and their rights in the UK. Such information includes the fact that a domestic worker's passport should not be taken from her without her consent. Contrary to this guidance, EK was interviewed by an entry clearance officer in the presence of Mrs Alibhai and was given no information about her migration status, the conditions of her employment, or what to do if she needed assistance.[132] To draw on the Tribunal's language, Mrs Alibhai was therefore able to trick EK into accompanying her and then to leave her with her parents, Mr and Mrs Dhanji.[133] The Dhanjis then took EK's passport from her and informed her that her permission as a domestic worker prevented her from leaving the UK.[134] It was not until some months after she had escaped that EK recovered her passport and discovered that her permission to remain had expired.[135] Significantly, EK's migration status provided the Dhanjis with a source of control over her even *after* she had left them. In the 'error of law determination' the Tribunal reported that Mr and Mrs Dhanji had used 'underhand methods' to try and have EK deported before she could bring her employment law claim against them or regularise her stay.[136] Mr and Mrs Dhanji also used the exclusions attendant on EK's status as a source of control, denying her access to medical treatment and informing her that she could not seek assistance from the police.[137] It is striking how similar these attempts by the Dhanjis to manipulate EK's migration status are to those that NA was subject to (as discussed in the previous chapter). In both cases, the perpetrator(s) of violence sought to harness the coercive power of the State to facilitate their wrongdoing and to evade responsibility for it.

EK's migration status and its attendant exclusions were also used by Mrs Kilumanga to 're-traffic' EK and to secure EK's labour in her home.[138] EK had 'overstayed' her domestic worker visa and was excluded from receiving housing or homelessness assistance. We may infer, therefore, that EK was faced with the choice of either living with and working for Mrs Kilumanga or being homeless and destitute. Mrs Kilumanga also denied EK medical treatment, telling her that she could not access it without payment.[139] The control exercised by Mr and Mrs Dhanji and Mrs Kilumanga over EK's access to healthcare had profound consequences. In addition to having a 'severe, complex and chronic form of post-traumatic distress disorder' (PTSD) because of her ill-treatment, EK had tuberculosis.[140] By the time the Upper Tribunal heard her case, an expert concluded that without access

[132] *EK (Article 4 ECHR: Anti-Trafficking Convention) Tanzania* (n 7) [28]; see also [29], [32].
[133] ibid [26].
[134] ibid [26].
[135] ibid [27].
[136] *EK v Secretary of State for the Home Department* (n 121) [7], [50].
[137] *EK (Article 4 ECHR: Anti-Trafficking Convention) Tanzania* (n 7) [26].
[138] ibid [60].
[139] ibid [44], [57].
[140] ibid [51].

to specialist care, she would have only a 50 per cent chance of surviving until the age of 50.[141] Such treatment was not available in Tanzania.

While many migrants are adversely affected by the restrictions that flow from the statuses they hold, women subject to violence experience a compounded disadvantage when these restrictions exclude them from those 'assets' that provide 'resilience' to it.[142] While EK had permission to remain as a domestic worker, she had 'no recourse to public funds' but full access to medical treatment provided by the NHS. Once EK had 'overstayed' she was subject to all the no-recourse rules described in chapter 4. This meant being excluded from, among other things, the already very limited support available to migrants from local authorities. Significantly, then, when Mr and Mrs Dhanji and Mrs Kilumanga told EK that she was not entitled to help or assistance they were not (entirely) misrepresenting her situation. Similarly, while we do not know whether or not the Dhanjis' comments to EK about the police included a threat that any report of *their* behaviour might result in *her* arrest, we do know that this is what happens in many such cases.[143] Disadvantageous rules, in combination with Home Office failures, resulted in EK having a migration status that enforced her dependency, which was precarious and restrictive, and which enabled the violence and exploitation she experienced.

The Upper Tribunal ruled that the Home Office's decision to refuse EK permission to remain was not in accordance with the UK's obligations under article 4 ECHR, in conjunction with the Trafficking Convention.[144] The relevant Trafficking Convention articles were 12, 14, and 16 concerning assistance to victims, the granting of residence permits, and repatriation.

First, the Tribunal found that the Home Office's instructions concerning the proper procedure for granting domestic worker visas fell within the ambit of the UK's positive article 4 ECHR anti-trafficking obligations.[145] Secondly, the Home Office's failure to follow its own instructions breached EK's article 4 rights, a breach that directly contributed to her illness.[146] Thirdly, article 14 of the Trafficking Convention had to be considered alongside article 16, which requires States to return trafficked persons with 'due regard' for their 'dignity'.[147] Finally, as EK's poor

[141] ibid [52].

[142] To draw once again on Martha Albertson Fineman, 'The Vulnerable Subject: Anchoring Equality in the Human Condition' (2008) 20 Yale Journal of Law and Feminism 1.

[143] As discussed in Her Majesty's Inspectorate of Constabulary and Fire and Rescue Services, College of Policing and Independent Office for Police Conduct, *Safe to Share? Liberty and Southall Black Sisters' Super-Complaint on Policing and Immigration Status* (17 December 2020).

[144] *EK (Article 4 ECHR: Anti-Trafficking Convention) Tanzania* (n 7) [65]–[66].

[145] ibid [35]–[39], drawing on *Rantsev v Cyprus and Russia* (n 9).

[146] *EK (Article 4 ECHR: Anti-Trafficking Convention) Tanzania* (n 7) [41]–[45], [56]–[59].

[147] ibid [60]–[61], [64]. The Tribunal rejected the Home Office's contention that EK did not have rights under the Trafficking Convention (because she entered the UK before it was ratified) finding that she was entitled to assistance no later than the point at which she received a positive CGD under the NRM.

health was linked to the breach of her article 4 ECHR rights, EK could not be removed to a country where she would receive inadequate healthcare and have a reduced life expectancy with the necessary 'due regard'.[148] EK should instead be granted a long-term permission to remain in the UK, such a grant being both reparation for the breach of her article 4 ECHR rights and required by articles 12, 14, and 16 of the Trafficking Convention.[149] The Upper Tribunal's analysis of what would be reparative of EK's situation—a secure migration status—and the international legal sources it draws on to conclude this are entirely consistent with chapter 4's arguments on compounded disadvantage.[150]

6.4 Evaluating the Trafficking Regime

EK sought permission to remain in the UK as a victim of trafficking. She finally received it, following adjudication, three years after the Home Office recognised her as a victim of trafficking and six years after she escaped Mr and Mrs Dhanji. In her detailed and compelling analysis of European responses to trafficking, Vladislava Stoyanova draws on EK's case to advance two separate lines of argument. In her first engagement with the case, Stoyanova discusses the failure of the police to investigate EK's treatment in the UK, using it to contend that the regime's preoccupation with how people are recruited and moved deflects attention from the abuses to which they are subject.[151] The response of the police to EK's situation certainly seems to bear this out. Because Mr and Mrs Dhanji had not arranged EK's entry into the UK but instead had 'received' and exploited her, the police appear to have concluded that no action could (or should?) be taken against them.[152] The regime's preoccupation with migration control left EK *without* the protection of the criminal law. Its focus on EK's movement and the person responsible for it obscured the role of both Mr and Mrs Dhanji and Mrs Kilumanga in EK's exploitation. To recap and connect with my arguments on compounded disadvantage: the Dhanjis tell EK that if she goes to the police they will not help her *and this is true*.

This is not the only way in which the trafficking regime may exacerbate, rather than remedy, compounded disadvantage. That EK was trafficked into, and then within, the UK does not appear to have been disputed at any point in EK's legal case(s). However, EK's recognition as a victim of trafficking did not yield any

[148] ibid [64].
[149] ibid [59], [63]–[67].
[150] Including, for example, UNGA, 'Trafficking in Persons, Especially Women and Children, Note by the Secretary-General' (9 August 2011) UN Doc A/66/283 [13], [41].
[151] Stoyanova, *Human Trafficking and Slavery Reconsidered* (n 59) 311–12. This also occurred in *CN v UK* (2013) 56 EHRR 24.
[152] *Kawogo v UK* (n 129). That the UK did not have a specific criminal offence relating to 'forced labour' at the relevant time formed part of a related admission.

significant improvement in her situation. Indeed, it initiated a process that culminated in the Home Office seeking to deport her. Although we do not know exactly what support EK received and when, we may assume that she received accommodation, healthcare, and other assistance once she received a positive RGD.[153] During this period of 'reflection and recovery', EK was protected from removal.[154] However, just one day after she received a positive CGD, EK was denied permission to remain in the UK. She was issued with removal directions soon after. EK's recovery and reflection period provided her with a very brief period of support. It did no more, as the final outcome of EK's NRM referral was exclusion and attempted deportation. We do not know what impact the compounded disadvantage EK experienced had on her health and well-being. We do know that by the time her case was finally concluded by the Upper Tribunal, the complex PTSD EK suffered from was exacerbated by a 'severe, chronic, major depressive disorder with an unspecified time of onset'.[155]

EK's case and its resolution add further support to my arguments for the granting of a secure, rights-bestowing migration status to those who have experienced compounded disadvantage.[156] Whether or not the Trafficking Convention provides such a status depends not only on the circumstances in which permits are granted but also on their duration. Significant rights do accrue to the holders of residence permits, including in relation to material assistance and access to the labour market. The permission to remain that they provide is, however, one that is precarious. Residence permits' length, the circumstances in which they can be renewed, and under which their holder can (ever) receive permanent residence is determined by each State Party's own immigration law.[157] As demonstrated by legislative developments in the UK from the Nationality and Borders Act 2022 onwards, the flexibility accorded to States in these matters provides cover for victims' rights to be eroded when it is politically expedient to do so.

How is this position altered by the EU's contribution to the law on trafficking? Would, for example, EK have been identified as a victim earlier than she was, or have been granted a residence permit any sooner? Are those in comparable situations to EK in the EU assisted by those rules which permit regularisation or provide rights? The Residence Permits Directive does not, it will be recalled, establish how victims should be identified. It seems unlikely, therefore, to have been able to facilitate EK's identification, or that of victims facing similar predicaments. Although the Directive does provide for a 'reflection period', it does not require MS to regularise a victim's stay for its duration, offering only protection from

[153] Pursuant to the Trafficking Convention, art 12.
[154] Her stay *should also* have been regularised for this period. See further the commentary at n 158.
[155] *EK (Article 4 ECHR: Anti-Trafficking Convention) Tanzania* (n 7) [51].
[156] ibid [66]–[68]. Here, the Upper Tribunal referred to both the granting of permanent residence and the need to correct injustice.
[157] Trafficking Convention, art 14(1), (3), (4).

removal.[158] EK's treatment during and after any such period may not have been substantially different, therefore, had it been under the auspices of EU law.[159]

Moving from reflection periods to residence, if EK had received the former under EU law, the failure of the police to investigate her allegations against the Dhanjis would have precluded her from receiving the latter. This would have been the case even though EK did everything in her power to hold Mr and Mrs Dhanji responsible for their conduct. It is also highly unlikely that any residence permit that was granted under EU law would provide a reparative response to compounded disadvantage. While rights do accrue to its holder, permits are granted for a minimum of six months.[160] Permits may be renewed, but are in any event to be coterminous with the length of any criminal proceedings.[161] Permits may also be withdrawn in a range of different situations, including when investigations are discontinued.[162] Where a permit is not renewed or is withdrawn, the victim becomes subject to the relevant MS' ordinary immigration law, thus rendering her both detainable and deportable.[163] In relation to both recovery and residence, then, the Residence Permits Directive is significantly less rights protective than the Trafficking Convention, the former offering what is at best a precarious stay on deportation.

The UK's brief engagement with the Trafficking Directive did benefit some victims, enabling them to challenge exclusions in relation to legal aid and compensation.[164] Within the EU context, the Directive has been credited with improving cross-border cooperation and strengthening support and protection services.[165] The Trafficking Directive does, it will be recalled, have provisions on assistance to victims before, during, and after the conclusion of criminal proceedings, and on unconditional support.[166] This indicates that MS should have victim identification and support systems that are separate from criminal justice processes and proceedings. The vagueness of these, in combination with their deference to the Residence Permits Directive, makes it difficult to assess their potential benefit. The European

[158] Compare Residence Permits Directive, art 6(3) with Trafficking Convention, art 13(1). While the former does not create any entitlement to residence, the latter states that a victim's stay 'shall' be authorised. Note that my analysis here may be contrary to the position set out in *R (EOG) v Secretary of State for the Home Department, R (KTT) v Secretary of State for the Home Department* [2022] EWCA Civ 307, [2023] QB 351.

[159] Indeed, less is offered in terms of either rights or protection; compare Residence Permits Directive, arts 6(2) and 7, with Trafficking Convention, arts 13(1)–(2) and 12(1)–(2).

[160] Residence Permits Directive, art 8(3).

[161] ibid arts 1 and 8(3).

[162] ibid art 14.

[163] ibid art 13(2).

[164] See, for example, *Puthenveetil v Alexander and George* UKEATPA/0125/14/LA (14 February 2014) (on legal aid in an employment case); *CICA v First-Tier Tribunal* JR/1309/2016 (28 November 2016) (concerning the refusal to grant compensation to a victim of trafficking who may have stopped cooperating with the police).

[165] European Commission, Evaluation (n 63) 56–59.

[166] Trafficking Directive, art 11(1), (3), (4).

Commission has noted a series of concerns about the Trafficking Directive's lack of clarity on unconditional assistance, identifying divergent practice between EU MS in relation to the treatment of victims.[167] The Commission intends to address this and other shortcomings in its proposed amended Directive.[168] EK, however, required a secure migration status, one that would enable her to receive the long-term medical treatment necessary to treat her tuberculosis, trauma, and depression. The Trafficking Directive would not have been able to deliver this, nor can its provisions assist those who are similarly situated in EU States.[169] This will not change, even with the adoption of a new Directive along the lines the Commission suggests.

6.5 Sketching a Way Forward for the Regime of Readmission

Much of both the trafficking-specific literature and emerging 'soft law' argues for, or asserts as the appropriate remedy, victims' voluntary repatriation, in conjunction with the provision of compensation or other legal redress.[170] What is notably absent from such work is, however, an acknowledgement that for any return to be voluntary, a victim must be able to make a meaningful choice as to the country in which they live. This tension is particularly striking in the more recent work of the Committee that monitors the UN Convention on the Elimination of All Forms of Discrimination against Women (CEDAW),[171] the CEDAW Committee. In its General Recommendation 38,[172] the Committee attempts to focus on either voluntary return or return that is in a child's best interests.[173] The Recommendation itself, however, only protects from forced return in circumstances where to do so would, in any event, be prohibited as *refoulement*.[174] References are made to either refugee protection or the provision of residence permits on humanitarian grounds.[175] Yet the Committee declines to delineate the circumstances in which

[167] European Commission, Evaluation (n 63) 50–51.

[168] ibid 56–65. See also the text of the proposed Directive referred to (n 64).

[169] EK might have benefited from Trafficking Directive, art 9, which requires EU MS to investigate and prosecute trafficking offences. Had the Dhanjis been investigated/prosecuted, EK might have been granted permission to remain per the Residents Permits Directive. However, for the reasons given, this would not provide EK with a reparative remedy because of the precarity of any such permit granted.

[170] Josephine A Suchecki, 'Remedies for Victims of Human Trafficking under the Palermo Protocol and United Nations Basic Principles: A Case Study Analysis' (2019) 9 Notre Dame Journal of International and Comparative Law 126.

[171] Convention on the Elimination of All Forms of Discrimination against Women (adopted 18 December 1979, entered into force 3 September 1981) 1249 UNTS 13 (CEDAW).

[172] UN Committee on the Elimination of Discrimination against Women, 'General Recommendation No 38 on Trafficking in Women and Girls in the Context of Global Migration' (20 November 2020) UN Doc CEDAW/C/GC/38.

[173] ibid [90]–[91].

[174] ibid [89].

[175] ibid [25], [88].

permits, or even recovery and reflection periods, should be granted.[176] A secure, independent, and rights-bestowing migration status would enable a victim to access support and reduce vulnerability to further exploitation and re-trafficking. It would also empower victims to engage with legal proceedings against those responsible for their ill-treatment, including for lost wages and compensation. Crucially, by enabling victims to make decisions on residence and return, the provision of such a status is consistent with the obligations the CEDAW Committee does identify. Such a remedy is both effective and reparative.

In contrast, the return of a victim of trafficking to her country of origin, involuntarily if necessary, is, as Stoyanova and now I have argued, what both the Trafficking Convention and EU law envisage.[177] In most cases, the relevant instrument does not provide status but enables return and secures readmission. EK's case is, therefore, exceptional in two ways: first, in her being granted permission to remain at all, and, secondly, in her being granted permission for a significant period of time.

The second time Stoyanova engages with EK's case, she does so to argue that positive obligations under article 4 of the ECHR, in conjunction with its article 13 right to a remedy, may offer victims protection by providing for non-removal as a form of relief.[178] In developing her arguments on this and related points, Stoyanova contrasts the assistance provided to victims by the European trafficking regime with that available under the ECHR, arguing that the former inappropriately builds protection measures for victims within a criminal law enforcement framework.[179]

There are some limitations to this argument, the first of which Stoyanova herself explains. First, as discussed in chapter 3, although the ECHR can protect an individual from removal in certain circumstances, the ECtHR has not generally required States to grant those who cannot be so removed a migration status. Stoyanova recognises that this position may 'feed the precariousness of the migrant's situation'.[180] Marie-Bénédicte Dembour is surely more accurate when she characterises an analogous situation as one that leaves migrants in a 'Kafkaesque stalemate' unable to live within, or leave, their country of residence.[181]

[176] ibid [25], [92], [104].

[177] Stoyanova, *Human Trafficking and Slavery Reconsidered* (n 59) 131–33.

[178] ibid 421–26, in her discussion of 'Anna'.

[179] ibid 185.

[180] ibid 416.

[181] Marie-Bénédicte Dembour, *When Humans Become Migrants: Study of the European Court of Human Rights with an Inter-American Counterpoint* (OUP 2015) 448–49 in her discussion of *Bonger v the Netherlands* App no 10154/04 (ECtHR, 15 September 2005). The role that both domestic and European law plays in constructing illegality and holding people in such a legal/illegal limbo is also explored in detail in Cathryn Costello, *The Human Rights of Migrants and Refugees in European Law* (OUP 2016).

Secondly, EK is granted a migration status not under *either* the Trafficking Convention *or* the ECHR but because of the relationships *between the two*. The Upper Tribunal is able to respond to compounded disadvantage because it understands the obligations of the ECHR and Trafficking Convention to be co-extensive and complementary. Stoyanova provides a detailed analysis of the respective strengths and weaknesses of the trafficking regime and the ECHR. My account of the interaction between these two builds on this analysis, contributing to the rights-protective arguments advanced by the second group of trafficking sceptics discussed in the introduction above. It is, therefore, significant that post-*EK*, co-extensive obligations have been at the heart of a number of cases, including those decided by the ECtHR.

In *Chowdury and Others v Greece* (2017),[182] the ECtHR found that article 4 of the ECHR 'must be construed' by reference to the Trafficking Convention, the Court being 'guided' in this respect by interpretations provided by GRETA.[183] In this case, Greece had breached its positive article 4 obligation to conduct an effective investigation by disregarding the Trafficking Convention's article 13 requirements on recovery and reflection periods.[184] As in *EK*, the Court's reasoning on the interaction between the ECHR and Trafficking Convention produced a judgment responsive to the relationships between migration status, vulnerability to rights violations, and remedies for them.[185] Although the ECtHR did not go so far as to find that articles 4 and 13 of the ECHR give rise to a more general obligation to regularise victims' stay, the judgment is, nevertheless, a step in this direction.

That the positive obligations of article 4 ECHR should be delineated by reference to the protective framework established by the Trafficking Convention is now well established at both the national UK and supranational level—see, for example, *MN and IXU* (2020),[186] *MS (Pakistan)* (2020),[187] *SM v Croatia* (2020),[188] and *VCL and AN v UK* (2021).[189] Of course, there have been cases where UK courts and tribunals have taken a restrictive approach to victims' residence rights. In *R (on the application of SV)* (2022),[190] the Upper Tribunal declined to find that an initial residence permit should be granted for a period coterminous with a victim's medical treatment.[191] In discussing the obligations assumed under the Trafficking

[182] *Chowdury v Greece* App no 21884/15 (ECtHR, 30 March 2017).
[183] ibid para 104.
[184] ibid paras 121–22.
[185] ibid paras 95–97.
[186] *MN and IXU* (n 93) [43]-[49], [97].
[187] *MS (Pakistan)* (n 95).
[188] *SM v Croatia* App no 60561/14 (ECtHR GC, 25 June 2020) (in which GRETA intervened and on whose reports and interpretation the Grand Chamber relied).
[189] *VCL and AN v UK* App nos 77587/12 and 74603/12 (ECtHR, 16 February 2021) para 150.
[190] *R (SV) v Secretary of State for the Home Department* [2022] UKUT 39, [2022] Imm AR 445.
[191] ibid [77].

Convention, the Tribunal was at pains to observe that the relevant guidance was not unlawful because the 'core question' concerned not the granting of permits but their duration.[192] Notably, the applicant in this case did not rely on ECHR obligations. What the more rights-protective jurisprudence shares is a focus on co-extensive obligations and the use of one instrument to remedy the defects of the other. Such defects include the Trafficking Convention's preoccupation with criminal and migration law enforcement on the one hand and the ECtHR's silence on regularisation on the other. GRETA has consistently advocated for the provision of unconditional assistance, including residence permits, to trafficking victims.[193] The ECtHR's engagement with GRETA's work in *Chowdhury* and the cases that followed offers the prospect of further positive developments in this area. The potential of the Trafficking Convention to provide respite and even reparation for compounded disadvantage may depend on the extent to which these strands in the jurisprudence, and synergies between courts and treaty bodies, are built upon.

The interaction between trafficking-specific instruments and more general human rights protections has also proven significant in EU law. In *Staatssecretaris van Justitie en Veiligheid v SS, NZ and SS* (2023),[194] the CJEU drew on article 47 of the CFREU to find that applicants who are refused residence permits must, as part of the right to an effective remedy, be able to challenge that decision.[195] Here, a CFREU-protected right filled a lacuna in the Residence Permits Directive as neither it, nor indeed the Trafficking Directive, contains provisions that enable victims to challenge their potential misapplication. However, giving effect to the right to a remedy does not preclude one EU MS transferring a potential victim to another involuntarily.[196] The protection offered to victims here is, therefore, generally of non-suspensive effect.

Finally, absent from all the cases discussed here which involved either discrimination or violence against women is any engagement with relevant non-discrimination provisions. It will be recalled that the ECtHR has applied article 14 of the ECHR inconsistently in its domestic violence jurisprudence. The Court has

[192] ibid [77].

[193] Group of Experts on Action Against Trafficking in Human Beings (GRETA), *8th General Report on GRETA's Activities covering the period 1 January to 31 December 2018* (Council of Europe, 2019) 6, 41–44. See also GRETA, *4th General Report on GRETA's Activities covering the period 1 August 2013 to 30 September 2014* (GRETA(2015)1, 2015) 29: 'GRETA has urged 12 countries either to adopt legislation or to ensure that victims of trafficking can fully benefit from the right to obtain a renewable residence permit, including victims who for various reasons do not co-operate with the authorities.'

[194] Case C–338/21 *Staatssecretaris van Justitie en Veiligheid v SS, NZ, SS* [2023] ECLI:EU:C:2023:269.

[195] ibid paras 39–42.

[196] ibid paras 42–48. The removal was pursuant to Regulation (EU) No 604/2013 of the European Parliament and of the Council of 26 June 2013 establishing the criteria and mechanisms for determining the Member State responsible for examining an application for international protection lodged in one of the Member States by a third-country national or a stateless person (recast) [2013] OJ L180/31. MS can make more favourable arrangements for victims. The CJEU was also careful to distinguish between a potential victim's removal from one EU MS to another and removal that may be *refoulement*.

never applied it in relation to trafficking, even where gendered stereotypes concerning women's appropriate behaviour and credibility were central to its finding of an article 4 breach.[197] Judges within the UK have found discrimination on the grounds of migration status, but not on the grounds of sex. In *R (JP and BS)* (2019),[198] for instance, the NRM policy in place at the relevant time was found to unlawfully discriminate against victims of trafficking who were also asylum seekers.[199]

A discrimination law-based analysis could be integrated into the jurisprudence in two ways. First, the prohibition could be applied to the relevant violence or exploitation itself and secondly, it could root an examination of States' responses to such rights violations. On the latter, domestic workers are disadvantaged by being accorded those statuses that enforce dependency, which are precarious and restrictive, and which increase vulnerability to violence. These rules both discriminate against women, per chapter 2, and fail to offer effective protection from violence, following chapter 3's discussion of *Opuz v Turkey* (2009)[200] and *Rantsev v Cyprus and Russia* (2010).[201] States should reform such discriminatory rules and regularise those they have subjected to compounded disadvantage.

The reasoning advanced in EK's case provides broad support for these arguments, even absent an article 14 ECHR, non-discrimination, analysis. Here, the article 4 breach concerned not the rules in force at the time but the Home Office's failure to follow its then instructions. Yet those granted permission as domestic workers now are, like EK following the Home Office's failure, unable in practice to extend their permission to remain, change employers, or access services.[202] The position of *all* domestic workers under the *current*, more restrictive, rules is similar to that EK was in following the Home Office's failure to follow its *historic* policy. In advancing this line of argument, one may question whether the article 4 breach in EK's case can bear the weight of all that the Upper Tribunal attaches to it: she would otherwise have got her passport back, understood her 'rights', and secured medical treatment. Nonetheless, the relationship between breach and status established in *EK* is one that connects compounded disadvantage with an

[197] *SM v Croatia* App no 60561/14 (ECtHR, 19 July 2018) paras 73–80. The Court's reasoning was upheld by the Grand Chamber. Interestingly, the applicant in SM characterised her ill-treatment, trafficking for the purposes of prostitution, as gender-based violence and initially relied on art 14 ECHR, *SM v Croatia (GC)* (n 188) para 220. The Court proceeded without examining the discrimination element of her case. ibid para 221.

[198] *R (JP and BS) v Secretary of State for the Home Department* [2019] EWHC 3346 (Admin), [2020] 1 WLR 918.

[199] ibid [167]. Similar discrimination/migration status arguments were made in *R (IJ (Kosovo)) v Secretary of State for the Home Department* [2020] EWHC 3487 (Admin), [2021] 1 WLR 2923.

[200] *Opuz v Turkey* App no 33401/02 (ECtHR, 9 June 2009).

[201] *Rantsev v Cyprus and Russia* (n 9).

[202] See further James Ewins QC, 'Independent Review of the Overseas Domestic Workers Visa' (*GOV.UK*, 17 December 2015) <www.gov.uk/government/publications/overseas-domestic-workers-visa-independent-review> accessed 26 April 2024.

independent, rights-bestowing migration status. Adjudicators have, in other cases, also been alive to the impact of the exclusions discussed in chapter 4 on victims of trafficking and have situated regularisation as an appropriate response to these.[203] The trafficking regime, in and of itself, cannot deliver such a remedy. I have argued here, however, that elements of it, interpreted in conjunction with human rights law, may be able to do so. Such reasoning, which is consistent with GRETA's position on unconditional assistance and residence, could be used to assert a victim's right to regularisation in a broader range of circumstances than is currently the case. It may also provide a means of contesting some of the UK's backsliding on refugee and trafficking victims' rights. On the Nationality and Borders Act 2022, national courts and tribunals could interpret section 65(2) on residence permits to acknowledge that a victim's (broader?) personal circumstances are determinative of their recovery. On the Illegal Migration Act 2023, the ECtHR could yet be called on to apply co-extensive ECHR and Trafficking Convention obligations to protect victims from removal from the UK to countries deemed 'safe' and to ensure their rights within it.

6.6 Conclusion

Criminalisation, enhanced border control measures, and mobility suppression: these are the responses States adopt under the guise of protecting trafficking victims, but which are harmful to them and others. Such responses are not all that the trafficking regime offers or provides, however. A European trafficking regime has emerged, one that departs in several key respects from the UN Protocol that inspired it. A more rights-based approach to trafficking and its victims is, for example, identifiable within both the Trafficking Convention and Residence Permits Directive. The Convention and Directive do, of course, differ from each other in several important respects. In relation to the residence rights they create, a central difference concerns the relevant permits' conditionality. The former instrument permits, but does not require, residence permits to be granted regardless of a victim's cooperation with criminal proceedings. In contrast, regularisation under the latter Directive depends entirely on such cooperation. The tension within and between both, between responses rooted in criminal law and migration control and those rooted in rights, have yet to be resolved. This is nowhere more evident than in the fact that, regardless of its legal source, *if* a victim is granted a residence permit, it may only defer and not preclude their subsequent deportation.

The obligations placed on States by the trafficking regime are significantly more complex and less clearly defined than the domestic violence rules considered in

[203] Albeit for the short term, see the discussion in *R (EOG), R (KTT)* (n 158) [40].

the previous chapter. Consequently, while NA's case could found broader claims about the shortcomings of the EU's domestic violence rule, one needs to be cautious about relying on EK's case, decided in the UK, to advance analogous claims about either the Trafficking Convention or EU law. This caveat notwithstanding, the analysis advanced here indicates that the tension between rights and return explored in this chapter may sometimes be resolved in an individual's favour. As *EK* demonstrates and *Chowdury* indicates, when trafficking-specific instruments are interpreted alongside those that offer broader human rights protections, a right of residence, even if of only short duration, may result. The development of co-extensive obligations, whether under the Trafficking Convention and ECHR, or between the Residence Permits Directive and CFREU, has improved the ability of the regime(s) to respond to compounded disadvantage, albeit from a very low base. Within the context of the UK, these developments may enable trafficking victims to secure more rights-protective interpretations of regressive legislation from domestic courts and contest any attempt to deport them before international ones.

7
The Istanbul Convention, an Alternative Approach?

7.1 Introduction

The Council of Europe Convention on Preventing and Combating Violence against Women and Domestic Violence (the Istanbul Convention)[1] is only the second international legal instrument to focus on violence against women.[2] It has, at present, been ratified by thirty-eight States and the European Union (EU). It has also been denounced by Turkey and subject to a range of reservations and interpretative declarations. The Convention is 'unique' and 'innovative' in rooting in international human rights law (that concerned with discrimination against women, as described in chapter 3) and Council of Europe conventions (including on trafficking) a holistic, practical, and predominantly gender-specific approach to gender-based violence.[3] This approach, the Convention's intersectional prohibition of discrimination and its protections for migrant and refugee women, have also made it the subject of both a populist backlash and legal contestation. This chapter explores the Convention within this challenging political and legal context, analysing its contribution to migrant women's protection from violence and the final two regimes of exception considered by this book, those created by article 59.

The Istanbul Convention's article 59 imposes two distinct obligations to grant permission to remain in the country of residence where experiences of violence against women and of migration control collide. Parties should grant victims whose migration status is dependent on a spouse or partner an 'autonomous residence permit' in some circumstances; in others it should grant victims a 'renewable residence permit'. I examine article 59 within the broader framework created by the Convention, exploring the latter's purposes, provisions, and

[1] Council of Europe Convention on Preventing and Combating Violence against Women and Domestic Violence (adopted 11 May 2011, entered into force 1 August 2014) CETS 210 (Istanbul Convention).

[2] Adopted seventeen years after the Inter-American Convention on the Prevention, Punishment and Eradication of Violence against Women (adopted 9 June 1994, entered into force 5 March 1995) (1994) 33 ILM 1534.

[3] Kevät Nousiainen and Christine Chinkin, *Legal Implications of EU Accession to the Istanbul Convention* (Publications Office of the European Union 2016) 39.

Violence against Women and Regimes of Exception. Catherine Briddick, Oxford University Press.
 DOI: 10.1093/9780191959899.003.0007

beneficiaries.[4] I also chart the EU's and UK's troubled relationship with it, considering both a partial accession and a relevant reservation. This chapter then evaluates article 59's ability to provide a reparative response to compounded disadvantage in three stages. First, I clarify ambiguities, offering an interpretation of the Convention's prohibition of discrimination and protection of residence status, one that is in line with the law on treaties. I then return to NA's and EK's cases. NA, it will be recalled from chapter 5, was unable to rely on the EU's domestic violence rule to retain the right of residence she had previously derived from her EU Citizen husband.[5] While subsequent case law offered the prospect of a rights-protective resolution to some cases that, like NA's, involved divorce following departure, lacunas remain, notably in relation to economic activity. EK, as discussed in the previous chapter, had been trafficked into and then within the UK.[6] She was able to rely on the European trafficking regime, read in conjunction with European human rights law, to receive a migration status. Having imagined how NA's and EK's cases might have been decided had they been able to rely on the Istanbul Convention, I review the impact it has had in States thus far. I conclude by considering whether the EU's or UK's *full* ratification of the Convention would improve the position of migrant women.

7.2 An Overview, an Accession, and a Reservation

The Istanbul Convention's purposes are ambitious. They include protecting women from violence, contributing to the elimination of discrimination, creating a comprehensive framework to assist victims, and eliminating violence against women and domestic violence.[7] As discussed in Part I, European and international human rights law imposes positive obligations on States and requires them to respond to violence against women with due diligence. Precisely what is entailed by these obligations in different circumstances continues, however, to be the subject of litigation (as evinced by the range of cases cited in chapter 3), scholarly debate, and, on the part of those who owe the obligations—States—obfuscation. In general, and as the previous chapter's discussion of the trafficking regime demonstrates, States have been quick(er) to accept legal obligations that give them greater enforcement powers, obligations that require the criminalisation of certain conduct,

[4] For an introduction to and overview of the Convention, see Ronagh JA McQuigg, *The Istanbul Convention, Domestic Violence and Human Rights* (Routledge 2019). For a more critical analysis, see Johanna Niemi, Lourdes Peroni, and Vladislava Stoyanova (eds), *International Law and Violence Against Women: Europe and the Istanbul Convention* (Routledge 2020).

[5] Case C-115/15 *Secretary of State for the Home Department v NA* [2016] ECLI:EU:C:2016:487 (*NA (CJEU Judgment)*).

[6] *EK (Article 4 ECHR: Anti-Trafficking Convention) Tanzania* [2013] UKUT 313 (IAC), [2013] Imm AR 895.

[7] Istanbul Convention, art 1.

for example, than they have been to provide civil remedies to, and specialist support for, the victims of those offences. One of the significant contributions that the Istanbul Convention makes to human rights law is, therefore, its establishment of a comprehensive, clear, and detailed framework of mutually reinforcing obligations that encompass policy, preventative, protective, *and* prosecution-based responses to violence against women.[8]

The obligations assumed by States under the Convention include, first, the adoption of integrated, coordinated, and properly resourced policies and programmes to challenge gender inequality and to monitor and respond to violence.[9] Secondly, education, training, and awareness-raising are to contribute to the prevention of violence.[10] Here, Parties are required to 'take into account and address the specific needs of persons made vulnerable by particular circumstances' and to 'place the human rights of all victims at their centre'.[11] Thirdly, States are required to protect and support victims via a range of legal and non-legal measures,[12] including by, fourthly, criminalising various forms of violence.[13] States must, with their protective measures, 'aim at the empowerment and economic independence of women victims of violence'.[14] To achieve this, victims should have access to those assets that enable their recovery from violence, including to refuges, financial assistance, and housing.[15] Fifthly, Parties should adopt measures that ensure the proper investigation, prosecution, and punishment of those responsible for violence and complement these with the provision of protective orders.[16] Finally, the Convention makes specific provision for migrant and refugee women, creating two regimes of exception for victims of violence and developing obligations in relation to asylum and *non-refoulement*.[17]

The beneficiaries of the Convention's expansive set of rights and protections, including its regimes of exception, are 'victims'. A 'victim' is, according to article

[8] See further Vladislava Stoyanova, 'Due Diligence versus Positive Obligations: Critical Reflections on the Council of Europe Convention on Violence Against Women' in Johanna Niemi, Lourdes Peroni, and Vladislava Stoyanova (eds), *International Law and Violence Against Women: Europe and the Istanbul Convention* (Routledge 2020).

[9] Istanbul Convention, ch II.

[10] ibid ch III. Here, art 12(1) (which focuses on the need to change attitudes and counter the stereotyping of women) draws on the Convention on the Elimination of All Forms of Discrimination against Women (adopted 18 December 1979, entered into force 3 September 1981) 1249 UNTS 13, art 5(a). This, the preamble of the Istanbul Convention, and its approach to violence, demonstrates the dialogue between these instruments. See further Dubravka Šimonović, 'Global and Regional Standards on Violence Against Women: The Evolution and Synergy of the CEDAW and Istanbul Conventions' (2014) 36 Human Rights Quarterly 590.

[11] Istanbul Convention, art 12(3).

[12] ibid ch IV.

[13] ibid ch V, including stalking (art 34), physical violence (art 35), sexual violence (art 36), forced marriage (art 37), FGM (art 38), and forced abortion and sterilisation (art 39).

[14] ibid art 18(3).

[15] ibid arts 20–25. Drawing again on Martha Albertson Fineman, 'The Vulnerable Subject: Anchoring Equality in the Human Condition' (2008) 20 Yale Journal of Law and Feminism 1.

[16] Istanbul Convention, ch VI, specifically arts 52 and 53.

[17] ibid ch VII. Discussed further in the Conclusion.

3, 'any person' subject to 'violence against women' 'and' 'domestic violence'. The structure of the Convention and its Explanatory Report indicate that the former's 'large number of references to victims' should be understood as referring to victims *both* of violence against women and of domestic violence.[18] The word 'and' in article 3(e) denotes the potential of the Convention's protections to apply to two, potentially distinct, groups of beneficiaries. The first group is women and girls subject to any form of violence against women (including domestic violence); the second is victims of domestic violence (including, potentially, men and boys).[19] The title of the Convention and this simultaneously gender-specific and gender-neutral approach to domestic violence reflects one of the tensions apparent in the European Court of Human Rights' (ECtHR) post-*Opuz v Turkey* (2009)[20] jurisprudence. Notably, it also offers the ECtHR (and others) a means of resolving this tension. I return to this issue and the broader impact of the Istanbul Convention on the ECtHR at the end of this chapter. For now, it is sufficient to acknowledge the Convention's dual approach to domestic violence and then to make three connected observations about violence and victimhood. First, the account of violence against women adopted in this book is, as explained in chapter 3, consonant with, but potentially narrower than, that taken by the Istanbul Convention.[21] Both encompass a range of harms and understand such violence, including domestic violence, to be a violation of women's human rights and entailing discrimination. Secondly, and building on the Convention's broad protection of equality, article 4(3) ensures that *all* rights of victims under the Convention are secured without discrimination. Thirdly, while the regimes considered in this book so far are available to victims *either* of domestic violence *or* of trafficking, the beneficiaries of article 59 include those who have experienced violence against women (including forms not covered by either UK or EU rules) and, in certain circumstances, victims of domestic violence who are men.

The implementation of the Istanbul Convention is monitored by the Group of Experts on Action against Violence against Women and Domestic Violence

[18] Council of Europe, *Explanatory Report to the Council of Europe Convention on Preventing and Combating Violence against Women and Domestic Violence* (CETS No 210) (2011) [45].

[19] Istanbul Convention, art 2(1): 'This Convention shall apply to all forms of violence against women, including domestic violence' and 2(2): 'Parties are encouraged to apply this Convention to all victims of domestic violence'. That the word 'and' is used to denote these two potentially distinct beneficiary groups is confirmed by the reference to 'women victims' in cases where a particular right/protection is available only to the former group (on economic empowerment, see art 18(3)). Where a right or protection is intended for victims of a particular form of violence, the relevant article limits its scope or beneficiary group to achieve this (on domestic violence and emergency barring orders, see art 52; on regaining a lost migration status in cases of forced marriage, art 59(4)). If the term 'and' was interpreted cumulatively, many of the Conventions' protections would be unavailable to women subjected to violence where the relevant acts were committed by someone they had no relationship with (as could be the case with, for example, stalking, sexual harassment, or sexual violence).

[20] *Opuz v Turkey* App no 33401/02 (ECtHR, 9 June 2009) and the cases that followed it, as discussed in chapter 3. Compare this with Council of Europe, *Explanatory Report* (n 18) [49].

[21] See further chapter 3's discussion of interpersonal versus structural violence.

(GREVIO), via a reporting and inquiry procedure.[22] This procedure is responsive, and GREVIO may carry out country visits and receive information from a range of sources. GREVIO may also make general recommendations and has intervened in litigation before the ECtHR.[23]

Finally, the integrity of the non-discrimination framework created by the Convention on the Elimination of All Forms of Discrimination against Women (CEDAW)[24] has been seriously undermined by the number and scope of reservations made to it.[25] Consequently, the drafters of the Istanbul Convention sought to protect the holistic approach it adopts towards violence against women by limiting Parties' ability to engage selectively with it.[26] These attempts have, however, been met with resistance from both the EU and States.

The Istanbul Convention itself envisages EU accession, something that the EU can do to the full extent of its competences.[27] Under the Treaty on the Functioning of the European Union (TFEU),[28] the procedure to be followed involves the Council, following a Commission proposal, adopting a decision that concludes the agreement.[29] The agreement must identify the legal bases for the EU's accession, bases derived from the EU's legal competence, its ability or power to act in a particular field. Subject to the consent of the European Parliament, this agreement is binding on the institutions of the EU and EU MS, to the extent of the competences involved.[30] The legal bases chosen for accession determine its scope.

The EU's competence in relation to violence against women is, potentially, extremely broad. As discussed in chapter 5, the EU has made a legal commitment to combat discrimination, including that based on sex, and to promote gender equality.[31] The relevant TFEU legal bases identified by the Commission in its Proposal to the Council for a decision to conclude the Convention were:

[22] Istanbul Convention, ch IX. There is also a Committee of the Parties.

[23] For example, see Group of Experts on Action against Violence against Women and Domestic Violence (GREVIO), 'General Recommendation No. 1 on the Digital Dimension of Violence against Women' GREVIO(2021)20 (adopted 20 October 2021); GREVIO, 'Third Party Intervention by the Group of Experts on Action against Violence against Women and Domestic Violence (GREVIO) pursuant to article 36 paragraph 2 of the European Convention on Human Rights Application no. 62903/15 Kurt v. Austria' (GREVIO/Inf(2020)3, 22 January 2020).

[24] Convention on the Elimination of All Forms of Discrimination against Women (adopted 18 December 1979, entered into force 3 September 1981) 1249 UNTS 13 (CEDAW).

[25] Judith Resnik, 'Comparative (In)Equalities: CEDAW, the Jurisdiction of Gender, and the Heterogeneity of Transnational Law Production' (2012) 10 International Journal of Constitutional Law 531; Marijke de Pauw, 'Women's Rights: from Bad to Worse? Assessing the Evolution of Incompatible Reservations to the CEDAW Convention' (2013) 29 Utrecht Journal of International and European Law 51.

[26] Istanbul Convention, arts 78 and 79. These limit Parties' ability to make reservations to the Convention and impose a (renewable) time limit on those that are made. Notwithstanding this, a number of States have made broad 'interpretative declarations' (reservations) that are impermissible and which have been objected to by other Parties.

[27] ibid art 75.

[28] Consolidated Version of the Treaty on the Functioning of the European Union [2012] OJ C326/47.

[29] ibid art 218.

[30] ibid arts 218 and 216(2).

[31] ibid arts 8, 10, 19(1).

> Article 16 (data protection), Article 19(1) (sex discrimination), Article 23 (consular protection for citizens of another Member State), Articles 18, 21, 46, 50 (free movement of citizens, free movement of workers and freedom of establishment), Article 78 (asylum and subsidiary and temporary protection), Article 79 (immigration), Article 81 (judicial cooperation in civil matters), Article 82 (judicial cooperation in criminal matters), Article 83 (definition of EU-wide criminal offences and sanctions for particularly serious crimes with a cross-border dimension), Article 84 (non-harmonising measures for crime prevention), and Article 157 (equal opportunities and equal treatment of men and women in areas of employment and occupation).[32]

The issue that then required consideration was whether, to accede to the Convention, the EU should rely on all these legal bases and if not, what the effect of selecting (and rejecting) particular bases might be. The Commission argued that it was appropriate to base a Council Decision on articles 82(2) and 84 TFEU because the 'predominant purpose' of the Istanbul Convention is to prevent violent crime and protect victims, other provisions being 'ancillary' to this.[33] The Commission's reading of the Convention's purposes here does not actually accord with them. Nonetheless, selecting these bases would have enabled the EU to 'exercise its competences over the entirety of the Convention'.[34] Accordingly, the Commission's proposed Council Decision refers to articles 82(2) and 84 TFEU and states, in its draft article 1 that:

> The Council of Europe Convention on preventing and combating violence against women and domestic violence is hereby approved on behalf of the Union.[35]

The decisions that the Council made, however, diverged significantly from this. Rather than adopting one decision, the Council adopted two. The first refers to article 82(2) and article 83(1) TFEU but states in article 1 that:

> The signing, on behalf of the European Union, of the Council of Europe Convention on preventing and combating violence against women and domestic violence *with regard to matters related to judicial cooperation in criminal matters* is hereby authorised, subject to the conclusion of the said Convention.[36]

[32] European Commission, 'Proposal for a Council Decision on the Conclusion, by the European Union, of the Council of Europe Convention on Preventing and Combating Violence against Women and Domestic Violence' (COM(2016) 109 final, 4 March 2016) 9.
[33] ibid 9.
[34] ibid 9–10.
[35] ibid 12.
[36] Council Decision (EU) 2017/865 of 11 May 2017 on the signing, on behalf of the European Union, of the Council of Europe Convention on preventing and combating violence against women and domestic violence with regard to matters related to judicial cooperation in criminal matters [2017] OJ L131/11 (emphasis added).

The second identifies article 78(2) TFEU as its legal base, stating in its article 1 that the signing of the Convention is 'with regard to *asylum and non-refoulement*'.[37] These decisions limited the legal obligations the EU accepted in relation to the Istanbul Convention *only* to those that concern judicial cooperation in criminal matters and to asylum and *non-refoulement*. These decisions not only differed from the Commission's proposals. They also diverged from the EU's ratification of the UN Convention on the Rights of Persons with Disabilities,[38] the Council decision concerning which was based on non-discrimination and covered the Convention in its entirety.[39] The European Parliament stated that it regretted the Council's approach, recommended 'a broad EU accession to the Convention without any limitations',[40] and sought the opinion of the Court of Justice of the EU (CJEU) to facilitate this.[41]

It was not just EU institutions that clashed during this period; also striking was a lack of 'common accord', or agreement, between EU MS. Repeated references were made, both in the European Parliament and in interpretative declarations made by States on ratification, to the Istanbul Convention's imposition of a 'gender ideology', or to its contribution to a new 'flood' of migrants.[42] Such 'concerns' have also been significant outside the EU, contributing to Turkey's denunciation of the Convention in 2021.[43] At issue before the CJEU was, therefore, both the correct

[37] Council Decision (EU) 2017/866 of 11 May 2017 on the signing, on behalf of the European Union, of the Council of Europe Convention on preventing and combating violence against women and domestic violence with regard to asylum and non-refoulement [2017] OJ L131/13 (emphasis added). In recital 9, the decision specifies that it concerns 'only' Istanbul Convention, arts 60 and 61.

[38] Convention on the Rights of Persons with Disabilities (adopted 13 May 2006, entered into force 3 May 2008) 2515 UNTS 3.

[39] Council Decision of 26 November 2009 concerning the conclusion, by the European Community, of the United Nations Convention on the Rights of Persons with Disabilities (2010/48/EC) [2010] OJ L23/35, art 1 (with one reservation).

[40] European Parliament resolution of 12 September 2017 on the proposal for a Council decision on the conclusion, by the European Union, of the Council of Europe Convention on preventing and combating violence against women and domestic violence (COM(2016)0109 – 2016/0062(NLE)) [2017] P8 TA(2017)0329 [9(d)], see also [2].

[41] European Parliament resolution of 4 April 2019 seeking an opinion from the Court of Justice on the compatibility with the Treaties of the proposals for the accession by the European Union to the Council of Europe Convention on preventing and combating violence against women and domestic violence and on the procedure for that accession (2019/2678(RSP)) [2019] P8 TA(2019)0357; Opinion 1/19: Request for an opinion submitted by the European Parliament pursuant to Article 218(11) TFEU [2019] OJ C413/21. For a critique of the legal bases selected at this stage, see Sara De Vido, 'The Ratification of the Council of Europe Istanbul Convention by the EU: A Step Forward in the Protection of Women from Violence in the European Legal System' (2017) 9 European Journal of Legal Studies 69; Catherine Briddick, 'Combatting or Enabling Domestic Violence? Evaluating the Residence Rights of Migrant Victims of Domestic Violence in Europe' (2020) 69 International and Comparative Law Quarterly 1013 (some of this chapter's arguments are developed from those first advanced in this latter piece).

[42] Valentine Berthet, 'Norm under Fire: Support for and Opposition to the European Union's Ratification of the Istanbul Convention in the European Parliament' (2022) 24 International Feminist Journal of Politics 675.

[43] Başak Çali and Laurence Helfer, 'The Gender of Treaty Withdrawal: Lessons from the Istanbul Convention' (*EJIL:Talk!*, 28 November 2022) <www.ejiltalk.org/the-gender-of-treaty-withdrawal-less

choice of legal basis for EU accession and whether or not such an accession could occur, given the lack of common accord between EU MS. These issues appear technical, concerning EU treaty-making powers and procedure, particularly in relation to 'mixed' agreements (those where competence is shared between the EU and its MS). They relate, however, to the EU's foundational legal commitments and fundamental values. That a Council of Europe instrument on violence against women generated such conflict, between EU institutions and EU MS, illustrates how contested an area women's human rights remains, both politically and legally.

In *Opinion 1/19* (2021),[44] the Court found that accession to the Istanbul Convention should have been based on TFEU articles 78(2) (asylum, subsidiary, and temporary protection); 82(2) (judicial cooperation in criminal matters); 84 (crime prevention); and 336 TFEU (staff regulations).[45] On the selection and rejection of particular legal bases, the Court took a narrow approach, focusing on the decisions the Council *did* make (rather than the decision(s) available to it) and leaving its discretion on this point unchecked.[46] Common accord between MS, while not legally required, may nonetheless be sought.[47] The EU could, therefore, accede to the Convention, even as some of its MS chose not to ratify it. Indeed, those non-ratifying States could 'no longer hold the EU hostage'.[48] Finally, 'split', or divided accession decisions were also justified in this case, given the Istanbul Convention's provisions on asylum and *non-refoulement* and certain MS' opt outs from related measures in the common European asylum system (CEAS).[49]

The EU's accession to the Istanbul Convention followed this decision relatively swiftly. It was concluded with another two Council Decisions, in June 2023, the Convention entering into force for the EU later that year. In line with *Opinion 1/19* (2021), the first decision covered the EU's 'institutions and public administration',[50] the second 'matters related to judicial cooperation in criminal matters

ons-from-the-istanbul-convention/> accessed 7 December 2022. Other relevant factors include the fading credibility of EU conditionality and domestic political considerations, see further Marella Bodur Ün and Harun Arikan, 'Europeanization and De-Europeanization of Turkey's Gender Equality Policy: The Case of the Istanbul Convention' (2022) 60 Journal of Common Market Studies 945.

[44] *Opinion 1/19 Opinion of the Court (Grand Chamber) of 6 October 2021* [2021] ECLI:EU:C:2021:832.

[45] ibid para 311.

[46] ibid para 282. See also Gesa Kübek, 'Facing and Embracing the Consequences of Mixity: Opinion 1/19, Istanbul Convention' (2022) 59 Common Market Law Review 1465, 1490 (on scrutiny of the Council); Matthias Möschel, 'The European Union's Actions in the Domain of Combating Gender-Based Violence' in Elena Brodeală, Ivana Jelić, and Silvia Şuteu (eds), *Violence Against Women under European Human Rights Law: From Supranational Standards to National Realities* (Edward Elgar 2024) (on the failure to rely on non-discrimination as a base).

[47] *Opinion 1/19* (n 44) paras 245–60, 274.

[48] Kübek 'Facing and Embracing the Consequences of Mixity' (n 46) 1481.

[49] *Opinion 1/19* (n 44) paras 336–37. The EU MS concerned are Ireland and Denmark.

[50] Council Decision (EU) 2023/1075 of 1 June 2023 on the conclusion, on behalf of the European Union, of the Council of Europe Convention on preventing and combating violence against women and domestic violence with regard to institutions and public administration of the Union [2023] OJ L143 I/1, art 1.

and to *asylum and non-refoulement, insofar as they fall within the exclusive competence of the Union*'.[51] Accordingly, while the Council's decisions concluding the Convention do differ from those it took when signing it, the EU's accession remains partial and selective. The EU appears to have assumed the obligations imposed by, for example, articles 60 and 61 of the Istanbul Convention in relation to the CEAS, but not those imposed by article 59 that could affect the regimes of exception created by the Citizens' Directive,[52] the Family Reunion Directive (FRD),[53] or the Residence Permits Directive.[54] As Advocate General Hogan observed when considering the Istanbul Convention's article 59 alongside the Citizens' Directive's domestic violence rule, judgments like *NA* (2016)[55] have 'given rise to doubts as to the minimum nature of some of the requirements' set out in the latter.[56] *Opinion 1/19* (2021) has rightly been described as a 'landmark' decision.[57] The Court's disinclination to subject the Council's decisions on the scope of accession to substantive scrutiny was, however, highly regrettable, given that those decisions have insulated swathes of EU law from the Convention's purview.[58]

Although the UK was a relatively early signatory to the Convention, in June 2012, ratification did not follow until a decade later, in July 2022.[59] Home Office reports on the UK's 'progress' towards ratification initially asserted that it was 'compliant'

[51] Council Decision (EU) 2023/1076 of 1 June 2023 on the conclusion, on behalf of the European Union, of the Council of Europe Convention on preventing and combating violence against women and domestic violence with regard to matters related to judicial cooperation in criminal matters, asylum and non-refoulement [2023] OJ L143 I/4, art 1 (emphasis added). See also Declaration concerning the competence of the European Union with regard to matters governed by the Council of Europe Convention on preventing and combating violence against women and domestic violence [2023] OJ C194/2.

[52] Directive 2004/38/EC of the European Parliament and of the Council of 29 April 2004 on the right of citizens of the Union and their family members to move and reside freely within the territory of the Member States amending Regulation (EEC) No 1612/68 and repealing Directives 64/221/EEC, 68/360/EEC, 72/194/EEC, 73/148/EEC, 75/34/EEC, 75/35/EEC, 90/364/EEC, 90/365/EEC and 93/96/EEC [2004] OJ L 158/77, and corrigenda ([2004] OJ L 229/35, [2005] OJ L 197/34, and [2007] OJ L 204/28) (Citizens' Directive).

[53] Council Directive 2003/86/EC of 22 September 2003 on the Right to Family Reunification [2003] OJ L 251/12 (FRD).

[54] Council Directive 2004/81/EC of 29 April 2004 on the residence permit issued to third-country nationals who are victims of trafficking in human beings or who have been the subject of an action to facilitate illegal immigration, who cooperate with the competent authorities [2004] OJ L261/19 (Residence Permits Directive). On the substantive point, in addition to the decisions themselves, see *Opinion 1/19* (n 44) paras 118–20.

[55] *NA (CJEU Judgment)* (n 5).

[56] *Opinion 1/19 (Istanbul Convention)* [2021] ECLI:EU:C:2021:198, Opinion of AG Hogan, para 107, see also paras 160–61. The Advocate General is able to dismiss such doubts by referring the issue back to MS. See further Catherine Briddick, 'Some Complex Legal Questions Examined from a Legal Perspective in a Partial and Passionate Manner' (2021) <http://eulawanalysis.blogspot.com/> accessed 3 April 2021.

[57] Kübek 'Facing and Embracing the Consequences of Mixity' (n 46) 1467.

[58] Note that it was 'common ground' that ch VII of the Istanbul Convention, arts 59–61, were within the scope of TFEU, art 78(2), *Opinion 1/19* (n 44) paras 302–03. See also ibid paras 118–20 and 122 on exclusive EU competence.

[59] Notwithstanding the adoption of primary legislation to expedite the process, Preventing and Combating Violence Against Women and Domestic Violence (Ratification of Convention) Act 2017.

with its putative article 59 obligations.[60] In doing so, reports highlighted the UK's domestic violence rule, the then destitute domestic violence concession, and the general power of the Home Secretary to regularise status as evidence of this.[61] This broad-brush approach failed to engage with the requirements of article 59, including its approach to victims. It also failed to engage with the non-discrimination provisions of the Convention, declaring them 'N/A', 'not applicable'.[62] How or why this was the case, given the raft of restrictions the UK applies to migrants, was left entirely unexplained. This position shifted with scrutiny of what came to be the Domestic Abuse Act 2021, the Home Office subsequently reporting that its compliance with both articles 4(3) (in relation to migration status) and 59 was 'under review', in part because of the difficulties that victims with 'no recourse' had in accessing women's refuges.[63] On ratification, the UK joined a number of other States and entered a reservation to article 59, this decision being criticised by, amongst others, the House of Lord's International Agreements Committee.[64] The UK could not enter a reservation to article 4(3), it not being permissible to do so under the Convention. It is, therefore, unsurprising that the UK's baseline report to GREVIO did not refer to this provision or to discrimination on the grounds of migration status.[65]

7.3 The Obligations Imposed

7.3.1 Discrimination against Migrant Women

The Istanbul Convention's approach to migrant women's experiences of violence appears, at first glance, to be more concerned with protection than prevention. As

[60] For example, Home Office, 'Ratification of the Council of Europe Convention on Combating Violence Against Women and Girls and Domestic Violence (Istanbul Convention)—2018 Report on Progress' (*GOV.UK*, 30 October 2018) 32 <www.gov.uk/government/publications/ratification-of-the-council-of-europe-convention-on-combating-violence-against-women-and-domestic-violence-progress-report> accessed 26 March 2024.

[61] For example, Home Office, 'Ratification of the Council of Europe Convention on Combating Violence Against Women and Domestic Violence (Istanbul Convention)—Report on Progress' (*GOV.UK*, 1 November 2017) 16 <www.gov.uk/government/publications/ratification-of-the-council-of-europe-convention-on-combating-violence-against-women-and-domestic-violence> accessed 26 March 2024; see also 40.

[62] ibid 25.

[63] Home Office, 'Istanbul Convention Implementation: Progress Report 2021' (*GOV.UK*, 1 November 2021) 8 <www.gov.uk/government/publications/istanbul-convention-implementation-progress-report-2021> accessed 26 March 2023.

[64] International Agreements Committee, *Scrutiny of International Agreements: Council of Europe Convention on Preventing and Combating Violence against Women and Domestic Violence* (HL Paper 24, 17 June 2022), [12]–[14]. The UK also entered a reservation to art 44(3).

[65] GREVIO, *Report submitted by the United Kingdom pursuant to Article 68, paragraph 1 of the Council of Europe Convention on preventing and combating violence against women and domestic violence (Baseline Report)* (GREVIO/Inf(2023)11, 3 July 2023).

explained in chapter 4, the Convention's Explanatory Report acknowledges that fear of deportation and loss of status is used by perpetrators to manipulate those they victimise and prevent them from seeking help.[66] Yet while States are obliged to address stereotyping and to criminalise certain conduct, they are not required to reduce or abolish probationary periods for partners, or eliminate the precarity and dependence of domestic workers. These and other omissions have prompted Fulvia Staiano to conclude that the Convention fails to respond to the role that migration law plays in increasing vulnerability to violence, a failure that article 59's focus on victims' residence status is unable to address.[67] If this argument is correct, the kinds of discrimination law-based arguments made in chapter 2 become all the more important to those concerned with migrant women's protection from violence. Staiano may, however, have dismissed the Convention's protective capacities too quickly. The failure of the drafters to make specific provision for prevention in relation to migration law is certainly notable. Nonethless, the Convention does have general obligations on discrimination and prevention that are highly relevant to migrant women's situation. Article 4(1)–(2) addresses all women's right to live free from violence and prohibits discrimination, while article 12(2) requires Parties to 'take the necessary legislative and other measures to prevent all forms of violence'.[68] These and related obligations apply as much to migration law and control as they do to those areas specifically addressed by the Convention. Such provisions, whether drawn on alone or in conjunction with other instruments' probitions on discrimination, could be relied on to challenge those facets of migration law that, like the probationary period, disadvantage women and increase their vulnerability to violence. GREVIO may also, as discussed at the end of the chapter, scrutinise States' policies in this regard. Space precludes a discussion of whether or not the Istanbul Convention's general obligations on discrimination and violence alone are sufficient to prevent compounded disadvantage. If violence does occur, however, article 4(3) offers victims significant protection from those exclusions, discussed in chapter 4, that contribute to its intensified experience.

Article 4(3) states:

> The implementation of the provisions of this Convention by the Parties, in particular measures to protect the rights of victims, shall be secured without discrimination on any ground such as sex, gender, race, colour, language, religion, political or other opinion, national or social origin, association with a national

[66] Council of Europe, *Explanatory Report* (n 18) [301].

[67] Fulvia Staiano, 'Protection beyond Victimisation: The Significance of the Istanbul Convention for Migrant Women' in Johanna Niemi, Lourdes Peroni, and Vladislava Stoyanova (eds), *International Law and Violence against Women: Europe and the Istanbul Convention* (Routledge 2020).

[68] See also the commentary to these provisions, notably Council of Europe, *Explanatory Report* (n 18) [49] and [54].

minority, property, birth, sexual orientation, gender identity, age, state of health, disability, marital status, migrant or refugee status, or other status.

This provision is notable for a number of reasons. First, it includes an explicit reference to sexual orientation and gender identity within its prohibition of discriminatory treatment. The extent to which this substantively improves the position of lesbian or trans women remains contested.[69] The expansive approach to grounds taken here has, however, generated some of the most trenchant opposition to the Convention, contributing to the lack of common accord between EU MS discussed above. This indicates that both the Convention's intersectional approach and the political stance of those advocating for it have been significant, expressively at least. Secondly, this provision has a structure similar to article 14 of the European Convention on Human Rights (ECHR).[70] It encompasses both direct and indirect discrimination between *victims*, but only in relation to the rights and protections that the Convention provides. The Explanatory Report states that the 'meaning of discrimination' here 'is identical to that given to it under Article 14 of the ECHR'.[71] The ECtHR has, when scrutinising disadvantageous treatment that relates to a protected ground, subjected different grounds to different levels of scrutiny.[72] As discussed in chapter 4, in relation to challenges to the UK's domestic violence rule, differential treatment on the grounds of sex, a suspect ground, must be justified by very weighty reasons.[73] In contrast, a wide margin of appreciation may be accorded to differential treatment on the grounds of migration status, it not being a suspect ground.[74] The standard of review adopted by the ECtHR is not, however, the same as that used by other courts or treaty bodies.[75] Nor should it be.[76] Significantly, there is nothing in the provision itself, related articles, the

[69] Johanna Niemi, Lourdes Peroni, and Vladislava Stoyanova, 'Introduction' in Johanna Niemi, Lourdes Peroni, and Vladislava Stoyanova (eds), *International Law and Violence against Women: Europe and the Istanbul Convention* (Routledge 2020); Guney Gizem, 'The Anti-Istanbul Convention Campaign: Rhetoric or Reality?: A Comparative Analysis of the Istanbul Convention and the ECHR on Same-Sex Marriage and the Legal Introduction of Third Sex' (2022) 6 European Human Rights Law Review 604.

[70] Convention for the Protection of Human Rights and Fundamental Freedoms (adopted 4 November 1950, entered into force 3 September 1953) ETS 5 (European Convention on Human Rights, as amended) (ECHR).

[71] Council of Europe, *Explanatory Report* (n 18) [52].

[72] Oddný Mjöll Arnardóttir, 'The Differences that Make a Difference: Recent Developments on the Discrimination Grounds and the Margin of Appreciation under Article 14 of the European Convention on Human Rights' (2014) 14 Human Rights Law Review 647.

[73] *Stec v UK* (2006) 43 EHRR 1017.

[74] *Bah v UK* App no 56328/07 (ECtHR, 27 September 2011); *Hode and Abdi v UK* App no 22341/09 (ECtHR, 6 November 2012).

[75] Dominic McGoldrick, 'A Defence of the Margin of Appreciation and an Argument for its Application by the Human Rights Committee' (2016) 65 International and Comparative Law Quarterly 21. See further Lukasz Gruszczynski and Wouter Werner, *Deference in International Courts and Tribunals: Standard of Review and Margin of Appreciation* (OUP 2014).

[76] As discussed in Catherine Briddick, 'Unprincipled and Unrealised: CEDAW and Discrimination Experienced in the Context of Migration Control' (2022) 22 International Journal of Discrimination and the Law 224.

Convention's purposes, or its Explanatory Report that suggests that GREVIO either could or should subject different Istanbul-protected grounds to different levels of scrutiny. States should, therefore, protect and support victims, including by providing safe accommodation, financial support, and access to healthcare, without discrimination on the grounds of migration status.[77]

7.3.2 The Residence Status of Victims of Violence

Having considered the Istanbul Convention's general approach to violence and migration, I can now move to its specific provision on residence status. Here, I analyse the obligations imposed by article 59, contrasting them, where illustrative, to those regimes considered in chapters 5 and 6. In doing so, it should be noted that article 59 must be interpreted in accordance with its terms' ordinary meaning, in light of the Convention's purposes.[78] Terms that have a particular meaning in, for example, EU law (with its focus on Citizens' rights) may not, therefore, have the same meaning when used in the context of the Istanbul Convention (given its objectives on the elimination of violence).

Article 59—Residence status

1. Parties shall take the necessary legislative or other measures to ensure that victims whose residence status depends on that of the spouse or partner as recognised by internal law, in the event of the dissolution of the marriage or the relationship, are granted in the event of particularly difficult circumstances, upon application, an autonomous residence permit irrespective of the duration of the marriage or the relationship. The conditions relating to the granting and duration of the autonomous residence permit are established by internal law.
2. Parties shall take the necessary legislative or other measures to ensure that victims may obtain the suspension of expulsion proceedings initiated in relation to a residence status dependent on that of the spouse or partner as recognised by internal law to enable them to apply for an autonomous residence permit.
3. Parties shall issue a renewable residence permit to victims in one of the two following situations, or in both:

[77] Council of Europe, *Explanatory Report* (n 18) [53]; Lorena Sosa and Ruth M Mestre i Mestre, *Ensuring the Non Discrimination Implementation of Measures against Violence against Women and Domestic Violence: Article 4, paragraph 3 of the Istanbul Convention: A collection of Papers on the Council of Europe Convention on Preventing and Combating Violence against Women and Domestic Violence* (Council of Europe, March 2022) 43–44.

[78] Vienna Convention on the Law of Treaties (adopted 23 May 1969, entered into force 27 January 1980) 1155 UNTS 331, art 31.

(a) where the competent authority considers that their stay is necessary owing to their personal situation;
(b) where the competent authority considers that their stay is necessary for the purpose of their co-operation with the competent authorities in investigation or criminal proceedings.

4. Parties shall take the necessary legislative or other measures to ensure that victims of forced marriage brought into another country for the purpose of the marriage and who, as a result, have lost their residence status in the country where they habitually reside, may regain this status.

Article 59 adopts a fourfold approach to victims' residence status. Article 59(1) requires States to grant victims whose migration status is dependent on a spouse or partner an 'autonomous residence permit' in certain circumstances. Article 59(2) protects victims whose migration status is, once again, dependent on a spouse or partner, from any expulsion proceedings initiated in relation to that status. Article 59(3) enables victims to be granted 'renewable residence permits' in two sets of circumstances, while 59(4) enables 'victims of forced marriage' to regain any migration status held in their country of habitual residence and lost because of that marriage. As noted above, the Istanbul Convention's regimes may be relied on by victims of any form of violence against women. As GREVIO explains, article 59's role within the Convention is to ensure that Parties' migration laws:

> do not turn a blind eye to the realities of women living in abusive relationships *or* subjected to sexual violence and exploitation and other forms of gender-based violence.[79]

The literature that engages with the Convention has yet to explore fully the implications of this breadth.

7.3.3 Article 59(1) and Autonomous Residence Permits

Article 59(1) addresses the predicament of victims of violence against women who are dependent for their migration status on their relationship with their spouse or partner. Unmarried partners, whether same-sex or opposite-sex, may benefit from

[79] GREVIO, *GREVIO Baseline Evaluation Report Denmark* (GREVIO/Inf(2017)14, 24 November 2017) [224] (emphasis added). This formulation in repeated in other reports, GREVIO, *GREVIO Baseline Evaluation Report Belgium* (GREVIO/Inf(2020)14, 21 September 2020) [206]. The only mention of trafficking or the Trafficking Convention in the Istanbul Convention is in its preamble, where it is referred to alongside the ECHR and other relevant human rights instruments. Of course, obligations imposed by the Trafficking Convention are not affected by those imposed by the Istanbul Convention; see art 71 of the latter.

this provision where their relationship meets conditions laid down by the relevant Party. The beneficiary class of article 59(1) is, therefore, significantly wider than that of the UK's domestic violence rule. The latter, it will be recalled, is only available to a limited group of dependent partners, those understood to have a reasonable expectation of living permanently in the UK.[80] From the vantage point of a potential applicant in the UK, the provision covers those who are married or in a relationship with someone who is British or resident here. Significantly, it also covers those who, like the partners of workers, are in a relationship with someone who also requires permission to remain. Article 59(1) mirrors and extends the EU's rules, both those of the Citizens' Directive' and of the FRD, covering third-country nationals (TCNs) who are in a relationship with an EU Citizen and those in a relationship with another TCN.[81] Where the potential applicant is dependent for her status on someone who themselves requires permission to remain, article 59(2) protects her from any expulsion proceedings taken against him, enabling proceedings to be suspended so that she may regularise her status.

Like both the EU's and UK's domestic violence rules, article 59(1) does not require the perpetrator of violence to be the person on whom the applicant is dependent for her migration status. Women who experience violence from other sources (harassment from other family members or from a work colleague) can rely on the rule if its other requirements are met. The violence also does not have to have caused the relationship to break down, in line with the EU's provisions and unlike the UK's domestic violence rule. The duration of the relationship is also irrelevant. This may all be helpful in cases where the cause and indeed timing of the relationship's breakdown is unclear or contested, such issues not being questions of fact, but of the judgment of particular facts.[82] Although the Citizens' Directive's domestic violence rule contains requirements which relate to the economic activity of both victims and perpetrators, no such criteria are imposed here. This may be significant for both TCN and EU Citizen victims of violence.[83]

There are three other aspects of article 59(1), the correct interpretation of which is less straightforward. The first is the rule's reference to 'particularly difficult circumstances'. This phrase appears to be drawn directly from EU law. According to the Citizens' Directive, rights may be retained where this is 'warranted by particularly difficult circumstances, *such as* having been a victim of domestic violence'.[84]

[80] Immigration Rules HC 590, Appendix Victim of Domestic Abuse, VDA 4.1.

[81] Recall that the Citizens' Directive, art 13(1) states that the rule is for the benefit of those whose marriage or registered partnership is terminated. This covers both same-sex and opposite-sex marriages/partnerships, per C–673/16 *Coman v Inspectoratul General pentru Imigrări and Ministerul Afacerilor Interne* [2018] ECLI:EU:C:2018:385. It excludes durable partners.

[82] As explained in *R (Balakoohi) v Secretary of State for the Home Department* [2012] EWHC 1439 (Admin) [68]–[69].

[83] EU Citizens may also have their rights affected by relationship breakdown, see Citizens' Directive, art 13(1) and the discussion of economic activity, gender, and citizenship in chapter 5.

[84] ibid art 13(2)(c) (emphasis added).

The rationale for using this phrase in article 59 is less clear. Vladislava Stoyanova argues that it may be interpreted to add a 'severity threshold', in terms of the violence experienced (a focus on past harm) or the applicant's personal circumstances (potentially a prospective test, considering the impact of removal on 'small' children for example).[85] Stoyanova appears to welcome such an approach, arguing that the definition of violence against women adopted by the Convention is 'far-reaching' and that:

> If this definition is to be followed without any restraints imposed by the qualifying words 'particularly difficult circumstances', the beneficiaries of Article 59 might be extended to unreasonable limits.[86]

This 'severity threshold' interpretation would be inconsistent with the purposes of the Istanbul Convention for two reasons. First, the Convention seeks to respond to all forms of violence against women, not just particularly harmful subsets or manifestations of it. The approach to violence and victimhood it adopts is, therefore, purposefully capacious to capture and enable a response to the many and varied forms of violence to which women are subject. Secondly, and as explained above, the Convention seeks to eliminate discrimination against women intersectionally. Per article 4(3), the rights and protections the Convention affords must be secured without discrimination. To interpret 'particularly difficult circumstances' as requiring a potential applicant to experience violence that is particularly severe, for example, is to impose on migrant women a higher eligibility threshold than must be met by other, 'normal', victims before the relevant protection is afforded.

Rather than interpreting 'particularly difficult circumstances' as *adding* a condition to the rule, I interpret it as *linking* its requirements: violence, dependency, and relationship dissolution. Without such a link, the potential beneficiary group of article 59(1) could, as Stoyanova observes, be unreasonably large. Why should, for example, an experience of sexual harassment perpetrated by a stranger generate a right of residence if, entirely unrelated to that harassment, the woman concerned divorces the person on whom she depends for her migration status? The migration status of victims of violence who wish to remain in a jurisdiction while that violence is investigated/prosecuted is covered by a separate provision, article 59(3), which requires Parties to grant *renewable* residence permits (as discussed in the next section). This being the case, for which 'particularly difficult circumstances' is bestowing an *autonomous* right of residence the appropriate response? Being deterred from ending a violent relationship because doing so may end your right to

[85] Vladislava Stoyanova, 'A Stark Choice: Domestic Violence or Deportation? The Immigration Status of Victims of Domestic Violence under the Istanbul Convention' (2018) 20 European Journal of Migration and Law 53, 62.

[86] ibid 62.

live in the UK or another State Party may be one such circumstance. Losing your migration status because you ended that relationship, or because the person on whom you depended for your status was imprisoned because of their conduct, may be two others.[87] Using 'particularly difficult circumstances' to link the rule's substantive requirements enables its benefit, the granting of an autonomous migration status, to be bestowed in a broad range of situations where a victim's dependent one is jeopardised in some way because of that victimhood. Such an interpretation is entirely consistent with the phrase's ordinary meaning in light of the Convention's purposes.[88]

The second feature of article 59(1) that requires more detailed consideration is its reference to victims 'whose residence status *depends* on that of the spouse or partner' (emphasis added). Must, therefore, a victim have a current, dependent migration status when she experiences violence, when her relationship ends, when she makes her immigration application, or at all three points? If article 59(1) were interpreted as requiring a woman to have a current, dependent migration status at the time she makes her application, the potential beneficiary group of the provision would be unreasonably small. Women who have overstayed their permission to remain because of their perpetrators' violence would, for example, be excluded from its ambit. Perpetrators of violence routinely manipulate the migration status of those they victimise, as discussed in chapter 4 and as both NA and EK experienced. Barring women who no longer have status from benefiting from article 59 reinforces, rather than undermines, this control. Any perpetrator who became aware of his partner's attempts to seek protection from him, or to gather evidence in support of an immigration application, could take action to have her permission curtailed, effectively depriving her of both. An alternative interpretation, one which is responsive to these issues and, therefore, consistent with the Convention's purposes, would require the victim to have had a dependent migration status at the time *any* of the factors referred to in the provision arose.[89] Such an approach would:

> allow victims to obtain the necessary protection from authorities without fearing that the perpetrator will retaliate by withdrawing or threatening to withdraw residence benefits under the perpetrator's control.[90]

[87] Per Case C-378/12 *Onuekwere v Secretary of State for the Home Department* [2014] ECLI:EU:C:2014:13, where the CJEU ruled that time spent in prison was not time legally residing in an EU MS; if an EU Citizen was imprisoned for his violence he would lose his right to reside. This could result in any family members who derived their rights from his also losing their rights, an issue that was discussed in chapter 5.

[88] Istanbul Convention, art 1. See also Council of Europe, *Explanatory Report* (n 18) [303].

[89] For a similar approach, see Sara De Vido, 'The Istanbul Convention as an Interpretative Tool at the European and National Levels' in Johanna Niemi, Lourdes Peroni, and Vladislava Stoyanova (eds), *International Law and Violence Against Women: Europe and the Istanbul Convention* (2020) 69–70.

[90] Council of Europe, *Explanatory Report* (n 18) [304].

The third element of article 59(1) that requires attention is the migration status that Parties are required to grant under it, the duration and rights that such a status bestows being determined by Parties' own migration law. As we saw in chapter 2, migration statuses can be of different durations, can be renewable (or not), and can bestow a variety of different rights (again, or not). Article 4(3) should enable migrant women to benefit from all the general and specialist support services that Parties are required to provide to victims. The Convention does not, however, contain provisions that relate to employment or to access to the labour market. This means that victims of violence will not have the right to work unless the migration status they are granted bestows it. The migration status that Parties grant under article 59 must be independent. Given that this permission to remain is not also required to be renewable, it will only meet the Convention's purposes and contribute to victims' empowerment if it is granted for a significant period of time (recall here the arguments made in chapter 4 which suggest three years *with the possibility of extension/naturalisation*). It must, in addition, bestow significant rights, including access to the labour market.

7.3.4 Article 59(3) and Renewable Residence Permits

The renewable residence permits provided by article 59(3) are available to any migrant victim able to meet one of its two conditions. In terms of migration status, this encompasses those with valid permission to remain and those without (overstayers and the undocumented). It includes those with a dependent migration status (certain family members) and those who have permission to remain in their own right (students and workers). It also covers those whose migration status is relatively secure (skilled labour migrants) and those whose permission to remain is for a short period of time (seasonal or domestic workers). Turning to the violence, this regime is also available to those who have experienced any form of violence against women covered by the Convention.[91] This includes victims of domestic violence, harassment, stalking, sexual violence, female genital mutilation (FGM), forced marriage, and trafficking. Article 59(3) is, therefore, the most expansive regime of exception covered in this book. It provides a route to a renewable residence permit in a broad range of situations not generally provided for by either UK or EU law. In terms of those whose predicaments have been discussed in preceding chapters, it may be particularly significant for domestic workers.

[91] The Explanatory Report's commentary on art 59(3) refers to victims of *domestic violence*, Council of Europe, *Explanatory Report* (n 18) [307]. Its introduction to the article as a whole, however, refers to victims both of violence against women and of domestic violence, ibid [301]. Limiting the Istanbul Convention's art 59(3) to victims of domestic violence only would not be consonant with the definitional approach set out in art 3(e). See also Stoyanova, 'A Stark Choice: Domestic Violence or Deportation?' (n 85) 61 and 77–78.

Those who experience harassment that is gender-based, for example, but whose ill-treatment does not constitute trafficking or servitude, are unable to rely on either the trafficking regime or UK provisions that enable some domestic workers to extend their permission to remain.[92] Women in this position would, however, be able to rely on article 59(3).

In terms of the conditions that a potential applicant has to meet, it is notable that subsections (a) and (b) of article 59(3) repeat, *almost* word-for-word, those of article 14 of the Council of Europe Convention on Action against Trafficking in Human Beings (the Trafficking Convention).[93] Indeed, this provision of the Trafficking Convention is described as providing inspiration to the drafters of the Istanbul Convention.[94] I explain these regimes' significant differences after exploring their apparent similarities.

Turning first to article 59(3)(a) and the requirement that a permit be granted to a victim where it is 'necessary owing to their personal situation'. This phrasing is, like the provision it draws on in the Trafficking Convention, deliberately expansive. It may be interpreted to include matters relating to a victim's health and welfare, encompassing, for example, her position in her country of residence and the circumstances she would have to confront if she were compelled to return to her country of origin.[95]

Article 59(3)(b) provides for status where it is necessary to enable cooperation with criminal proceedings. It also repeats a formulation used in the Trafficking Convention and may, consequently, be open to criticism on a similar basis. Granting a residence permit to someone who is cooperating with criminal proceedings could assist that person (and the State) in holding a perpetrator to account for their conduct. However, in making permits conditional on such cooperation, the Convention is, once again, imposing dependency, not on a person or relationship, but on a process over which the victim has no control. The police may not properly investigate a victim's allegations (as occurred in EK's case). The perpetrator may flee the jurisdiction (as occurred in NA's). A perpetrator may be investigated but not prosecuted for his or her violent conduct, or a prosecution may be discontinued for a variety of 'good' reasons (the unavailability of other witnesses or evidence, for example). Any of these factors could result in a victim being ineligible for a permit or its renewal *if* she is not also able to rely on article 59(3)(a). This 'if' is central, because the Istanbul Convention differs from the Trafficking Convention in two key respects.

92 Immigration Rules HC 590, Appendix Domestic Worker who is a Victim of Modern Slavery, as discussed in chapters 2 and 4.

93 Council of Europe Convention on Action against Trafficking in Human Beings (adopted 16 May 2005, entered into force 1 February 2008) CETS 197 (Trafficking Convention).

94 Council of Europe, *Explanatory Report* (n 18) [307].

95 ibid [307].

First, article 14(1) of the Trafficking Convention requires residence permits to be granted 'in one or other of the two following situations or in both'. In contrast, under the Istanbul Convention, permits must be granted 'in one of the two following situations, or in both'. Such a reformulation is intentional, 'or other' is removed to change both the phrase and the obligation. This addresses what Stoyanova highlights as a key deficiency of the Trafficking Convention: States' ability to provide permits *only* to those who are cooperating with criminal proceedings per article 14(1)(b).[96] The Istanbul Convention's reconfiguration of this aspect of the Trafficking Convention's regime requires Parties to provide residence permits where either of the 'two requirements' are met.[97] This crucial difference tempers criticisms, like those aired above, concerning article 59(3)(b)'s potential conditionality. It may also, however, affect how States engage with the Convention, influencing their decision to enter reservations to it.[98]

The second difference between the Trafficking and Istanbul Conventions concerns not the wording of provisions but their context. It will be recalled that the Trafficking Convention requires Parties to facilitate the re-documentation and removal of victims. The granting of residence permits under the broader regime operating as a narrow, and usually temporary, exception to migration law's default position of 'return or be removed'. The Istanbul Convention does not contain any analogous provisions. This means that victims who are ineligible for a status under article 59 will not, at least, have their removal facilitated by the Convention. They will also continue to benefit from the other protections the Convention provides to victims on a non-discriminatory and unconditional basis. Differences between the Trafficking and Istanbul Conventions, in their approach to both the residence status of victims and to their protection and support needs are, consequently, much greater than an initial comparison of the relevant provisions in isolation would suggest. One consequence of this is the potential of the two Conventions to deliver markedly different outcomes in substantively similar cases.

[96] Vladislava Stoyanova, *Human Trafficking and Slavery Reconsidered: Conceptual Limits and States' Positive Obligations in European Law* (CUP 2017) 134; Stoyanova, 'A Stark Choice: Domestic Violence or Deportation?' (n 85) 78–79. See also, however, chapter 6's discussion of the role of GRETA (the group that monitors the Convention) in championing the provision of unconditional assistance to victims.

[97] Council of Europe, *Explanatory Report* (n 18) [307]. This approach is consistent with the approach taken by GREVIO; see, for example, GREVIO, *GREVIO Baseline Evaluation Report Greece* (GREVIO/Inf(2023)23, 26 October 2023) [316]–[317]. See also Stoyanova, 'A Stark Choice: Domestic Violence or Deportation?' (n 85) 78–79.

[98] As appeared to be the case with one of Germany's (now withdrawn) reservations. 'Reservations and Declarations for Treaty No. 210—Council of Europe Convention on Preventing and Combating Violence against Women and Domestic Violence (CETS No 210): Reservation handed over by the State Secretary for Foreign Affairs of Germany to the Secretary General of the Council of Europe at the time of signature of the instrument, on 11 May 2011—Or. Engl., confirmed and completed in a letter from the Federal Minister for Foreign Affairs of Germany, deposited with the instrument of ratification on 12 October 2017—Or. Engl' (*Council of Europe*) <www.coe.int/en/web/conventions/full-%20list?module=declarations-by-treaty&numSte=210&codeNature=0> accessed 30 March 2023.

Finally, the residence permit granted under article 59(3) must be renewable. The comments made above as to the rights that this status should bestow also apply here.

7.4 The Istanbul Convention in Theory: An Exercise of the Legal Imagination

7.4.1 NA's Case

When we left NA in chapter 4, her attempt to secure permanent residence under the EU's domestic violence rule had failed, the CJEU ruling that KA's sudden departure, occurring before their divorce, had extinguished her derivative right of residence.[99] NA had sought the stability permanent residence provides. What she received *under EU law* was another precarious and dependent status. Although the Court took the first opportunity it had to correct its position, this restrictive ruling remained determinative of many victims' position for five years. This changed with *X v Belgian State* (2021),[100] where the CJEU found that rights could indeed be retained providing divorce proceedings are initiated within a reasonable period. TCN victims of domestic violence may now, therefore, be able to secure an independent right of residence where the EU Citizen spouse or registered partner has resided in the relevant EU MS in accordance with the Citizens' Directive, being economically active as a worker or self-employed person, for example. The TCN partner must also be economically active (or the family member of someone else who is), such activity needing to be maintained if permanent residence is to be secured.

How might, therefore, someone in NA's position be assisted by the Istanbul Convention? As a victim of domestic violence, and one able to evidence this, NA is a 'victim' as defined by the Convention and entitled (in this exercise) to the rights and protections it provides. Had NA been able to rely on the Convention, she might have sought help from the general and specialist support services States are required to provide to all victims, including healthcare, housing and financial support, counselling, and legal advice. Although we do not know what (if any) support NA received while her case progressed to the CJEU, we do know that KA's departure might have led to her exclusion, legally and/or practically, from a range of support services that provide resilience to violence, including welfare benefits and housing. By prohibiting Parties from discriminating against migrant women in their provision of support services, the Istanbul Convention has the potential to transform the position of migrant women, like NA, who are subject to violence.

[99] *NA (CJEU Judgment)* (n 5).
[100] Case C-930/19 *X v Belgian State* [2021] ECLI:EU:C:2021:657.

Could someone in NA's position benefit from the regimes created by article 59? Turning first to article 59(1), NA's migration status *did depend* on that of her spouse. Her loss of that status may be connected to the violence she experienced. It may also be connected to the dissolution of her relationship. Indeed, in NA's case, the three conditions of the rule—violence, dependency, and relationship breakdown—seem both legally and practically inseparable.[101] The difficulty arises from the requirement that the applicant 'depends' on another for her migration status. NA had lost her dependent status by the time that she made her immigration application. An interpretation of article 59(1) that prevented women in NA's position from benefiting from it would replicate deficiencies (partially) corrected by the CJEU. It would strengthen, rather than counter, the control that perpetrators of violence exercise over their migrant partners. Such consequences would be manifestly contrary to the Convention's protective purposes. Rather than interpreting article 59(1) by reference to the evolving EU rule that it draws on, I have argued for an approach to 'depends' that relates to a potential applicant's migration status at the time that *any* of the substantive requirements of the rule arise. Following this interpretation, women who lose their residence rights because the person who they derive them from abandons them (or otherwise no longer meets the Directive's 'qualified person' requirements) may be eligible for an autonomous migration status. Similarly protected are women who overstay their permission because of their partner's violent and controlling behaviour. Centrally, if being a victim of violence is regarded by the Council of Europe as a ground for converting a dependent migration status into one that is autonomous, the ability to do so cannot depend on whether the perpetrator of that violence chooses to remain in the relevant Party's territory or chooses to remain in work.[102] Finally, in chapter 5 I argued that what the EU's domestic violence rule offers victims are the rights provided by market citizenship, notably to be an economic actor in accordance with a particular gendered conception of labour. The rule's passing of the economic activity requirement from the EU Citizen to the TCN makes it less protective as the vulnerability of the individual it purports to protect increases. Article 59(1)'s silence on such matters would ensure that, post *X v Belgian State*, TCNs' ability to support themselves economically, whether for the short or longer term, does not determine their access to an independent residence status.

Article 59(2) could have benefited NA if KA had remained in the jurisdiction. If KA had been investigated for his violent conduct, or if immigration

[101] Adopting the interpretation of 'particularly difficult circumstances' set out above and using the phrase to link the rule's substantive requirements. NA's predicament at the relevant time (a victim of potentially criminal violence, pregnant, and caring for another young child) would make her eligible for status under art 59(1) whether or not my or Stoyanova's 'severity threshold' interpretation is preferred. Stoyanova, 'A Stark Choice: Domestic Violence or Deportation?' (n 85).

[102] To draw on and paraphrase Case C-115/15 *Secretary of State for the Home Department v NA* [2016] ECLI:EU:C:2016:259, Opinion of AG Wathelet, para 76.

proceedings had been brought against him, NA's dependent migration status could have been affected. In such circumstances, article 59(2) could protect a victim's position, preventing removal and providing time to seek an alternative residence status.

Finally, NA could also seek a renewable residence permit under article 59(3)(a) (in addition to, or instead of a permit under article 59(1)), her stay being necessary owing to her personal circumstances. As article 59(3) is silent as to the migration status of any potential applicant (or indeed, perpetrator), issues as to NA's dependency (or not) on KA do not arise. Of course, the evidential requirements, application process, and permission granted under article 59(1) or (3) are all determined by Parties' own migration laws. Whether or not a woman applies for either an autonomous or renewable residence permit will, in practice, be determined by issues relating to these processes, as well as by the rights that attach to each form of permission granted. In both cases, I have argued that, in line with the purposes of the Convention, any permission granted must be non-temporary (particularly important given that leave granted under article 59(1) does not have to be renewable) and must bestow significant rights, including the right to access State support and the labour market.

In chapter 4, I also explored the potential of the UK's Migrant Victims of Domestic Abuse Concession (MVDAC),[103] and domestic violence rule,[104] to remedy compounded disadvantage. Those eligible for the concession and accompanying rule are, I argued, only a small proportion of those subject to both domestic violence and migration control. My exploration of NA's reimagined UK case revealed that, where a victim's status depends on someone who is not British or resident here, seeking support under the MVDAC could result in their loss of status and involuntary departure from the UK. Here it is worth returning to the case of *R (on the application of SWP)* (2023)[105] which concerned the wife of a skilled worker. SWP's partner had threatened her with deportation; leaving their violent relationship and protecting their child had left SWP destitute.[106] SWP sought the assistance of the then domestic violence concession and rule, a combination that may provide short-term financial support and a route to permanent residence. SWP's discrimination law challenge to her exclusion from these protections failed.[107] Article 59(1)'s concern with all victims whose residence depends on that of a spouse or partner would ensure that women like SWP no longer have to choose between safety and status.

[103] Home Office, *Migrant Victims of Domestic Abuse Concession (formerly the destitute domestic violence concession (DDVC))* (Version 4, 4 April 2024).
[104] Appendix Victim of Domestic Abuse (n 80).
[105] *R (SWP) v Secretary of State for the Home Department* [2023] EWCA Civ 439, [2023] 4 WLR 37.
[106] ibid [16]–[22].
[107] ibid [50].

7.4.2 EK's Case

Unlike NA, EK did eventually receive permission to remain in the UK under the Trafficking Convention, read with the positive obligations imposed by article 4 of the ECHR.[108] However, that permission was granted in 2013, seven years after she had first been trafficked into the UK (by Mrs Alibhai in 2006), six years after she had been re-trafficked (by Mrs Kilumanga in 2007), and three years after she was officially recognised as a victim (in 2010, when her claim for asylum was also refused). EK should have received assistance when, having been referred into the National Referral Mechanism (NRM) (in 2010), she was granted a brief 'recovery and reflection period'. However, before her formal identification (and, indeed, potentially after it) EK's migration status, 'an overstayer', left her excluded from receiving a variety of sources of State support. These exclusions provided Mr and Mrs Dhanji with a powerful source of control over EK. They may have enabled, or at least facilitated, her re-trafficking: when she escaped the Dhanjis, EK was faced with the prospect of either being homeless and destitute or 'working for' Mrs Kilumanga. Finally, these exclusions may also have contributed to her extremely poor physical and mental health. EK believed the partially correct assertions of her traffickers that the police would not assist her and that she would have to pay for medical treatment.

EK would also be considered a 'victim' under the Istanbul Convention and therefore entitled (in this scenario, again if not in fact) to the rights and protections it provides. By prohibiting Parties from discriminating against migrant women, the Convention also has the potential to alter radically EK's position. She might have received support from the general and specialist support services States are required to provide to all victims, a greater array of which are available to victims under the Istanbul Convention than the trafficking regime.[109] Crucially, the receipt of such support might have enabled her to escape the Dhanjis sooner and decreased her risk of being re-trafficked. In either case, the physical and psychological consequences of EK's ill-treatment by the Dhanjis, or by Mrs Kilumanga, could have been significantly reduced, or even averted.

EK would not be entitled to an autonomous residence permit under article 59(1) of the Convention because she was not dependent for her migration status on a spouse or partner but potentially on her employer (following the misapplication of the then rules and policy). EK also could not rely on article 59(2) to obtain the suspension of any expulsion proceedings initiated against her (which, as we saw, the Dhanjis attempted to procure). This protection is, it will be recalled, also

[108] *EK (Article 4 ECHR: Anti-Trafficking Convention) Tanzania* (n 6).

[109] See art 3 in conjunction with arts 20, 22, and 57, for example, and compare these with the rights provided by the trafficking regime, as summarised in the previous chapter.

limited to proceedings brought in relation to a status that is dependent on that of a spouse or partner.

As article 59(3)(a) of the Istanbul Convention repeats, almost verbatim, the provision of the trafficking regime under which EK was eventually granted permission to remain, she would, we can imagine, be entitled to a renewable residence permit under it. This provision of the trafficking regime had, however, to be interpreted with article 4 of the ECHR (the prohibition on slavery and servitude) to produce this result. The Istanbul Convention's focus on violence, prevention, and its rights-based reparation (rather than the means by which someone enters the jurisdiction, per the migration control/criminal law approach to trafficking discussed in the preceding chapter) should produce such a result independent of any other claim a person has.

Finally, EK would not be entitled to a residence permit under article 59(3)(b) as, despite her best efforts, no criminal proceedings were brought against those responsible for her ill-treatment. EK's case also reveals, therefore, the importance of the Istanbul Convention's requirement that States provide residence permits under *both* article 59(3)(a) and (b). It will be recalled that the support provided by the EU's Residence Permits Directive is entirely dependent on first, there being criminal proceedings against any suspected trafficker(s) and secondly, the victim cooperating with those proceedings.[110] As discussed above, many States also provide residence permits in just one of the two circumstances listed in article 14(1) of the Trafficking Convention (cooperation and/or personal circumstances). Recent, regressive developments in the UK have taken advantage of this to limit the situations in which a victim of trafficking may regularise their status.[111] Article 59(3) may, in certain circumstances, offer a corrective to this and any partial conditionality that results. Notably, it also offers a route to regularisation to a much broader group of migrant women, including domestic workers who are not trafficked or held in servitude, but who are subject to other forms of violence against women, including sexual harassment and physical abuse.

7.5 The Istanbul Convention in Practice

This chapter's analysis of the Istanbul Convention has been conducted in a different register to that of the other regimes considered in this book. This is, in part, because the EU and UK have sought, in different ways and to different extents, to limit or

[110] Residence Permits Directive, art 8(1).

[111] Compare Trafficking Convention, art 14(1)(a) with Nationality and Borders Act 2022, s 65(2)(a) and Immigration Rules HC 590, Appendix Temporary Permission to Stay for Victims of Human Trafficking or Slavery, VTS 3.1–3.4. As explained in chapter 6, the grounds on which permission may be granted, set out in the Act at s 65(2), do not appear to map onto both limbs of the Trafficking Convention's art 14.

evade certain of the Convention's obligations. The EU's accession to the Istanbul Convention has, as will be discussed in the Conclusion, had a significant impact on the rights of asylum-seeking and refugee women.[112] The EU's partial and highly selective engagement with it appears, however, to leave intact much of its current legislative framework on violence experienced in the context of migration control. The situation in the UK is also complicated. Article 59 has already been drawn on in discrimination law-based challenges to the domestic violence rule and this has, in some cases, contributed to its expansion, including to the partners of refugees.[113] The UK's reservation to article 59, however, precludes further positive developments in this area. It has already been observed that the UK operates a range of rules that appear, on their face, to be incompatible with the Convention when applied to victims of violence. The potential impact of the Convention's non-discrimination provisions on these is hard to predict. Victims of violence in the UK cannot rely directly on article 4(3) or other relevant provisions in litigation because the Istanbul Convention has not been incorporated into domestic law.[114] For now, therefore, the impact of the Convention in the UK will depend on GREVIO's scrutiny and the UK's response to it. The impact of the Convention on migrant women in Europe is also, again in different ways and to different extents, contingent on GREVIO's analysis of and engagement with the Convention's Parties. It is fruitful, therefore, to consider briefly GREVIO's approach to both discrimination and residence status.

GREVIO has consistently adopted an intersectional approach to discrimination, its observations and recommendations on migration status being consonant with the interpretation of article 4(3) provided above. The exclusions that women without a valid migration status are subject to in Denmark have, for example, been described as 'counter' to the spirit of the Convention, the Danish authorities being urged to implement its protections in full and without discrimination.[115] GREVIO has similarly called for Austria to remove barriers to services based on migration status.[116] GREVIO has also discussed article 4(3) in its General Reports, affirming the rights of asylum-seeking and refugee women, amongst others, to receive the Convention's benefits.[117] It has, consequently,

[112] Notably Case C–621/21 *WS v Intervyuirasht organ na Darzhavna agentsia za bezhantsite pri Ministerskia savet* [GC] [2024] ECLI:EU:C:2024:47.

[113] Following *A v Secretary of State for the Home Department* [2016] CSIH 38, [2016] SC 776 (before ratification and the reservation), but see *R (FA (Sudan))* [2021] EWCA Civ 59, [2021] 4 WLR 22.

[114] There is, however, a 'strong presumption' in favour of interpreting relevant policies and rules so as not to place the UK in breach of its obligations under international law. This was discussed in relation to the Trafficking Convention in chapter 6. See further *R (Atamewan) v Secretary of State for the Home Department* [2013] EWHC 2727, [2014] 1 WLR 1959 [103]; *R (PK (Ghana)) v Secretary of State for the Home Department* [2018] EWCA Civ 98, [2018] 1 WLR 3955; *MN and IXU v Secretary of State for the Home Department* [2020] EWCA Civ 1746, [2021] 1 WLR 1956.

[115] GREVIO, *Baseline Evaluation Report Denmark* (n 79) 14.

[116] GREVIO, *GREVIO Baseline Evaluation Report Austria* (GREVIO/Inf(2017)4, 27 September 2017) 31–33.

[117] GREVIO, *1st General Report on GREVIO's Activities* (Council of Europe, April 2020) [55].

identified and expressed concerns about intersectional discrimination, including on the grounds of migration status, when reviewing the reports of Austria, Portugal, Sweden, Italy, and Belgium.[118] GREVIO has similarly commented on the exclusion of migrant and asylum-seeking women from shelters in Austria, Belgium, France, Serbia, Spain, and, indirectly, in Malta.[119] Finally, GREVIO has acknowledged the impact of the Covid-19 pandemic specifically on migrant victims of violence.[120]

The picture is slightly less clear when we turn to the Convention's regimes of exception. This is, in part, because some of GREVIO's reports have lacked detail and precision including, for example, on victimhood and the different obligations imposed by different subsections of article 59.[121] More recently, GREVIO has expressed a range of concerns about Parties' rules on residence status. Given the very significant differences between Parties, and between Parties' provisions and the Convention, GREVIO has repeatedly called on States to undertake, and then act on, a formal review of their rules.[122] More specifically, GREVIO has expressed concern about the Danish requirement that dependent spouses/partners demonstrate 'attachment' to the State in some way (through taking a language course, for example), such requirements adding 'to the power which abusive men in Denmark have over foreign brides/wives'.[123] This may prove significant, indicating GREVIO's preparedness to use article 59 to explore both responses to violence and those elements of the rules that increase vulnerability to it.[124] GREVIO has also expressed concern about the position of unmarried partners in Greece and rules limiting a victim's access to status by reference to the nationality of their spouse.[125] Finally, GREVIO has encouraged both Ireland and Sweden to ensure that victims who are dependent for their status on those who are refugees or beneficiaries of subsidiary protection are also able to secure an independent migration status.[126] The response of States to these and to other relevant recommendations is, as yet, unclear. GREVIO's increasingly robust reviews of Parties, particularly regarding discrimination and hierarchies of migration status and protection are, however, most welcome.

118 GREVIO, *2nd General Report on GREVIO's Activities* (Council of Europe, April 2021) [66].

119 ibid [81].

120 GREVIO, *4th General Report on GREVIO's Activities* (Council of Europe, September 2023) 17.

121 GREVIO, *GREVIO Baseline Evaluation Report Luxembourg* (GREVIO/Inf(2023)4, 10 July 2023) [218], which limits its discussion to domestic violence.

122 GREVIO, *Baseline Evaluation Report Belgium* (n 79) [215]; GREVIO, *Baseline Evaluation Report Greece* (n 97) [320].

123 GREVIO, *Baseline Evaluation Report Denmark* (n 79) [226].

124 ibid [227]–[228]. GREVIO also questioned the imposition of such a requirement in 'domestic violence rule'/art 59(1) scenarios and invited the Danish Immigration Service to reconsider it.

125 GREVIO, *Baseline Evaluation Report Greece* (n 97) [313].

126 GREVIO, *GREVIO Baseline Evaluation Report Sweden* (GREVIO/Inf(2018)15, 21 January 2019) [240]; GREVIO, *GREVIO Baseline Evaluation Report Ireland* (GREVIO/Inf(2023)22, 14 November 2023) [316].

7.6 Conclusion

I have argued that the Istanbul Convention has the capacity to transform the position of women who, like NA and EK, are profoundly disadvantaged by both the migration status they hold and the violence they have experienced. The Convention's general obligations in relation to discrimination, prevention, and violence may enable those aspects of migration law that increase women's vulnerability to violence to be contested. If violence does occur, the specific rights and protections that must be accorded to *all* victims may enable migrant women to both access support and regularise their status. The Istanbul Convention may, therefore, both avert and provide a remedy for compounded disadvantage. GREVIO's analysis and engagement with Parties will be crucial in realising this potential, early indications in this regard being positive.

While the EU's and UK's limited engagement with the Istanbul Convention may be permissible, it can and should change. There is nothing in *Opinion 1/19* that precludes the EU's full accession, the CJEU having accepted that chapter VII of the Istanbul Convention is within the scope of relevant provisions of the TFEU.[127] Germany has withdrawn the reservation that it entered to article 59.[128] The UK should do the same, particularly as its current position appears inconsistent with its obligations under CEDAW and other international instruments.[129] GREVIO could also be more robust in engaging with Parties to secure these outcomes.[130]

There is another way, however, that the Istanbul Convention and its monitoring body have been and may be yet more influential: their relationship with the ECHR and ECtHR. In chapter 3, I explained that the ECtHR has struggled, on occasion, to explain the relationships between domestic violence and discrimination. The Court may draw on the Istanbul Convention's definitions and approach to find domestic violence a form of discrimination against women, as it did in cases like *Bălşan v Romania* (2017)[131] and *Tkhelidze v Georgia* (2021).[132] It could make a similar move in cases that relate to other forms of violence against women, including trafficking. The rights and protections the Istanbul Convention provides may also continue to inform the ECtHR's analysis of States' response to violence,

[127] *Opinion 1/19* (n 44) [302]–[303].
[128] See the text and reference at n 98.
[129] 'Letter from Mandates of the Special Rapporteur on violence against women and girls, its causes and consequences; the Special Rapporteur on the human rights of migrants; the Special Rapporteur on trafficking in persons, especially women and children and the Working Group on discrimination against women and girls to the UK' (OL GBR 11/2022, 22 August 2022).
[130] As argued in Wojciech Burek, 'Reservations to the Istanbul Convention and the Role of GREVIO: A Call for New Approach' (2022) 22 Human Rights Law Review 1.
[131] *Bălşan v Romania* App no 49645/09 (ECtHR, 23 May 2017) para 79.
[132] *Tkhelidze v Georgia* App no 33056/17 (ECtHR, 8 July 2021), the Court drawing on this reasoning in a case that followed (also referred to in chapter 3), *A and B v Georgia* App no 73975/16 (ECtHR, 10 February 2022).

as they did in *Kurt v Austria* (2021).[133] States' non-ratification of the Convention may also be significant, indicating, as it did in *AE v Bulgaria* (2023)[134] their (lack of sufficient) commitment to 'fighting' domestic violence.[135] States' immigration rules should offer all women 'practical and effective' protection from violence.[136] In chapter 6, I discussed how domestic courts and the ECtHR interpreted positive ECHR obligations by reference to those of the Trafficking Convention. I ended by discussing *Chowdury v Greece* (2017),[137] where the denial of a Trafficking Convention reflection period contributed to a breach of the ECHR's article 4.[138] If and when a case concerning the treatment of a migrant victim of violence against women comes before the ECtHR, the Istanbul Convention's obligations on discrimination and residence status, and the views of GREVIO, may inform similar reasoning. Following the above, such a case could be highly significant, whether or not it comes from the UK, from another Party to the Convention (with or without a relevant reservation), or from a non-ratifying State.

[133] *Kurt v Austria* App no 62903/15 (ECtHR GC, 15 June 2021).
[134] *AE v Bulgaria* App no 53891/20 (ECtHR, 23 May 2023) para 121.
[135] ibid para 121.
[136] *Rantsev v Cyprus and Russia* (2010) 51 EHRR 1.
[137] *Chowdury v Greece* App no 21884/15 (ECtHR, 30 March 2017).
[138] ibid paras 121–22.

8
Conclusion: The Exceptions that Prove the Rule

8.1 Undoing Discrimination in Migration Law

I began this book with quotes from two women, one a partner, the other a domestic worker. They shared an experience, being made dependent for their permission to remain on a person, or persons, who were violent towards them. This book analyses some of the different forms of discrimination that impacted upon and determined these women's situations. To do so, it considers migration law's forging of status and international law's understanding of violence. It identifies patterns of disadvantage in the UK and draws analogies between these and the migration laws of other States and of the European Union (EU). It conceptualises and then delineates obligations in relation to violence against women. Centrally, it brings together six legal responses to violence experienced in the context of migration control and offers a new framework for their evaluation, one that focuses on the provision of a secure, rights-bestowing permission to remain. At the heart of this book is, therefore, an argument concerning the difference that migration status makes to an experience of violence, one in which disadvantage is compounded, and the remedy for it, an independent migration status. Related to this is an argument on discrimination against women and pre-emptive migration status reform. Flowing from it are arguments on scrutiny and different discrimination law grounds, and on co-extensive obligations. The analysis offered here has been an exercise in legal scholarship and in the legal imagination. The arguments I advance on migration status, discrimination, intersectionality, and violence are all rooted in the relevant rules, instruments, and jurisprudence. Different strands of these could, therefore, be drawn on before a court or tribunal (subject to the case and jurisdiction) or relied on in dialogue with a policymaker or legislator. Yet it is not these actors that this book centres on. Instead, the analysis is structured around and developed from the legal challenges brought by migrant women to the rules that determine their status.

Siobhán Mullally contends that the 'nexus between access to safe migration routes, obligations of due diligence, and compliance with human rights standards is rarely acknowledged by states'.[1] The arguments on discrimination made

[1] Siobhán Mullally, 'Migration, Gender, and the Limits of Rights' in Ruth Rubio-Marín (ed), *Human Rights and Immigration* (OUP 2014) 170. Mullally is specifically referring to the predicament of domestic workers here, but the point has broader relevance.

Violence against Women and Regimes of Exception. Catherine Briddick, Oxford University Press.
 DOI: 10.1093/9780191959899.003.0008

here provide a means of recognising such connections, establishing States' obligations to end their disadvantageous treatment of women, to offer effective protection from violence, and to provide victims with a reparative remedy. The analysis starts in the UK and then broadens to engage with EU law. In doing so, it captures a particular legal moment in the UK/EU's post-Brexit divergence, one which takes place within shared legal, institutional, and political contexts: the Council of Europe and a populist backlash against migrants' and women's rights. Scholarship from a range of European and common law jurisdictions is also drawn upon to indicate the relevance of arguments on status and disadvantage to the migration laws of other States, both within and outside the EU. Consequently, while this book focuses on regimes of exception in the UK and Europe, the legal and analytical framework that it contributes for their evaluation could be applied in a broader range of jurisdictions and contexts.[2]

UK immigration law is constantly being revised, 'reformed', and contested. Yet while rules and policies change on an almost monthly basis, broad and enduring patterns of advantage and disadvantage can be discerned. In chapter 2, I engage in a doctrinal and statistical analysis of the fragmented and shifting hierarchy that migration law creates, one conducted at a high level of generality, to map who is where within it. I then use the effects-based concept of indirect discrimination to scrutinise the rules that determine status within this hierarchy. The legal framework at the heart of this analysis is the prohibition of discrimination found in article 14 of the European Convention on Human Rights (ECHR).[3] This scrutiny yields two insights. First, women, particularly racialised women, are disadvantaged by immigration law's creation and distribution of migration statuses. Secondly, such disadvantage is, at least in some cases, produced by rules that indirectly discriminate on the grounds of sex. Arguing discrimination in this context requires paying careful attention to the role of comparators and to the wrong of stereotyping. If it is accepted that the statuses of partner and domestic worker are based on stereotypes, women's comparative disadvantage, their experiences as probationary wives and precarious workers, cannot be justified. Indeed, establishing this may, in and of itself, be sufficient to impugn the relevant rules as discriminatory.

Having drawn, in chapter 2, on the European Court of Human Rights' (ECtHR) article 14 jurisprudence to understand the UK's distribution of migration statuses, chapter 3 starts by examining its application in cases involving domestic violence. I argue that the ECtHR's failure in *Opuz v Turkey* (2009)[4] to explain when

[2] An interesting starting point could be the US' domestic violence regime of exception, see further Natalie Nanasi, 'The U Visa's Failed Promise for Survivors of Domestic Violence' (2018) 29 Yale Journal of Law & Feminism 271.

[3] Convention for the Protection of Human Rights and Fundamental Freedoms (adopted 4 November 1950, entered into force 3 September 1953) ETS 5 (European Convention on Human Rights, as amended) (ECHR).

[4] *Opuz v Turkey* App no 33401/02 (ECtHR, 9 June 2009).

such violence, as distinct from States' responses to it, is discrimination contrary to article 14, has generated contradictory lines of reasoning. In response to this ambiguity, I advance a juridical account of violence against women. The core of this legal wrong is identified by reference to five international legal instruments' definitions of such violence, including those relevant to the Convention on the Elimination of All Forms of Discrimination against Women (CEDAW),[5] and set out in the Council of Europe Convention on Preventing and Combating Violence against Women and Domestic Violence (the Istanbul Convention).[6] These definitions cohere around three elements: conduct that causes certain kinds of harm, conduct that is interpersonal, and, crucially, conduct that is gender-based. This approach combines narrowness and breadth. Its narrowness comes from my exclusion of structural violence and focus on conduct that is interpersonal. Its breadth comes from my understanding of that conduct primarily in terms of acts but also as encompassing threats, attempts, and omissions. Narrowness and breadth are simultaneously present in my approach to violence and women. While I include acts that are directed at a woman because she is woman, or which affect women disproportionately, I exclude from my account conduct experienced by women that is not so gender-based.

Some forms of violence are more readily understood as entailing (or also entailing) violence against women than others. Consequently, the international consensus on interpersonal, gender-based conduct that causes harm is drawn on to provide an uncontentious foundation to my claim that domestic violence and trafficking are, in some circumstances and situations, violence against women. My analysis of migration law's treatment of women and the remedy for compounded disadvantage is underpinned by what flows from this: States' obligations to provide 'effective measures of prevention, protection, punishment and reparation'.[7]

Compounded disadvantage arises from the interaction between migration status and violence against women. While this interaction will produce a diverse

[5] Convention on the Elimination of All Forms of Discrimination against Women (adopted 18 December 1979, entered into force 3 September 1981) 1249 UNTS 13. Relevant definitions can be found in UN Committee for the Elimination of All Forms of Discrimination against Women, 'General Recommendation No 19' in 'Note by the Secretariat, Compilation of General Comments and General Recommendations Adopted by Human Rights Treaty Bodies' (29 July 1994) UN Doc HRI/GEN/1/Rev.1 [6] (CEDAW's GR 19); UN Committee on the Elimination of Discrimination against Women, 'General Recommendation No 35 on Gender-Based Violence Against Women, Updating General Recommendation No 19' (26 July 2017) UN Doc CEDAW/C/GC/35 [9] (CEDAW's GR 35).

[6] Council of Europe Convention on Preventing and Combating Violence against Women and Domestic Violence (adopted 11 May 2011, entered into force 1 August 2014) CETS 210, art 3(a) and (d) (Istanbul Convention). See also Declaration on the Elimination of Violence against Women UNGA Res 48/104 (20 December 1993) art 1; Inter-American Convention on the Prevention, Punishment and Eradication of Violence against Women (adopted 9 June 1994, entered into force 5 March 1995) (1994) 33 ILM 1534, art 1; Protocol to the African Charter on Human and Peoples' Rights on the Rights of Women in Africa (adopted 11 July 2003, entered into force 25 November 2005) OAU Doc Cab/Leg/66.6, art 1(j).

[7] Rashida Manjoo, 'State Responsibility to Act with Due Diligence in the Elimination of Violence against Women' (2013) 2 International Human Rights Law Review 240, 245.

array of experiences, in chapter 4 I explain that what these share is control, exclusion, and an intensified experience of violence. In the fashioning and distribution of migration statuses, States may generate or amplify vulnerability to different forms of ill-treatment, including violence and other rights violations. These statuses and the legal frameworks in which they are imbricated may also exclude victims from those services that provide protection from and resilience to such harm. Yet this is not what is required of States, ethically or legally. Drawing on the work of Martha Albertson Fineman and others, and weaving this scholarship together with the jurisprudence of the ECtHR, I explore States' obligations in relation to vulnerability, the embodied, the embedded, and the constructed and imposed.[8] In doing so, I connect the assets that the responsive State should provide (ethically) with those obligations States have chosen to assume (legally), different facets of compounded disadvantage illuminating States' failure to discharge these obligations to migrant victims of violence against women.

Two allied arguments rest on Part I's analysis of migration status and violence against women. First, States are required to remedy their disadvantageous and discriminatory treatment of women, reviewing how they achieve their aims in migration law and, if necessary, changing the means they adopt to do so.[9] The resulting reforms would not, of course, preclude States from differentiating between citizens and migrants, or between different types of migrants. They would, however, require States to address gendered patterns of disadvantage and stereotyping. They would also require them to ensure that however statuses differ, they nonetheless afford basic protections from violence and other rights violations through, for example, their independence, the rights they bestow, their duration, and/or their renewability.

Secondly, States should provide those subject to compounded disadvantage with an independent, rights-bestowing migration status. Such a status offers both effective protection from, and a reparative remedy for, compounded disadvantage. A secure permission to remain would enable a woman to leave a violent home or workplace, access support, and recover from her experience. Such a status would reduce vulnerability to further violence, enable someone to bring legal proceedings against those responsible for it, and put the victim in the position of being able to make a meaningful decision as to the jurisdiction in which they make their home.

[8] Including Martha Albertson Fineman, 'The Vulnerable Subject and the Responsive State' (2010) 60 Emory Law Journal 251; Lourdes Peroni and Alexandra Timmer, 'Vulnerable Groups: The Promise of an Emerging Concept in European Human Rights Convention Law' (2013) 11 International Journal of Constitutional Law 1056; Martha Albertson Fineman, 'Vulnerability and Inevitable Inequality' (2017) 4 Oslo Law Review 133; Shahrzad Fouladvand and Tony Ward, 'Human Trafficking, Vulnerability and the State' (2019) 81 Journal of Criminal Law 39.

[9] Drawing on Sandra Fredman, 'Addressing Disparate Impact: Indirect Discrimination and the Public Sector Equality Duty' (2014) 43 Industrial Law Journal 349.

My account of the wrong and its gender-sensitive remedy provides the basis for my analysis of selected national and supranational responses to violence experienced in the context of migration control. When, in Part II, I approach the rules that determine status, I do not provide a detailed definitional account of what does, or does not, constitute a regime of exception. The use of the term 'regime' is apt because it captures broad combinations of law and policy that, taken together, may determine rights and status. As the regimes are all departures from the general position that, absent a claim for international protection, a person who no longer has valid permission to remain should leave the jurisdiction, it also seems appropriate to highlight their exceptionality. The regimes evaluated have different legal sources and bestow different packages of rights. They also operate in parallel with refugee and other protections from *refoulement* (a point I will return to). Taking a broad and flexible approach enables the evaluation of regimes which, while differing in a number of key respects, share one key element: they enable some migrants, who have experienced some forms of violence, to receive a migration status.

Chapter 5 evaluates two regimes which determine the status of migrant victims of domestic violence in the EU and UK respectively: article 13(2)(c) of the Citizens' Directive[10] and Appendix Victim of Domestic Abuse.[11] Chapter 6 examines provisions in the Convention on Action against Trafficking in Human Beings (the Trafficking Convention)[12] and the EU's Residence Permits Directive,[13] which require States to protect and regularise the stay of some victims of trafficking. The final regimes considered, those created by the Istanbul Convention's article 59, are analysed in chapter 7. Part II's evaluation of these regimes by reference to the legal and normative framework established in Part I reveals their failure, in different ways and to different extents, to remedy compounded disadvantage.

8.2 Perpetuating Discrimination in Migration Law

The domestic violence and trafficking regimes, taken together, are exceptions to migration law's 'return or be removed' position, exceptions that prove and enforce the rule. Not only do these regimes normalise the denial of status to many victims of violence but they may also facilitate their deportation.

[10] Directive 2004/38/EC of the European Parliament and of the Council of 29 April 2004 on the right of citizens of the Union and their family members to move and reside freely within the territory of the Member States amending Regulation (EEC) No 1612/68 and repealing Directives 64/221/EEC, 68/360/EEC, 72/194/EEC, 73/148/EEC, 75/34/EEC, 75/35/EEC, 90/364/EEC, 90/365/EEC and 93/96/EEC [2004] OJ L 158/77, and corrigenda ([2004] OJ L 229/35, [2005] OJ L 197/34, and [2007] OJ L 204/28).

[11] Immigration Rules HC 590, Appendix Victim of Domestic Abuse.

[12] Council of Europe Convention on Action against Trafficking in Human Beings (adopted 16 May 2005, entered into force 1 February 2008) CETS 197.

[13] Council Directive 2004/81/EC of 29 April 2004 on the residence permit issued to third-country nationals who are victims of trafficking in human beings or who have been the subject of an action to facilitate illegal immigration, who cooperate with the competent authorities [2004] OJ L261/19.

To the extent that the Court of Justice of the EU (CJEU) has been required to interpret the EU's domestic violence rule, it has been consistent in approaching it as a 'derogation', relevant only in 'exceptional cases'.[14] The Court, in *X v Belgian State* (2021),[15] does amend its position on divorce and departure, remedying the exclusionary interpretation offered in *Secretary of State for the Home Department v NA* (2016).[16] This change will improve the position of some victims of violence, enabling them to retain their residence rights. For them, and for those whose circumstances fall within the rule's ambit, a more secure and then potentially permanent status may be reparative of compounded disadvantage. This 'fall within' is crucial, however, as the rule transfers the right/requirement to be economically active in particular (gendered) ways from the EU Citizen to the third-country national (TCN). Consequently, the more vulnerable the TCN is—the more severe the violence is, for example, or the more onerous the caring responsibilities—the less likely it is that they will receive a status, for both the short and longer term. Such a position is starkly at odds with the rule's protective purpose.[17]

Two connected elements make up the UK's domestic violence regime of exception: the Migrant Victims of Domestic Abuse Concession (MVDAC)[18] and Appendix Victims of Domestic Abuse. These offer short-term regularisation and then a route to permanent residence. Once again, the status on offer is one that may be reparative of compounded disadvantage. A significant proportion of those subject to such disadvantage are, however, excluded from the scope of the concession, while a significant proportion of those who may benefit from the concession are, in turn, excluded from the rule. Some, such as those who are the partners of people who are British or resident here but who do not have permission in this category, may be unable to access either the concession or the rule. Others, such as the partners of labour migrants, may benefit from the former but not the latter, and so face being required to leave the UK once their three-month permission to remain has expired.[19] The MVDAC does offer short-term support in the form of a status that grants access to welfare benefits and the labour market. Yet accessing it may result in a victim being made destitute and deportable.

Chapter 6's account of the trafficking regime reveals a tension between responses to trafficking that are rights-based and those that remain dominated by criminal

[14] Case C–115/15 *Secretary of State for the Home Department v NA* [2016] ECLI:EU:C:2016:487, paras 41–42. This formulation is repeated in Case C–930/19 *X v Belgian State* [2021] ECLI:EU:C:2021:657, paras 34–35.

[15] *X v Belgian State* (n 14).

[16] *NA (CJEU Judgment)* (n 14).

[17] For an approach to which, see Case C–115/15 *Secretary of State for the Home Department v NA* [2016] ECLI:EU:C:2016:259, Opinion of AG Wathelet, paras 67–76 (and the Opinion more broadly).

[18] Home Office, *Migrant Victims of Domestic Abuse Concession (formerly the destitute domestic violence concession (DDVC))* (Version 4, 4 April 2024).

[19] Unless, for example, another application can be made (eg for international protection).

and migration law enforcement imperatives. Rather than offering regularisation, both the Trafficking Convention and Residence Permits Directive operate, in different ways and to different extents, to secure the readmission of a victim to their country of origin. As a consequence, legal advances on victims' 'rights' are stripped of their substance by the deportation of those victims from the very States obliged to uphold them. Indeed, within the UK, legislation and policy seek to resolve the tension between rights and return in favour of the latter by recasting victims as threats to public order.[20] The extent to which the trafficking regime is able to offer a reparative response to compounded disadvantage depends on a number of factors. These include the individual's circumstances, the States' identification procedures, the basis on which any residence permit is granted, and, of course, its duration. In some circumstances and States, the regime may actually exacerbate or reinstitute disadvantage. Its focus on the means by which a person enters a jurisdiction has deflected attention from the violence, exploitation, or other rights violations they are subject to, denying the victim concerned a remedy.[21] The conditionality built into EU law, and to a lesser extent the Trafficking Convention, restricts the possibility of securing a permit. Compounded disadvantage may, therefore, be exacerbated or reinstated through either the denial of status following the recovery period or the imposition of new forms of dependency, on the continuation of criminal proceedings for example. It will be recalled that in *EK (Article 4 ECHR: Anti-Trafficking Convention) Tanzania*,[22] EK's identification as a trafficking victim coincided with the Home Office deciding to deport her.[23]

Two brief conclusions may be drawn from the above. First, the domestic violence and trafficking regimes provide, in different ways, a short-term period of stay to some (eg retention of rights, under the MVDAC, or through a recovery period), this being followed by the provision of a longer-term permission to remain in certain limited circumstances. Such temporariness may benefit States, including by enabling victims to be identified and encouraging them to cooperate with criminal proceedings. A person who fears deportation may, however, be deterred from doing either or both of these things. For all the reasons advanced in chapters 3 and 4, such a situation does not provide effective protection from violence. Nor does it offer a reparative and gender-sensitive response to compounded disadvantage. Some victims of violence may have, in such a period, the rights and time they need to recover from their experiences. However, by denying those who have already been subject to violence and discrimination the ability to make long-term,

[20] Explanatory Notes: Illegal Migration Act 2023 [147]. See also *In re NIHRC* [2024] NIKB 35 [150]–[158].
[21] *CN v UK* (2013) 56 EHRR 24; *Kawogo v UK* App no 56921/09 (ECtHR, 3 September 2013).
[22] *EK (Article 4 ECHR: Anti-Trafficking Convention) Tanzania* [2013] UKUT 313 (IAC), [2013] Imm AR 895.
[23] ibid [65].

meaningful, decisions about their lives, such temporary relief may itself constitute a separate injustice.[24]

Secondly, compounded disadvantage may be exacerbated and enforced for those who face removal, whether immediately or following some form of stay, in the relevant jurisdiction. Once again, this constitutes a breach of victims' human rights and an additional, further injustice.[25] This book has sought to make the wrong of removal (or the threat thereof) under such circumstances more legible. It has done so by illuminating the role of the State in constructing vulnerability to violence, denying effective protection from it, and then rendering a significant proportion of those it has so disadvantaged destitute, detainable, and deportable. I explore this and related issues further in the three sections that follow. I also make some tentative suggestions for how this situation could be challenged or changed.

8.3 Identifying Grounds, Situating the Claim

Of all the cases discussed in chapter 5, *A v Secretary of State for the Home Department* (2016)[26] offers the most clarity on the relationship between the relevant domestic violence rule and States' obligations in relation to discrimination against women. Drawing on some of the instruments and elements relied on in chapter 3, including CEDAW and the Istanbul Convention, the Inner House recognised that the violence the rule was responding to was gender-based.[27] As a consequence, and placing both the rule and its analysis within the context of the UK's international obligations to eliminate violence against women, the Inner House concluded that an overly restrictive approach to eligibility would be indirectly discriminatory to women.[28] This framing ensured that a comparatively high level of scrutiny was applied to the justifications offered for the differential treatment of refugee spouses in comparison with those who were the partner of someone who was British or settled in the UK.[29]

This approach to a regime of exception is, itself, exceptional. Neither domestic violence nor protection nor discrimination find substantive treatment in *NA*. This is the case notwithstanding that these issues were raised (in the domestic litigation at least) and engaged with by the Advocate General.[30] The UK cases, from

[24] Drawing on Rebecca Buxton, 'Justice in Waiting: The Harms and Wrongs of Temporary Refugee Protection' (2023) 22 European Journal of Political Theory 51. With thanks to Cathryn Costello for drawing my attention to this article.

[25] Drawing on Deborah Hellman, 'Indirect Discrimination and the Duty to Avoid Compounding Injustice' in Hugh Collins and Tarunabh Khaitan (eds), *Foundations of Indirect Discrimination Law* (Hart 2018).

[26] *A v Secretary of State for the Home Department* [2016] CSIH 38, [2016] SC 776.

[27] ibid [29], [64], [65], [79].

[28] ibid [79].

[29] ibid [38], [47]–[56].

[30] *Opuz v Turkey* (n 4) was referred to in the domestic litigation, *Ahmed (Amos; Zambrano; reg 15A(3)(c) 2006 EEA Regs)* [2013] UKUT 00089 (IAC) [17]. See also *NA (AG Opinion)* (n 17) [67]-[76].

A onwards, are also remarkable for their cursory treatment of discrimination.[31] This is not just limited to arguments like those advanced here, which focus on discrimination against women. The justification analysis provided in relation to migration status in *R (on the application of SWP)* (2023)[32] is startlingly superficial when compared with the facts of the case or the representations the Court received. Analogous conclusions may be drawn in relation to the CJEU's contrived assessment of comparators and equality in *X v Belgian State* (2021).[33] Finally, the consequence of arguing cases on multiple grounds, as per *R (on the application of FA (Sudan))* (2021),[34] seems to be a *lowering* of the standard of review.[35] Discrimination law challenges to the domestic violence rule have, therefore, to be careful in selecting their grounds and in calibrating the standard of review accordingly. Women's identity as migrants should not displace the discrimination they are subject to as migrant women. Finally, and related to this, claims could also be strengthened by reference to arguments on intersectional discrimination, in addition to that which contends single-axis discrimination on a range of grounds.[36]

Conspicuous in their absence from the relevant trafficking jurisprudence are arguments concerning violence and discrimination against women.[37] As discussed in chapters 3 and 6, this may be remedied by drawing together reasoning like that found in *Opuz* and *Rantsev v Cyprus and Russia* (2010)[38] to argue that migration law's failure to protect women from violence and exploitation that is gender-based denies them the equal protection of the law.

The apparent 'munificence' of both the domestic violence and trafficking regimes operates to mask their relative inaccessibility.[39] This position has been challenged, in some cases successfully, by reference to arguments rooted in discrimination law. As SWP's circumstances remind us, the consequences when these challenges fail may be devastating. However, this book's situating of the regimes of exception within States' obligations to offer women effective protection from, and a reparative remedy for, violence experienced in the context of migration control

[31] With the possible exception of *R (AM) v Secretary of State for the Home Department* [2022] EWHC 2591, [2023] 1 WLR 732, which concerned discrimination on the grounds of location.

[32] *R (SWP) v Secretary of State for the Home Department* [2023] EWCA Civ 439, [2023] 4 WLR 37.

[33] In addition to the arguments on this point in chapter 5, see further Francesca Strumia, 'Speaking Too Little, Yet Saying Too Much. The Wrong Signals about EU Values: *X. v. Belgian State*' (2022) 59 Common Market Law Review 1195.

[34] *R (FA (Sudan))* [2021] EWCA Civ 59, [2021] 4 WLR 22.

[35] ibid [48].

[36] On which, see Shreya Atrey, *Intersectional Discrimination* (OUP 2019).

[37] There have been successful challenges based on migration status, see further *R (JP and BS) v Secretary of State for the Home Department* [2019] EWHC 3346 (Admin), [2020] 1 WLR 918.

[38] *Rantsev v Cyprus and Russia* (2010) 51 EHRR 1.

[39] Drawing on, Audrey Macklin, 'Dancing across Borders: "Exotic Dancers", Trafficking, and Canadian Immigration Policy' (2003) 37 International Migration Review 464, 495. Macklin makes this argument in relation to trafficking, but it can also be applied to other situations where compounded disadvantage arises.

provides one avenue by which exclusions from those regimes may be contested. In this regard, the Inner House in *A* offers an example that could be built upon.

8.4 Developing Co-extensive Obligations: Systemic Integration

I have drawn on a wealth of different legal instruments and materials to advance this book's arguments on migration and violence. These include Council of Europe Conventions, EU Directives, international treaties, the decisions of regional and supranational courts, the recommendations and decisions of treaty bodies, and the reports of UN Special Rapporteurs. The proliferation of different sources of obligation and of (quasi)-judicial bodies, expert committees, and Special Procedures has prompted an interest in the fragmentation (or diversification) of international law and in systemic integration.[40] Systemic integration, broadly understood, avoids norm conflict by interpreting one source of legal obligation by reference to other relevant rules of international law.[41] While the term has not been used in any of the cases this book engages with, this interpretative approach is evident in many of them and in the arguments that these cases support.

It will be recalled that the CEDAW Committee positions both domestic violence and trafficking within that Convention's framework on discrimination against women.[42] In contrast, the ECtHR jurisprudence on both lacks clarity on the relationships between violence and discrimination. This is true even in cases like *Opuz*, where the Court draws on the work of the CEDAW Committee to aid its interpretation of the ECHR's non-discrimination obligations.[43] I have, in this book and elsewhere, suggested different ways in which the ECtHR's lack of clarity here could be resolved.[44] Nonetheless, my own conclusion, that violence against women

[40] International Law Commission, *Fragmentation of International Law: Difficulties Arising from the Diversification and Expansion of International Law: Report of the Study Group of the International Law Commission: Finalized by Martti Koskenniemi* (UN Doc A/CN4/L682, 13 April 2006).

[41] ibid [37]-[43], [410]-[432]. One of the report's conclusions was that this could be achieved by drawing on art 31(3)(c) of the Vienna Convention on the Law of Treaties (adopted 23 May 1969, entered into force 27 January 1980) 1155 UNTS 331. I have drawn on the report and provision here. See further Campbell McLachlan, 'The Principle of Systemic Integration and Article 31(3)(c) of the Vienna Convention' (2005) 54 International and Comparative Law Quarterly 279; Violeta Moreno-Lax, 'Systematising Systemic Integration: 'War Refugees', Regime Relations, and a Proposal for a Cumulative Approach to International Commitments' (2014) 12 Journal of International Criminal Justice 907; Anuscheh Farahat, 'Enhancing Constitutional Justice by Using External References: The European Court of Human Rights' Reasoning on the Protection against Expulsion' (2015) 28 Leiden Journal of International Law 303.

[42] CEDAW's GR 19 (n 5); CEDAW's GR 35 (n 5); UN Committee on the Elimination of Discrimination against Women 'General Recommendation No 38 on Trafficking in Women and Girls in the Context of Global Migration' (20 November 2020) UN doc CEDAW/C/GC/38.

[43] *Opuz v Turkey* (n 4) [184]-[187]. For a critical analysis of this, see Adamantia Rachovitsa, 'The Principle of Systemic Integration in Human Rights Law' (2017) 66 International and Comparative Law Quarterly 557.

[44] In addition to the arguments made in chapters 3 and 7, see also Catherine Briddick, 'Resisting Domestic Violence' (2024) 36 International Journal of Refugee Law 106.

is discriminatory and a breach of women's human rights, does not rest on whether or not it is (also) understood to be discrimination by reference to *both* CEDAW and the ECHR. This leaves open an alternative approach, one which allows for diversity in different instruments' understandings of discrimination but which nonetheless promotes dialogue between them. *AE v Bulgaria* (2023)[45] provides an illustration of what such a line of argument could achieve. Here, the Court drew on CEDAW to understand domestic violence as 'discrimination against women' and to inform its interpretation of the ECHR obligations States have to respond to it.[46] Yet, it was the State's failure to take steps to counter violence it understood was gender-based that generated the finding that article 14 had been breached.[47] Space precludes any further discussion of all the different forms that (unlawful?) discrimination against women could take, or what may flow from this in terms of those who hold duties in relation to it. The observations made here, however, raise interesting questions about the nature of its prohibition in domestic, regional, and international law, and the extent to which there is a shared consensus between these as to what this entails.

Systemic integration has also been influential in the jurisprudence relating to the regimes of exception. The Inner House's CEDAW-based reasoning on violence and discrimination in *A* may, for example, be understood by reference to it. It is in the trafficking jurisprudence, however, that the approach is most evident. Exceptional for a number of reasons here is *EK (Article 4 ECHR: Anti-Trafficking Convention) Tanzania*. First, the Upper Tribunal's approach to positive obligations and reparative remedies offers additional support for this book's arguments on compounded disadvantage and an independent migration status.[48] Secondly and relatedly, the Upper Tribunal is able to make connections between these because it understands the obligations of the ECHR and Trafficking Convention to be co-extensive and complementary.[49] That the positive obligations of article 4 of the ECHR should be understood by reference to the protective framework established by the Trafficking Convention is, as chapter 6 explains, now well established in both the UK and at the ECtHR.[50] Analogous interpretative moves have also been made by the CJEU.[51] The trafficking regime's preoccupation with migration control is, therefore, being countered, and its own rights-based approach to victims

[45] *AE v Bulgaria* App no 53891/20 (ECtHR, 23 May 2023).
[46] ibid paras 46–49, 116.
[47] ibid paras 119–23.
[48] *EK (Article 4 ECHR: Anti-Trafficking Convention) Tanzania* (n 22) [66]–[68]. Here, the Upper Tribunal referred to both the granting of permanent residence and the need to correct injustice.
[49] ibid [65].
[50] Cases discussed here include *MN and IXU v Secretary of State for the Home Department* [2020] EWCA Civ 1746, [2021] 1 WLR 1956; *MS (Pakistan) v Secretary of State for the Home Department* [2020] UKSC 9, [2020] 1 WLR 1373; *SM v Croatia* App no 60561/14 (ECtHR GC, 25 June 2020); *VCL and AN v UK* App nos 77587/12 and 74603/12 (ECtHR, 16 February 2021).
[51] On the relationship between EU law on trafficking and fundamental rights, see Case C-338/21 *Staatssecretaris van Justitie en Veiligheid v SS, NZ, SS* [2023] ECLI:EU:C:2023:269.

strengthened, by reference to the ECHR's focus on effective protection. At the same time, the ECtHR's failure to require States to regularise is being mitigated, in some cases at least, by reference to those provisions that enable the regularisation of victims' stay. Cases like *A*, *EK*, and others support the conclusion that arguments which engage with systemic integration, which rely on and develop co-extensive obligations, may yield more rights- and residence-protective responses to violence experienced in the context of migration control.[52]

8.5 Protecting Women from Violence, Recognising Women as Refugees: The Istanbul Convention

The regimes of exception created by the Istanbul Convention go further than any of the others this book considers in providing a response to compounded disadvantage that is, or has the potential to be, reparative of it. This conclusion may not be unrelated to the EU's and UK's reluctance to assume the obligations that article 59 imposes. Article 59 may carve out more expansive exceptions to the 'return or be removed' position discussed above, but these remain, nonetheless, exceptions. One criticism that could be made of the Istanbul Convention is, therefore, that it offers a solution to what is, in effect, the wrong problem. Article 59 seeks to mitigate the disadvantage caused by migration statuses that enforce dependency, that are precarious, and that bestow few rights. Yet it does so by requiring victims to be granted a status that is less injurious (and potentially only marginally so). It does not explicitly prohibit Parties from according such disadvantageous statuses to women in the first place.[53]

Two aspects of the Convention militate against such a conclusion being drawn. First, its general obligations on discrimination and prevention apply to migration law in the same way as they do to those other areas engaged with by the Convention. As explained in chapter 7, such provisions, whether drawn on alone or in conjunction with article 14 of the ECHR, could be relied on to challenge aspects of the rules which, like the probationary period, increase vulnerability to violence.[54] Promising here is the concern expressed by the Group of Experts on Action against Violence against Women and Domestic Violence (GREVIO) about integration requirements that may contribute to compounded disadvantage and deny women a remedy for it.[55] Secondly, by enabling victims to benefit

[52] Notably *Chowdury v Greece* App no 21884/15 (ECtHR, 30 March 2017). Here, I am assuming some co-extensiveness between co-extensive obligations and systemic integration.

[53] See further Fulvia Staiano, 'Protection beyond Victimisation: the Significance of the Istanbul Convention for Migrant Women' in Johanna Niemi, Lourdes Peroni, and Vladislava Stoyanova (eds), *International Law and Violence against Women: Europe and the Istanbul Convention* (Routledge 2020).

[54] Relevant here would be Istanbul Convention, arts 4(1)–(2), 12(2).

[55] See, for example, Group of Experts on Action against Violence against Women and Domestic Violence (GREVIO), *GREVIO Baseline Evaluation Report Denmark* (GREVIO/Inf(2017)14, 24 November 2017) [226].

from the rights and protections it provides on a non-discriminatory and unconditional basis, the Convention may, in some circumstances, avert compounded disadvantage. EK may not, for example, have been re-trafficked had she been able to access advice and accommodation. By prohibiting Parties from discriminating intersectionally, including against *migrant* women, the Istanbul Convention offers victims protection from violence that is practical and effective.

Article 59(1), when interpreted as set out in chapter 7, has the potential to remedy deficiencies in both the EU's and UK's domestic violence rules. All victims who are dependent on their spouse or partner for their permission to remain may have that dependent status converted into one that is autonomous. Victims should also not be required to divorce at particular times or to maintain particular types of economic activity. Similar arguments can be made in relation to article 59(3). Renewable residence permits should be granted to victims who are co-operating with criminal proceedings *and* to those whose stay is necessary owing to their personal situation. The Convention also offers the prospect of regularisation to women (and potentially others) who are currently excluded from either the domestic violence or trafficking regimes evaluated in the book. Given the UK's and EU's troubled and troubling accession and ratification processes, GREVIO's ability to engage constructively with its Parties may prove crucial to realising the Convention's potential to offer a reparative response to compounded disadvantage. Equally significant may be GREVIO's engagement with the ECtHR and the latter's willingness, when presented with a migrant victim of violence, to interpret positive ECHR obligations by reference to those on discrimination and residence assumed under the Istanbul Convention. Arguments made along these lines should engage with cases like *Kurt v Austria* (2021),[56] in which, following a GREVIO intervention, the Court indicated such a willingness.

There is one further way in which the Istanbul Convention offers protection to migrant victims of violence against women: facilitating their recognition as refugees. According to article 1A(2) of the Convention relating to the Status of Refugees (the Refugee Convention),[57] a refugee is a person who, being outside their country of origin, is unable to return owing to a well-founded fear of being persecuted for reasons of race, religion, nationality, membership of a particular social group, or political opinion. This definition, 'properly interpreted', includes gender-related protection claims.[58] Yet, one theme of the rich and diverse literature concerned

[56] *Kurt v Austria* App no 62903/15 (ECtHR GC, 15 June 2021); GREVIO, 'Third Party Intervention by the Group of Experts on Action against Violence against Women and Domestic Violence (GREVIO) pursuant to article 36 paragraph 2 of the European Convention on Human Rights Application no. 62903/15 Kurt v. Austria' (GREVIO/Inf(2020)3, 22 January 2020). See also *Chowdury v Greece* (n 52).

[57] Convention relating to the Status of Refugees (adopted 28 July 1951, entered into force 22 April 1954) 189 UNTS 137.

[58] UNHCR, 'Guidelines on International Protection No 1: Gender-Related Persecution Within the Context of Article 1A(2) of the 1951 Convention and/or its 1967 Protocol relating to the Status of Refugees' (7 May 2002) UN Doc HCR/GIP/02/01 [6]. See also UNHCR, 'Guidelines on International

with gender and asylum is the array of practical and legal barriers that continue to operate to deny women protection.[59] As a consequence, victims of both domestic violence and trafficking may struggle to fit their experiences of (discriminatory) violence and (discriminatory) State (lack of) protection within the refugee definition.[60] They may also be prevented from accessing a jurisdiction that is safe to make such a claim, or be unable to evidence it to the satisfaction of the relevant decision-maker.[61]

There are a number of women in this book who are in refugee-like situations or who are the family members of refugees. We do not know, for example, whether or not NA considered making an asylum claim in the UK. We do know that her violent husband sought her return to their country of origin, the country where he lived following his departure from the UK.[62] NA may, therefore, have feared that if she returned 'home' she would face further violence, violence that the State may not have been willing or able to protect her from.[63] In contrast, EK did make a claim for asylum. This was refused, such claims being 'a less easy fit' within the relevant jurisprudence.[64] Discrimination law has also been used both to protect refugees' rights to family reunion and, in *A* for example, to secure their status in the event of relationship breakdown.[65] GREVIO has also expressed concerns about

Protection No. 7: The Application of Article 1A(2) of the 1951 Convention and/or 1967 Protocol relating to the Status of Refugees to Victims of Trafficking and Persons At Risk of Being Trafficked' (7 April 2006) UN Doc HCR/GIP/06/07.

59 For an introduction to which, see Efrat Arbel, Catherine Dauvergne, and Jenni Millbank (eds), *Gender in Refugee Law: From the Margins to the Centre* (Routledge 2014); Catherine Dauvergne, 'Women in Refugee Jurisprudence' in Cathryn Costello, Michelle Foster, and Jane McAdam (eds), *The Oxford Handbook of International Refugee Law* (OUP 2021).

60 See Catherine Briddick and Vladislava Stoyanova, 'Human Trafficking and Refugees' in Cathryn Costello, Michelle Foster, and Jane McAdam (eds), *The Oxford Handbook of International Refugee Law* (OUP 2021); Briddick, 'Resisting Domestic Violence' (n 44) (and the references cited in both).

61 On access to protection, legal and policy measures adopted to 'fight' trafficking have, as chapter 6 explains, been implicated in the adoption of non-entrée regimes that compel people to undertake dangerous journeys and contain them in places that are unsafe. See further Thomas Gammeltoft-Hansen and James C Hathaway, '*Non-Refoulement* in a World of Cooperative Deterrence' (2015) 53 Columbia Journal of Transnational Law 235; Theodore Baird and Thomas Spijkerboer, 'Carrier Sanctions and the Conflicting Legal Obligations of Carriers: Addressing Human Rights Leakage' (2019) 11 Amsterdam Law Forum 4. These measures have gendered consequences. See further Sharon Pickering and Brandy Cochrane, 'Irregular Border-Crossing Deaths and Gender: Where, How and Why Women Die Crossing Borders' (2013) 17 Theoretical Criminology 27. On decision-making, see Debora Singer, 'Falling at Each Hurdle: Assessing the Credibility of Women's Asylum Claims in Europe' in Efrat Arbel, Catherine Dauvergne, and Jenni Millbank (eds), *Gender in Refugee Law: From the Margins to the Centre* (Routledge 2014); Helen Baillot, Sharon Cowan, and Vanessa E Munro, 'Reason to Disbelieve: Evaluating the Rape Claims of Women Seeking Asylum in the UK' (2014) 10 International Journal of Law in Context 105.

62 *NA (AG Opinion)* (n 17) para 14.

63 As the applicants did in *Islam v Secretary of State for the Home Department; R v Immigration Appeal Tribunal, ex p Shah* [1999] 2 AC 629; [1999] 2 WLR 1015.

64 *EK (Article 4 ECHR: Anti-Trafficking Convention) Tanzania* (n 22) [65]; *EK v Secretary of State for the Home Department* AA/16743/2010 (27 February 2012) [5].

65 On the former, see *Hode and Abdi v UK* App no 22341/09 (ECtHR, 6 November 2012) (discussed in chapters 2 and 5).

the number of refugee family members who are excluded from rules giving effect to States' obligations under article 59.[66] Relevant to all these cases and predicaments, therefore, are articles 60 and 61 of the Istanbul Convention.

Article 60 provides that:

1. Parties shall take the necessary legislative or other measures to ensure that gender-based violence against women may be recognised as a form of persecution within the meaning of Article 1, A (2), of the 1951 Convention relating to the Status of Refugees and as a form of serious harm giving rise to complementary/subsidiary protection.
2. Parties shall ensure that a gender-sensitive interpretation is given to each of the Convention grounds and that where it is established that the persecution feared is for one or more of these grounds, applicants shall be granted refugee status according to the applicable relevant instruments.
3. Parties shall take the necessary legislative or other measures to develop gender-sensitive reception procedures and support services for asylum-seekers as well as gender guidelines and gender-sensitive asylum procedures, including refugee status determination and application for international protection.

Article 61 complements this provision by affirming the international prohibition of *refoulement* and its application to victims of violence against women.

There are, at present, somewhat divergent views as to the ability of these provisions to provide either more gender-sensitive interpretations of the refugee definition or more gender-sensitive processes in relation to it.[67] It is notable that the drafters of the Convention did not, for example, follow the approach adopted by the CEDAW Committee and invite Parties to consider adding sex/gender as a 'sixth ground' to refugee definitions in their domestic law and policy.[68] Yet these provisions of the Istanbul Convention have already had a significant impact on

[66] GREVIO, *GREVIO Baseline Evaluation Report Sweden* (GREVIO/Inf(2018)15, 21 January 2019) [240]; GREVIO, *GREVIO Baseline Evaluation Report Ireland* (GREVIO/Inf(2023)22, 14 November 2023) [316].

[67] Dolores Morondo Taramundi, 'Gender-based Violence against Women and International Protection Needs: The Contribution of the Istanbul Convention' in Johanna Niemi, Lourdes Peroni, and Vladislava Stoyanova (eds), *International Law and Violence against Women: Europe and the Istanbul Convention* (Routledge 2020); Catherine Warin, 'Gender in European Union Asylum Law: The Istanbul Convention as a Game Changer?' International Journal of Refugee Law <https://doi.org/10.1093/ijrl/eeae004> accessed 27 May 2024.

[68] UN Committee for the Elimination of All Forms of Discrimination against Women, 'General Recommendation No. 32 on the Gender-Related Dimensions of Refugee Status, Asylum, Nationality and Statelessness of Women' (14 November 2014) UN Doc CEDAW/C/GC/32 [13], [38]. See also Talia Inlender, 'Status Quo or Sixth Ground? Adjudicating Gender Asylum Claims' in Seyla Benhabib and Judith Resnick (eds), *Migrations and Mobilities: Citizenship, Borders, and Gender* (New York University Press 2009).

refugee protection within the EU.[69] *WS* (2024)[70] concerned the circumstances in which women may be considered members of a particular social group, the connection between group membership and persecution, and the availability of subsidiary protection in cases involving the risk of fatal violence.[71] The Opinion of Advocate General Richard de la Tour was given before the EU was legally bound by the Istanbul Convention; the judgment was handed down after it. As the Advocate General explained, central to the case were the arguments of:

> those who consider that refugee status cannot be granted to all women who are victims of domestic violence, since it is a problem common to all States, and those who, on the other hand, deplore the fact that subsidiary protection is only protection granted 'by default' to those women, thus leading to non-recognition of the reasons for gender-related persecution.[72]

While the Advocate General found that neither the Istanbul Convention nor CEDAW could be relied on to assist in the interpretation of the Directive, the Grand Chamber of the CJEU took a different view. It drew on both to find that women may be regarded as belonging to a particular social group 'where it is established that, in their country of origin, they are, on account of their gender, exposed to physical or mental violence, including sexual violence and domestic violence'.[73] The judgment as a whole and this conclusion in particular is significantly more alive to the relationships between violence, discrimination, and gender than either the Advocate General's opinion or the decisions that preceded it.[74] The Grand Chamber recognises this, connecting its reasoning to the EU's accession to the Istanbul Convention and the obligations imposed by article 60.[75] In chapter 7, I argued that the Istanbul Convention has the potential to transform the position of

[69] The EU and its MS have developed a regional asylum framework, the Common European Asylum System, which purports to be based on and give effect to the Refugee Convention. See further Consolidated Version of the Treaty on the Functioning of the European Union [2012] OJ C326/47, art 78; Charter of Fundamental Rights of the European Union [2007] OJ C303/01, art 18.

[70] Case C–621/21 *WS v Intervyuirasht organ na Darzhavna agentsia za bezhantsite pri Ministerskia savet* [GC] [2024] ECLI:EU:C:2024:47.

[71] ibid para 34. See also Directive 2011/95/EU of the European Parliament and of the Council of 13 December 2011 on standards for the qualification of third-country nationals or stateless persons as beneficiaries of international protection, for a uniform status for refugees or for persons eligible for subsidiary protection, and for the content of the protection granted (recast) [2011] OJ L337/9, recital 30, art 9(2)(a) and (f), art 10(1)(d).

[72] Case C–621/21 *WS v Intervyuirasht organ na Darzhavna agentsia za bezhantsite pri Ministerskia savet* [2023] ECLI:EU:C:2023:314, Opinion of AG Richard de la Tour, para 3.

[73] *WS (CJEU GC)* (n 70) para 57.

[74] Christel Querton, 'One Step Forward, Two Steps Back? Interpreting "Particular Social Group" in the European Union' (2022) 71 International and Comparative Law Quarterly 425; Matthias Möschel, 'The European Union's Actions in the Domain of Combating Gender-Based Violence' in Elena Brodeală, Ivana Jelić, and Silvia Şuteu (eds), *Violence Against Women under European Human Rights Law: From Supranational Standards to National Realities* (Edward Elgar 2024).

[75] *WS (CJEU GC)* (n 70) paras 46–48.

migrant women subject to violence. *WS* confirms this and indicates that one of the ways this may be achieved is by decreasing women's reliance on the regimes of exception in circumstances where refugee protection is, or should be, available.

8.6 Concluding Remarks

This book's doctrinal and normative analysis of migration law's treatment of women shields from view the material and psychological demands of making applications and challenging negative decisions. The different forms of evidence required to substantiate a claim—the application form; the supporting statement; the process by which it is submitted, decided, reviewed, and then challenged—all warrant their own research and analysis. Whether or not a particular application is made will also depend on a number of other factors, including the availability or otherwise of safe accommodation and financial support. Addressing gendered disadvantage in this context requires more than migration law reform. Legal aid and specialist support services must, as a starting point, be properly funded. The arguments advanced here risk, therefore, being of academic value in both the positive and pejorative senses of the word, of being both related to scholarship and having little practical relevance.

Yet the rules that determine rights and status have been shaped by the challenges that women have brought to them. This book builds on these, examining violence experienced in the context of migration control and the different ways that the regimes of exception respond to it. The resulting analysis may inform future litigation. Advocates should ensure that courts apply the correct level of scrutiny in cases involving discrimination against women and draw on specialist legal instruments in their response to it. Centrally, however, the existence of regimes that enable some, and, it is to be hoped, an increasing number of women who have experienced compounded disadvantage to receive a status reparative of it should not deflect our attention from those rules that create it. The response provided by the Istanbul Convention to violence experienced in the context of migration is unique in this respect. Its focus on prevention (albeit circumscribed) and protection speaks to both the rules that increase vulnerability to violence and those that respond to it, in addition to addressing women's protection as refugees and from *refoulement*. The Convention and its monitoring body may not be able to bear the weight of all I have attached to it, either in chapter 7 or here. There are, nonetheless, strong arguments both for welcoming the EU's partial accession to the Convention and for seeking to expand upon it. There are similarly strong arguments for encouraging European States, including the UK, to ratify the Convention in full. Those seeking to secure such outcomes have, therefore, to challenge those political and legal movements that seek to exclude migrants, women, and racialised 'others' from both the protections the Convention provides and from their/our political communities. At the heart of human rights law is a recognition of the 'equal and inalienable rights of all members of the human family' and the concomitant promise of rights and protection without discrimination.[76] This book's arguments on violence against women and the regimes of exception are my contribution to the effort to keep this promise.

[76] Universal Declaration of Human Rights (adopted 10 December 1948) UNGA Res 217A (III) preamble, art 2.

Select Bibliography of Scholarly Works

Achiume ET, 'Migration as Decolonization' (2019) 71 Stanford Law Review 1509
—— 'Race, Refugees, and International Law' in C Costello, M Foster, and J McAdam (eds), *The Oxford Handbook of International Refugee Law* (OUP 2021)
—— 'Racial Borders' (2022) 110 The Georgetown Law Journal 445
Agustín LM, 'A Migrant World of Services' in S van Walsum and T Spijkerboer (eds), *Women and Immigration Law: New Variations on Classical Feminist Themes* (Routledge Cavendish 2006)
Alcoff L, 'Cultural Feminism versus Post-Structuralism: The Identity Crisis in Feminist Theory' (1988) 13 Signs 405
—— *Visible Identities: Race, Gender, and the Self* (OUP 2006)
Alexander L, 'What Makes Wrongful Discrimination Wrong? Biases, Preferences, Stereotypes, and Proxies' (1992) 141 University of Pennsylvania Law Review 149
Alksnis C, Desmarais S, and Curtis J, 'Workforce Segregation and the Gender Wage Gap: Is "Women's" Work Valued as Highly as "Men's"?' (2008) 38 Journal of Applied Social Psychology 1416
Allain J, '*Rantsev v Cyprus and Russia*: The European Court of Human Rights and Trafficking as Slavery' (2010) 10 Human Rights Law Review 546
—— *Slavery in International Law: Of Human Exploitation and Trafficking* (Brill 2013)
—— 'No Effective Trafficking Definition Exists: Domestic Implementation of the Palermo Protocol' (2014) 7 Albany Government Law Review 111
Altun S and others, 'Mental Health and Human Trafficking: Responding to Survivors' Needs' (2017) 14 BJPsych International 21
Amanor-Boadu Y and others, 'Immigrant and Nonimmigrant Women: Factors That Predict Leaving an Abusive Relationship' (2012) 18 Violence Against Women 611
Anderberg D and others, 'Unemployment and Domestic Violence: Theory and Evidence' (2016) 126 The Economic Journal 1947
Anderson B, 'Mobilizing Migrants, Making Citizens: Migrant Domestic Workers as Political Agents' (2009) 33 Ethnic and Racial Studies 60
—— 'Migration, Immigration Controls and the Fashioning of Precarious Workers' (2010) 24 Work, Employment & Society 300
—— *Us and Them?: The Dangerous Politics of Immigration Control* (OUP 2013)
—— 'Trafficking' in E Fiddian-Qasmiyeh and others (eds), *The Oxford Handbook of Refugee and Forced Migration Studies* (OUP 2014)
—— and Andrijasevic R, 'Sex, Slaves and Citizens: the Politics of Anti-Trafficking' (2008) 40 Soundings 135
Anderson E, 'Recent Thinking about Sexual Harassment: A Review Essay' (2006) 34 Philosophy & Public Affairs 284
Andrijasevic R, 'Beautiful Dead Bodies: Gender, Migration and Representation in Anti-Trafficking Campaigns' (2007) 86 Feminist Review 24
Anitha S, 'No Recourse, No Support: State Policy and Practice towards South Asian Women Facing Domestic Violence in the UK' (2010) 40 British Journal of Social Work 462
—— 'Legislating Gender Inequalities' (2011) 17 Violence Against Women 1260
—— Roy A, and Yalamarty H, 'Gender, Migration, and Exclusionary Citizenship Regimes: Conceptualizing Transnational Abandonment of Wives as a Form of Violence Against Women' (2018) 24 Violence Against Women 747
—— Yalamarty H, and Roy A, 'Changing Nature and Emerging Patterns of Domestic Violence in Global Contexts: Dowry Abuse and the Transnational Abandonment of Wives in India' (2018) 69 Women's Studies International Forum 67

Arbel E, Dauvergne C, and Millbank J (eds), *Gender in Refugee Law: From the Margins to the Centre* (Routledge 2014)
Arnardóttir OM, 'The Differences that Make a Difference: Recent Developments on the Discrimination Grounds and the Margin of Appreciation under Article 14 of the European Convention on Human Rights' (2014) 14 Human Rights Law Review 647
—— 'Vulnerability under Article 14 of the European Convention on Human Rights' (2017) 4 Oslo Law Review 150
Atrey S, 'Lifting as We Climb: Recognising Intersectional Gender Violence in Law' (2015) 5 Oñati Socio-Legal Series 1512
—— 'From Progress to Transformation, An Intersectional Response to Martha Nussbaum' (2018) 40 Human Rights Quarterly 859
—— *Intersectional Discrimination* (OUP 2019)
—— 'Structural Racism and Race Discrimination' (2021) 74 Current Legal Problems 1
—— Briddick C, and Foster M, 'Contesting and Undoing Discriminatory Borders' (2022) 22 International Journal of Discrimination and the Law 210
Baillot H, Cowan S, and Munro VE, 'Reason to Disbelieve: Evaluating the Rape Claims of Women Seeking Asylum in the UK' (2014) 10 International Journal of Law in Context 105
Baird T and Spijkerboer T, 'Carrier Sanctions and the Conflicting Legal Obligations of Carriers: Addressing Human Rights Leakage' (2019) 11 Amsterdam Law Forum 4
Balgamwalla S, 'Bride and Prejudice: How US Immigration Law Discriminates Against Spousal Visa Holders' (2014) 29 Berkeley Journal of Gender, Law & Justice 25
Barnard C, Ludlow A, and Butlin SF, 'Beyond Employment Tribunals: Enforcement of Employment Rights by EU-8 Migrant Workers' (2018) 47 Industrial Law Journal 226
Baumgärtel M, *Demanding Rights: Europe's Supranational Courts and the Dilemma of Migrant Vulnerability* (CUP 2019)
—— 'Facing the Challenge of Migratory Vulnerability in the European Court of Human Rights' (2020) 38 Netherlands Quarterly of Human Rights 12
Berthet V, 'Norm under Fire: Support for and Opposition to the European Union's Ratification of the Istanbul Convention in the European Parliament' (2022) 24 International Feminist Journal of Politics 675
Bhambra GK, 'The Current Crisis of Europe: Refugees, Colonialism, and the Limits of Cosmopolitanism' (2017) 23 European Law Journal 395
Bhuyan R and Bragg B, 'Epistemologies of Bordering: Domestic Violence Advocacy with Marriage Migrants in the Shadow of Deportation' (2021) 9 Migration Studies 159
Blackstone W, *Commentaries on the Laws of England: Book I: Of the Rights of Persons* (OUP 2016)
Block L and Bonjour S, 'Fortress Europe or Europe of Rights? The Europeanisation of Family Migration Policies in France, Germany and the Netherlands' (2013) 15 European Journal of Migration and Law 203
Bogoeski V and Costamagna F, 'Law and the Production of Precarious Work in Europe: An Introduction' (2022) 1 European Law Open 660
Bonjour S and Block L, 'Ethnicizing Citizenship, Questioning Membership. Explaining the Decreasing Family Migration Rights of Citizens in Europe' (2016) 20 Citizenship Studies 779
Bosma A and Rijken C, 'Key Challenges in the Combat of Human Trafficking: Evaluating the EU Trafficking Strategy and EU Trafficking Directive' (2016) 7 New Journal of European Criminal Law 315
Bosworth M, Fili A, and Pickering S, 'Women and Border Policing at the Edges of Europe' (2018) 44 Journal of Ethnic and Migration Studies 2182
—— Hoyle C, and Madden Dempsey M, 'Researching Trafficked Women: On Institutional Resistance and the Limits to Feminist Reflexivity' (2011) 17 Qualitative Inquiry 769
Boucher A, *Gender, Migration and the Global Race for Talent* (Manchester University Press 2016)
Boucher AK and Gest J, *Crossroads: Comparative Immigration Regimes in a World of Demographic Change* (CUP 2018)
Briddick C, 'Secretary of State for the Home Department v NA' (2016) 30 Journal of Immigration Asylum and Nationality Law 368

—— 'Combatting or Enabling Domestic Violence? Evaluating the Residence Rights of Migrant Victims of Domestic Violence in Europe' (2020) 69 International and Comparative Law Quarterly 1013
—— 'Precarious Workers and Probationary Wives: How Immigration Law Discriminates Against Women' (2020) 29 Social & Legal Studies 201
—— 'When Does Migration Law Discriminate against Women?' (2021) 115 AJIL Unbound 356
—— 'Unprincipled and Unrealised: CEDAW and Discrimination Experienced in the Context of Migration Control' (2022) 22 International Journal of Discrimination and the Law 224
—— 'Resisting Domestic Violence' (2024) 36 International Journal of Refugee Law 106
—— and Costello C, 'Introduction to the Symposium on Undoing Discriminatory Borders' (2021) 115 AJIL Unbound 328
—— and Stoyanova V, 'Human Trafficking and Refugees' in Costello C, Foster M, and McAdam J (eds), *The Oxford Handbook of International Refugee Law* (OUP 2021)
Burek W, 'Reservations to the Istanbul Convention and the Role of GREVIO: A Call for New Approach' (2022) 22 Human Rights Law Review 1
Burman M, 'Immigrant Women Facing Male Partner Violence—Gender, Race and Power in Swedish Alien and Criminal Law' (2012) 2 feminists@law 1
Busby N, 'Crumbs of Comfort: Pregnancy and the Status of "Worker" under EU Law's Free Movement Provisions' (2015) 44 Industrial Law Journal 134
Butler J, *Undoing Gender* (Routledge 2004)
Buxton R, 'Justice in Waiting: The Harms and Wrongs of Temporary Refugee Protection' (2023) 22 European Journal of Political Theory 51
Calvo JM, 'Spouse-Based Immigration Laws: The Legacies of Coverture' (1991) 28 San Diego Law Review 593
Canning V, *Gendered Harm and Structural Violence in the British Asylum System* (Routledge 2017)
—— 'Degradation by Design: Women and Asylum in Northern Europe' (2019) 61 Race & Class 46
—— 'Corrosive Control: State-Corporate and Gendered Harm in Bordered Britain' (2020) 28 Critical Criminology 259
Carens JH, *The Ethics of Immigration* (OUP 2013)
Carver N, '"For Her Protection and Benefit": The Regulation of Marriage-Related Migration to the UK' (2016) 39 Ethnic and Racial Studies 2758
Cassidy K, Yuval-Davis N, and Wemyss G, 'Intersectional Border(ing)s' (2018) 66 Political Geography 139
Chantler K, 'Independence, Dependency and Interdependence: Struggles and Resistances of Minoritized Women Within and on Leaving Violent Relationships' (2006) 82 Feminist Review 27
Charlesworth H, 'What are "Women's International Human Rights?"' in RJ Cook (ed), *Human Rights of Women: National and International Perspectives* (University of Pennsylvania Press 2012)
Charsley K and Benson M, 'Marriages of Convenience, and Inconvenient Marriages: Regulating Spousal Migration to Britain' (2012) 26 Journal of Immigration Asylum and Nationality Law 10
—— and others, 'Marriage-Related Migration to the UK' (2012) 46 International Migration Review 861
Chinkin C and Freeman MA, 'Introduction' in MA Freeman, C Chinkin, and B Rudolf (eds), *The UN Convention on the Elimination of all Forms of Discrimination Against Women: A Commentary* (OUP 2012)
Cho S, Crenshaw K, and McCall L, 'Toward a Field of Intersectionality Studies: Theory, Applications, and Praxis' (2013) 38 Signs 785
Choudhry S, 'Towards a Transformative Conceptualisation of Violence Against Women—A Critical Frame Analysis of Council of Europe Discourse on Violence Against Women' (2016) 79 Modern Law Review 406
—— and Herring J, 'Opuz v Turkey' in L Hodson and T Lavers (eds), *Feminist Judgments in International Law* (Hart 2019)

Chuang JA, 'Exploitation Creep and the Unmaking of Human Trafficking Law' (2014) 108 The American Journal of International Law 609

Clarke HM, 'Gender Stereotypes and Gender-Typed Work' in KF Zimmermann (ed), *Handbook of Labor, Human Resources and Population Economics* (Springer 2020)

Collins H, 'Discrimination, Equality and Social Inclusion' (2003) 66 Modern Law Review 16

—— and Khaitan T, *Foundations of Indirect Discrimination Law* (Hart 2018)

Conaghan J, *Law and Gender* (OUP 2013)

Cook RJ, 'Women's International Human Rights Law: The Way Forward' in RJ Cook (ed), *Human Rights of Women: National and International Perspectives* (University of Pennsylvania Press 2012)

Costello C, *The Human Rights of Migrants and Refugees in European Law* (OUP 2016)

Cowan S, '"Gender is No Substitute for Sex": A Comparative Human Rights Analysis of the Legal Regulation of Sexual Identity' (2005) 13 Feminist Legal Studies 67

Crawford J and Olleson S, 'The Character and Forms of International Responsibility' in MD Evans (ed), *International Law* (5th edn, CUP 2018)

Crenshaw K, 'Demarginalizing the Intersection of Race and Sex: A Black Feminist Critique of Antidiscrimination Doctrine, Feminist Theory and Antiracist Politics' [1989] University of Chicago Legal Forum 139

—— 'Mapping the Margins: Intersectionality, Identity Politics, and Violence against Women of Color' (1991) 43 Stanford Law Review 1241

Czaika M and De Haas H, 'The Effectiveness of Immigration Policies' (2013) 39 Population and Development Review 487

D'Aoust A-M, 'A Moral Economy of Suspicion: Love and Marriage Migration Management Practices in the United Kingdom' (2018) 36 Environment and Planning D: Society and Space 40

Dąbrowska-Kłosińska P, 'The Right to Family Reunion vs Integration Conditions for Third-Country Nationals: The CJEU's Approach and the Road Not Taken' (2018) 20 European Journal of Migration and Law 251

Danewid I, 'White Innocence in the Black Mediterranean: Hospitality and the Erasure of History' (2017) 38 Third World Quarterly 1674

Dauvergne C, *The New Politics of Immigration and the End of Settler Societies* (CUP 2016)

—— 'Women in Refugee Jurisprudence' in C Costello, M Foster, and J McAdam (eds), *The Oxford Handbook of International Refugee Law* (OUP 2021)

de Hart B, 'Superdads. Migrant Fathers' Right to Family Life before the European Court of Human Rights' (2015) 18 Men and Masculinities 448

—— and Bonjour S, 'A Proper Wife, a Proper Marriage: Constructions of "Us" and "Them" in Dutch Family Migration Policy' (2013) 20 The European Journal of Women's Studies 61

de Noronha L, 'Deportation, Racism and Multi-status Britain: Immigration Control and the Production of Race in the Present' (2019) 42 Ethnic and Racial Studies 2413

de Pauw M, 'Women's Rights: From Bad to Worse? Assessing the Evolution of Incompatible Reservations to the CEDAW Convention' (2013) 29 Utrecht Journal of International and European Law 51

De Vido S, 'The Ratification of the Council of Europe Istanbul Convention by the EU: A Step Forward in the Protection of Women from Violence in the European Legal System' (2017) 9 European Journal of Legal Studies 69

—— 'The Istanbul Convention as an Interpretative Tool at the European and National Levels' in J Niemi, L Peroni, and V Stoyanova (eds), *International Law and Violence Against Women: Europe and the Istanbul Convention* (Routledge 2020)

de Vries K and Spijkerboer T, 'Race and the Regulation of International Migration. The Ongoing Impact of Colonialism in the Case Law of The European Court of Human Rights' (2021) 39 Netherlands Quarterly of Human Rights 291

Del Real D, 'Toxic Ties: The Reproduction of Legal Violence within Mixed-Status Intimate Partners, Relatives, and Friends' (2019) 53 International Migration Review 548

Dembour M-B, *When Humans Become Migrants: Study of the European Court of Human Rights with an Inter-American Counterpoint* (OUP 2015)

Dias-Abey M, 'Path Dependent Policymaking in the Post-Brexit United Kingdom: What's New about the 'Points-Based' Labour Migration System?' (2022) 1 European Law Open 720
Docquier F, Lowell BL, and Marfouk A, 'A Gendered Assessment of Highly Skilled Emigration' (2009) 35 Population and Development Review 297
Doezema J, 'Loose Women or Lost Women? The Re-Emergence of the Myth of White Slavery in Contemporary Discourses of Trafficking in Women' (1999) 18 Gender Issues 23
Dorevitch A and Foster M, 'Obstacles on the Road to Protection: Assessing the Treatment of Sex-Trafficking Victims under Australia's Migration and Refugee Law' (2008) 9 Melbourne Journal of International Law 1
Dudley RG, 'Domestic Abuse and Women with "No Recourse to Public Funds": The State's Role in Shaping and Reinforcing Coercive Control' (2017) 6 Families, Relationships and Societies 201
Edwards A, *Violence Against Women under International Human Rights Law* (CUP 2011)
Egan S, 'Protecting the Victims of Trafficking: Problems and Prospects' (2008) 1 European Human Rights Law Review 106
El-Enany N, *Bordering Britain: Law, Race and Empire* (Manchester University Press 2020)
Ellermann A, 'Discrimination in Migration and Citizenship' (2020) 46 Journal of Ethnic and Migration Studies 2463
Emir A, *Selwyn's Law of Employment* (22nd edn, OUP 2022)
England P and Folbre N, 'The Cost of Caring' (1999) 561 The ANNALS of the American Academy of Political and Social Science 39
Erez E, 'Migration/Immigration, Domestic Violence and the Justice System' (2002) 26 International Journal of Comparative and Applied Criminal Justice 277
Ewing AP, 'Establishing State Responsibility for Private Acts of Violence against Women under the American Convention on Human Rights' (1995) 26 Columbia Human Rights Law Review 751
Farahat A, 'Enhancing Constitutional Justice by Using External References: The European Court of Human Rights' Reasoning on the Protection against Expulsion' (2015) 28 Leiden Journal of International Law 303
Farcy J-B, 'Equality in Immigration Law: An Impossible Quest?' (2020) 20 Human Rights Law Review 725
Feldman R, 'Maternity Care for Undocumented Migrant Women: The Impact of Charging for Maternity Care' (2016) 24 British Journal of Midwifery 52
Fineman MA, 'The Vulnerable Subject: Anchoring Equality in the Human Condition' (2008) 20 Yale Journal of Law and Feminism 1
—— 'The Vulnerable Subject and the Responsive State' (2010) 60 Emory Law Journal 251
—— 'Beyond Identities: The Limits of an Anti-Discrimination Approach to Equality' (2012) 92 Boston University Law Review 1713
—— 'Equality and Difference—The Restrained State' (2015) 66 Alabama Law Review 609
—— 'Vulnerability and Inevitable Inequality' (2017) 4 Oslo Law Review 133
—— 'Beyond Equality and Discrimination' (2020) 73 SMU Law Review Forum 51
—— 'Populations, Pandemics, and Politics' (2021) 21 International Journal of Discrimination and the Law 184
Fouladvand S and Ward T, 'Human Trafficking, Vulnerability and the State' (2019) 81 Journal of Criminal Law 39
Fredman S, 'Addressing Disparate Impact: Indirect Discrimination and the Public Sector Equality Duty' (2014) 43 Industrial Law Journal 349
—— 'Emerging from the Shadows: Substantive Equality and Article 14 of the European Convention on Human Rights' (2016) 16 Human Rights Law Review 273
—— 'Direct and Indirect Discrimination: Is There Still a Divide?' in H Collins and T Khaitan (eds), *Foundations of Indirect Discrimination Law* (Hart 2018)
Freedland M and Costello C, 'Migrants at Work and the Division of Labour Law' in C Costello and M Freedland (eds), *Migrants at Work: Immigration and Vulnerability in Labour Law* (OUP 2014)
Fudge J, 'The Precarious Migrant Status and Precarious Employment: The Paradox of International Rights for Migrant Workers' (2012) 34 Comparative Labor Law & Policy Journal 95

—— and Strauss K, 'Migrants, Unfree Labour, and the Legal Construction of Domestic Servitude: Migrant Domestic Workers in the UK' in C Costello and M Freedland (eds), *Migrants at Work: Immigration and Vulnerability in Labour Law* (OUP 2014)

Gallagher A, 'Human Rights and the New UN Protocols on Trafficking and Migrant Smuggling: A Preliminary Analysis' (2001) 23 Human Rights Quarterly 975

Gallagher AT, *The International Law of Human Trafficking* (CUP 2010)

Galtung J, 'Violence, Peace, and Peace Research' (1969) 6 Journal of Peace Research 167

Gammeltoft-Hansen T and Hathaway JC, '*Non-Refoulement* in a World of Cooperative Deterrence' (2015) 53 Columbia Journal of Transnational Law 235

Gardner J, 'On the Ground of Her Sex(uality)' (1988) 18 Oxford Journal of Legal Studies 167

Gentleman A, *The Windrush Betrayal: Exposing the Hostile Environment* (Faber 2019)

Ghezelbash D, 'Legal Transfers of Restrictive Immigration Laws: A Historical Perspective' (2017) 66 International and Comparative Law Quarterly 235

Gibney MJ, 'Is Deportation a Form of Forced Migration?' (2013) 32 Refugee Survey Quarterly 116

Gill A and Harrison K, 'Police Responses to Intimate Partner Sexual Violence in South Asian Communities' (2016) 10 Policing 446

—— and Sharma K, 'Response and Responsibility: Domestic Violence and Marriage Migration in The UK' in S van Walsum and T Spijkerboer (eds), *Women and Immigration Law: New Variations on Classical Feminist Themes* (Routledge Cavendish 2007)

Gizem G, 'The Anti-Istanbul Convention Campaign: Rhetoric or Reality?: A Comparative Analysis of the Istanbul Convention and the ECHR on Same-Sex Marriage and the Legal Introduction of Third Sex' (2022) 6 European Human Rights Law Review 604

Goldscheid J, 'Gender Neutrality, the "Violence against Women" Frame, and Transformative Reform' (2014) 82 UMKC Law Review 623

Grans L, 'The Impact of Vulnerability on State Obligations in Criminal Proceedings on Domestic Violence: Interpreting the Istanbul Convention and the European Convention on Human Rights' Women & Criminal Justice <https://doi.org/10.1080/08974454.2023.2296624> accessed 2 May 2024

Griffiths M and Yeo C, 'The UK's Hostile Environment: Deputising Immigration Control' (2021) 41 Critical Social Policy 521

Gruszczynski L and Werner W, *Deference in International Courts and Tribunals: Standard of Review and Margin of Appreciation* (OUP 2014)

Guild E, Peers S, and Tomkin J, *The EU Citizenship Directive: A Commentary* (2nd edn, OUP 2019)

Hathaway JC, 'The Human Rights Quagmire of "Human Trafficking"' (2008–09) 49 Virginia Journal of International Law 1

Havelková B, 'Judicial Scepticism of Discrimination at the ECtHR' in H Collins and T Khaitan (eds), *Foundations of Indirect Discrimination Law* (Hart 2018)

Hayes L, *Stories of Care: A Labour of Law* (Palgrave 2017)

Heise LL and Kotsadam A, 'Cross-national and Multilevel Correlates of Partner Violence: An Analysis of Data From Population-Based Surveys' (2015) 3 Lancet Global Health 332

Hellman D, 'Indirect Discrimination and the Duty to Avoid Compounding Injustice' in H Collins and T Khaitan (eds), *Foundations of Indirect Discrimination Law* (Hart 2018)

Herring J, 'The Istanbul Convention: Is Domestic Abuse Violence Against Women?' in G Douglas, M Murch, and V Stephens (eds), *International and National Perspectives on Child and Family Law: Essays in Honour of Nigel Lowe* (Intersentia 2018)

Hester M, 'Who Does What to Whom? Gender and Domestic Violence Perpetrators in English Police Records' (2013) 10 European Journal of Criminology 623

Holtmaat R, 'The CEDAW: A Holistic Approach to Women's Equality and Freedom' in A Hellum and HS Aasen (eds), *Women's Human Rights: CEDAW in International, Regional and National Law* (CUP 2013)

Hoyle C, Bosworth M, and Dempsey M, 'Labelling the Victims of Sex Trafficking: Exploring the Borderland between Rhetoric and Reality' (2011) 20 Social & Legal Studies 313

Inlender T, 'Status Quo or Sixth Ground? Adjudicating Gender Asylum Claims' in S Benhabib and J Resnick (eds), *Migrations and Mobilities: Citizenship, Borders, and Gender* (New York University Press 2009)

Irving H, *Citizenship, Alienage, and the Modern Constitutional State: A Gendered History* (CUP 2016)

Jayasinghe U and Baglay S, 'Protecting Victims of Human Trafficking Within a "Non-Refoulement" Framework: Is Complementary Protection an Effective Alternative in Canada and Australia?' (2011) 3 International Journal of Refugee Law 489

Jelinic AB, 'Australia's Family Violence Provisions in Migration Law: A Comparative Study' (2020) 21 Flinders Law Journal 259

Jenson J, 'The Talents of Women, the Skills of Men: Flexible Specialization and Women' in S Wood (ed), *The Transformation of Work: Skill, Flexibility and the Labour Process* (Unwin Hyman 1989)

Johnson MP, 'Conflict and Control: Gender Symmetry and Asymmetry in Domestic Violence' (2006) 12 Violence Against Women 1003

Joppke C, *Selecting by Origin: Ethnic Migration in the Liberal State* (Harvard University Press 2005)

—— 'Immigration in the Populist Crucible: Comparing Brexit and Trump' (2020) 8 Comparative Migration Studies 49

Juss SS, 'Recognizing Refugee Status for Victims of Trafficking and the Myth of Progress' (2015) 34 Refugee Survey Quarterly 107

Juverdeanu C, 'The Different Gears of EU Citizenship' (2021) 47 Journal of Ethnic and Migration Studies 1596

—— 'The EU Market Citizenship Paradigm: Embraced or Abandoned?' (2022) 44 Journal of European Integration 1011

Kavanagh A, *The Collaborative Constitution* (CUP 2023)

Khaitan T, *A Theory of Discrimination Law* (OUP 2015)

Kim SY, 'Les Vulnérables: Evaluating the Vulnerability Criterion in Article 14 Cases by the European Court of Human Rights' (2021) 41 Legal Studies 617

Kiss L and others, 'Health of Men, Women, and Children in Post-Trafficking Services in Cambodia, Thailand, and Vietnam: An Observational Cross-sectional Study' (2015) 3 The Lancet Global Health 154

Kneebone S, 'The Refugee–Trafficking Nexus: Making Good (The) Connections' (2010) 29 Refugee Survey Quarterly 137

Kochenov D, '*Ius Tractum* of Many Faces: European Citizenship and the Difficult Relationship between Status and Rights' (2009) 15 Columbia Journal of European Law 169

Kofman E, 'Gendered Labour Migrations in Europe and Emblematic Migratory Figures' (2012) 39 Journal of Ethnic and Migration Studies 579

Krivenko EY, 'The Role and Impact of Soft Law on the Emergence of the Prohibition of Violence against Women within the Context of the CEDAW' in S Lagoutte, T Gammeltoft-Hansen, and J Cerone (eds), *Tracing the Roles of Soft Law in Human Rights* (OUP 2016)

Kübek G, 'Facing and Embracing the Consequences of Mixity: Opinion 1/19, Istanbul Convention' (2022) 59 Common Market Law Review 1465

Levanon A, England P, and Allison P, 'Occupational Feminization and Pay: Assessing Causal Dynamics Using 1950–2000 US Census Data' (2009) 88 Social Forces 865

Lewis G, 'Unsafe Travel: Experiencing Intersectionality and Feminist Displacements' (2013) 38 Signs 869

Lim D, 'The Indirect Gender Discrimination of Skill-Selective Immigration Policies' (2019) 22 Critical Review of International Social and Political Philosophy 906

Lloyd-Jones L, 'International Law before United Kingdom Courts: A Quiet Revolution' (2022) 71 International and Comparative Law Quarterly 503

Macklin A, 'Dancing across Borders: "Exotic Dancers", Trafficking, and Canadian Immigration Policy' (2003) 37 International Migration Review 464

Madden Dempsey M, *Prosecuting Domestic Violence: A Philosophical Analysis* (OUP 2009)

Manjoo R, 'State Responsibility to Act with Due Diligence in the Elimination of Violence against Women' (2013) 2 International Human Rights Law Review 240
—— and Jones J, *The Legal Protection of Women From Violence: Normative Gaps in International Law* (Routledge 2019)
Mantouvalou V, '"Am I Free Now?" Overseas Domestic Workers in Slavery' (2015) 42 Journal of Law and Society 329
—— 'The UK Modern Slavery Act 2015 Three Years On' (2018) 81 Modern Law Review 1017
—— 'The UK Seasonal Worker Visa' (2022) 1 European Law Open 711
McGlynn C, 'Rape, Torture and the European Convention on Human Rights' (2009) 58 International & Comparative Law Quarterly 565
McGoldrick D, 'A Defence of the Margin of Appreciation and an Argument for its Application by the Human Rights Committee' (2016) 65 International and Comparative Law Quarterly 21
McLachlan C, 'The Principle of Systemic Integration and Article 31(3)(c) of the Vienna Convention' (2005) 54 International and Comparative Law Quarterly 279
McNeilly K, 'Gendered Violence and International Human Rights: Thinking Non-discrimination Beyond the Sex Binary' (2014) 22 Feminist Legal Studies 263
McQuigg RJA, *The Istanbul Convention, Domestic Violence and Human Rights* (Routledge 2019)
—— 'The European Court of Human Rights and Domestic Violence: *Volodina v. Russia*' (2021) 10 International Human Rights Law Review 155
McWilliams M, Yarnell PNR, and Churchill M, 'Forced Dependency and Legal Barriers: Implications of the UK's Immigration and Social Security Policies for Minoritized Women Living in Abusive Intimate Relationships in Northern Ireland' (2015) 5 Oñati Socio-Legal Series 1536
Menjívar C, 'The Racialization of "Illegality"' (2021) 150 Daedalus 91
—— and Salcido O, 'Immigrant Women and Domestic Violence: Common Experiences in Different Countries' (2002) 16 Gender & Society 898
Merry SE and Ramachandran V, 'The Limits of Consent: Sex and the Problem of International Paternalism' in MN Barnett (ed), *Paternalism Beyond Borders* (CUP 2016)
Mikkola M, *The Wrong of Injustice: Dehumanization and its Role in Feminist Philosophy* (OUP 2016)
Minnow M, 'Adjudicating Differences: Conflicts Among Feminist Lawyers' in M Hirsch and EF Keller (eds), *Conflicts in Feminism* (Routledge 1990)
—— 'Archetypal Legal Scholarship: A Field Guide' (2013) 63 Journal of Legal Education 65
Mirza N, 'The UK Government's Conflicting Agendas and "Harmful" Immigration Policies: Shaping South Asian Women's Experiences of Abuse and "Exit"' (2016) 36 Critical Social Policy 592
Montoya C and Rolandsen Agustín L, 'The Othering of Domestic Violence: The EU and Cultural Framings of Violence against Women' (2013) 20 Social Politics 534
Moreau S, 'What Is Discrimination?' (2010) 38 Philosophy & Public Affairs 143
—— 'In Defense of a Liberty-Based Account of Discrimination' in D Hellman and S Moreau (eds), *Philosophical Foundations of Discrimination law* (OUP 2013)
Moreau SR, 'The Wrongs of Unequal Treatment' (2004) 54 University of Toronto Law Journal 291
—— 'Equality Rights and the Relevance of Comparator Groups' (2006) 5 Journal of Law and Equality 81
Moreno-Lax V, 'Systematising Systemic Integration: "War Refugees", Regime Relations, and a Proposal for a Cumulative Approach to International Commitments' (2014) 12 Journal of International Criminal Justice 907
Möschel M, 'The Strasbourg Court and Indirect Race Discrimination: Going Beyond the Education Domain' (2017) 80 Modern Law Review 121
—— 'The European Union's Actions in the Domain of Combating Gender-Based Violence' in M Brodeală, I Jelić, and S Şuteu (eds), *Violence Against Women under European Human Rights Law: From Supranational Standards to National Realities* (Edward Elgar 2024)
Mullally S, 'Migration, Gender, and the Limits of Rights' in R Rubio-Marín (ed), *Human Rights and Immigration* (OUP 2014)

—— and Murphy C, 'Migrant Domestic Workers in the UK: Enacting Exclusions, Exemptions, and Rights' (2014) 36 Human Rights Quarterly 397
Murphy C, 'The Enduring Vulnerability of Migrant Domestic Workers in Europe' (2013) 62 International and Comparative Law Quarterly 599
Muzio D and Bolton SC, 'Feminisation and Paradox: Stratification and Segmentation in Professional Contexts' (2006) 27 Irish Journal of Management 79
Nanasi N, 'The U Visa's Failed Promise for Survivors of Domestic Violence' (2018) 29 Yale Journal of Law & Feminism 271
Niemi J, Peroni L, and Stoyanova V (eds), *International Law and Violence Against Women: Europe and the Istanbul Convention* (Routledge 2020)
Nussbaum MC, *Women and Human Development: The Capabilities Approach* (CUP 2000)
—— 'Women's Bodies: Violence, Security, Capabilities' (2005) 6 Journal of Human Development 167
O'Brien C, '"I trade, therefore I am": Legal Personhood in the European Union' (2013) 50 Common Market Law Review 1643
—— 'The Pillory, the Precipice and the Slippery Slope: the Profound Effects of the UK's Legal Reform Programme Targeting EU Migrants' (2015) 37 Journal of Social Welfare and Family Law 111
—— 'Civis Capitalist Sum: Class as the New Guiding Principle of EU Free Movement Rights' (2016) 53 Common Market Law Review 937
—— 'The ECJ Sacrifices EU Citizenship in Vain: *Commission v. United Kingdom*' (2017) 54 Common Market Law Review 209
Ó'Cinnéide C, 'Why Challenging Discrimination at Borders is Challenging (and Often Futile)' (2021) 115 AJIL Unbound 362
Oosterom-Staples H, 'The Family Reunification Directive: A Tool Preserving Member State Interest or Conducive to Family Unity?' in A Baldaccini, E Guild, and H Toner (eds), *Whose Freedom, Security and Justice? EU Immigration and Asylum Law and Policy* (Bloomsbury 2007)
—— 'Residence Rights for Caring Parents Who Are Also Victims of Domestic Violence' (2017) 19 European Journal of Migration and Law 396
Otto D, 'Queering Gender [Identity] in International Law' (2015) 33 Nordic Journal of Human Rights 299
Peers S and others, 'Family Reunion' in S Peers and others (eds), *EU Immigration and Asylum Law (Text and Commentary): Second Revised Edition* (2nd edn, Brill | Nijhof 2012)
Peroni L, 'Violence Against Migrant Women: The Istanbul Convention Through a Postcolonial Feminist Lens' (2016) 24 Feminist Legal Studies 49
—— and Timmer A, 'Vulnerable Groups: The Promise of an Emerging Concept in European Human Rights Convention Law' (2013) 11 International Journal of Constitutional Law 1056
Phillips A and Taylor B, 'Sex and Skill: Notes towards a Feminist Economics' (1980) 6 Feminist Review 79
Pickering S and Cochrane B, 'Irregular Border-Crossing Deaths and Gender: Where, How and Why Women Die Crossing Borders' (2013) 17 Theoretical Criminology 27
Querton C, 'One Step Forward, Two Steps Back? Interpreting "Particular Social Group" in the European Union' (2022) 71 International and Comparative Law Quarterly 425
Rachovitsa A, 'The Principle of Systemic Integration in Human Rights Law' (2017) 66 International and Comparative Law Quarterly 557
Raj A and Silverman J, 'Violence Against Immigrant Women: The Roles of Culture, Context, and Legal Immigrant Status on Intimate Partner Violence' (2002) 8 Violence Against Women 367
Réaume DG, 'What's Distinctive about Feminist Analysis of Law?: A Conceptual Analysis of Women's Exclusion from Law' (1996) 2 Legal Theory 265
—— 'Discrimination and Dignity' (2003) 63 Louisiana Law Review 645
—— 'Dignity, Equality, and Comparison' in D Hellman and SR Moreau (eds), *Philosophical Foundations of Discrimination Law* (OUP 2013)
Renzetti CM, *Violent* Reiertsen M, *Effective Remedies and the European Court of Human Rights* (CUP 2022)

Betrayal: Partner Abuse in Lesbian Relationships (Sage 1992)
Resnik J, 'Comparative (In)Equalities: CEDAW, the Jurisdiction of Gender, and the Heterogeneity of Transnational Law Production' (2012) 10 International Journal of Constitutional Law 531
Rodenhäuser T, 'Another Brick in the Wall: Carrier Sanctions and the Privatization of Immigration Control' (2014) 26 International Journal of Refugee Law 223
Rodó JV, 'A Preliminary Analysis of the Intersection Between Domestic Violence, Coercive Control and Migration Statuses in Ireland and Spain' (2022) 9 Deusto Journal of Human Rights 13
Rosenblum D, 'Unsex CEDAW, Or What's Wrong with Women's Rights' (2011) 20 Columbia Journal of Gender and Law 98
Rubio-Marín R and Sandoval C, 'Engendering the Reparations Jurisprudence of the Inter-American Court of Human Rights: The Promise of the *Cotton Field* Judgment' (2011) 33 Human Rights Quarterly 1062
Sánchez SI, 'Fundamental Rights Protection for Third Country Nationals and Citizens of the Union: Principles for Enhancing Coherence' (2013) 15 European Journal of Migration and Law 137
Saul B, 'Migrating to Australia with Disabilities: Non-Discrimination and the Convention on the Rights of Persons with Disabilities' (2010) 16 Australian Journal of Human Rights 63
Scott JW, 'Gender: Still a Useful Category of Analysis?' (2010) 225 Diogenes 7
Sedacca N, 'Migrant Domestic Workers and the Right to a Private and Family Life' (2019) 37 Netherlands Quarterly of Human Rights 288
—— 'Domestic Workers, the 'Family Worker' Exemption from Minimum Wage, and Gendered Devaluation of Women's Work' (2022) 51 Industrial Law Journal 771
—— 'Migrant Work, Gender and the Hostile Environment: A Human Rights Analysis' (2024) 53 Industrial Law Journal 63
Segrave M, 'Temporary Migration and Family Violence: How Perpetrators Weaponise Borders' (2021) 10 International Journal for Crime, Justice and Social Democracy 26
Shivakoti R, Henderson S, and Withers M, 'The Migration Ban Policy Cycle: A Comparative Analysis of Restrictions on the Emigration of Women Domestic Workers' (2021) 9 Comparative Migration Studies 1
Sikkink K, *Evidence for Hope: Making Human Rights Work in the 21st Century* (Princeton University Press 2017)
Silver S, 'Twenty Years After the Passage of the Palermo Protocol: Identifying Common Flaws in Defining Trafficking through the First Global Study of Domestic Anti-Trafficking Laws' (2021) 40 Yale Law & Policy Review 336
Šimonović D, 'Global and Regional Standards on Violence Against Women: The Evolution and Synergy of the CEDAW and Istanbul Conventions' (2014) 36 Human Rights Quarterly 590
Singer D, 'Falling at Each Hurdle: Assessing the Credibility of Women's Asylum Claims in Europe' in E Arbel, C Dauvergne, and J Millbank (eds), *Gender in Refugee Law: From the Margins to the Centre* (Routledge 2014)
Sosa L, *Intersectionality in the Human Rights Legal Framework on Violence against Women: At the Centre or the Margins?* (CUP 2017)
—— 'The Istanbul Convention in the Context of Feminist Claims' in J Niemi, L Peroni, and V Stoyanova (eds), *International Law and Violence Against Women: Europe and the Istanbul Convention* (Routledge 2020)
Sosa LPA, 'Inter-American Case Law on *Femicide*: Obscuring Intersections?' (2017) 35 Netherlands Quarterly of Human Rights 85
Staiano F, 'Protection beyond Victimisation: The Significance of the Istanbul Convention for Migrant Women' in J Niemi, L Peroni, and V Stoyanova (eds), *International Law and Violence against Women: Europe and the Istanbul Convention* (Routledge 2020)
Stark E, *Coercive Control: The Entrapment of Women in Personal Life* (OUP 2007)
Steinberg RJ, 'Social Construction of Skill: Gender, Power, and Comparable Worth' (1990) 17 Work and Occupations 449

Stoyanova V, *Human Trafficking and Slavery Reconsidered: Conceptual Limits and States' Positive Obligations in European Law* (CUP 2017)

—— 'A Stark Choice: Domestic Violence or Deportation? The Immigration Status of Victims of Domestic Violence under the Istanbul Convention' (2018) 20 European Journal of Migration and Law 53

—— 'On the Bride's Side? Victims of Domestic Violence and their Residence Rights under EU and Council of Europe Law' (2019) 37 Netherlands Quarterly of Human Rights 311

—— 'Due Diligence versus Positive Obligations: Critical Reflections on the Council of Europe Convention on Violence Against Women' in J Niemi, L Peroni, and V Stoyanova (eds), *International Law and Violence Against Women: Europe and the Istanbul Convention* (Routledge 2020)

—— *Positive Obligations under the European Convention on Human Rights: Within and Beyond Boundaries* (OUP 2023)

Strid S, Walby S, and Armstrong J, 'Intersectionality and Multiple Inequalities: Visibility in British Policy on Violence Against Women' (2013) 20 Social Politics 558

Strumia F, 'Divorce Immediately, or Leave. Rights of Third Country Nationals and Family Protection in the Context of EU Citizens' Free Movement: *Kuldip Singh and Others*' (2016) 53 Common Market Law Review 1373

—— 'Speaking Too Little, Yet Saying Too Much. The Wrong Signals about EU Values: *X. v. Belgian State*' (2022) 59 Common Market Law Review 1195

Suchecki JA, 'Remedies for Victims of Human Trafficking under the Palermo Protocol and United Nations Basic Principles: A Case Study Analysis' (2019) 9 Notre Dame Journal of International and Comparative Law 126

Szigeti PD, 'No Country for Old Men: Restrictions on the Immigration of Elderly Family Members' (2023) 68 McGill Law Journal 1

Tanha M and others, 'Sex Differences in Intimate Partner Violence and the Use of Coercive Control as a Motivational Factor for Intimate Partner Violence' (2010) 25 Journal of Interpersonal Violence 1836

Taramundi DM, 'Gender-based Violence against Women and International Protection Needs: The Contribution of the Istanbul Convention' in J Niemi, L Peroni, and V Stoyanova (eds), *International Law and Violence against Women: Europe and the Istanbul Convention* (Routledge 2020)

Timmer A, 'Toward an Anti-Stereotyping Approach for the European Court of Human Rights' (2011) 11 Human Rights Law Review 707

Ün MB and Arikan H, 'Europeanization and De-Europeanization of Turkey's Gender Equality Policy: The Case of the Istanbul Convention' (2022) 60 Journal of Common Market Studies 945

Vasanthakumar A, 'Epistemic Privilege and Victims' Duties to Resist their Oppression' (2018) 35 Journal of Applied Philosophy 465

Vasil S, '"I Came Here, and it Got Worse Day by Day": Examining the Intersections Between Migrant Precarity and Family Violence Among Women with Insecure Migration Status in Australia' (2023) <https://journals.sagepub.com/doi/abs/10.1177/10778012231159414> accessed 4 May 2024

Vishnuvajjala R, 'Insecure Communities: How an Immigration Enforcement Program Encourages Battered Women to Stay Silent' (2012) 32 Boston College Journal of Law & Social Justice 185

Voolma H, '"I Must Be Silent Because of Residency": Barriers to Escaping Domestic Violence in the Context of Insecure Immigration Status in England and Sweden' (2018) 24 Violence Against Women 1830

Walker A, 'One Child of One's Own: A Meaningful Digression Within the Work(s)' in *In Search of Our Mothers' Gardens: Womanist Prose* (Phoenix 2005)

Warin C, 'Gender in European Union Asylum Law: The Istanbul Convention as a Game Changer?' International Journal of Refugee Law <https://doi.org/10.1093/ijrl/eeae004> accessed 27 May 2024

Weiler JHH, 'Thou Shalt Not Oppress a Stranger: On the Judicial Protection of the Human Rights of Non-EC Nationals—A Critique' (1992) 3 European Journal of International Law 65

Weiss A, 'Transnational Families in Crisis: An Analysis of the Domestic Violence Rule in E.U. Free Movement Law' (2009) 30 Michigan Journal of International Law 841

Wessels J, 'The Boundaries of Universality—Migrant Women and Domestic Violence Before the Strasbourg Court' (2019) 37 Netherlands Quarterly of Human Rights 336

Wong MYY, 'The Unequal Price of Love: A Critical Race Feminist Critique of the £18,600 Minimum Income Requirement for Family Reunification under Article 14 ECHR' (2019) 33 Journal of Immigration Asylum and Nationality Law 302

Wray H, *Regulating Marriage Migration into the UK: A Stranger in the Home* (Ashgate 2011)

—— '"A Thing Apart": Controlling Male Family Migration to the United Kingdom' (2015) 18 Men and Masculinities 424

—— Agoston A, and Hutton J, 'A Family Resemblance? The Regulation of Marriage Migration in Europe' (2014) 16 European Journal of Migration and Law 209

Yahyaoui Krivenko E, 'Reassessing the Relationship between Equality and Vulnerability in Relation to Refugees and Asylum Seekers in the ECtHR: The *MSS* Case 10 Years On' (2022) 34 International Journal of Refugee Law 192

Yeo C, *Welcome to Britain: Fixing Our Broken Immigration System* (Biteback 2022)

Yong A, 'A Gendered EU Settlement Scheme: Intersectional Oppression of Immigrant Women in a Post-Brexit Britain' (2022) 32 Social & Legal Studies 756

York S, 'The "Hostile Environment"—How Home Office Immigration Policies and Practices Create and Perpetuate Illegality' (2018) 32 Journal of Immigration Asylum and Nationality Law 363

Yoshida K, 'Towards Intersectionality in the European Court of Human Rights: The Case of *B.S. v Spain*' (2013) 21 Feminist Legal Studies 195

Yusran R, 'The ASEAN Convention Against Trafficking in Persons: A Preliminary Assessment' (2018) 8 Asian Journal of International Law 258

Yuval-Davis N, Wemyss G, and Cassidy K, 'Everyday Bordering, Belonging and the Reorientation of British Immigration Legislation' (2018) 52 Sociology 228

Zimmerman C, Hossain M, and Watts C, 'Human Trafficking and Health: A Conceptual Model to Inform Policy, Intervention and Research' (2011) 73 Social Science & Medicine 327

Index

For the benefit of digital users, indexed terms that span two pages (e.g., 52–53) may, on occasion, appear on only one of those pages.